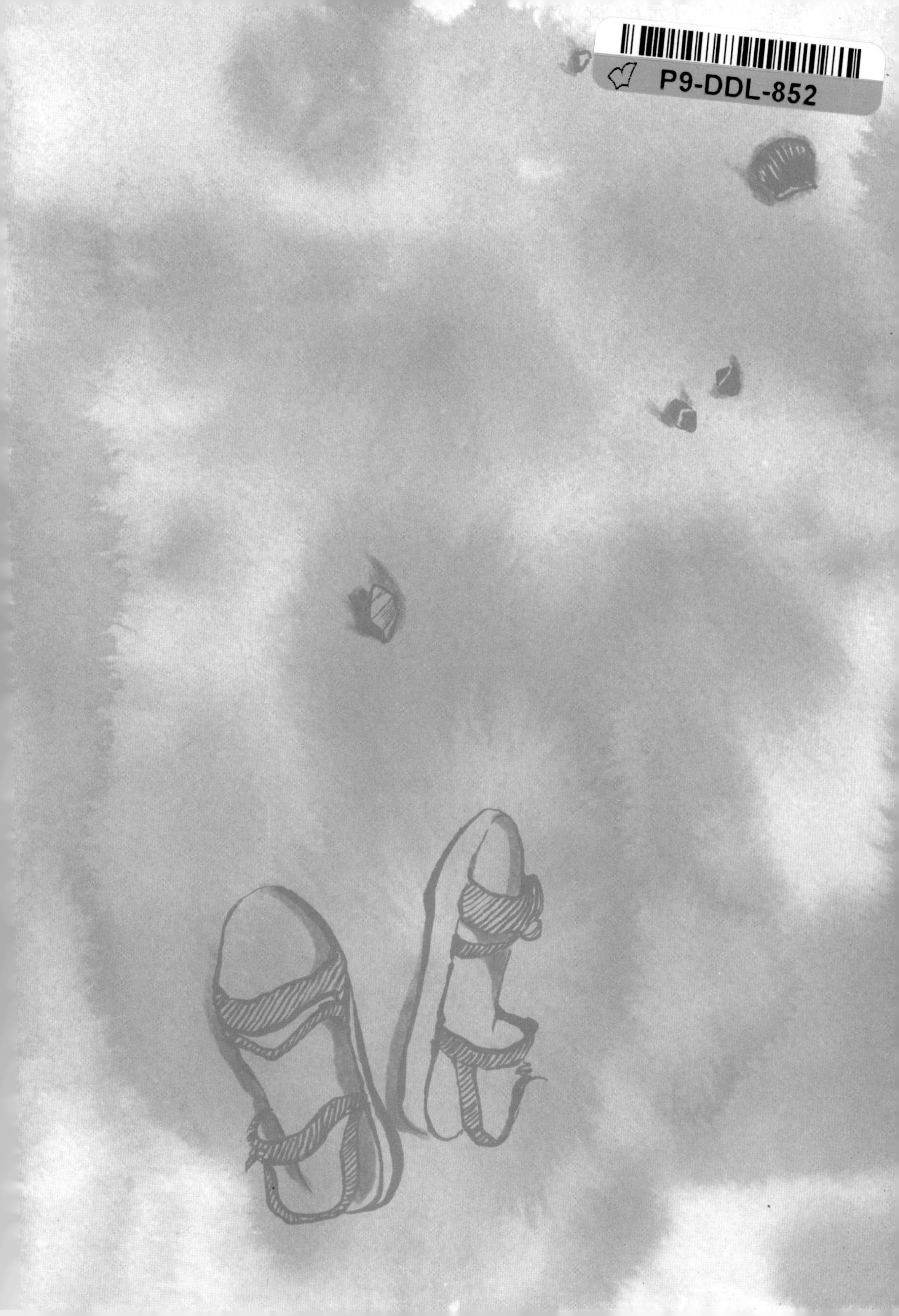

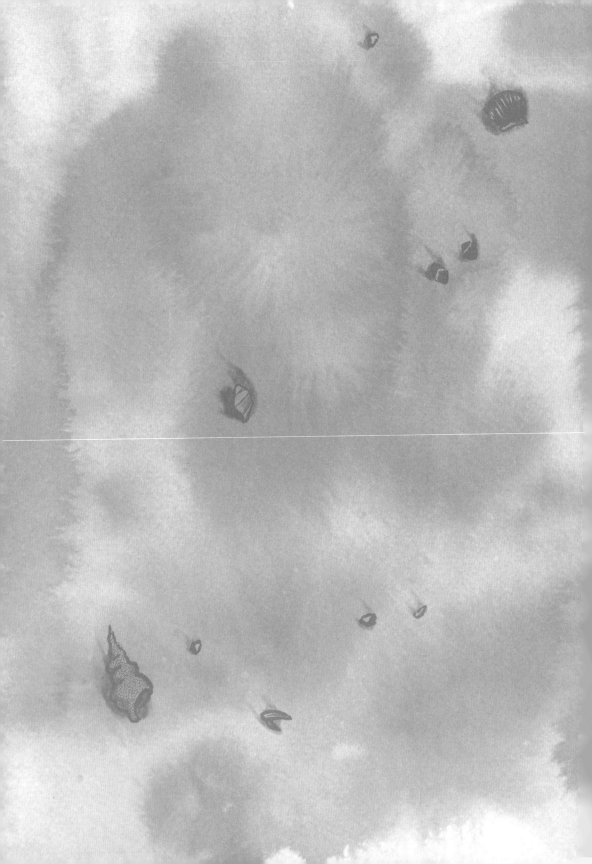

THE BEST WE COULD DO

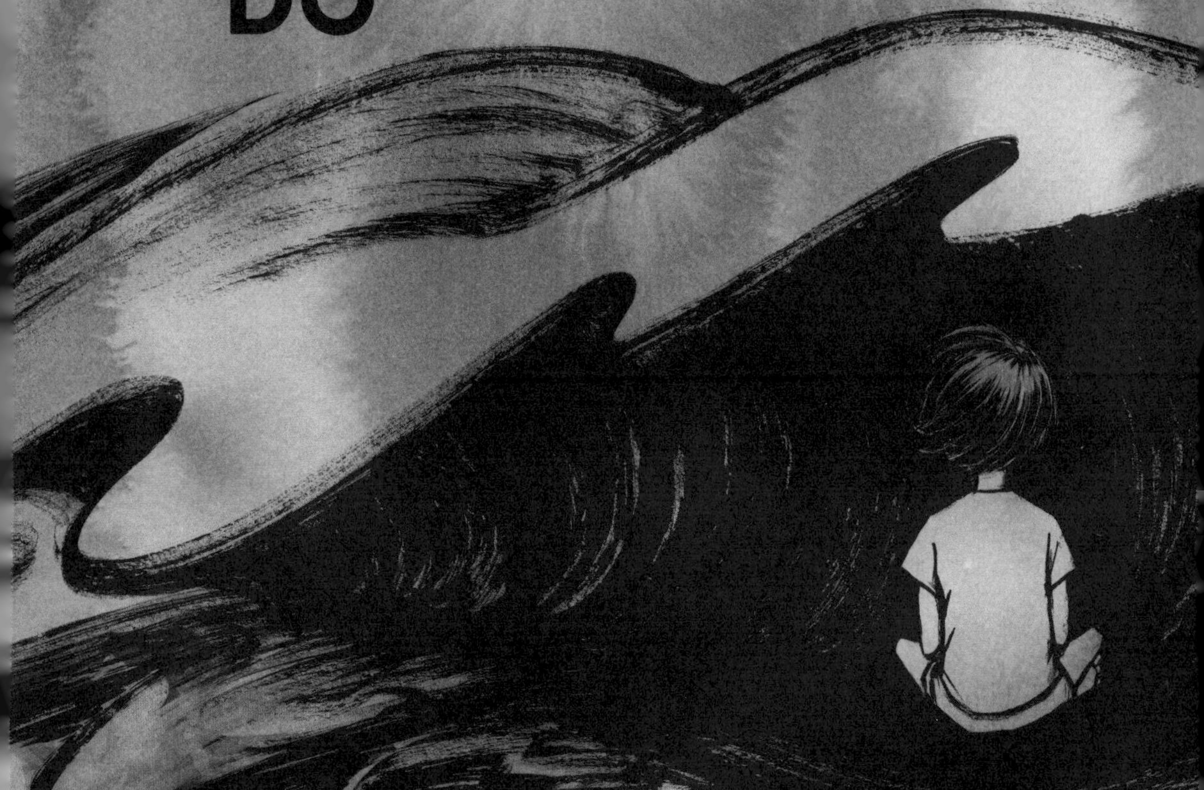

AN ILLUSTRATED MEMOIR

THI BUI

ABRAMS COMICARTS • NEW YORK

Editor: Clarissa Wong
Project Manager: Charles Kochman
Designer: Pamela Notarantonio
Managing Editor: Michael Clark
Production Manager: Kathy Lovisolo

Library of Congress Control Number: 2016940170

ISBN: 978-1-4197-1877-9

Printed and bound in U.S.A.
10 9 8 7 6 5 4 3

Abrams ComicArts books are available at special discounts when
purchased in quantity for premiums and promotions as well as fundraising
or educational use. Special editions can also be created to specification.
For details, contact specialsales@abramsbooks.com or the address below.

ABRAMS The Art of Books
115 West 18th Street, New York, NY 10011
abramsbooks.com

PREFACE

The seeds of this book were planted around 2002, when I was a graduate student and took a detour from my art education training to get lost in the world of oral history. The transcripts of my family's stories (and the clumsy, homemade book that I produced) from that time were more meaningful than any art I had made before. I was trying to understand the forces that caused my family, in the late seventies, to flee one country and start over in another. I titled my project "Buis in Vietnam and America: A Memory Reconstruction." It had photographs and some art, but mostly writing, and it was pretty academic. However, I didn't feel like I had solved the storytelling problem of how to present history in a way that is human and relatable and not oversimplified. I thought that turning it into a graphic novel might help. So then I had to learn how to do comics! I drew the initial draft of the first pages in 2005, and it's been a steep learning curve working in this medium.

For that and other reasons, this book has taken me a very long time to make. When my son was one, and the book was also just a baby, my family and I moved from New York to California. I helped open an alternative public high school for immigrants in Oakland, where I taught for the next seven years. It was difficult to carve out the time and headspace to work on something that not only required a lot of historical research, but was also intensely personal and at times painful. I often wanted to quit. With my mind on current immigration issues and the lives of my students, I gave my book the name *Refugee Reflex* and worked on it during school holidays. Besides sounding an awful lot like "reflux," this title was problematic because it didn't quite encompass everything the book was about. In 2011, while I was reorganizing my life so that my aging parents could be more involved in it, I realized that the book was about parents and children, and it became *The Best We Could Do*.

On the long road to getting this book made, I received many gifts from the people I encountered: The opportunity to pitch this book to a wonderful publisher. Unwavering support and generous guidance from artists, writers, and editors I admire. The camaraderie of storytellers and magic makers. And the unconditional love and trust that were placed in me by my family. My head spins in amazement. My heart swells with gratitude.

—Thi

Thi Bui
Berkeley, California
July 2016

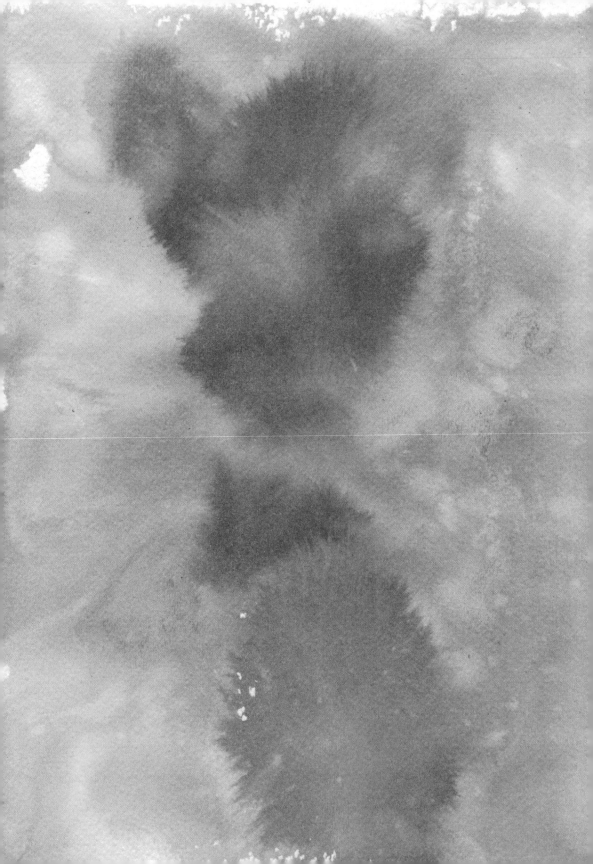

CONTENTS

CHAPTER 1

LABOR

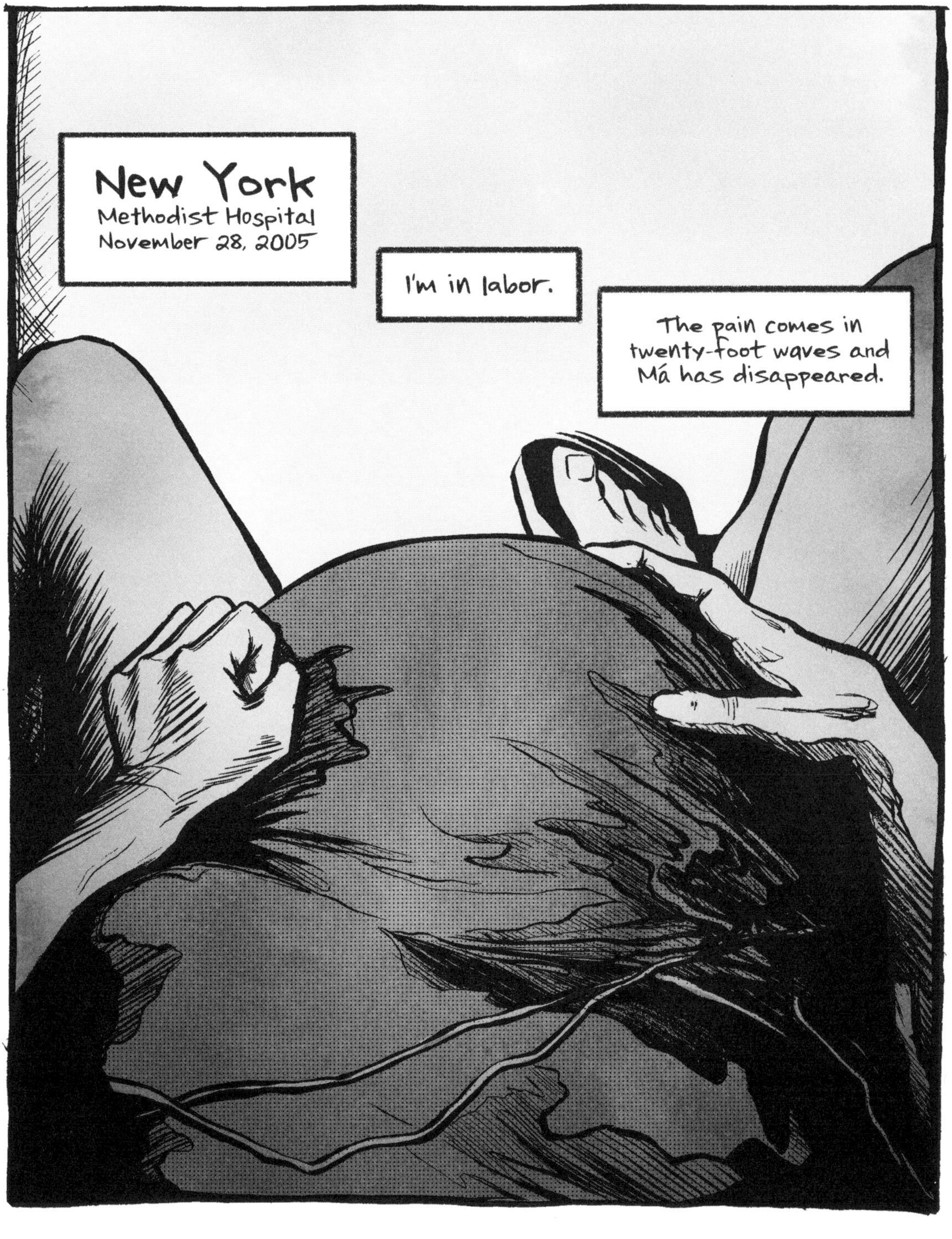
New York
Methodist Hospital
November 28, 2005
I'm in labor.
The pain comes in twenty-foot waves and Má has disappeared.

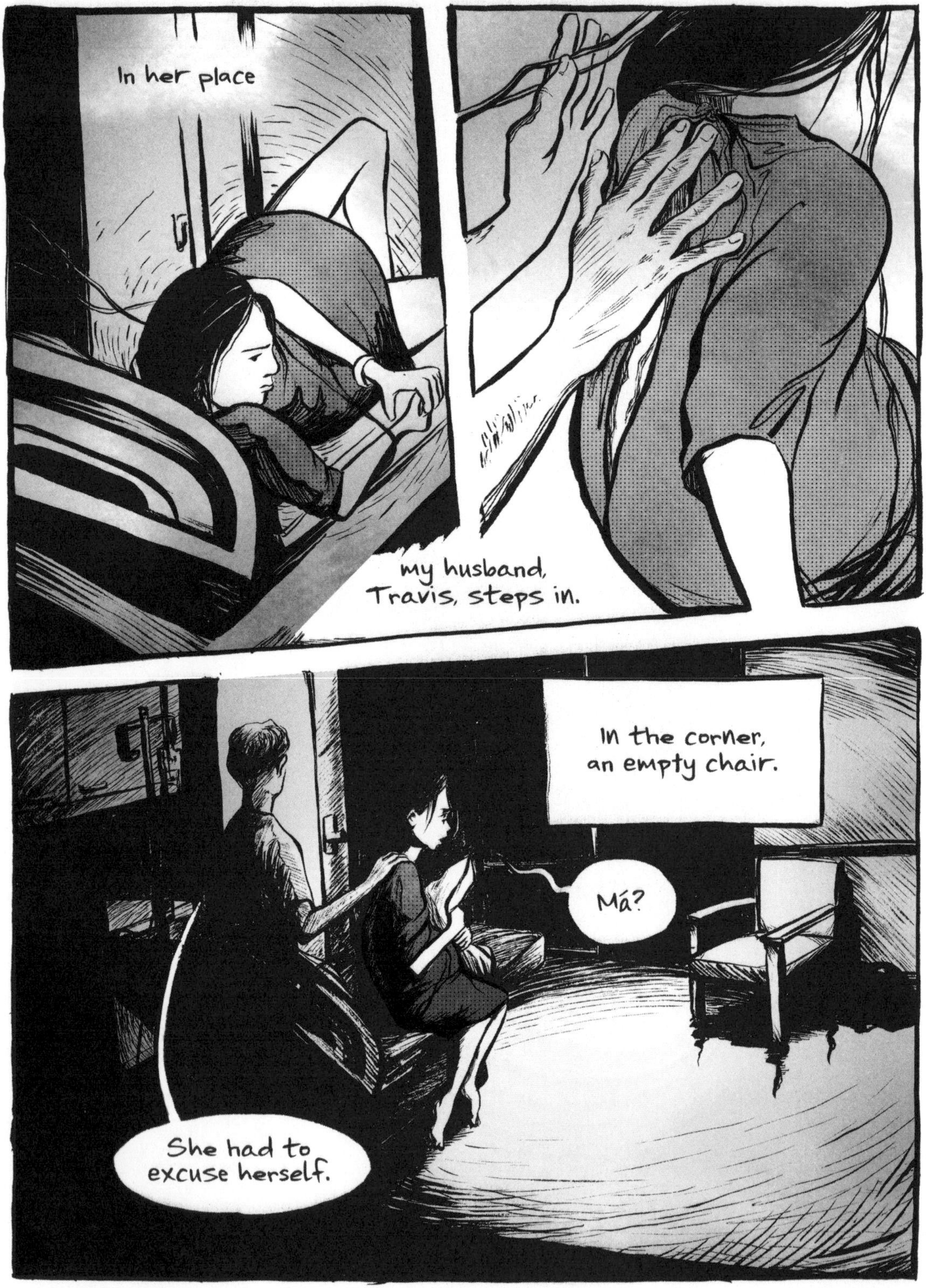
In her place
my husband, Travis, steps in.
In the corner, an empty chair.
Má?
She had to excuse herself.

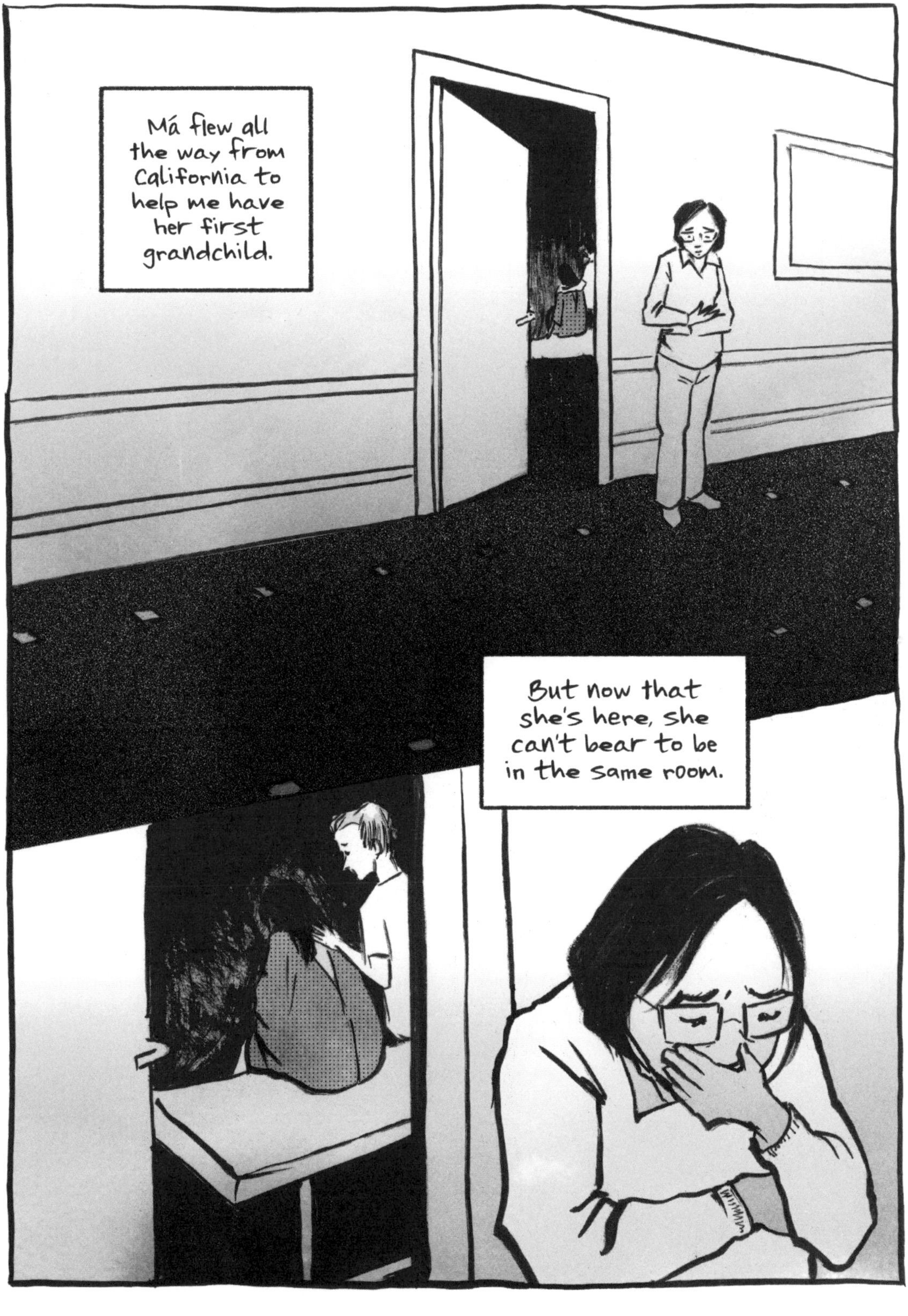
Má flew all the way from California to help me have her first grandchild.
But now that she's here, she can't bear to be in the same room.

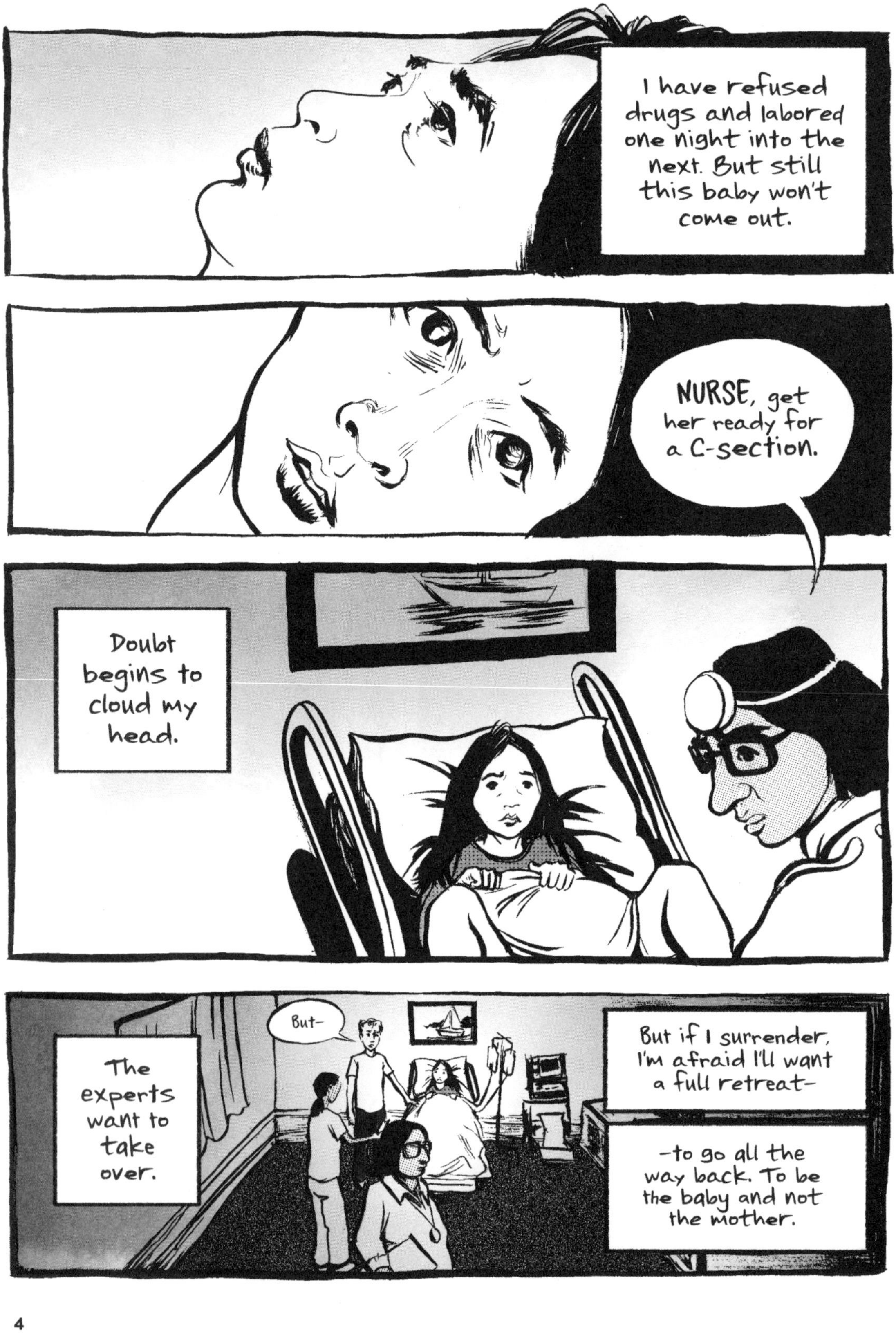
I have refused drugs and labored one night into the next. But still this baby won't come out.
NURSE, get her ready for a C-section.
Doubt begins to cloud my head.
The experts want to take over.
But-
But if I surrender, I'm afraid I'll want a full retreat-
-to go all the way back. To be the baby and not the mother.

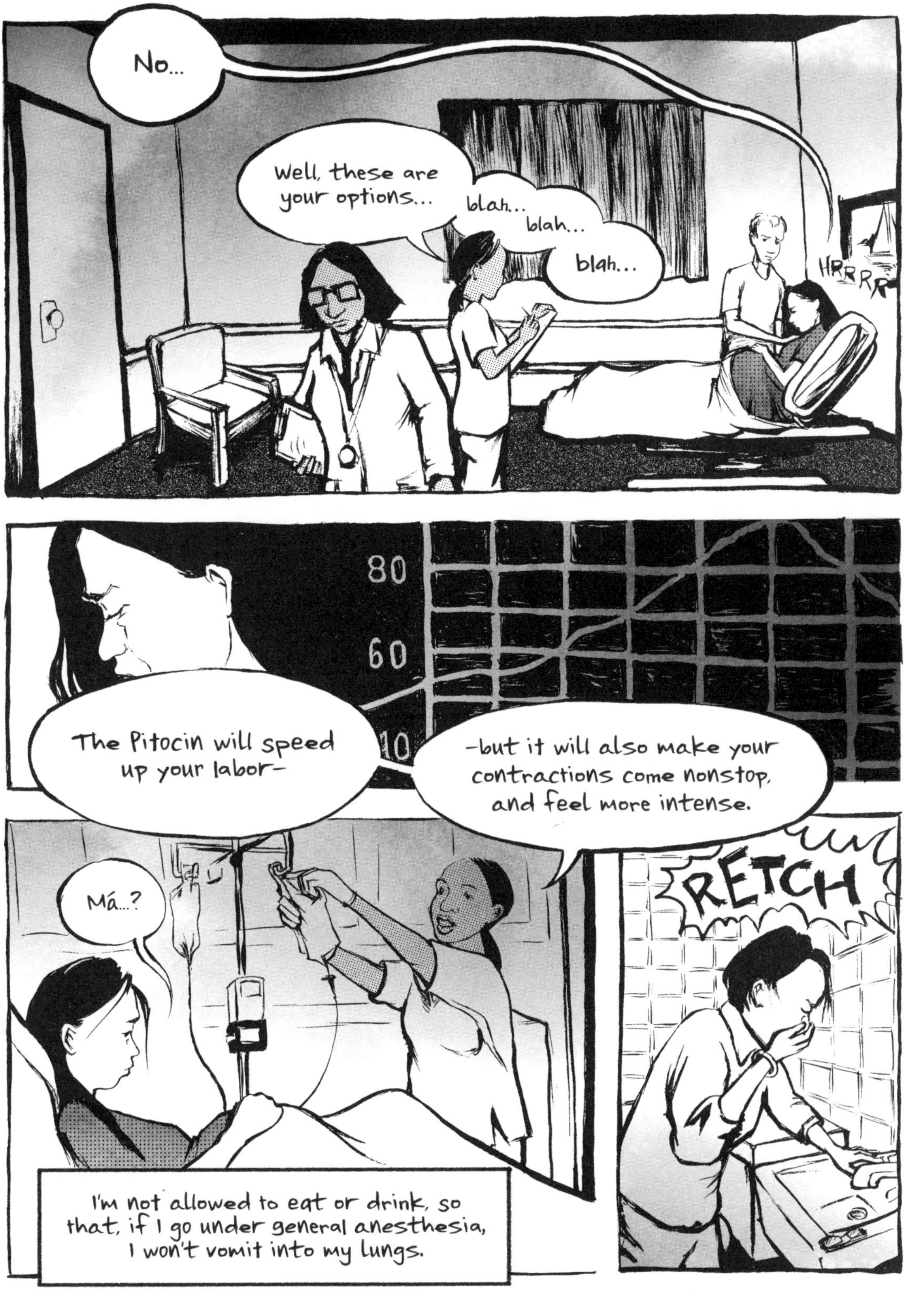
No...
Well, these are your options...
blah...
blah...
blah...
HRRRR
80
60
10
The Pitocin will speed up your labor—
—but it will also make your contractions come nonstop, and feel more intense.
Má...?
RETCH
I'm not allowed to eat or drink, so that, if I go under general anesthesia, I won't vomit into my lungs.

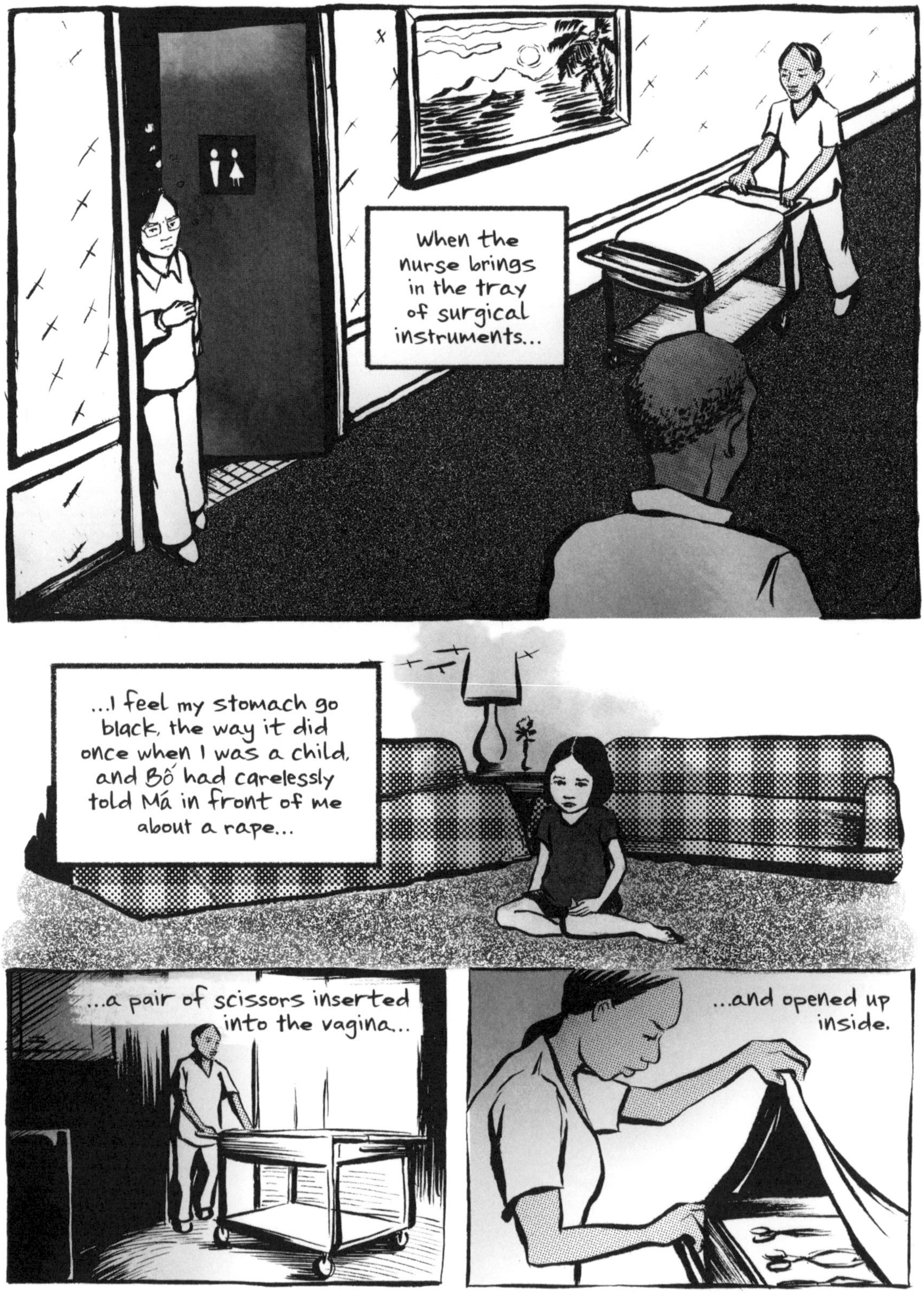
When the nurse brings in the tray of surgical instruments...
...I feel my stomach go black, the way it did once when I was a child, and Bố had carelessly told Má in front of me about a rape...
...a pair of scissors inserted into the vagina...
...and opened up inside.

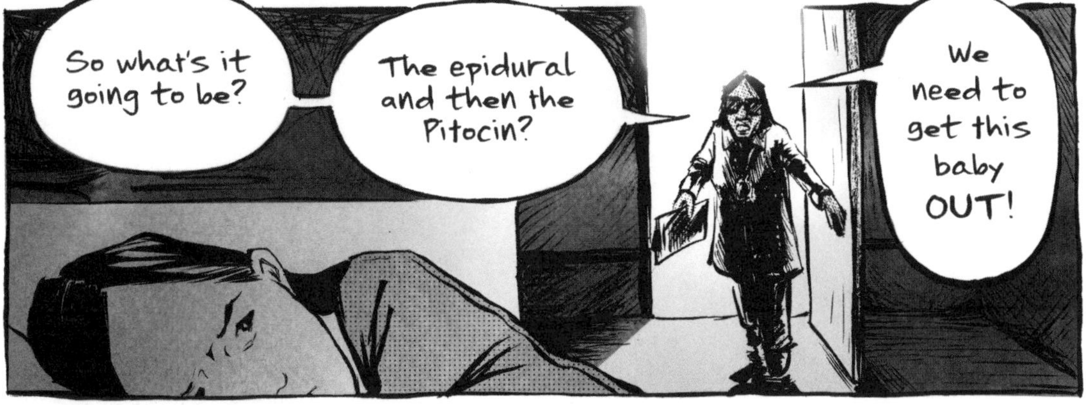
So what's it going to be?
The epidural and then the Pitocin?
We need to get this baby OUT!

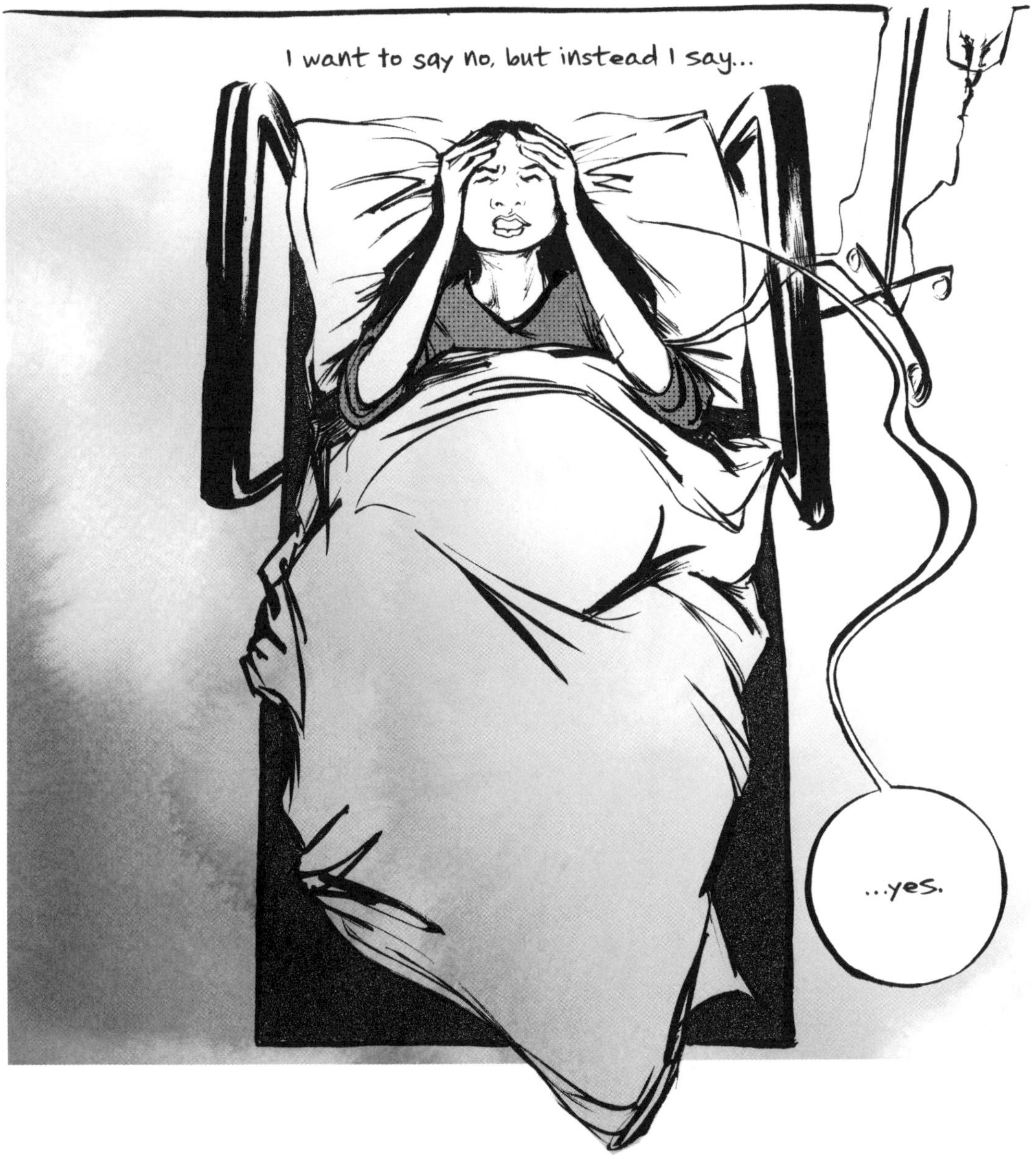
I want to say no, but instead I say...
...yes.

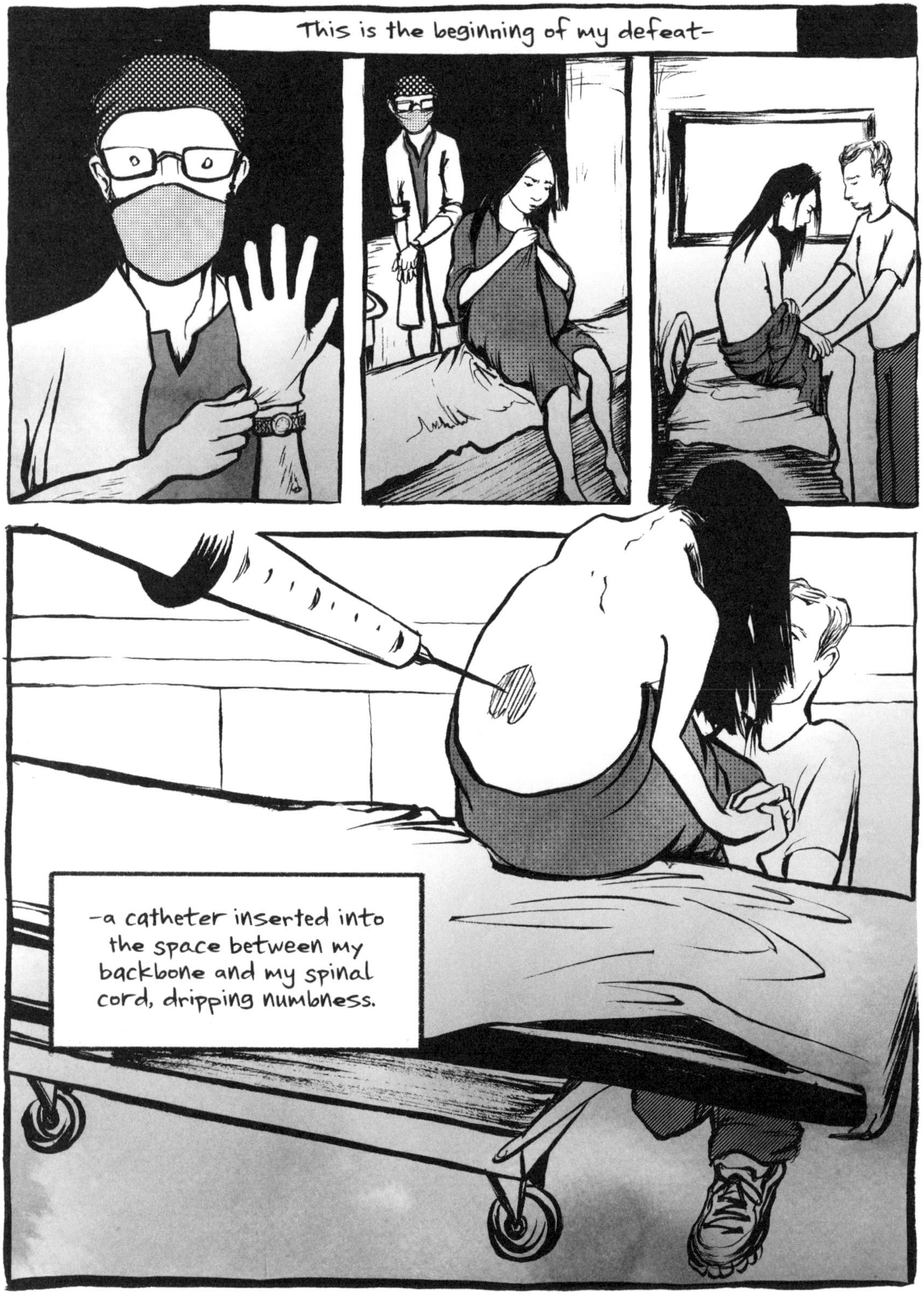
This is the beginning of my defeat-
-a catheter inserted into the space between my backbone and my spinal cord, dripping numbness.

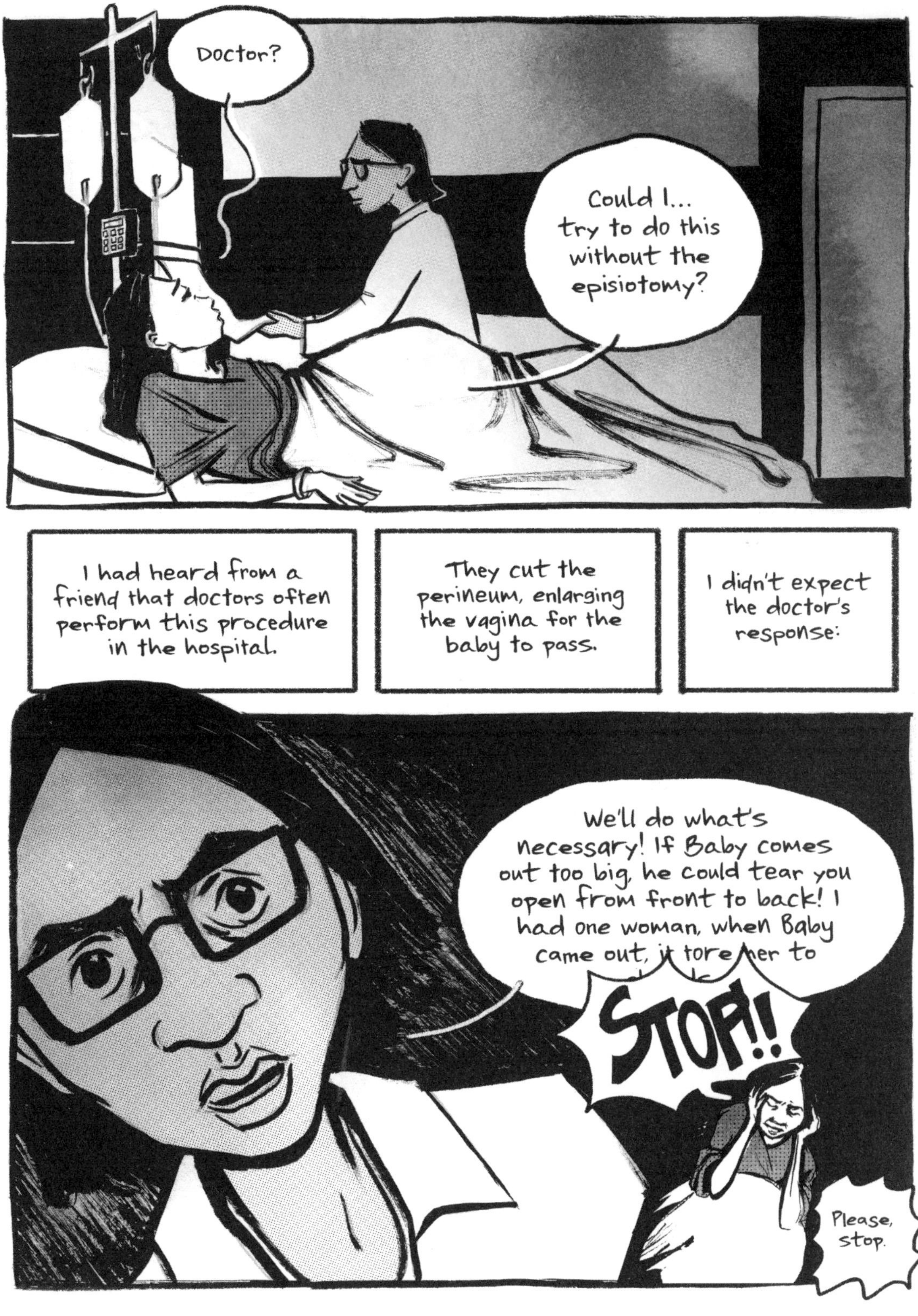
Doctor?
Could I... try to do this without the episiotomy?
I had heard from a friend that doctors often perform this procedure in the hospital.
They cut the perineum, enlarging the vagina for the baby to pass.
I didn't expect the doctor's response:
We'll do what's necessary! If Baby comes out too big, he could tear you open from front to back! I had one woman, when Baby came out, it tore her to
STOP!!
Please, stop.

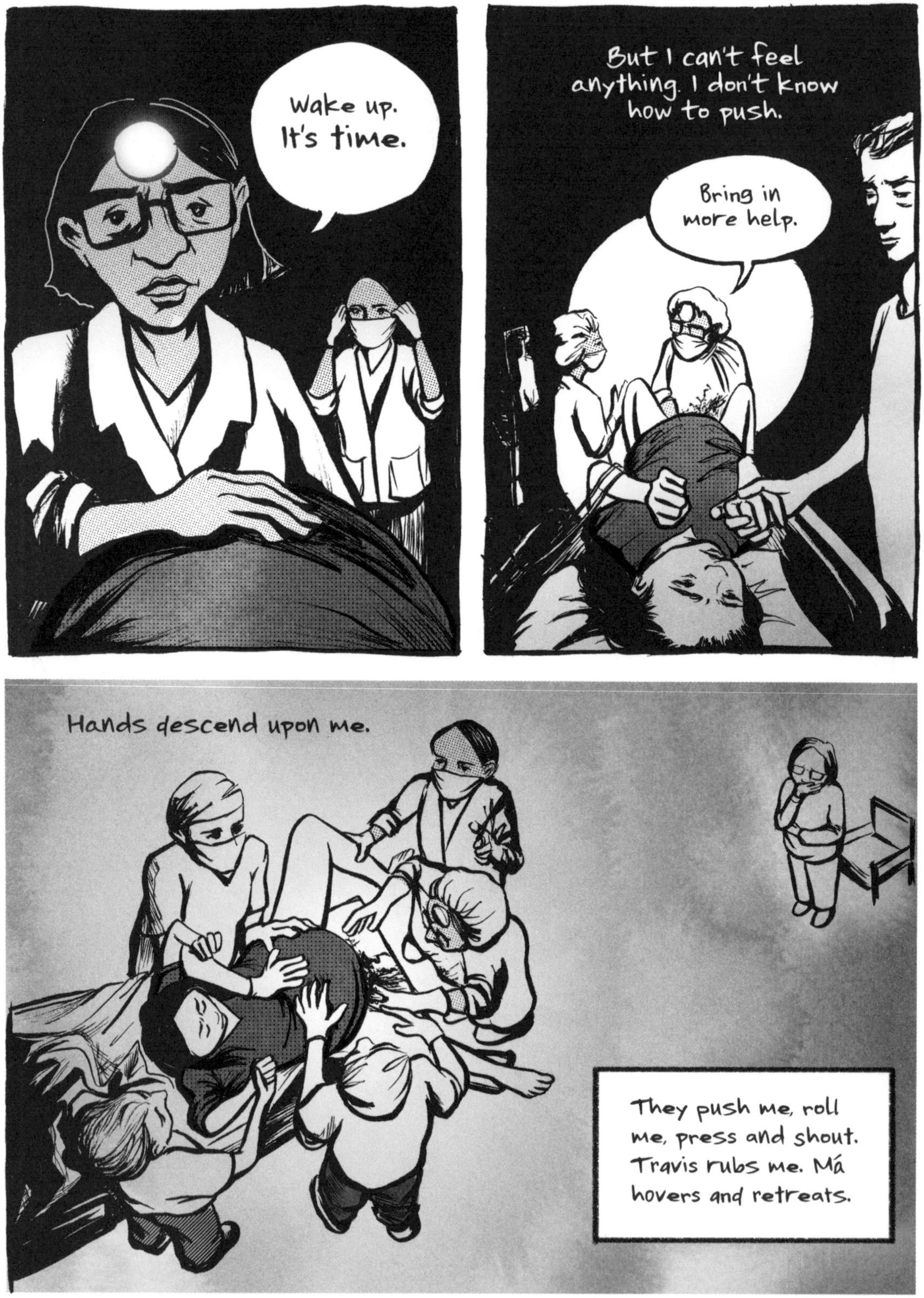

Wake up.
It's time.
But I can't feel anything. I don't know how to push.
Bring in more help.
Hands descend upon me.
They push me, roll me, press and shout. Travis rubs me. Má hovers and retreats.

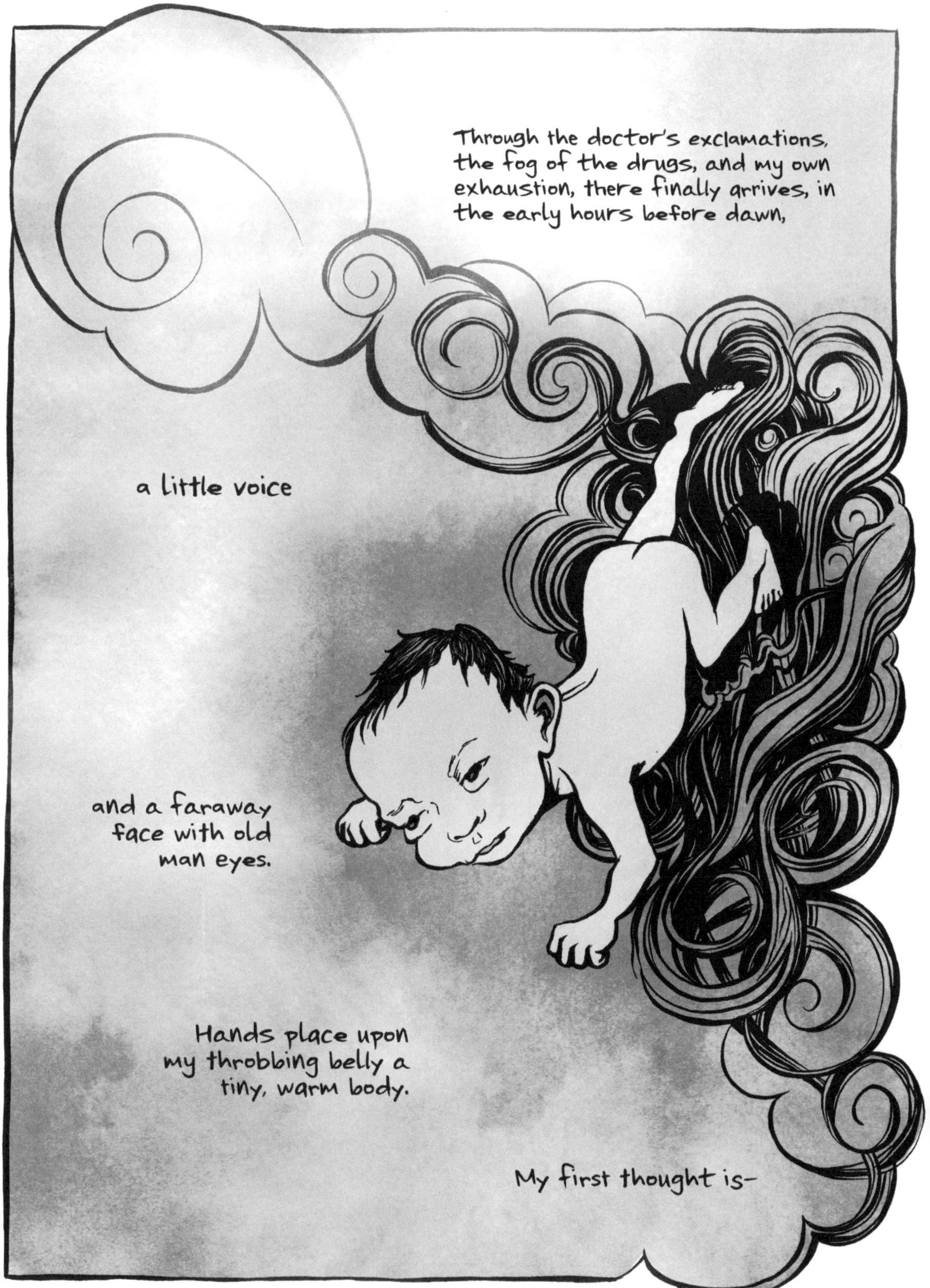
Through the doctor's exclamations, the fog of the drugs, and my own exhaustion, there finally arrives, in the early hours before dawn,
a little voice
and a faraway face with old man eyes.
Hands place upon my throbbing belly a tiny, warm body.
My first thought is—

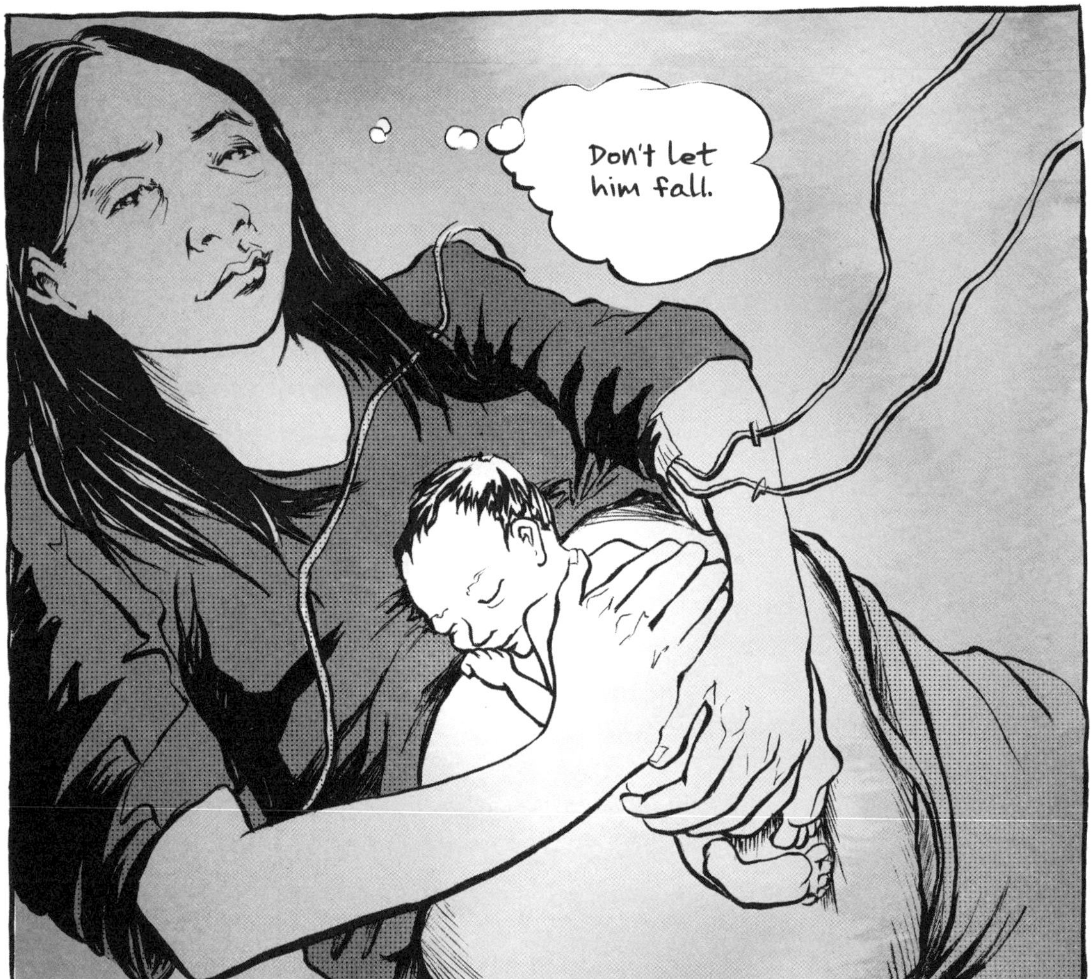
Don't let him fall.

Then hands lift him away.

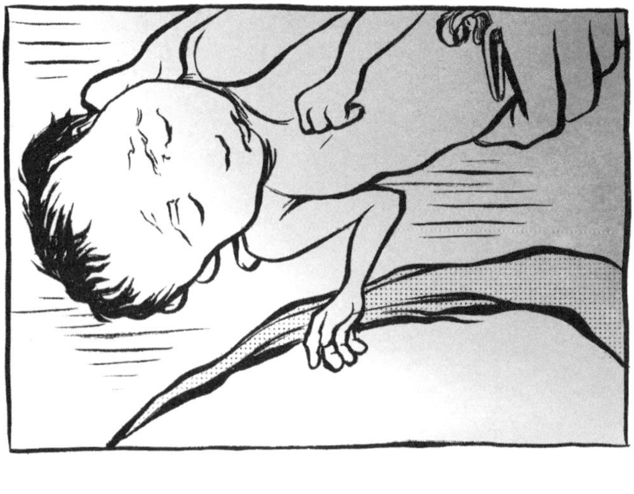

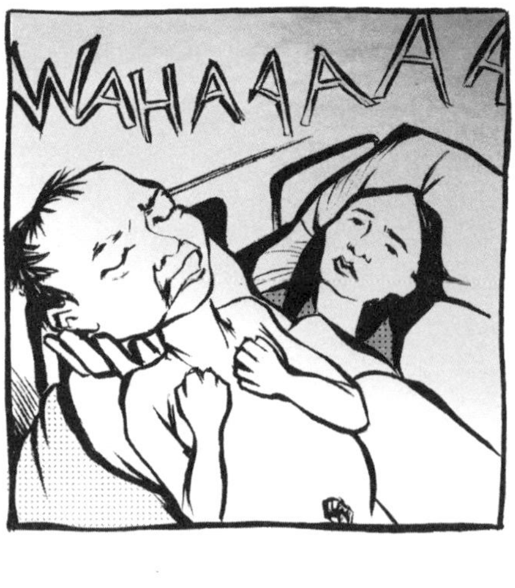
WAHAAAAA

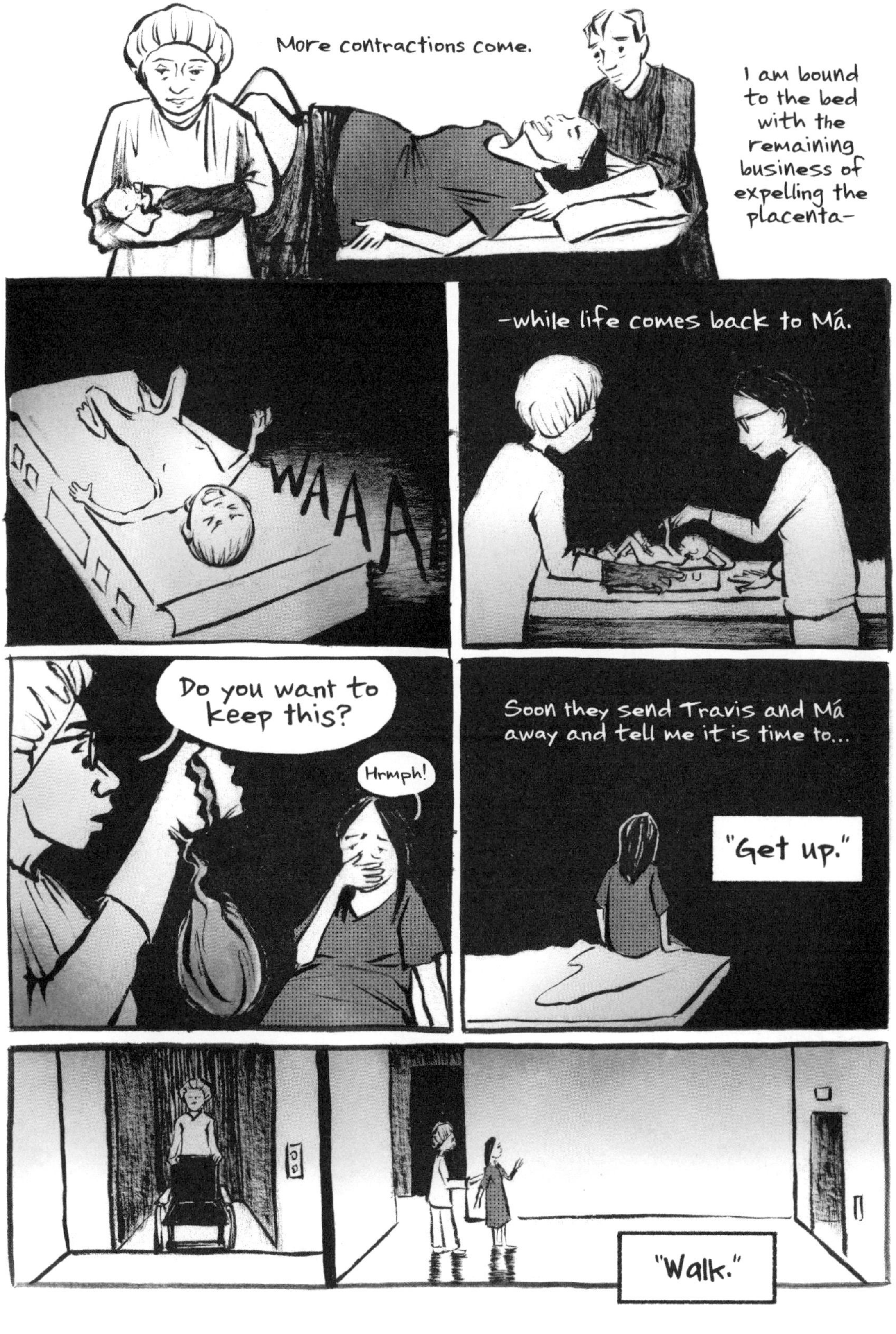
More contractions come.
I am bound to the bed with the remaining business of expelling the placenta-
WAAA
-while life comes back to Má.
Do you want to keep this?
Hrmph!
Soon they send Travis and Má away and tell me it is time to...
"Get up."
"Walk."

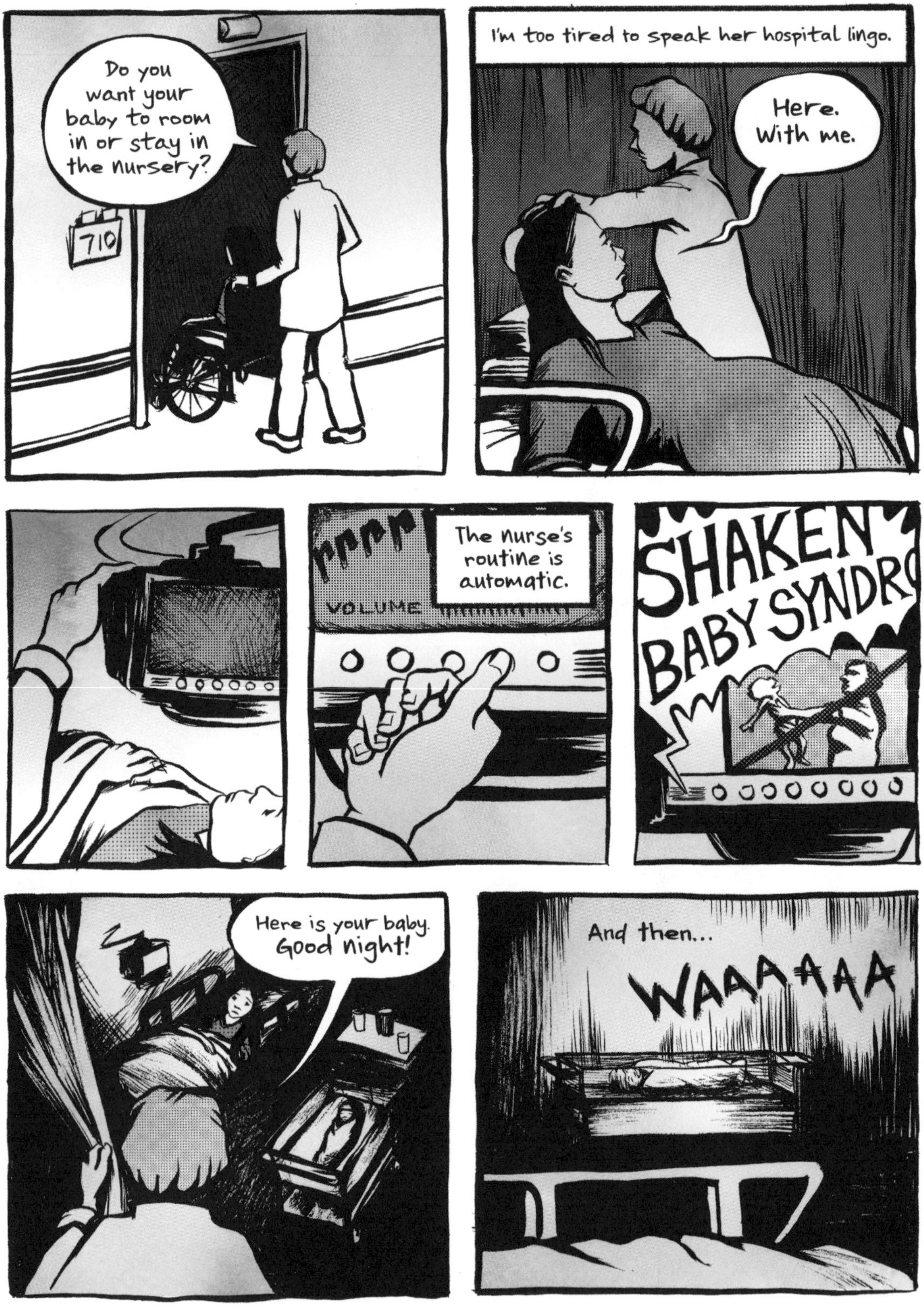

Do you want your baby to room in or stay in the nursery?
710
I'm too tired to speak her hospital lingo.
Here. With me.
rrrr
VOLUME
The nurse's routine is automatic.
SHAKEN BABY SYNDRO
Here is your baby. Good night!
And then...
WAAAAAA

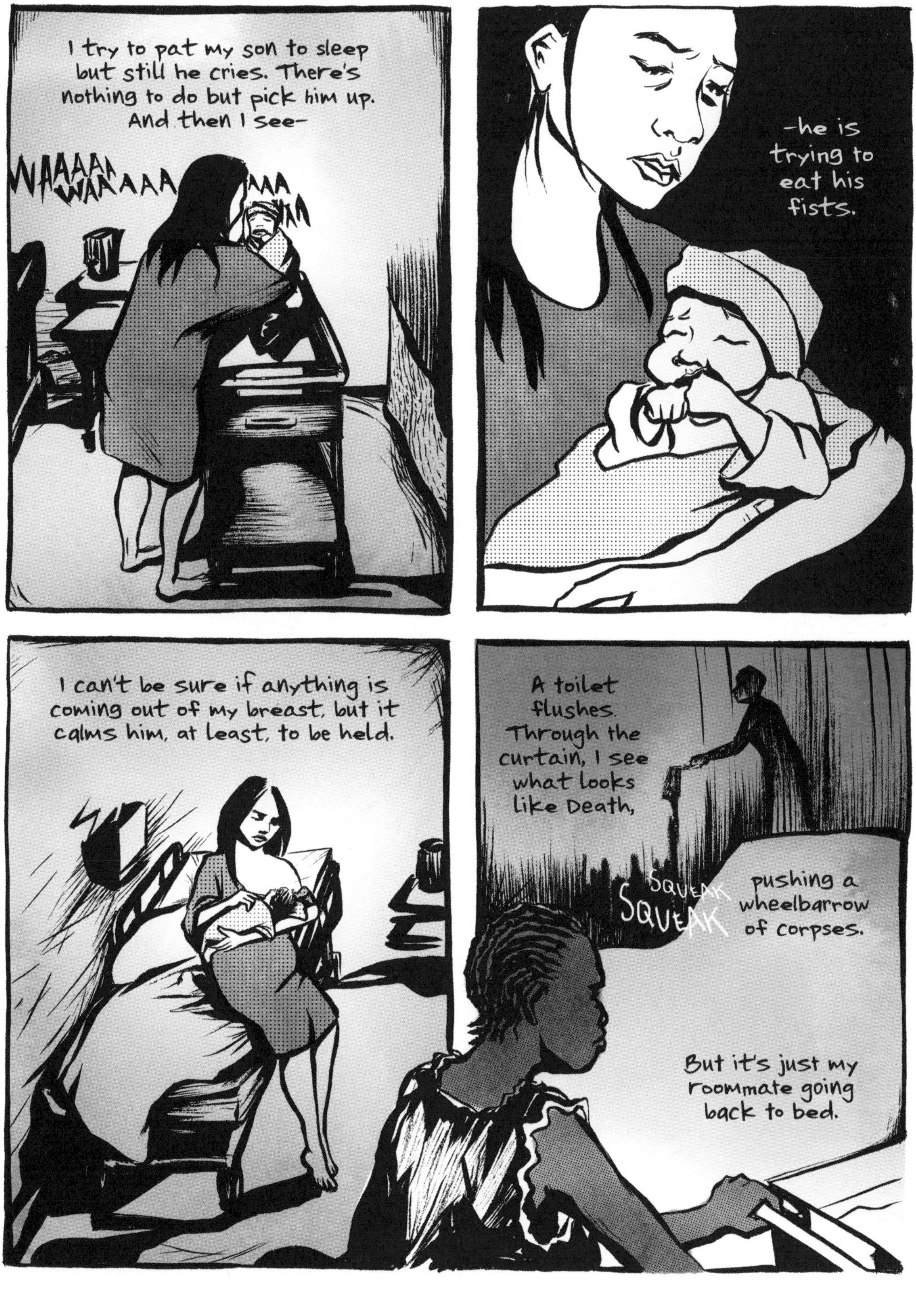
I try to pat my son to sleep but still he cries. There's nothing to do but pick him up. And then I see—
WAAAAA WAAAAA
AAA WAA
—he is trying to eat his fists.
I can't be sure if anything is coming out of my breast, but it calms him, at least, to be held.
A toilet flushes. Through the curtain, I see what looks like Death,
SQUEAK SQUEAK
pushing a wheelbarrow of corpses.
But it's just my roommate going back to bed.

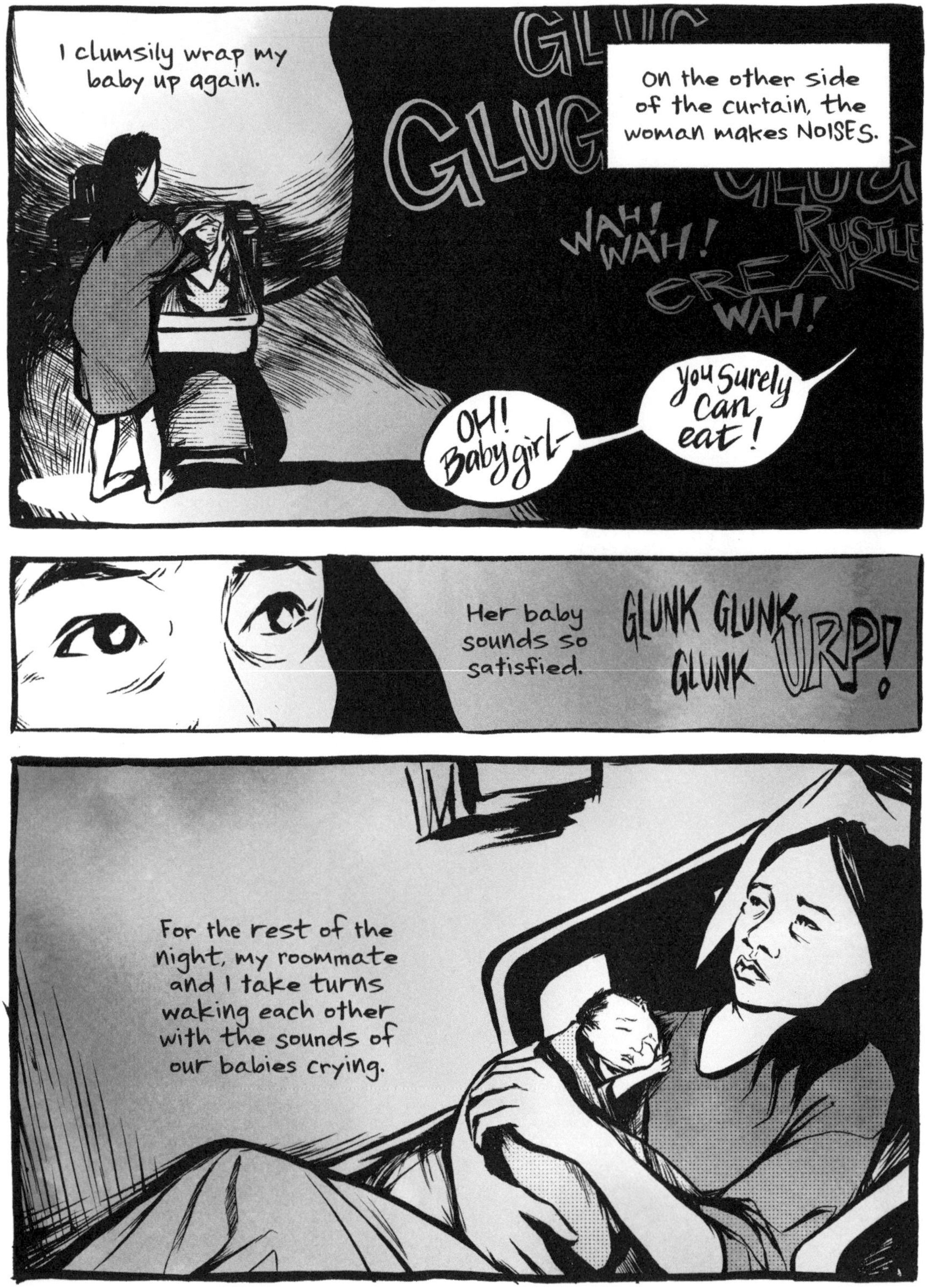
I clumsily wrap my baby up again.
GLUG
GLUG
On the other side of the curtain, the woman makes NOISES.
GLUG
WAH! WAH!
RUSTLE
CREAK
WAH!
OH! Baby girl–
You surely can eat!
Her baby sounds so satisfied.
GLUNK GLUNK GLUNK
URP!
For the rest of the night, my roommate and I take turns waking each other with the sounds of our babies crying.

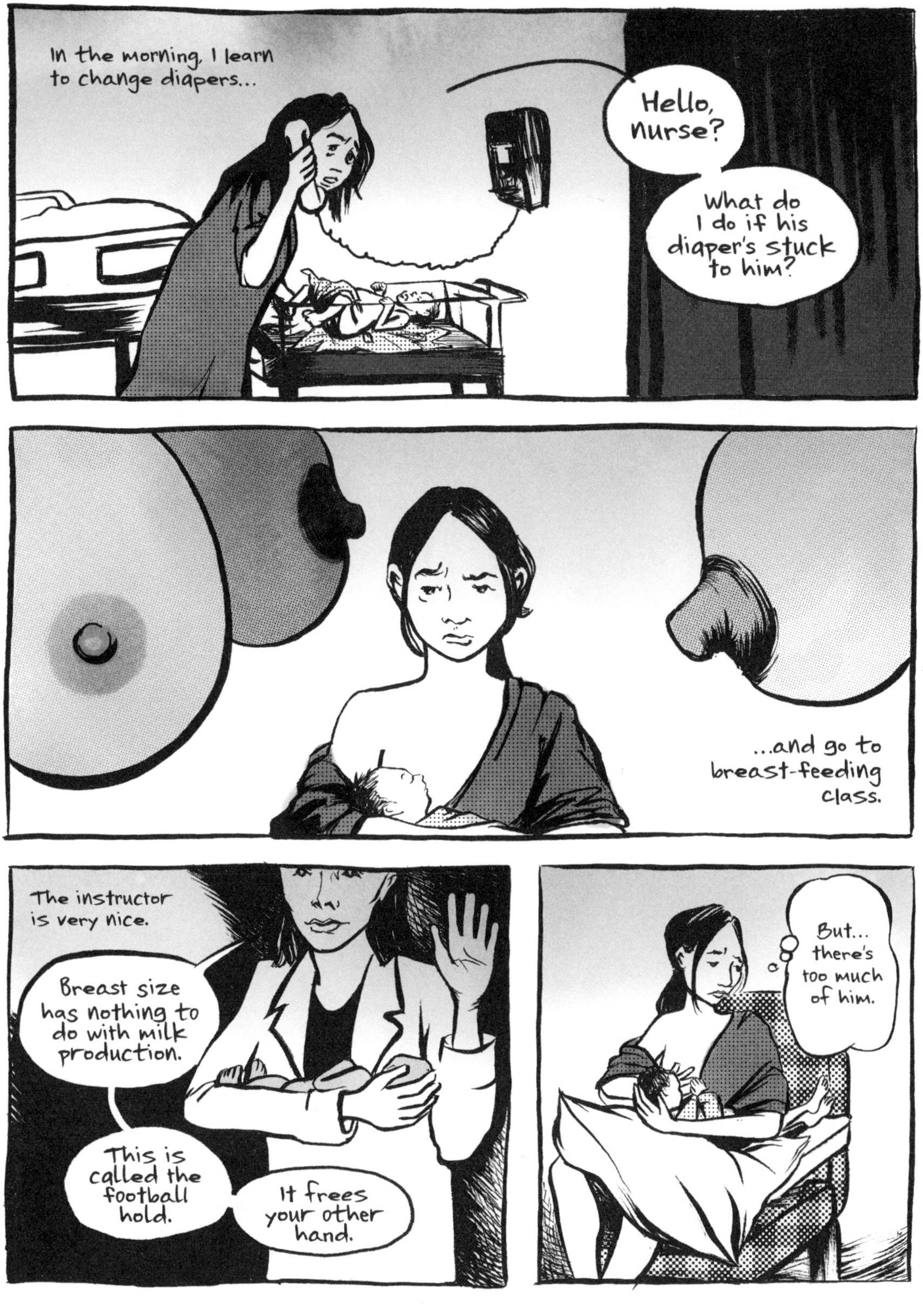
In the morning, I learn to change diapers...
Hello, nurse?
What do I do if his diaper's stuck to him?
...and go to breast-feeding class.
The instructor is very nice.
Breast size has nothing to do with milk production.
This is called the football hold.
It frees your other hand.
But... there's too much of him.

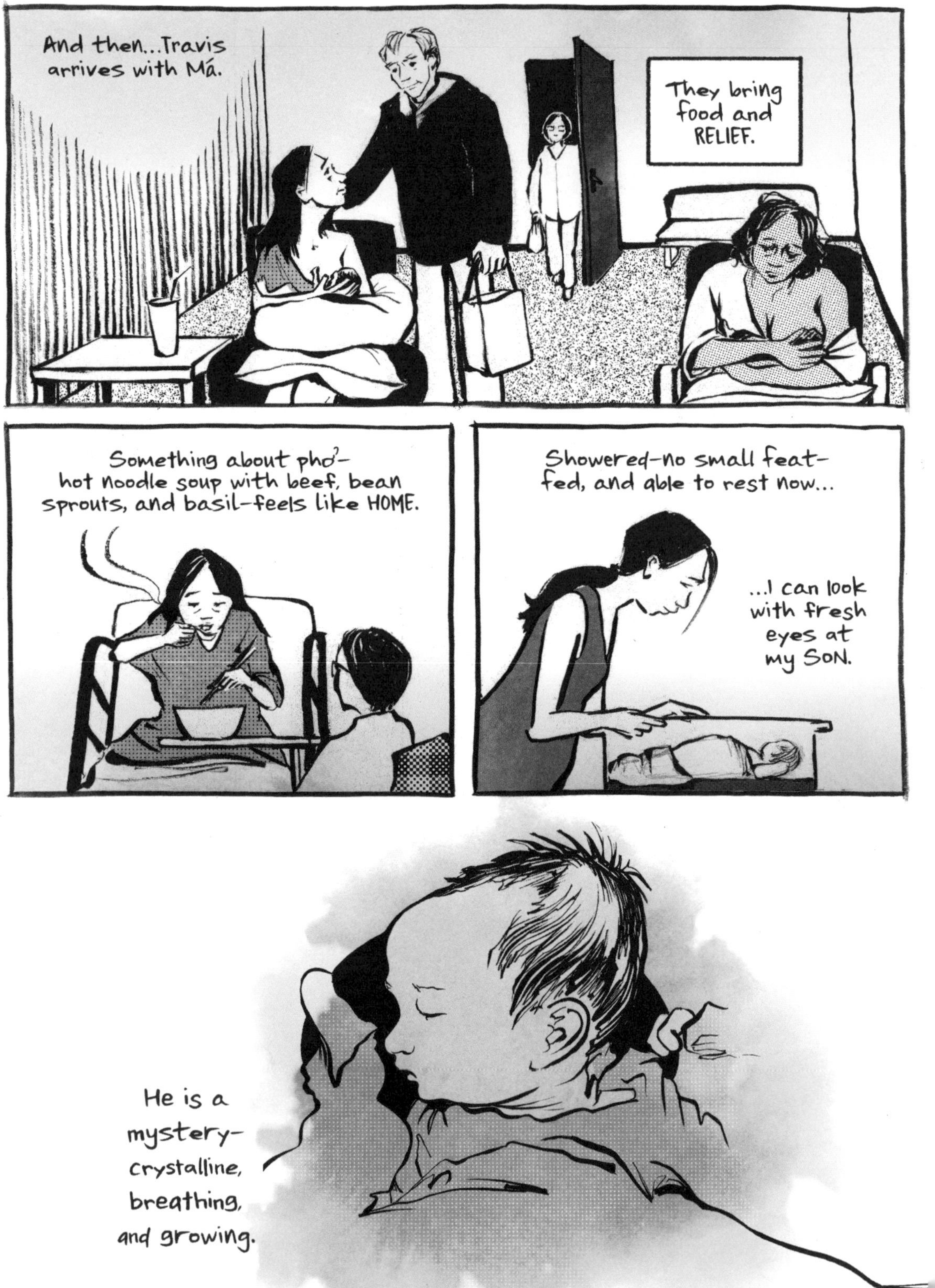
And then...Travis arrives with Má.
They bring food and RELIEF.
Something about phở– hot noodle soup with beef, bean sprouts, and basil–feels like HOME.
Showered–no small feat– fed, and able to rest now...
...I can look with fresh eyes at my SON.
He is a mystery– crystalline, breathing, and growing.

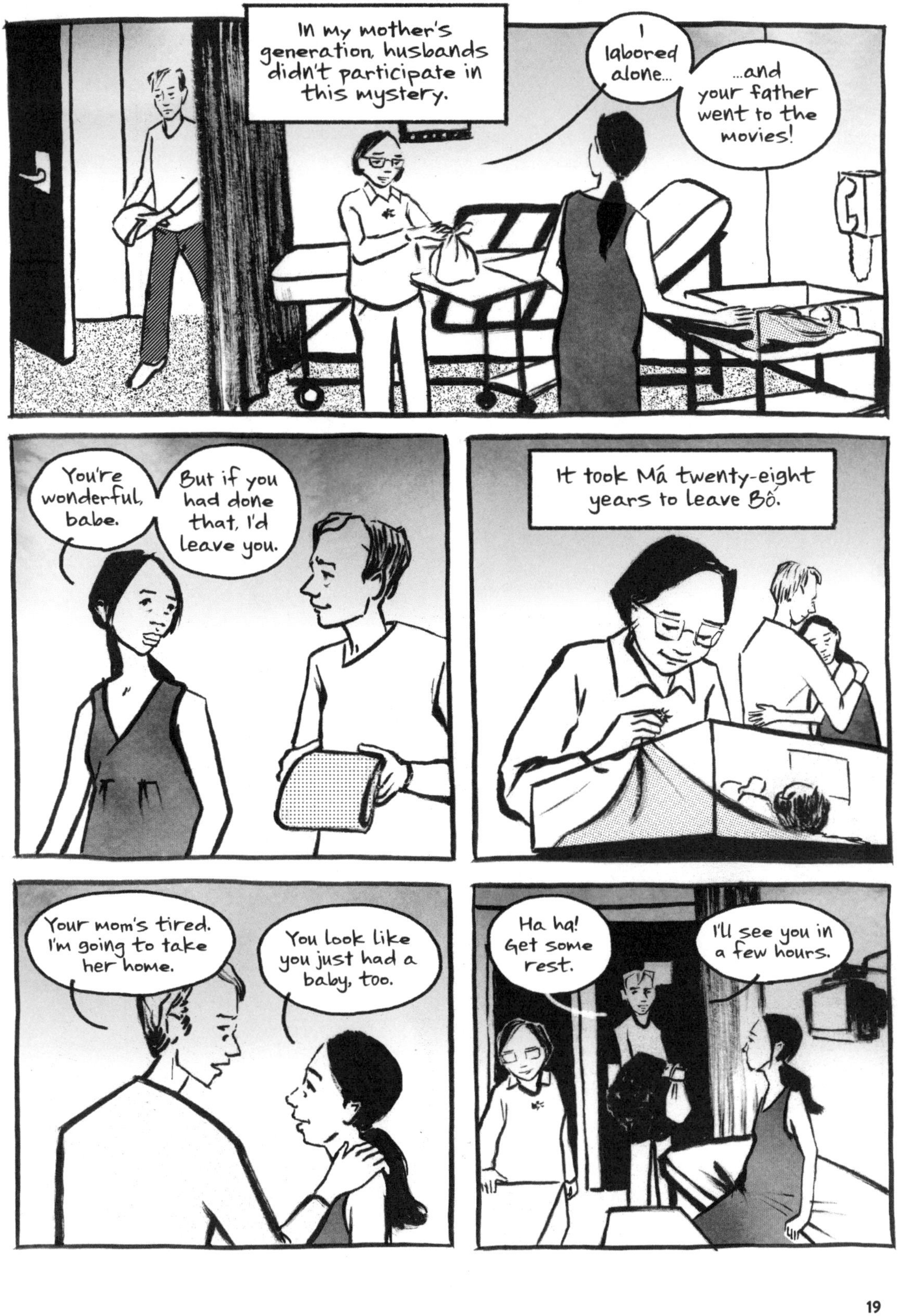
In my mother's generation, husbands didn't participate in this mystery.
I labored alone...
...and your father went to the movies!
You're wonderful, babe.
But if you had done that, I'd leave you.
It took Má twenty-eight years to leave Bố.
Your mom's tired. I'm going to take her home.
You look like you just had a baby, too.
Ha ha! Get some rest.
I'll see you in a few hours.

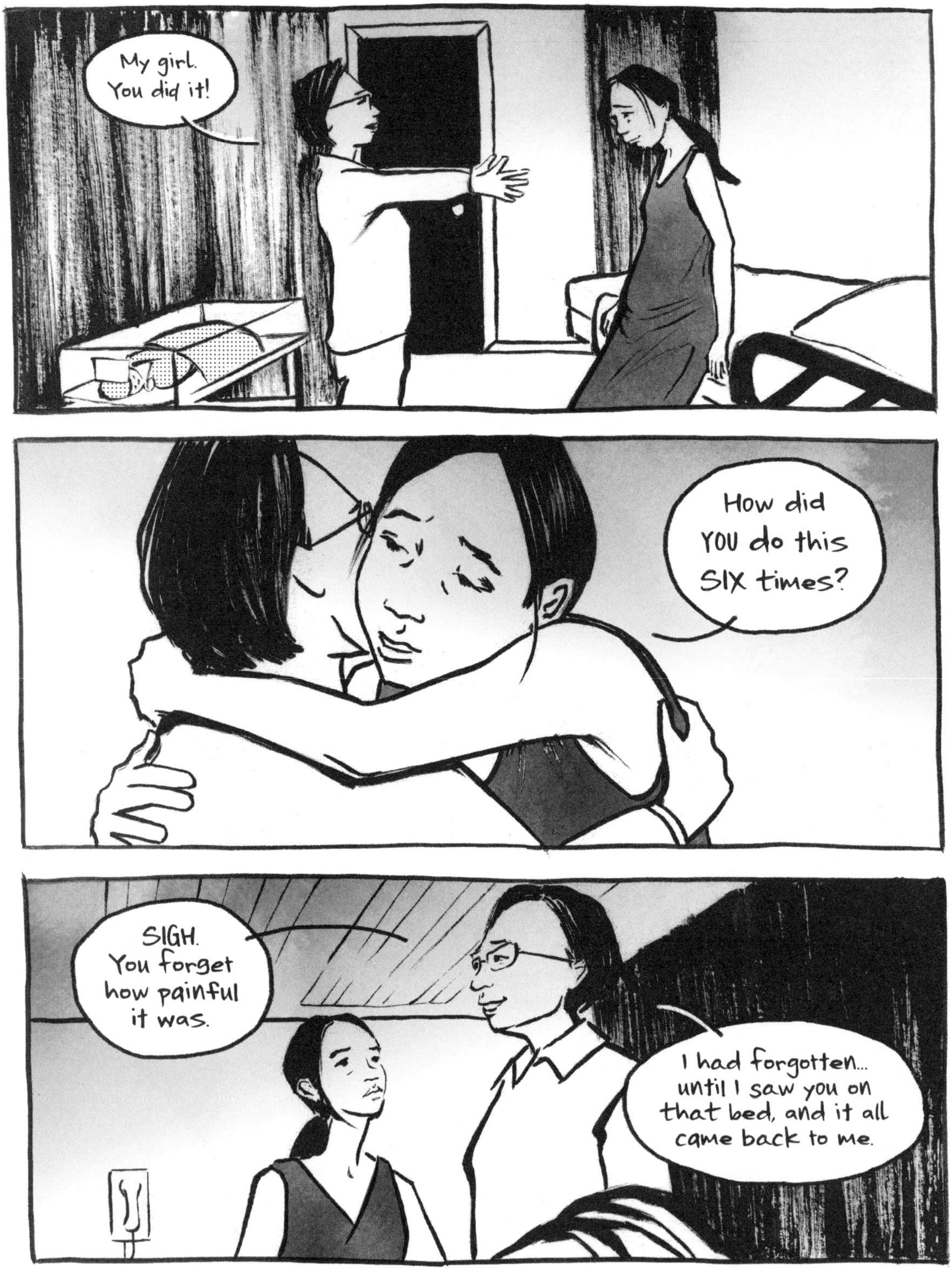
My girl. You did it!
How did YOU do this SIX times?
SIGH. You forget how painful it was.
I had forgotten... until I saw you on that bed, and it all came back to me.

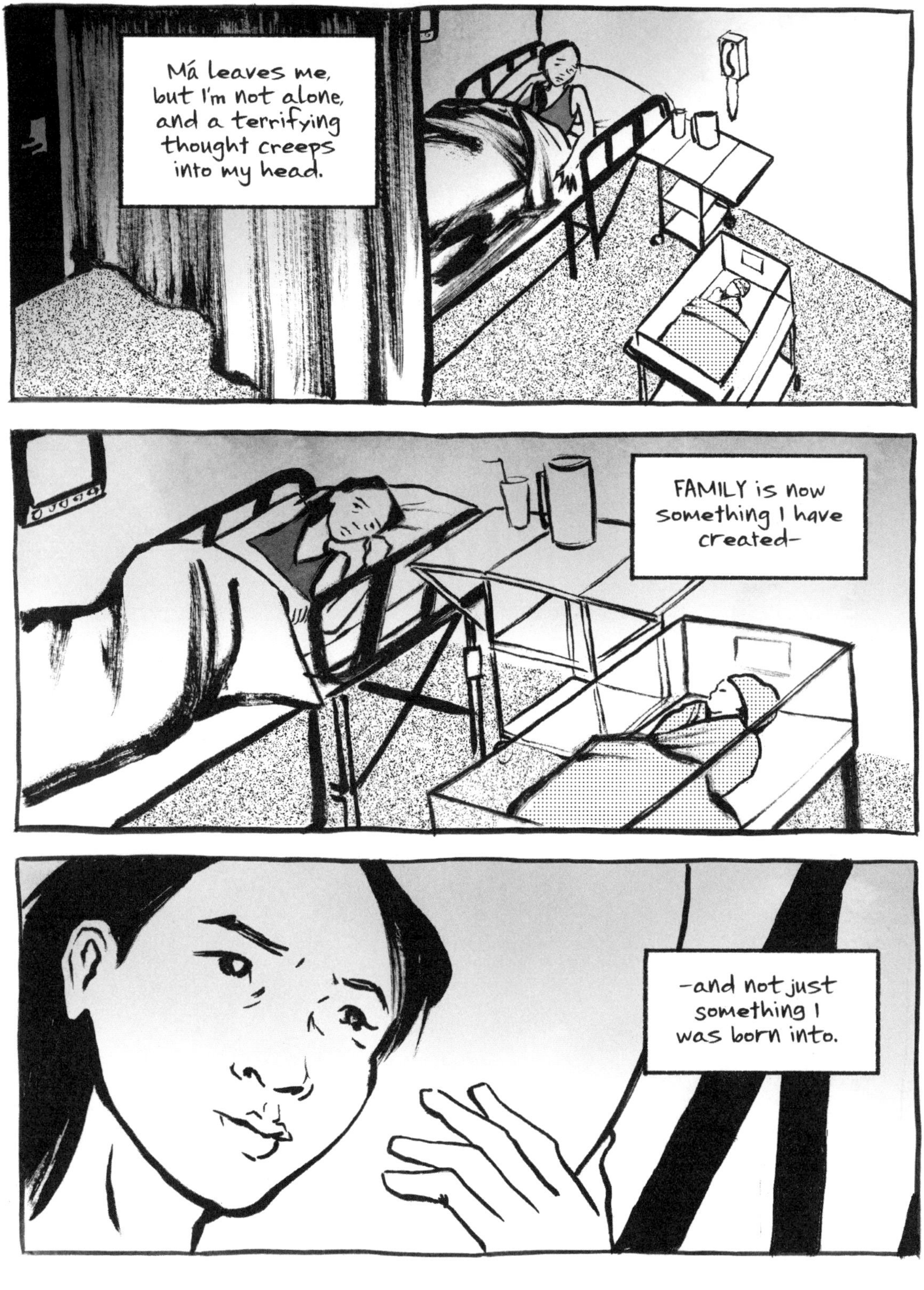
Má leaves me, but I'm not alone, and a terrifying thought creeps into my head.
FAMILY is now something I have created-
-and not just something I was born into.

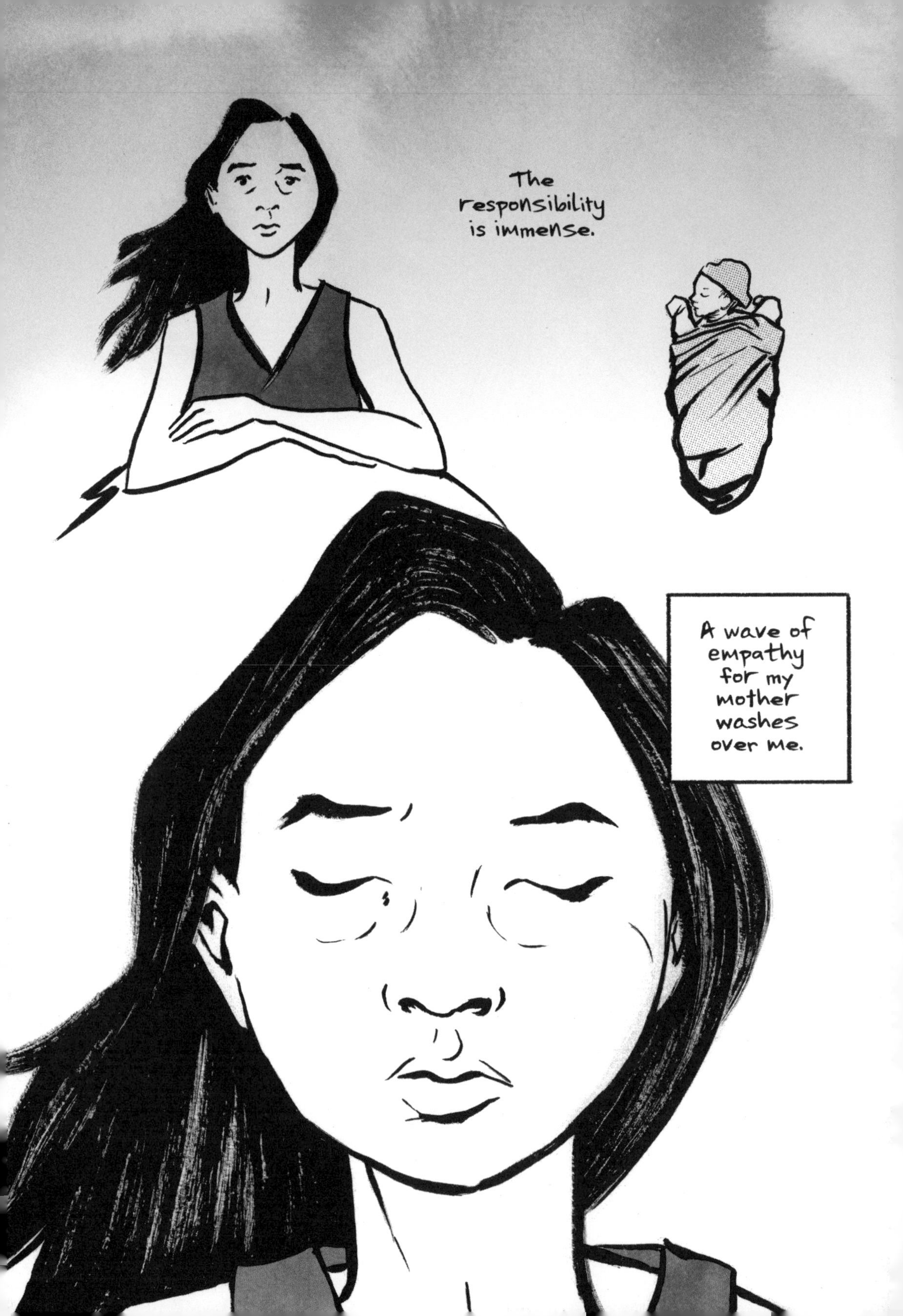
The responsibility is immense.
A wave of empathy for my mother washes over me.

CHAPTER 2

REWIND, REVERSE

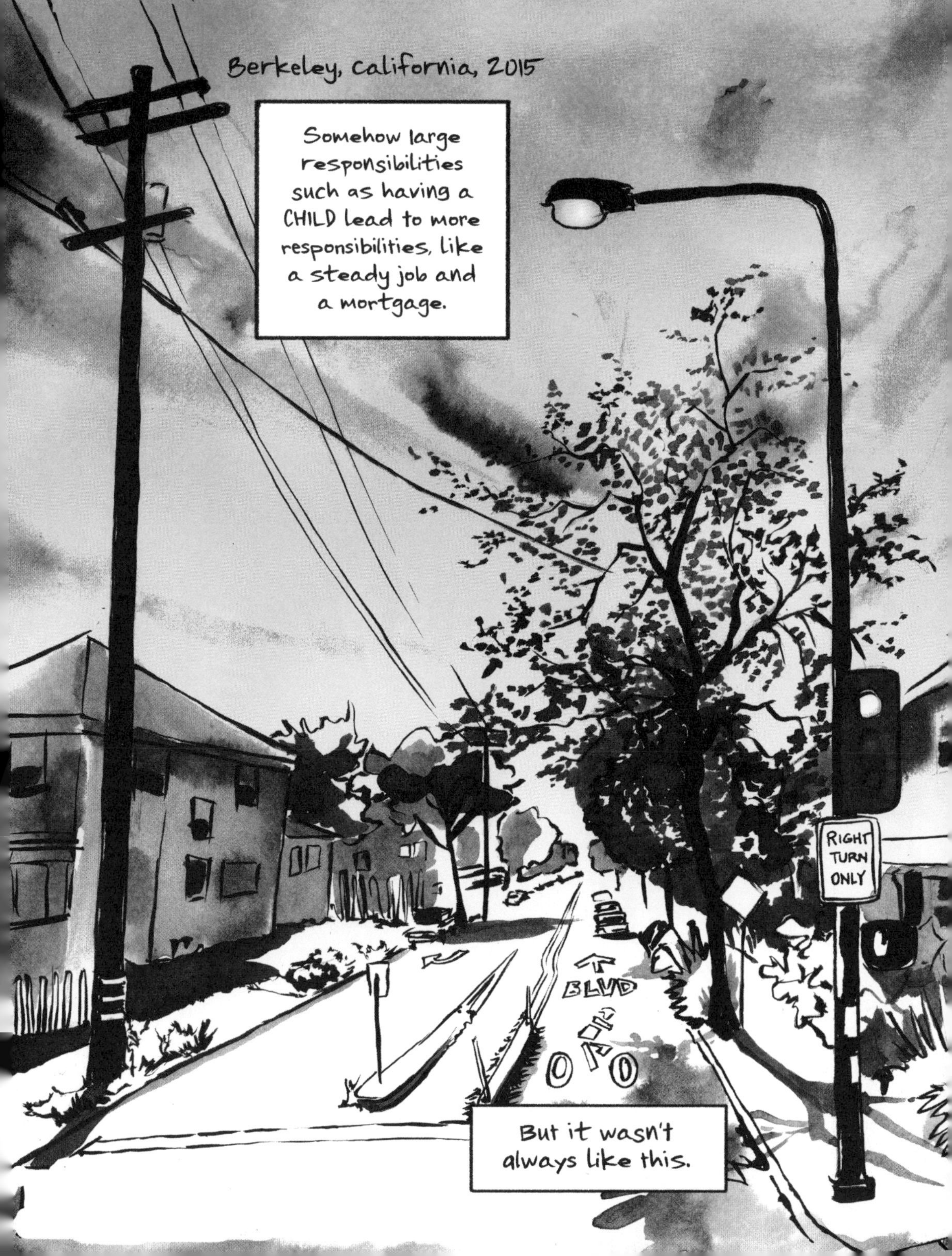
Berkeley, California, 2015
Somehow large responsibilities such as having a CHILD lead to more responsibilities, like a steady job and a mortgage.
RIGHT TURN ONLY
BLVD
But it wasn't always like this.

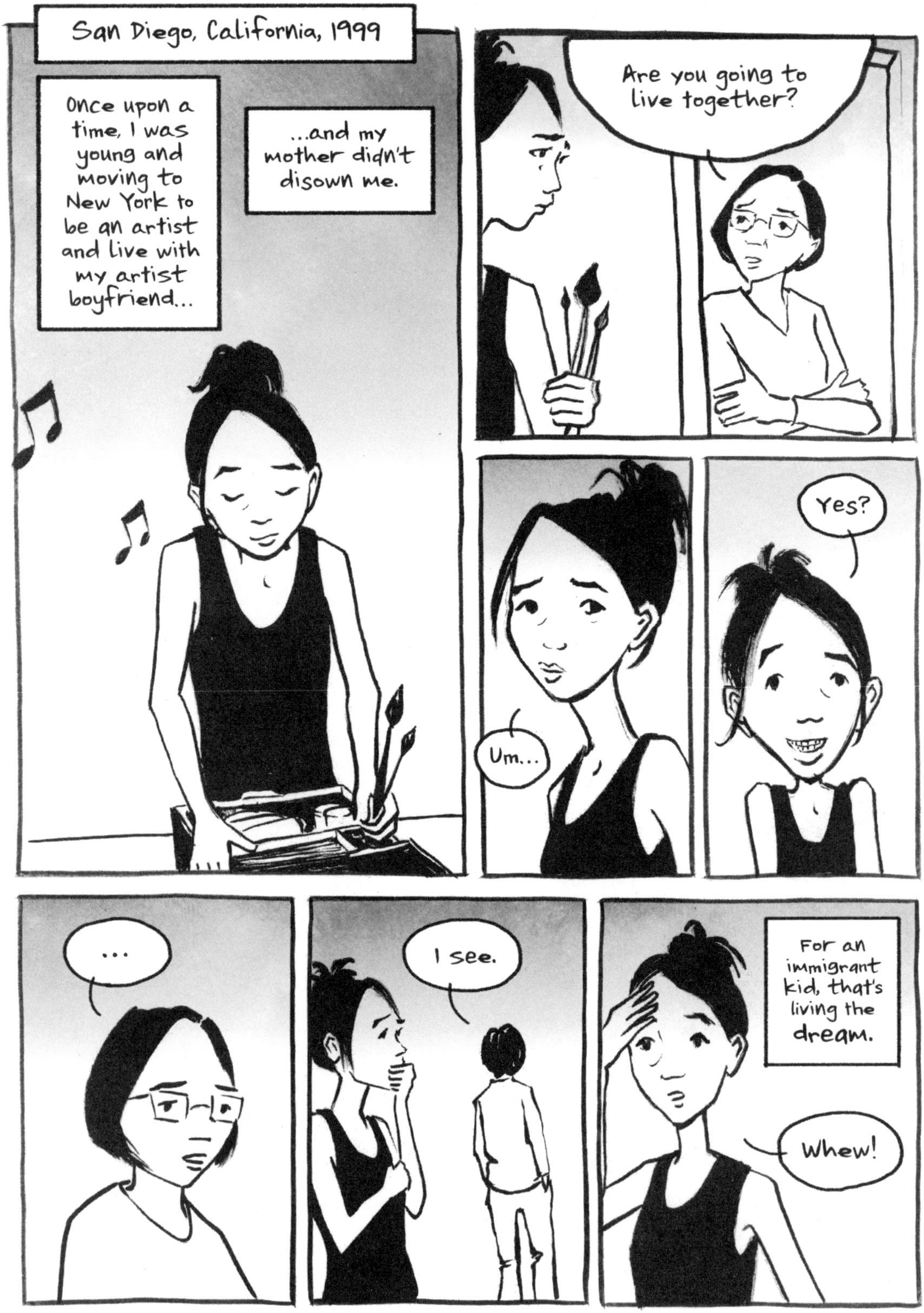
San Diego, California, 1999
Once upon a time, I was young and moving to New York to be an artist and live with my artist boyfriend...
...and my mother didn't disown me.
Are you going to live together?
Um...
Yes?
...
I see.
For an immigrant kid, that's living the dream.
Whew!

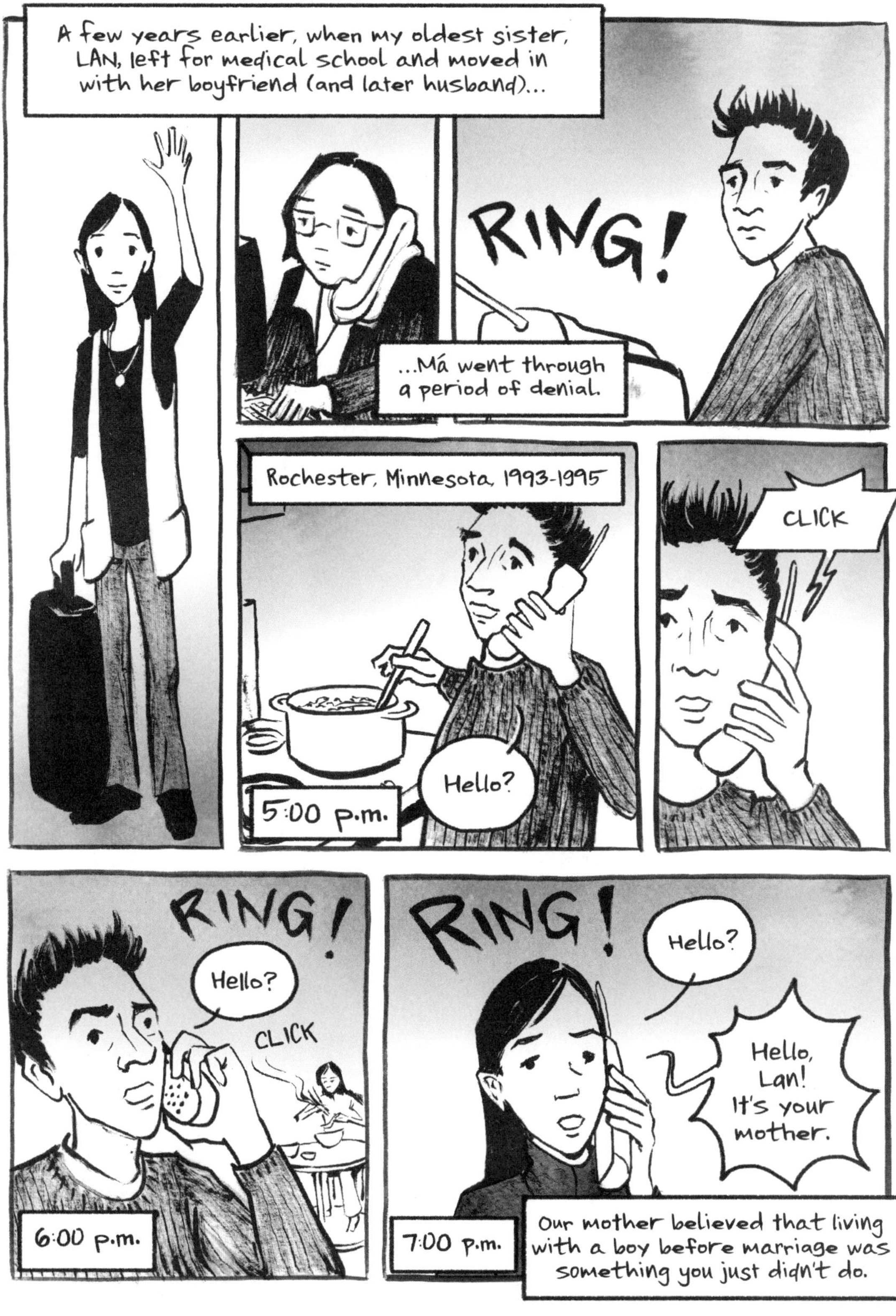
A few years earlier, when my oldest sister, LAN, left for medical school and moved in with her boyfriend (and later husband)...
...Má went through a period of denial.
RING!
Rochester, Minnesota, 1993-1995
5:00 p.m.
Hello?
CLICK
6:00 p.m.
RING!
Hello?
CLICK
7:00 p.m.
RING!
Hello?
Hello, Lan! It's your mother.
Our mother believed that living with a boy before marriage was something you just didn't do.

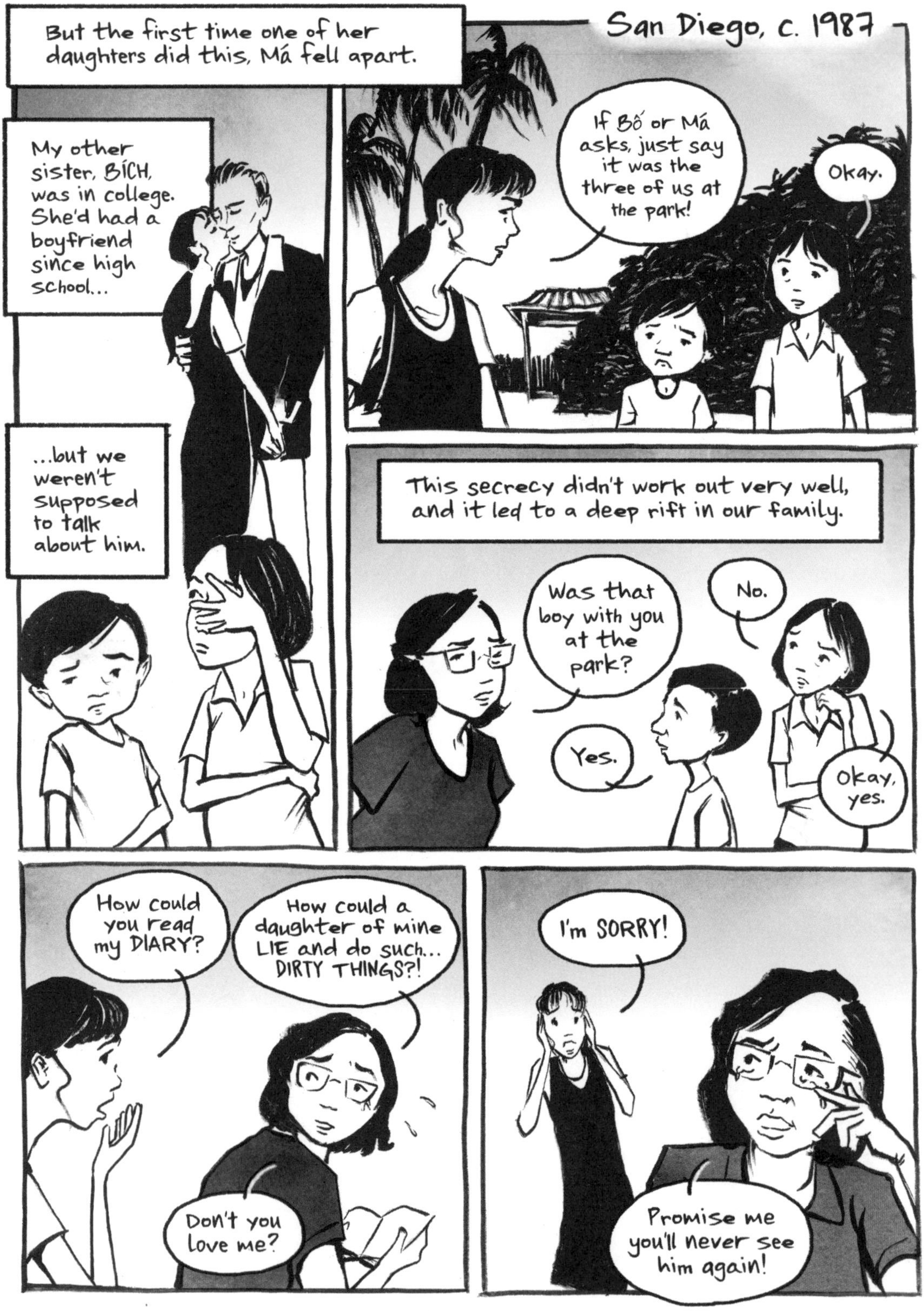
But the first time one of her daughters did this, Má fell apart.
San Diego, c. 1987
My other sister, BÍCH, was in college. She'd had a boyfriend since high school...
...but we weren't supposed to talk about him.
If Bố or Má asks, just say it was the three of us at the park!
Okay.
This secrecy didn't work out very well, and it led to a deep rift in our family.
Was that boy with you at the park?
No.
Yes.
Okay, yes.
How could you read my DIARY?
How could a daughter of mine LIE and do such... DIRTY THINGS?!
Don't you love me?
I'm SORRY!
Promise me you'll never see him again!

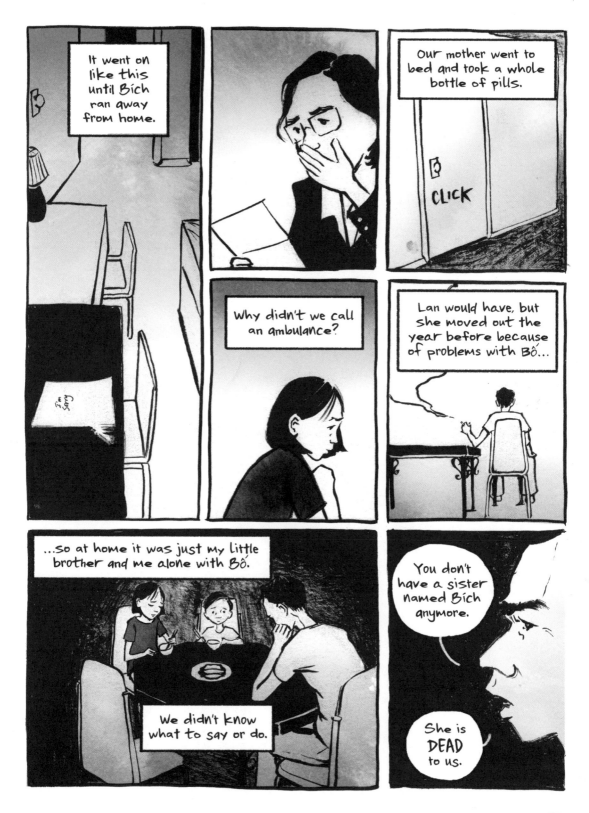

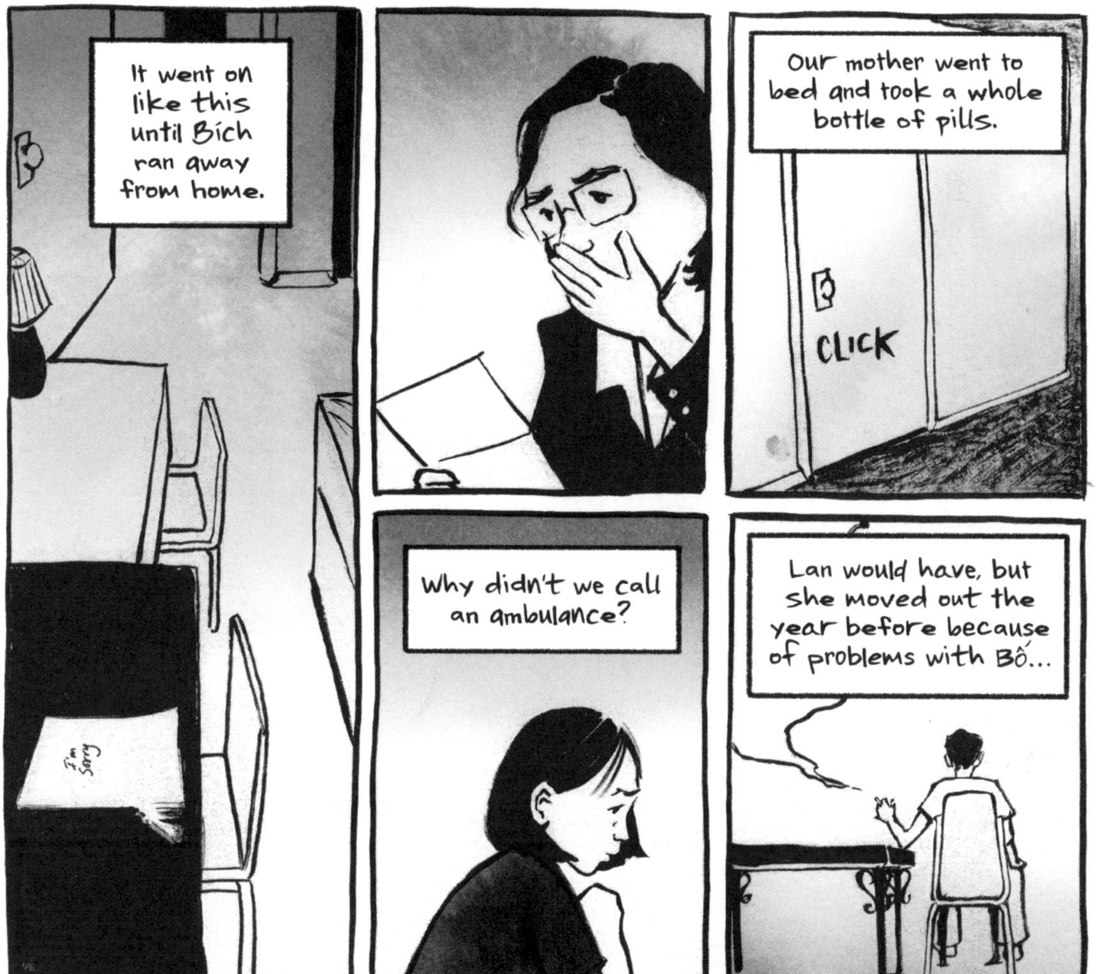
It went on like this until Bích ran away from home.
I'm Sorry
Our mother went to bed and took a whole bottle of pills.
CLICK
Why didn't we call an ambulance?
Lan would have, but she moved out the year before because of problems with Bố...
...so at home it was just my little brother and me alone with Bố.
We didn't know what to say or do.
You don't have a sister named Bích anymore.
She is DEAD to us.

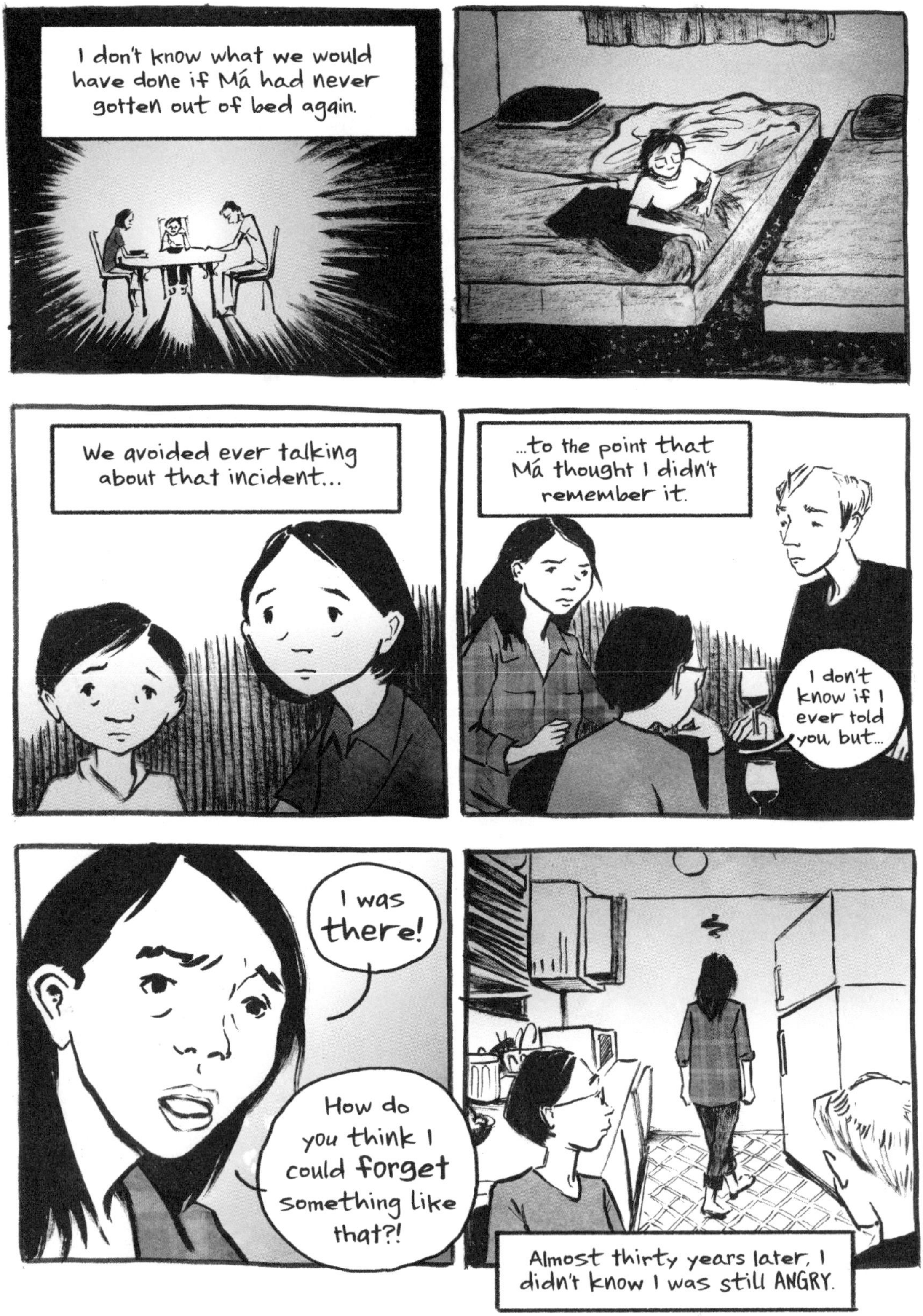
I don't know what we would have done if Má had never gotten out of bed again.
We avoided ever talking about that incident...
...to the point that Má thought I didn't remember it.
I don't know if I ever told you, but...
I was there!
How do you think I could forget something like that?!
Almost thirty years later, I didn't know I was still ANGRY.

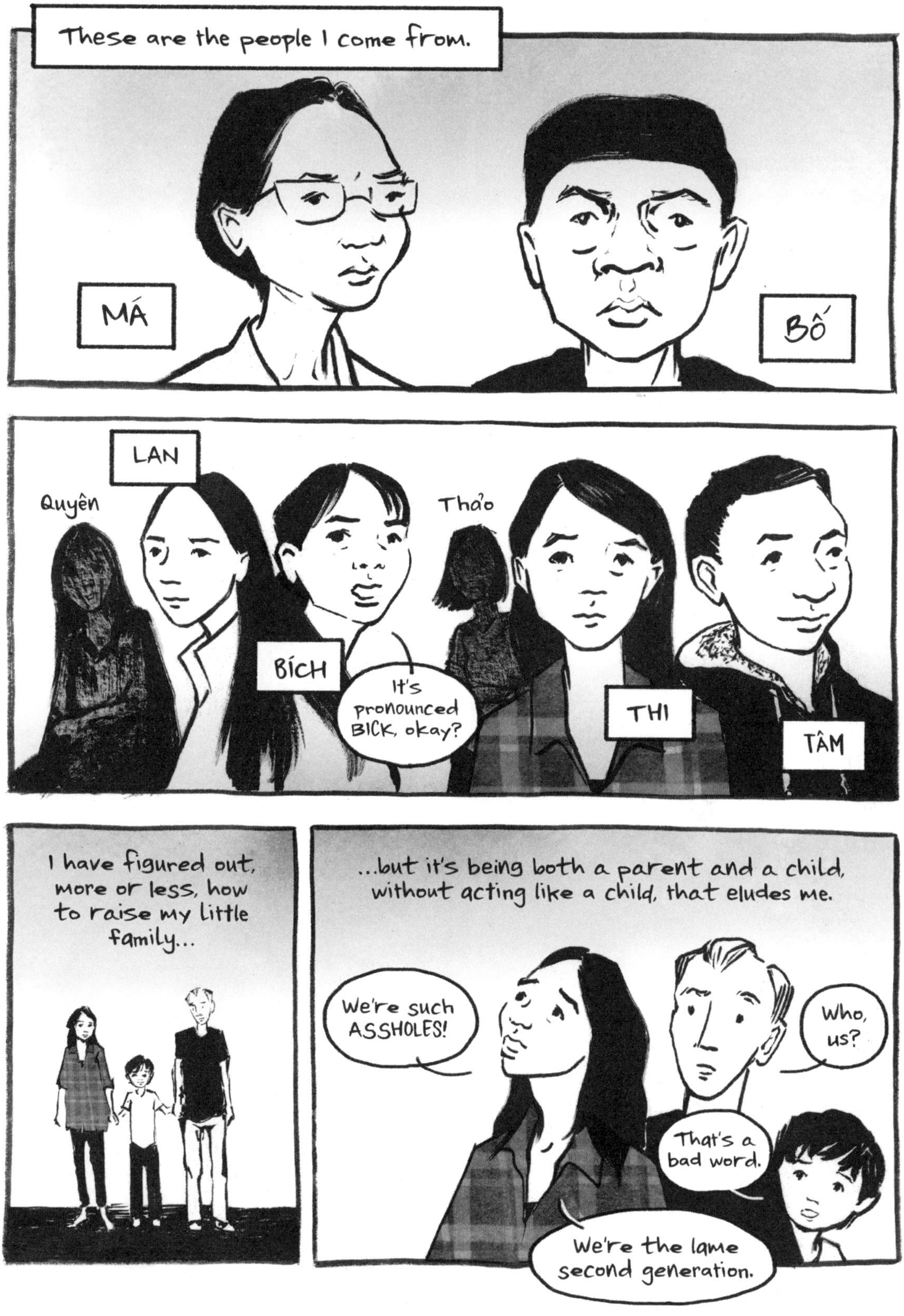

These are the people I come from.
MÁ
BỐ
LAN
Quyên
BÍCH
It's pronounced BICK, okay?
Thảo
THI
TÂM
I have figured out, more or less, how to raise my little family...
...but it's being both a parent and a child, without acting like a child, that eludes me.
We're such ASSHOLES!
Who, us?
That's a bad word.
We're the lame second generation.

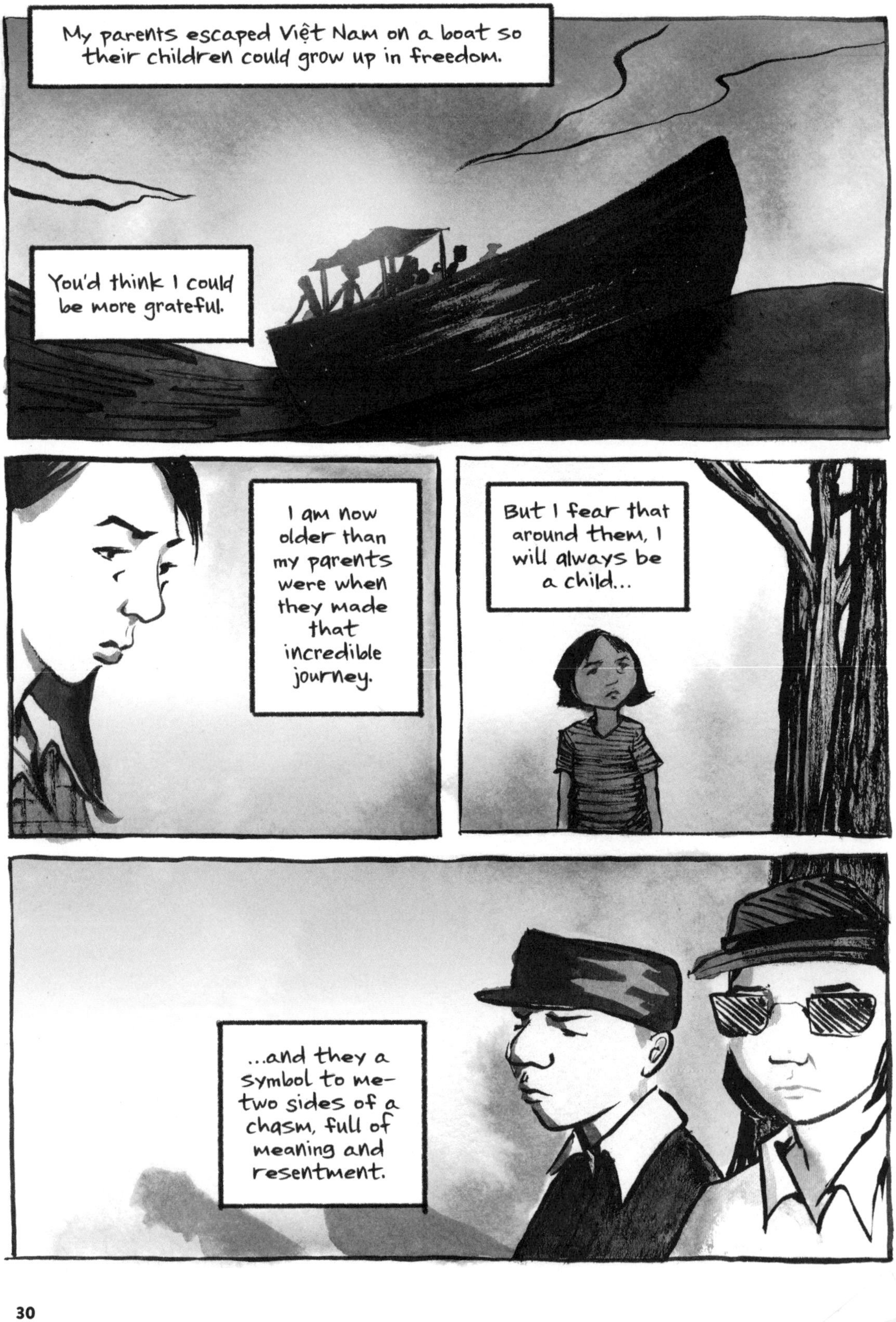
My parents escaped Việt Nam on a boat so their children could grow up in freedom.
You'd think I could be more grateful.
I am now older than my parents were when they made that incredible journey.
But I fear that around them, I will always be a child...
...and they a symbol to me— two sides of a chasm, full of meaning and resentment.

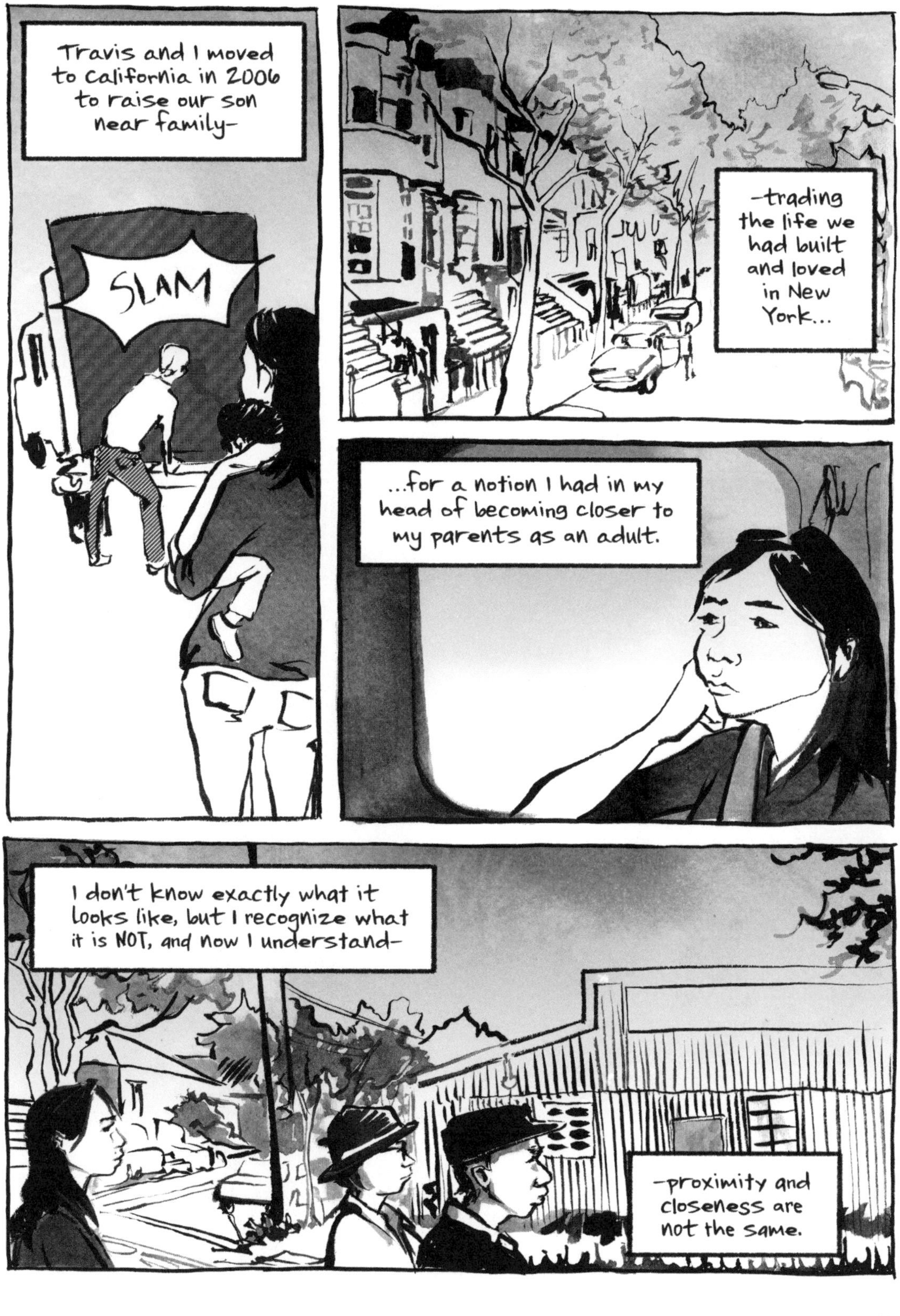
Travis and I moved to California in 2006 to raise our son near family-
SLAM
-trading the life we had built and loved in New York...
...for a notion I had in my head of becoming closer to my parents as an adult.
I don't know exactly what it looks like, but I recognize what it is NOT, and now I understand-
-proximity and closeness are not the same.

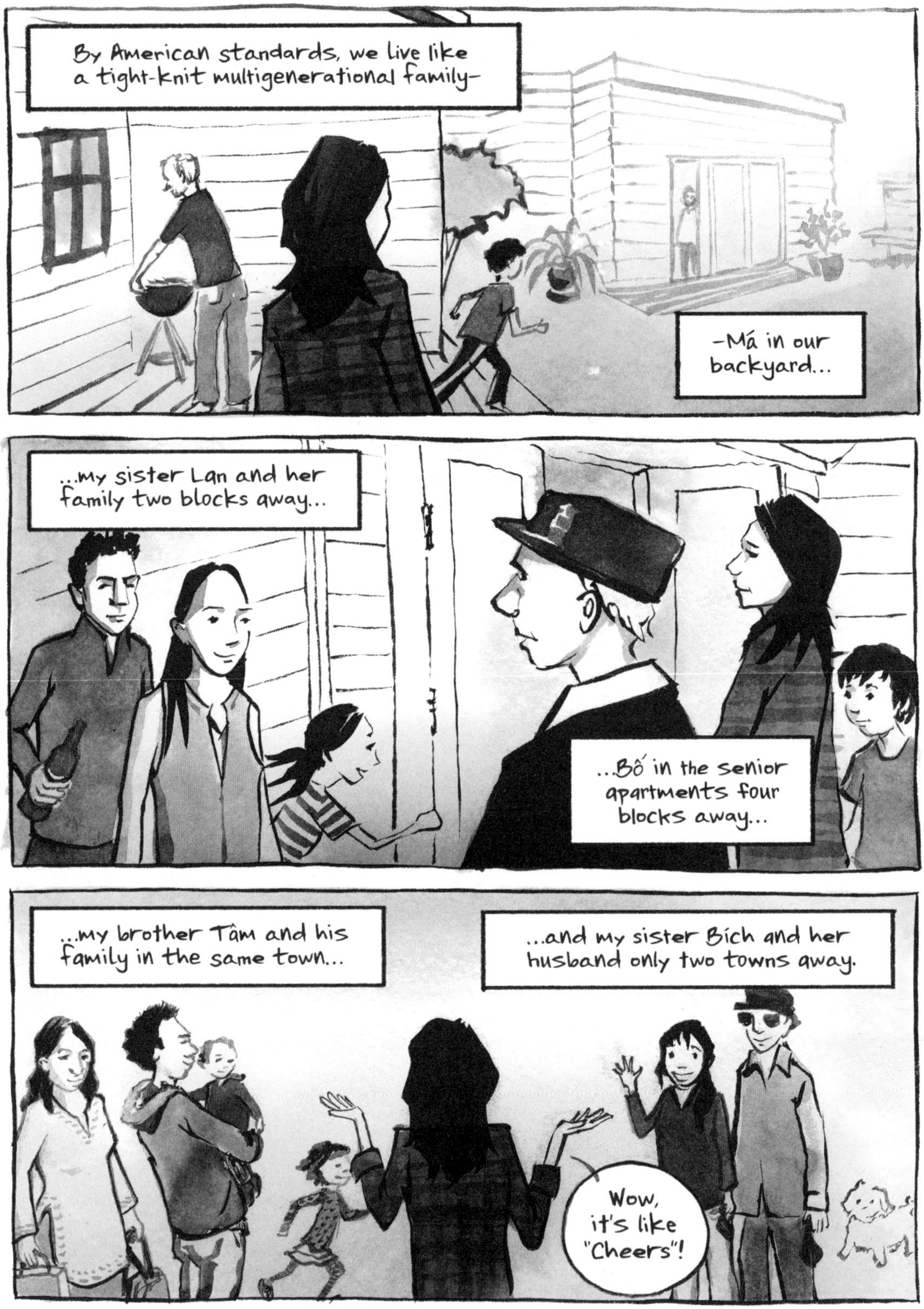
By American standards, we live like a tight-knit multigenerational family-
-Má in our backyard...
...my sister Lan and her family two blocks away...
...Bố in the senior apartments four blocks away...
...my brother Tâm and his family in the same town...
...and my sister Bích and her husband only two towns away.
Wow, it's like "Cheers"!

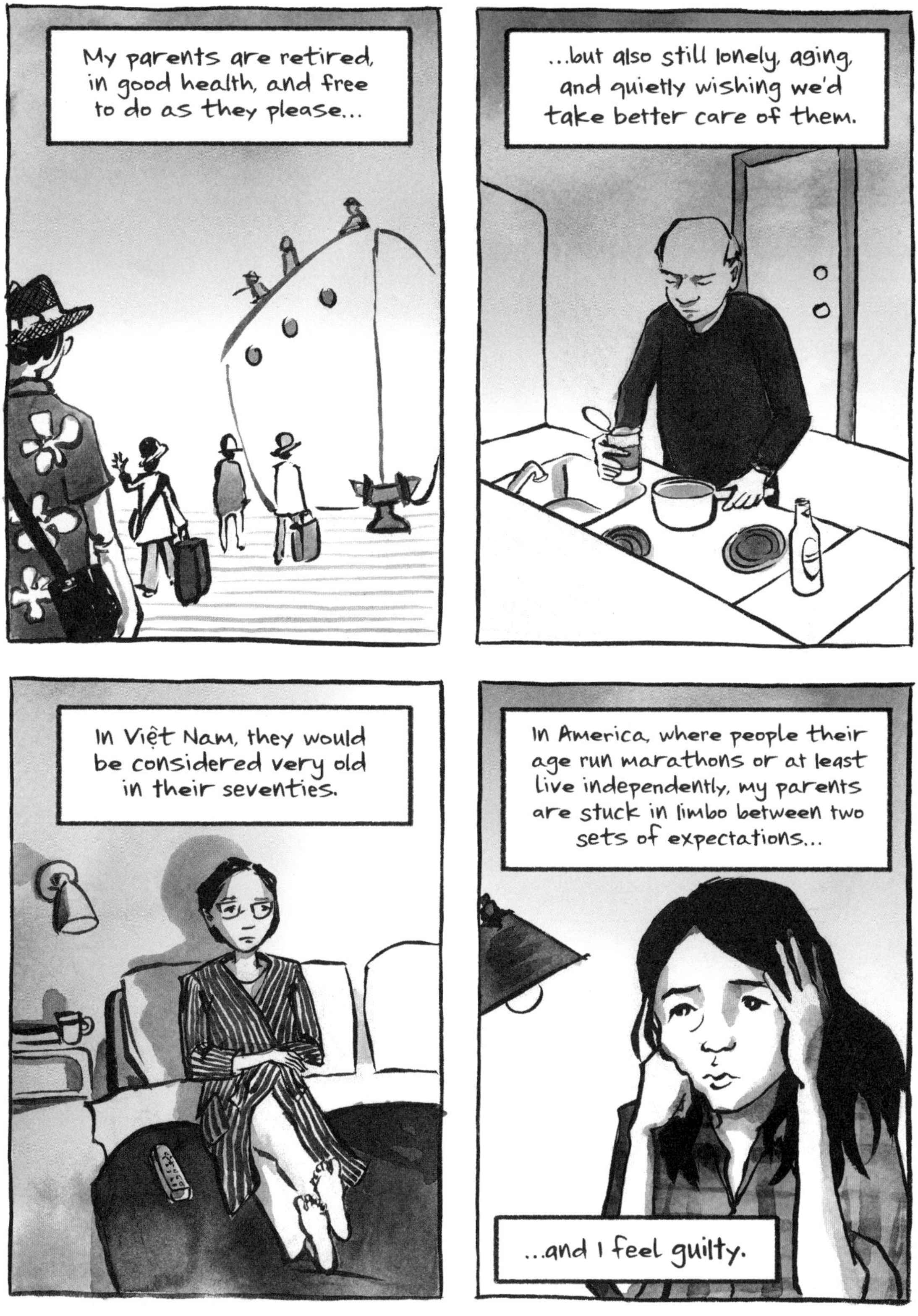
My parents are retired, in good health, and free to do as they please...
...but also still lonely, aging, and quietly wishing we'd take better care of them.
In Việt Nam, they would be considered very old in their seventies.
In America, where people their age run marathons or at least live independently, my parents are stuck in limbo between two sets of expectations...
...and I feel guilty.

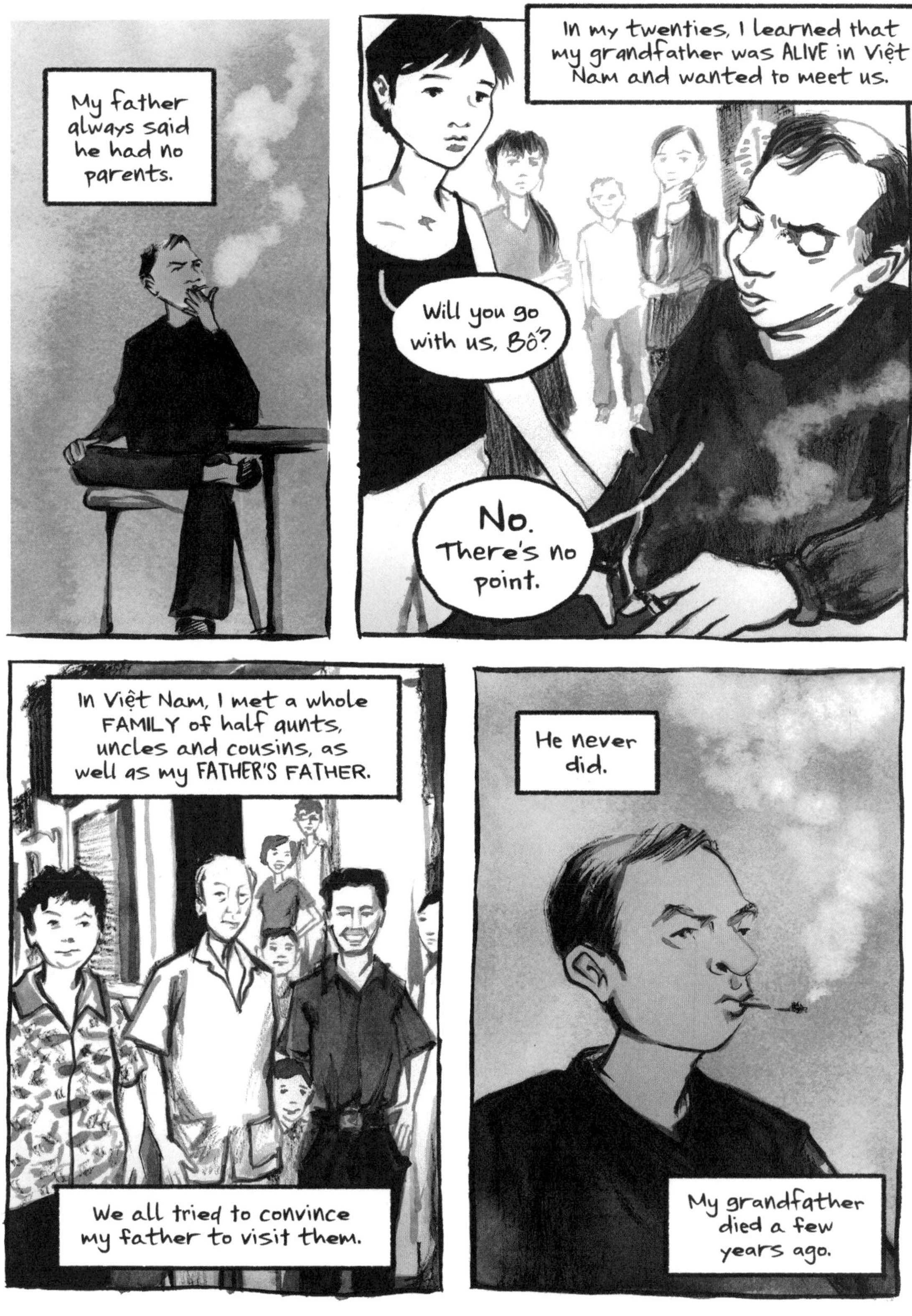
My father always said he had no parents.
In my twenties, I learned that my grandfather was ALIVE in Việt Nam and wanted to meet us.
Will you go with us, Bố?
No. There's no point.
In Việt Nam, I met a whole FAMILY of half aunts, uncles and cousins, as well as my FATHER'S FATHER.
We all tried to convince my father to visit them.
He never did.
My grandfather died a few years ago.

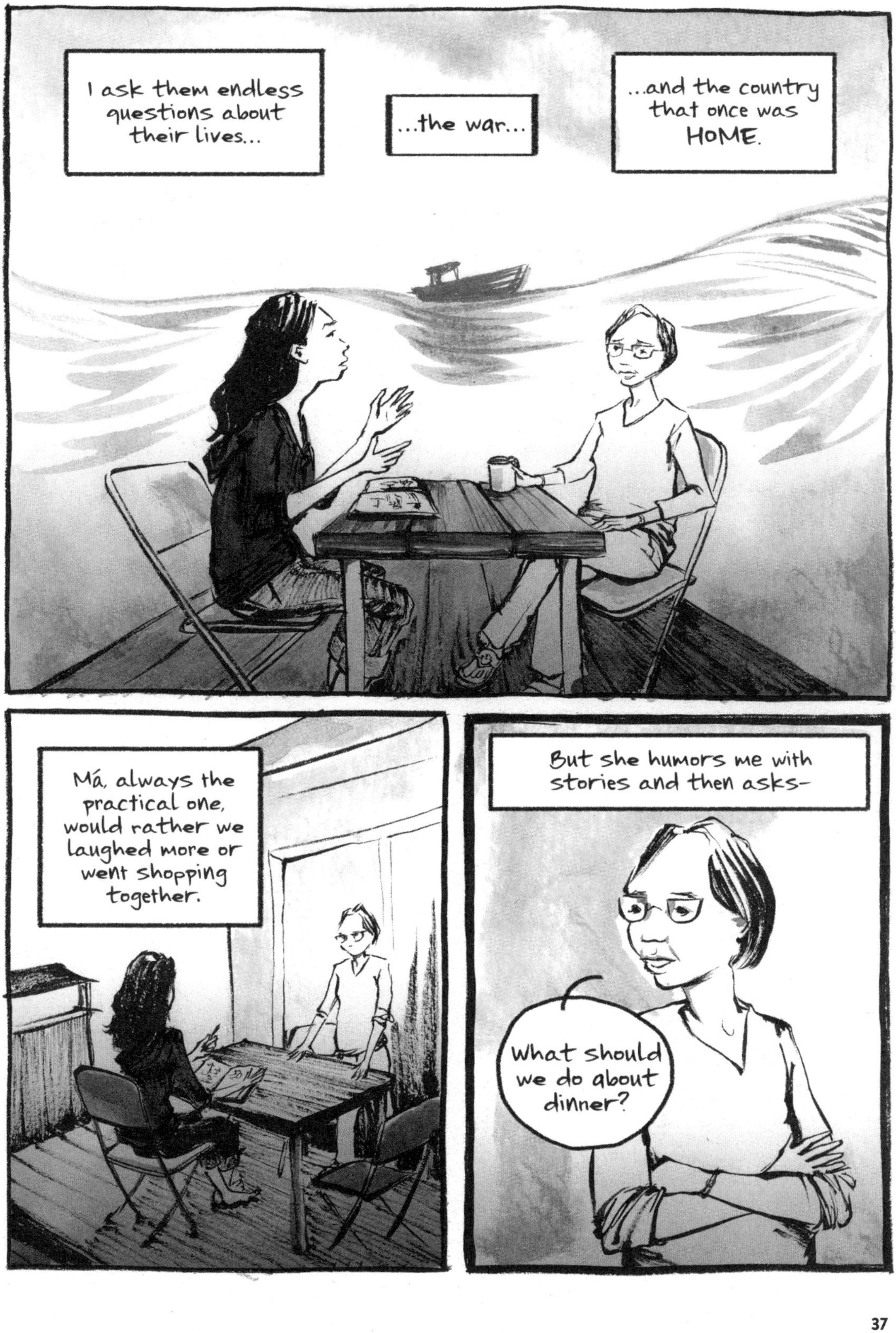
I ask them endless questions about their lives...
...the war...
...and the country that once was HOME.
Má, always the practical one, would rather we laughed more or went shopping together.
But she humors me with stories and then asks-
What should we do about dinner?

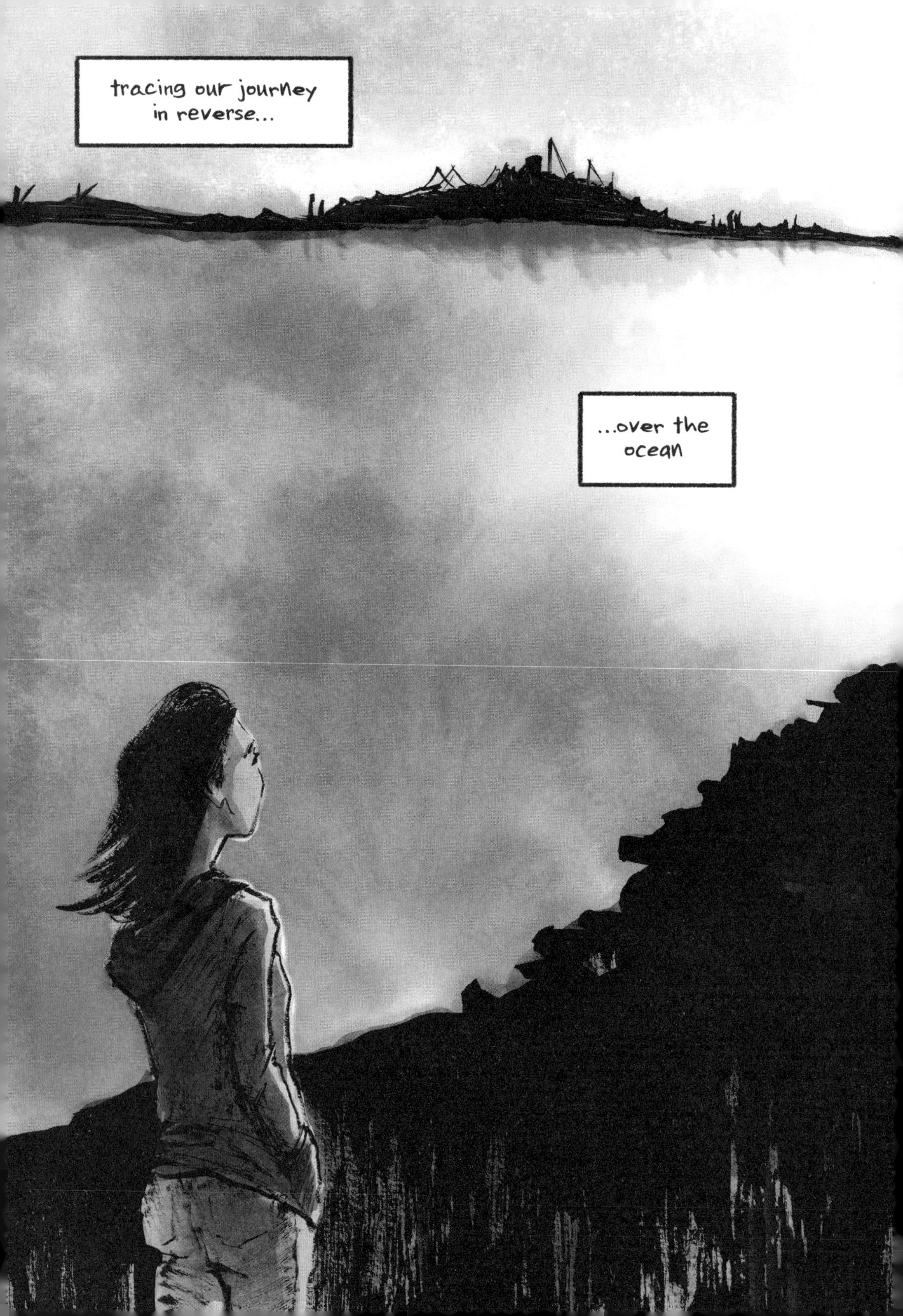
tracing our journey in reverse...
...over the ocean

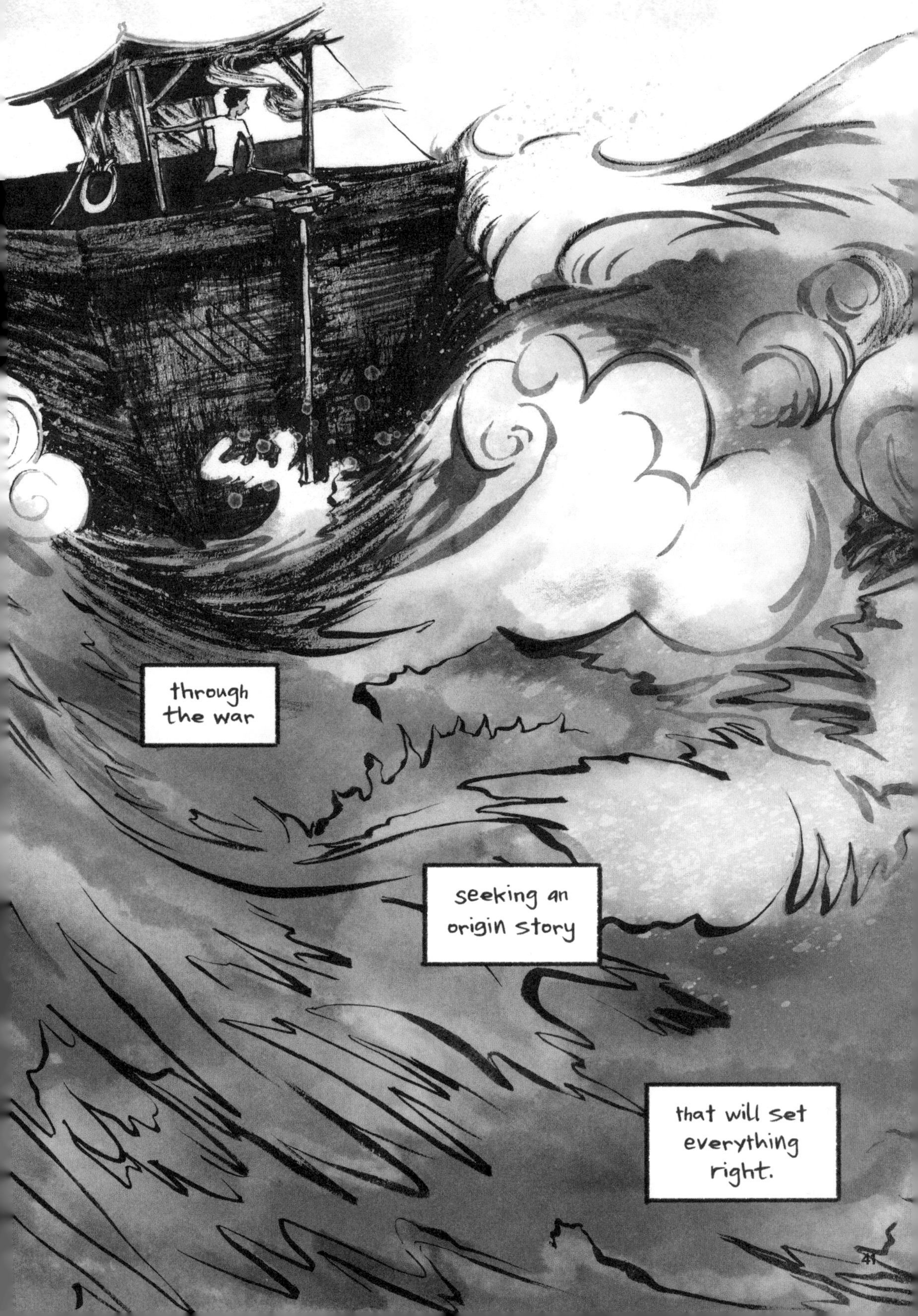
through the war
seeking an origin story
that will set everything right.

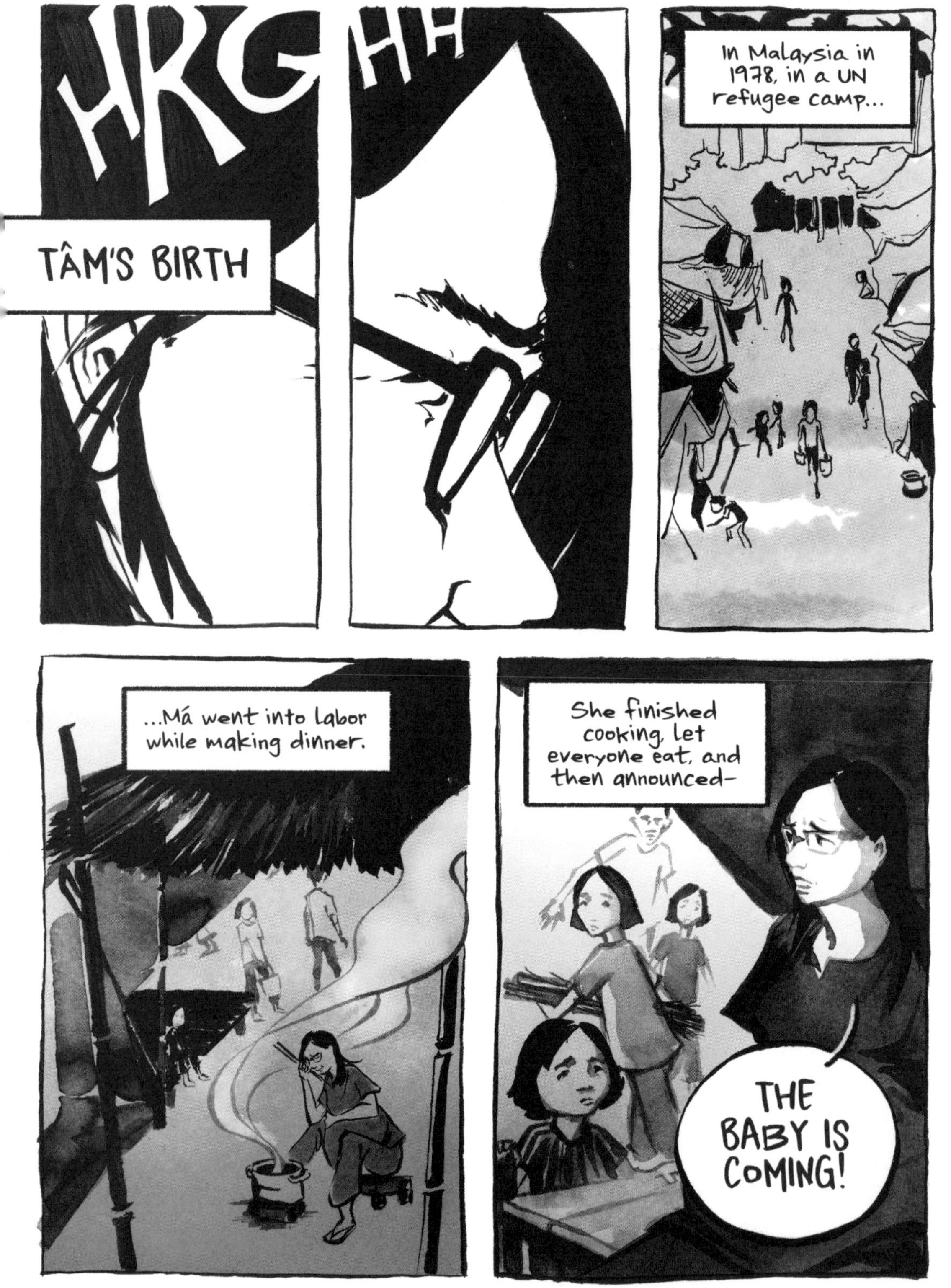
HRGHH
TÂM'S BIRTH
In Malaysia in 1978, in a UN refugee camp...
...Má went into labor while making dinner.
She finished cooking, let everyone eat, and then announced-
THE BABY IS COMING!

43

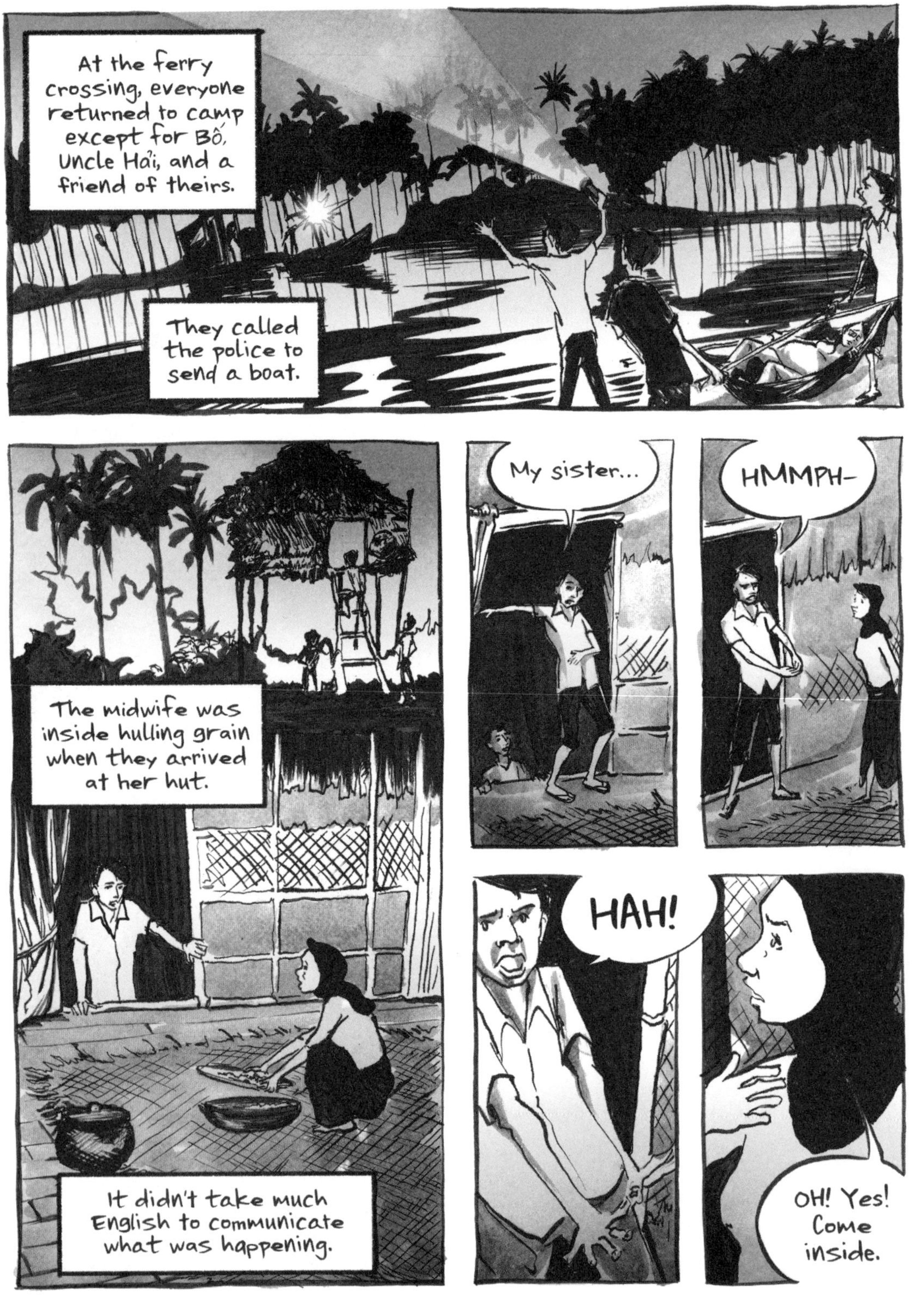
At the ferry crossing, everyone returned to camp except for Bố, Uncle Hải, and a friend of theirs.
They called the police to send a boat.
The midwife was inside hulling grain when they arrived at her hut.
It didn't take much English to communicate what was happening.
My sister...
HMMPH-
HAH!
OH! Yes! Come inside.

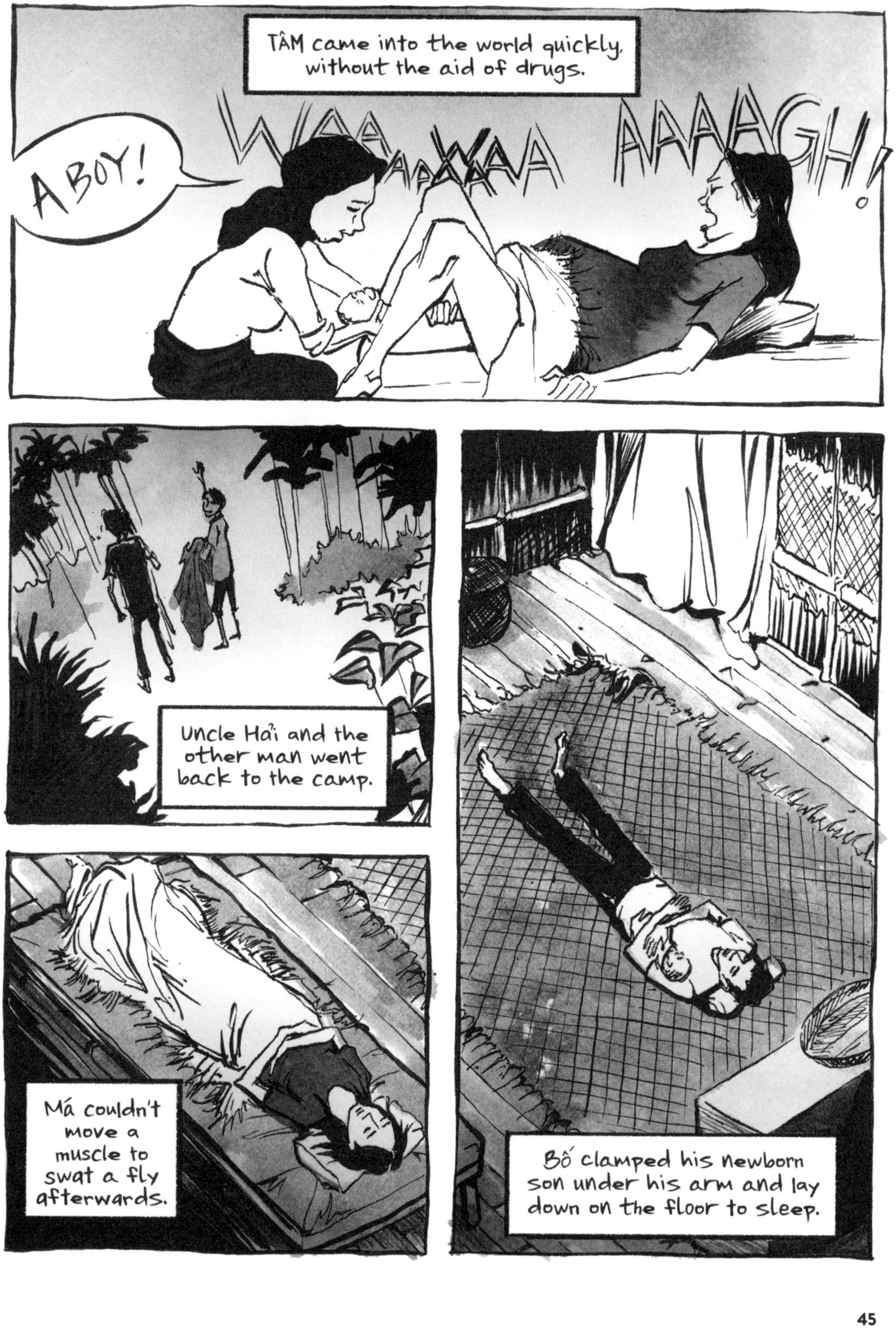
TÂM came into the world quickly, without the aid of drugs.
A BOY!
WAA AAA WAA AAA
AAAAGH!
Uncle Hải and the other man went back to the camp.
Má couldn't move a muscle to swat a fly afterwards.
Bố clamped his newborn son under his arm and lay down on the floor to sleep.

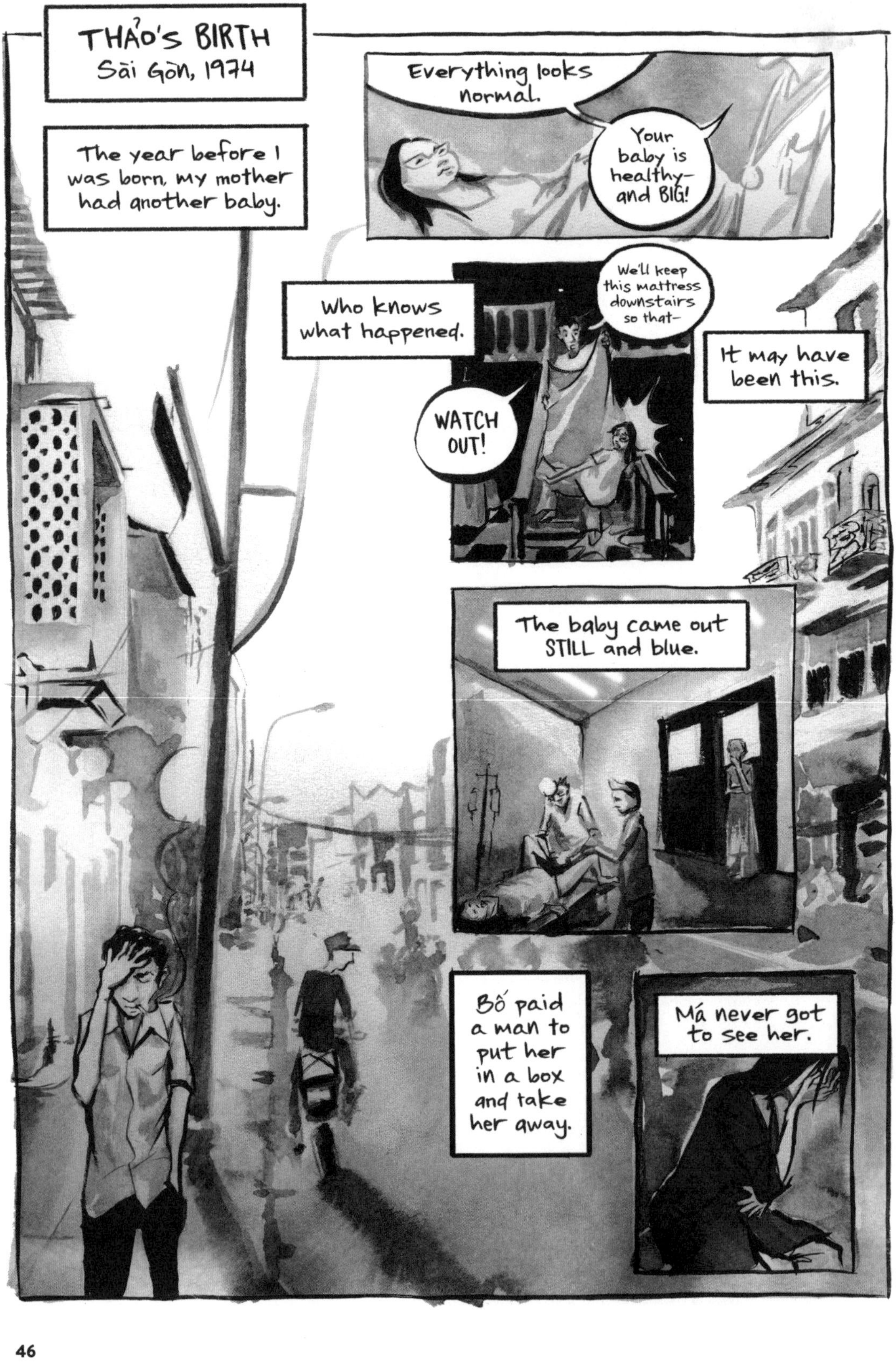
THẢO'S BIRTH
Sài Gòn, 1974
The year before I was born, my mother had another baby.
Everything looks normal.
Your baby is healthy— and BIG!
Who knows what happened.
We'll keep this mattress downstairs so that—
WATCH OUT!
It may have been this.
The baby came out STILL and blue.
Bố paid a man to put her in a box and take her away.
Má never got to see her.

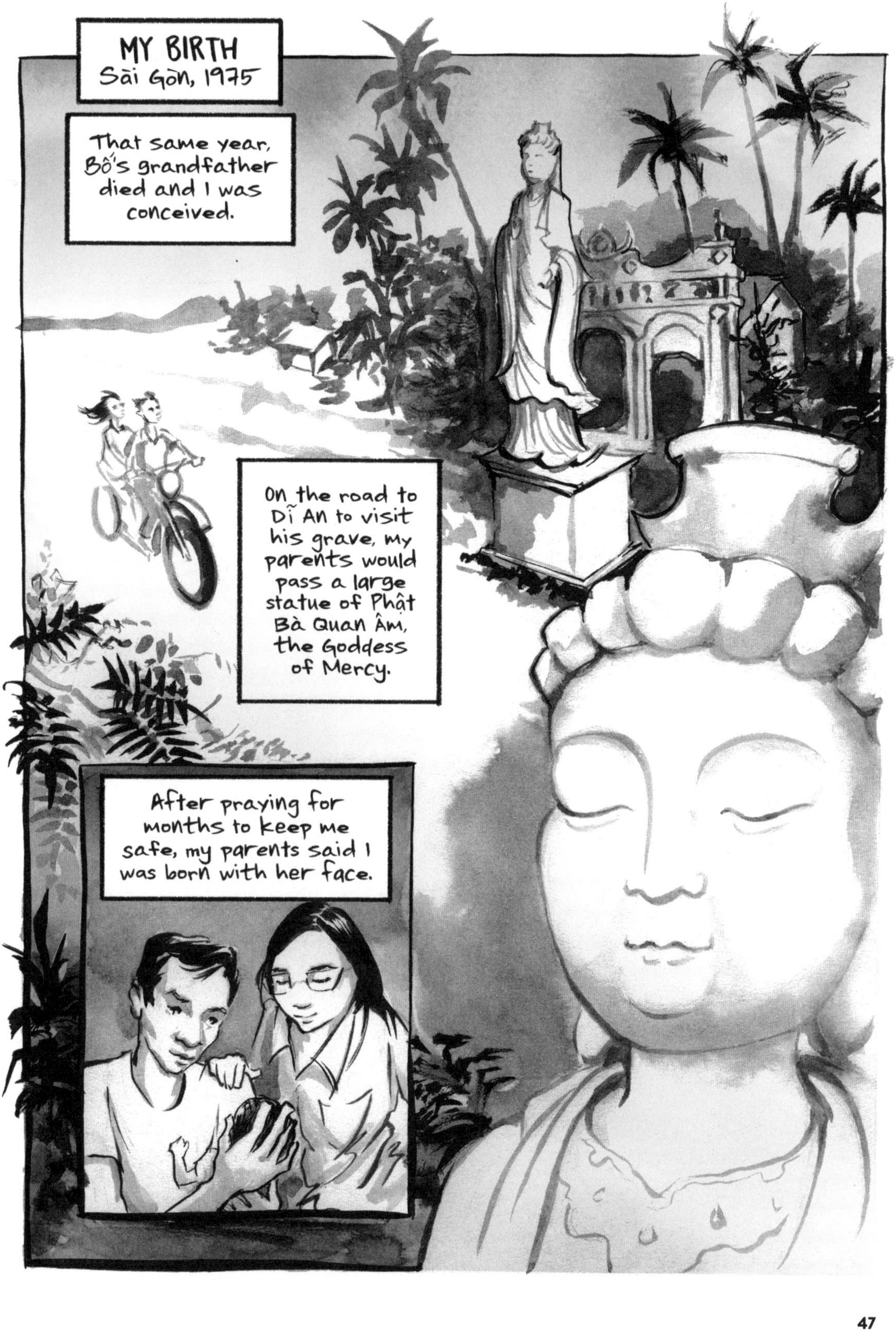
MY BIRTH
Sài Gòn, 1975
That same year, Bố's grandfather died and I was conceived.
On the road to Dĩ An to visit his grave, my parents would pass a large statue of Phật Bà Quan Âm, the Goddess of Mercy.
After praying for months to keep me safe, my parents said I was born with her face.

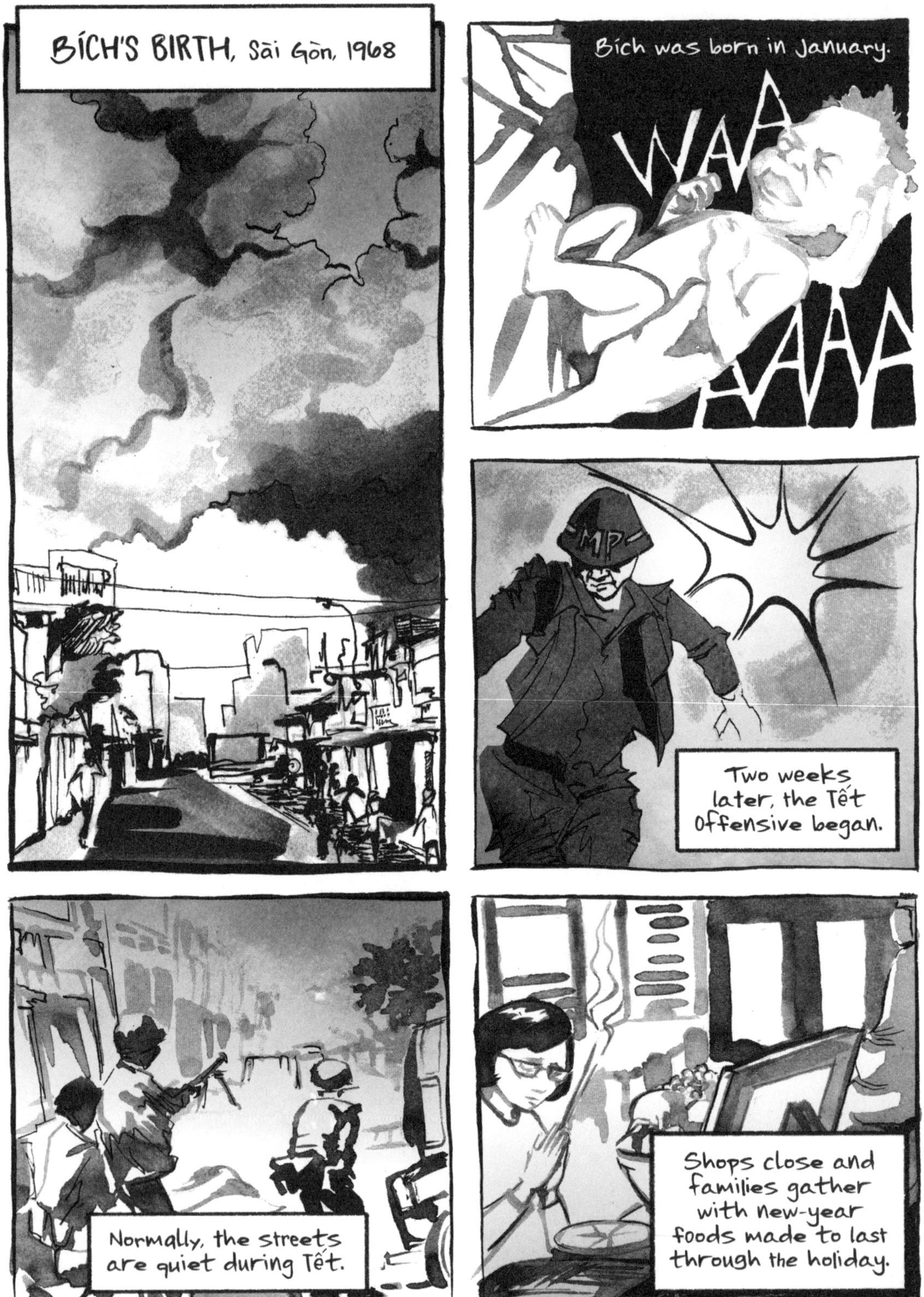
BÍCH'S BIRTH, Sài Gòn, 1968
Bích was born in January.
WAAAAAAAA
Two weeks later, the Tết Offensive began.
Normally, the streets are quiet during Tết.
Shops close and families gather with new-year foods made to last through the holiday.

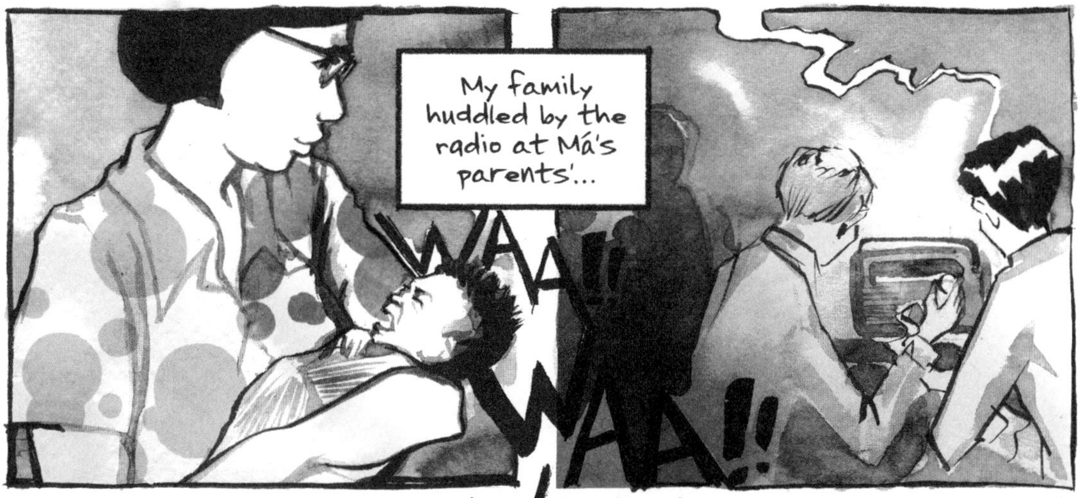
My family huddled by the radio at Má's parents'...
WAA!!
WAA!!
WAA!
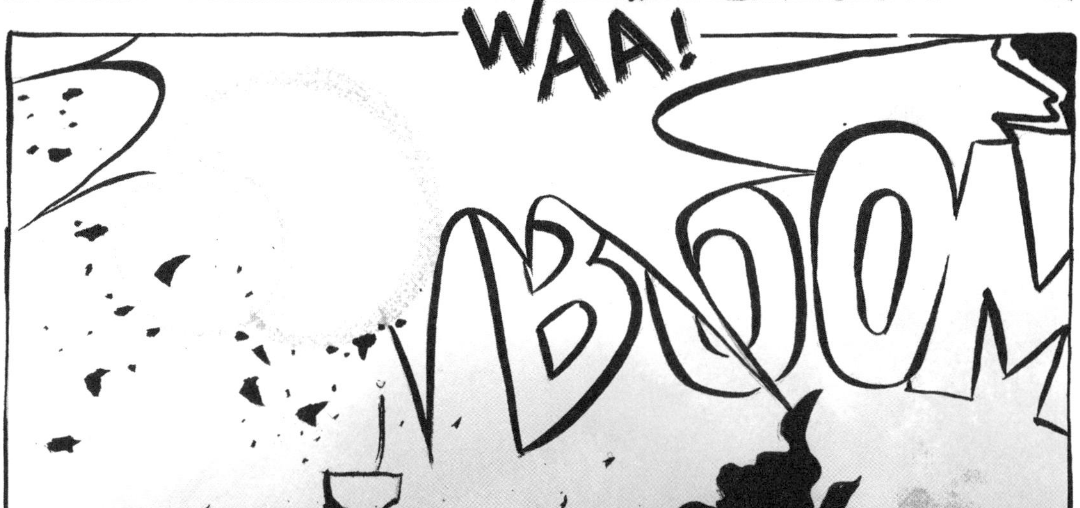
BOOOM
...while the fighting raged on outside.

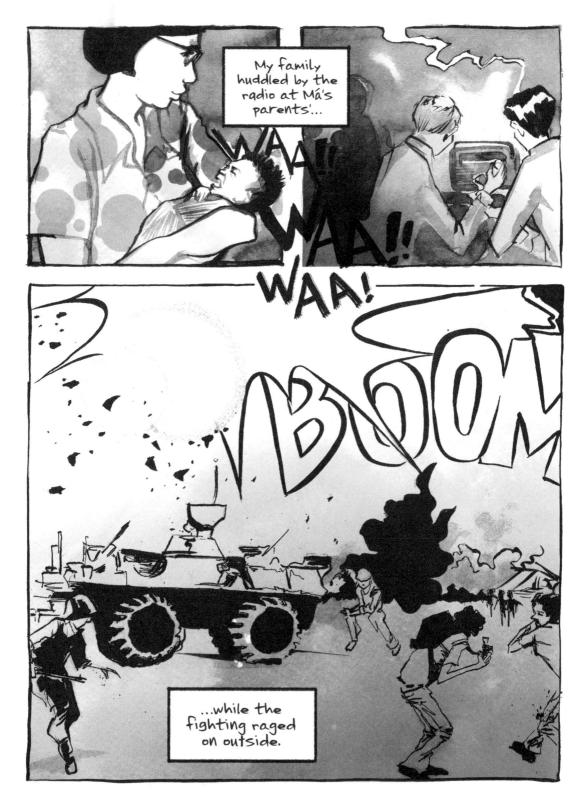

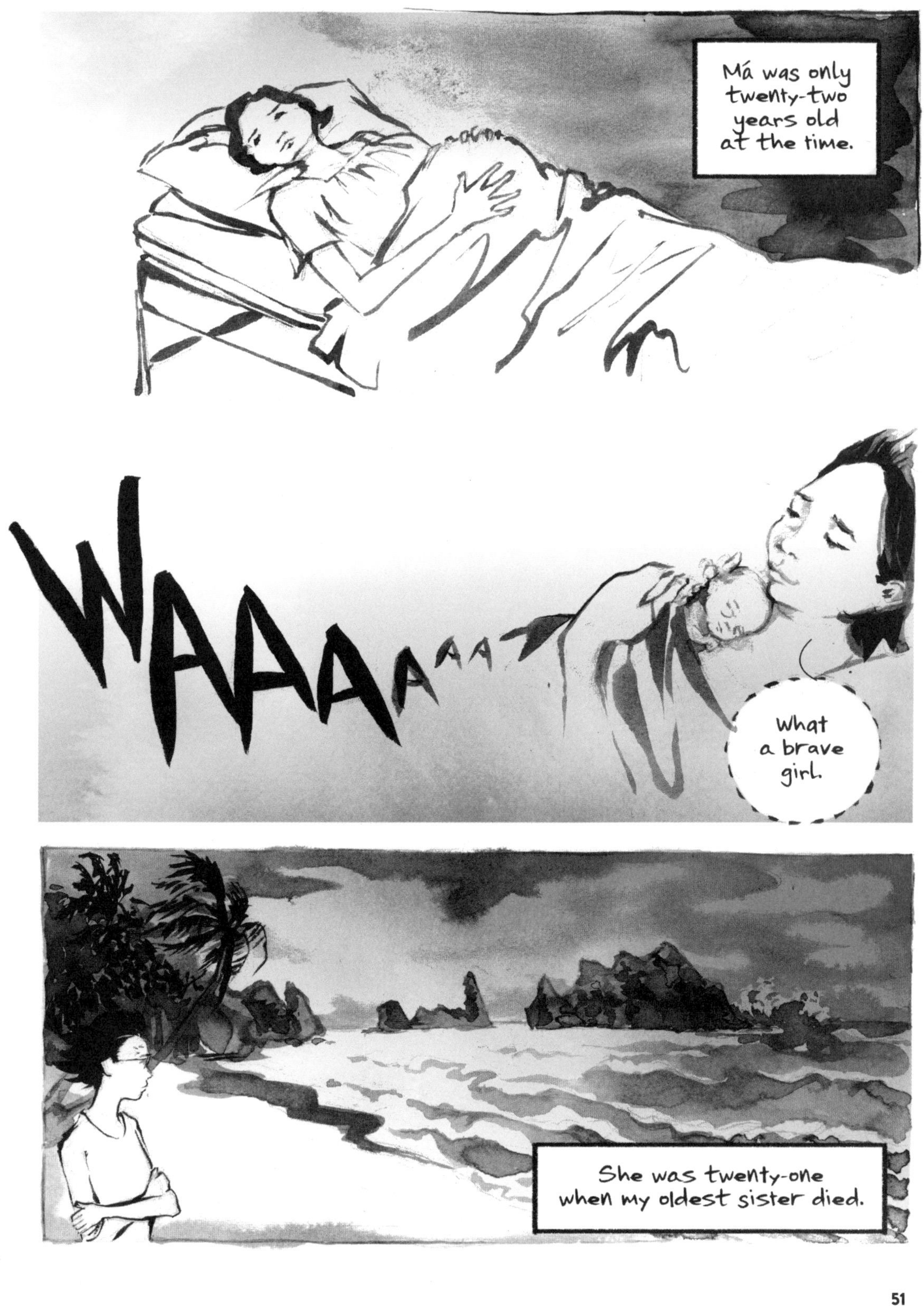
Má was only twenty-two years old at the time.
WAAAAAAA
What a brave girl.
She was twenty-one when my oldest sister died.

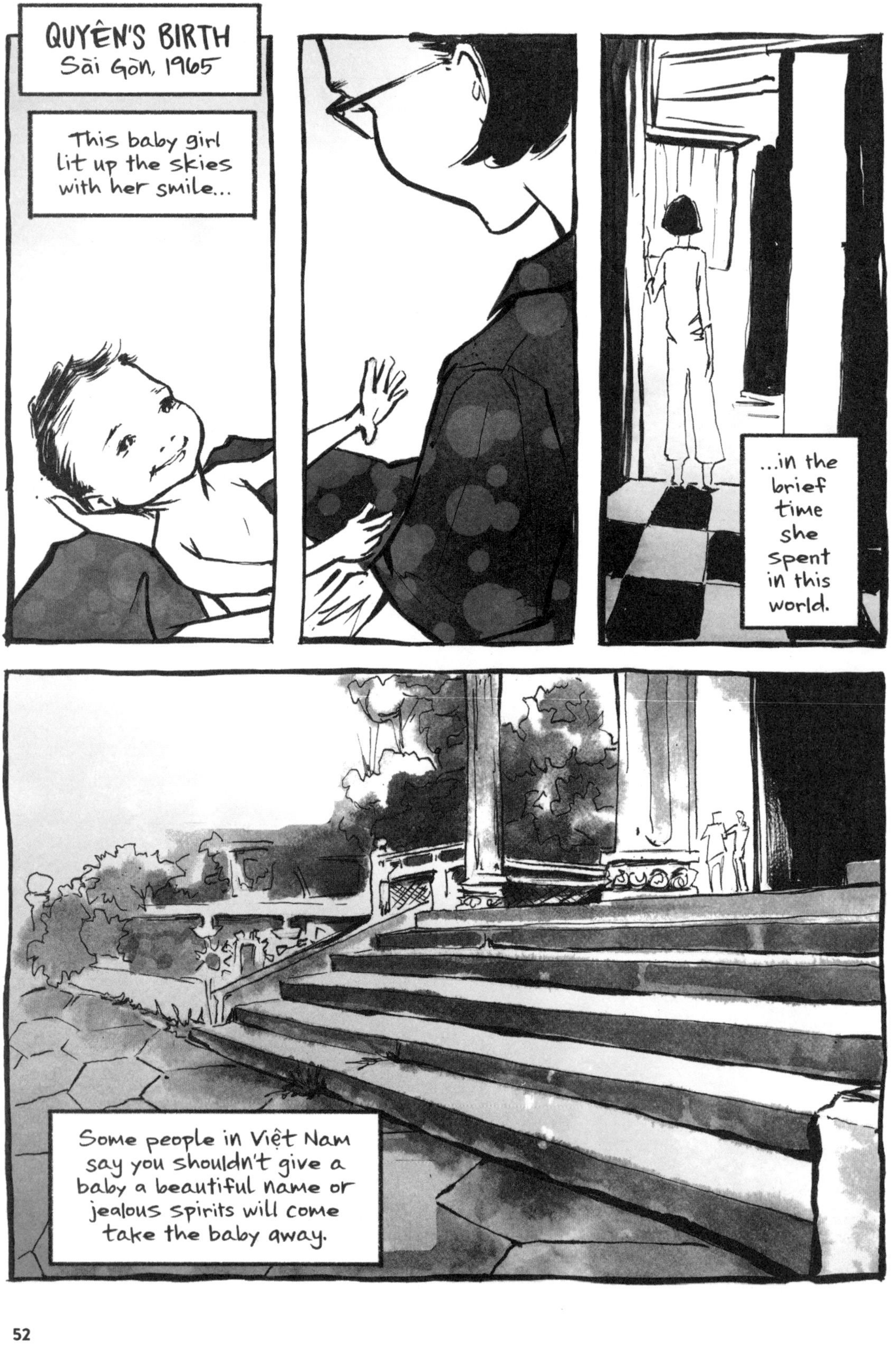
QUYÊN'S BIRTH
Sài Gòn, 1965
This baby girl lit up the skies with her smile...
...in the brief time she spent in this world.
Some people in Việt Nam say you shouldn't give a baby a beautiful name or jealous spirits will come take the baby away.

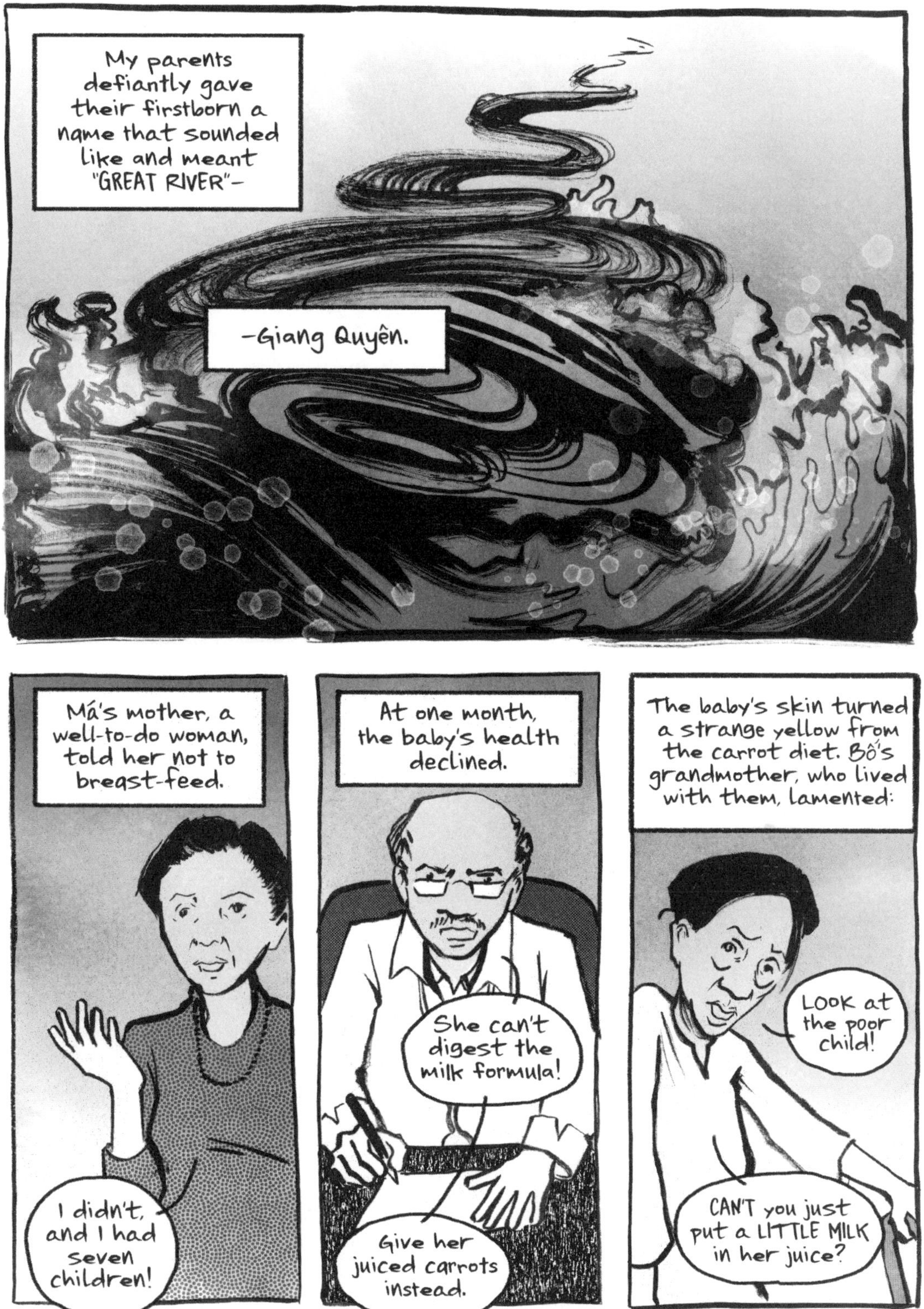
My parents defiantly gave their firstborn a name that sounded like and meant "GREAT RIVER"–
–Giang Quyên.
Má's mother, a well-to-do woman, told her not to breast-feed.
I didn't, and I had seven children!
At one month, the baby's health declined.
She can't digest the milk formula!
Give her juiced carrots instead.
The baby's skin turned a strange yellow from the carrot diet. Bố's grandmother, who lived with them, lamented:
LOOK at the poor child!
CAN'T you just put a LITTLE MILK in her juice?

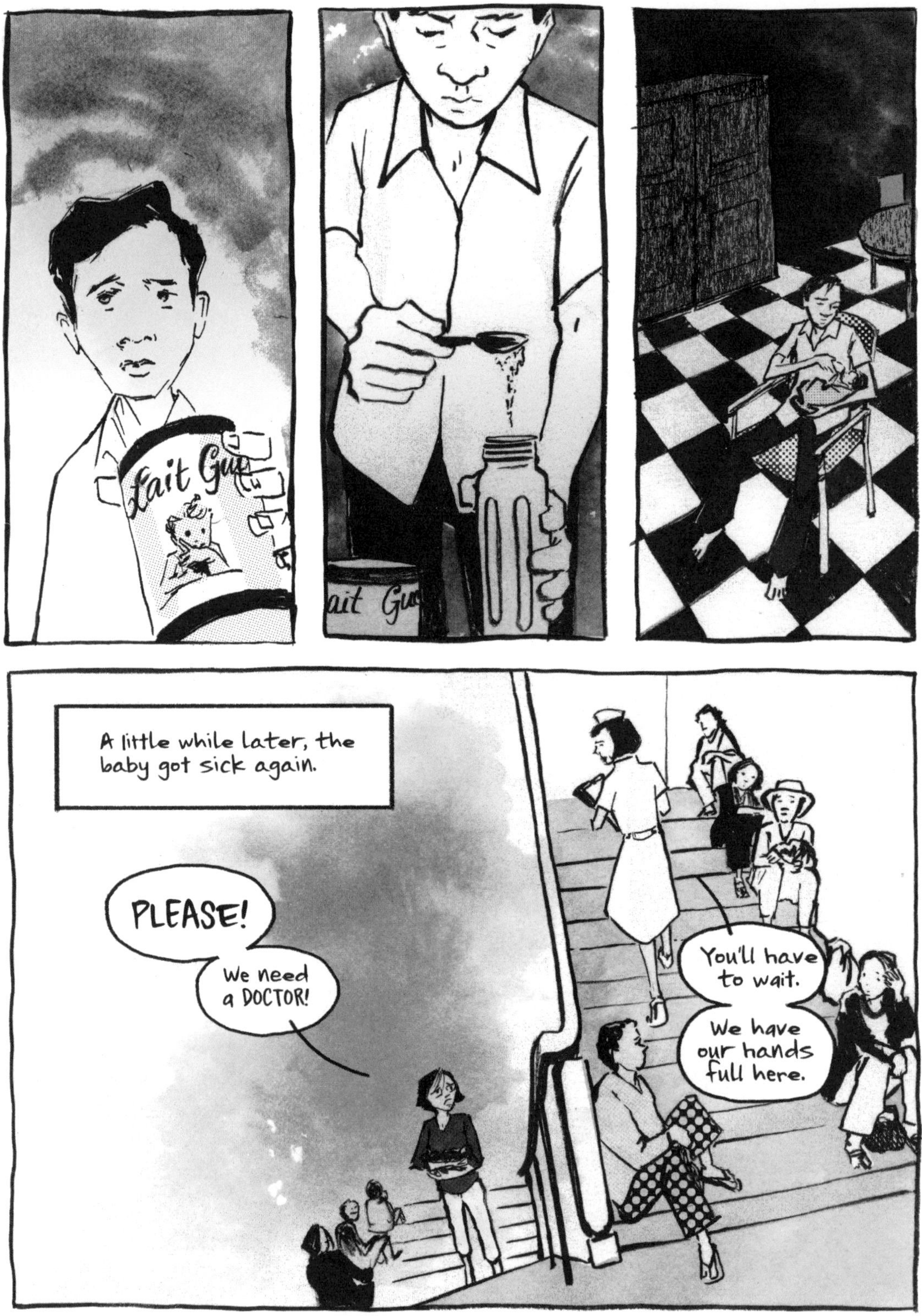
A little while later, the baby got sick again.
PLEASE!
We need a DOCTOR!
You'll have to wait.
We have our hands full here.

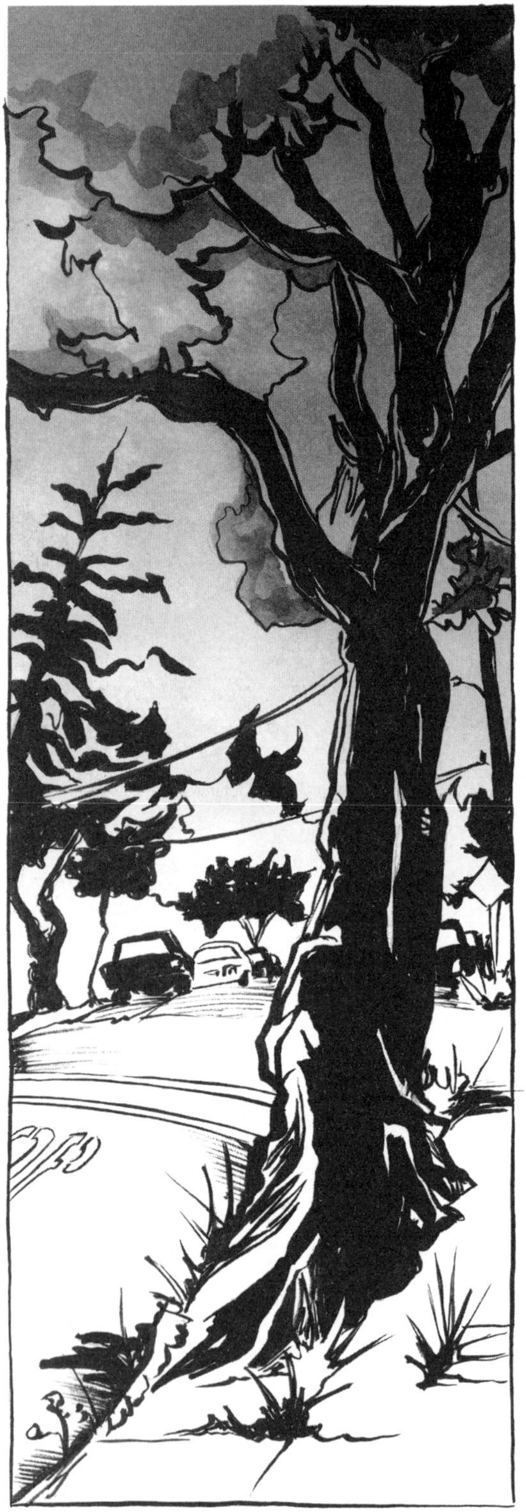

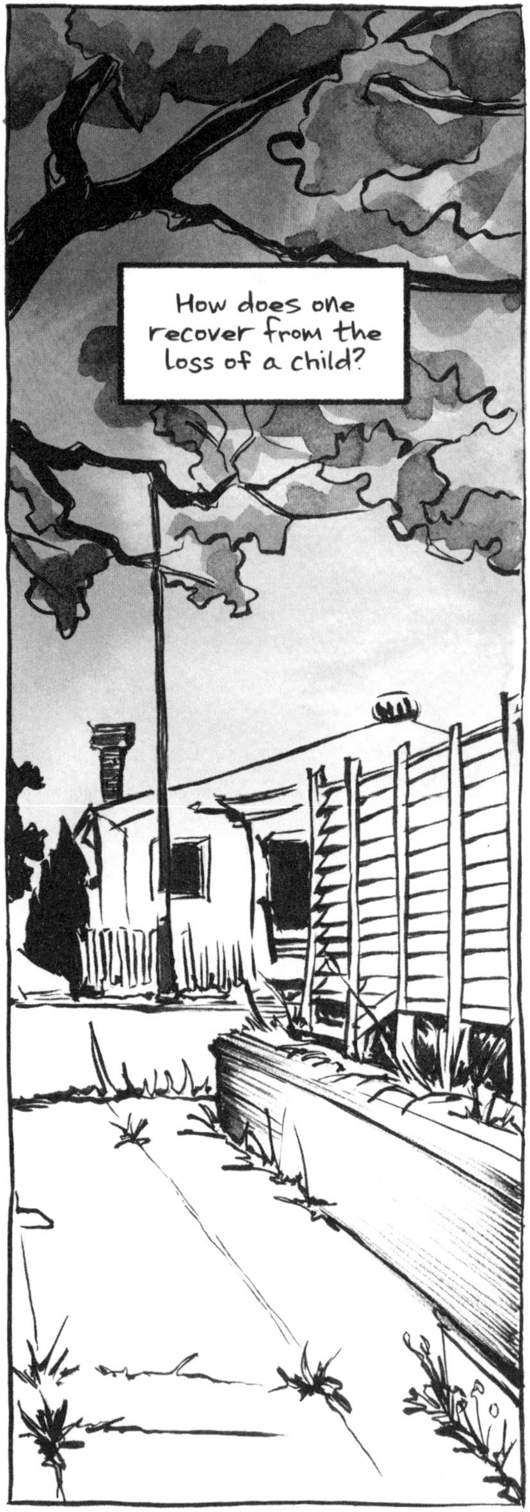

How does one recover from the loss of a child?

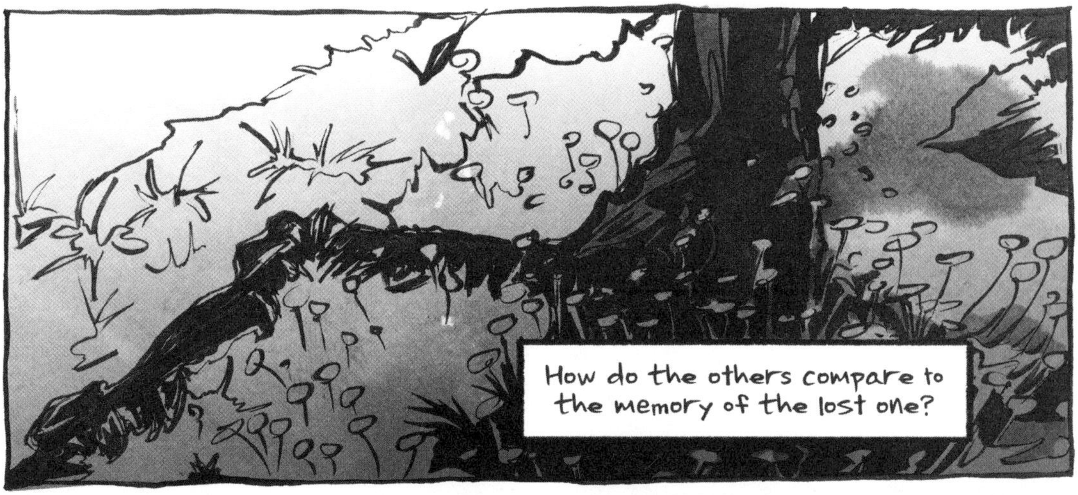
How do the others compare to the memory of the lost one?

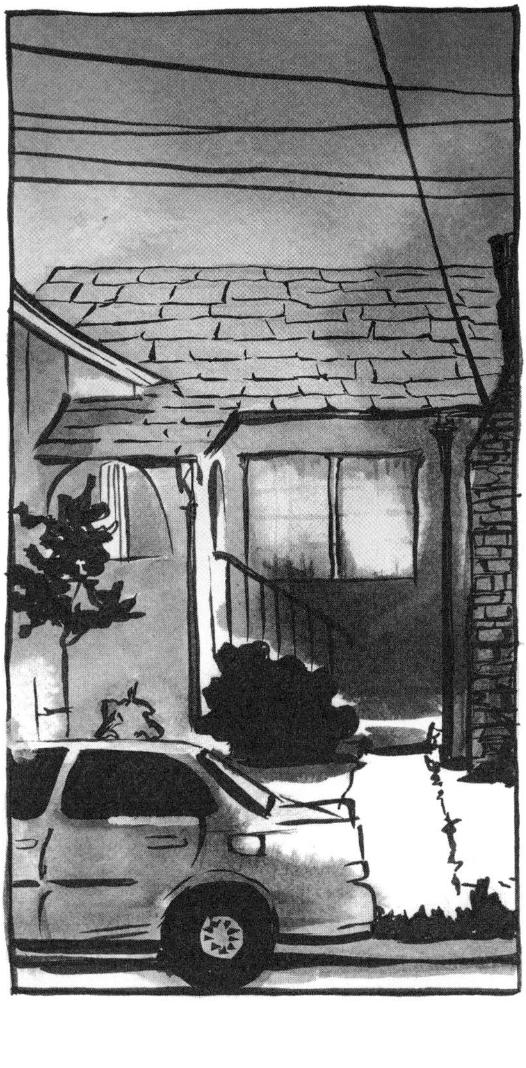

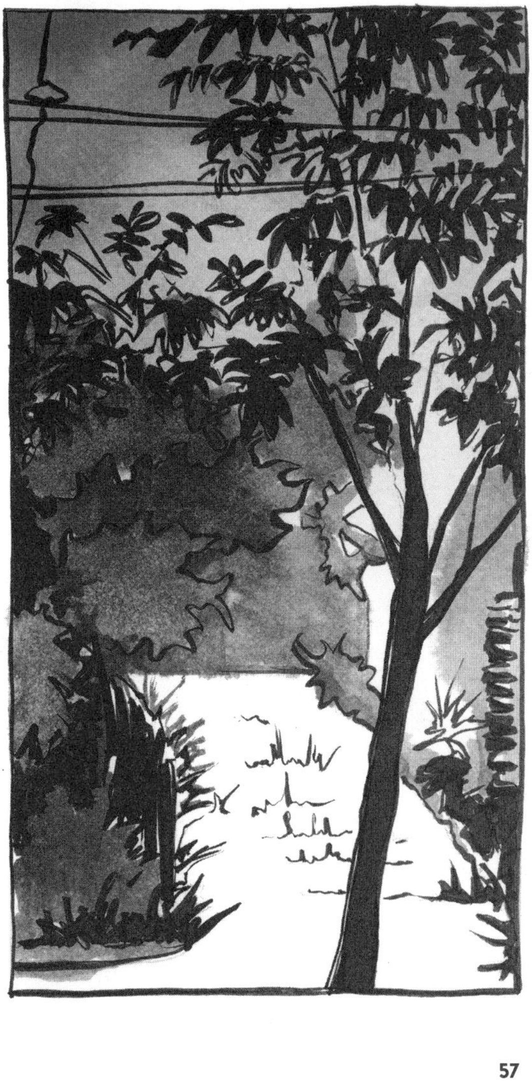

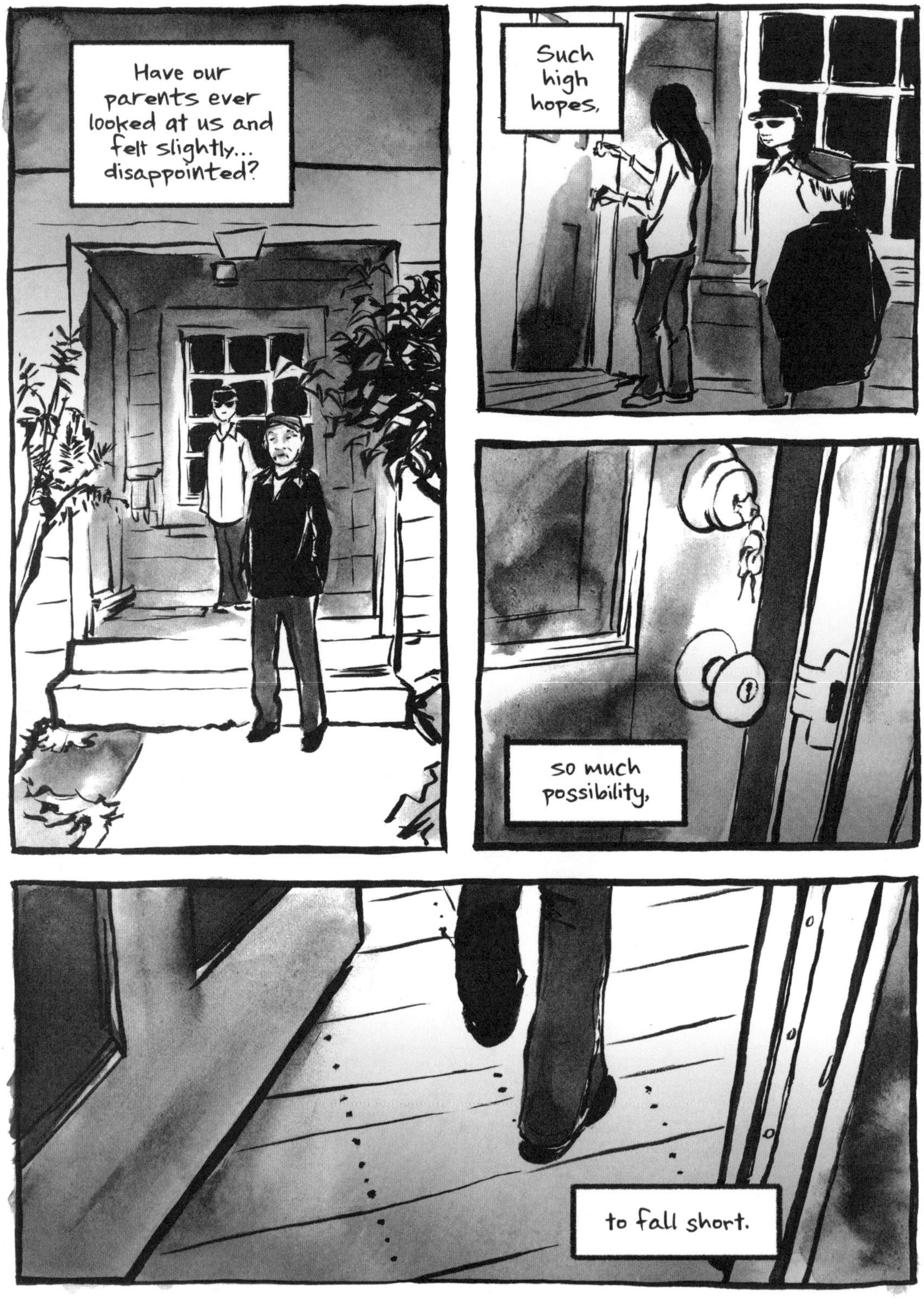
Have our parents ever looked at us and felt slightly... disappointed?
Such high hopes,
so much possibility,
to fall short.

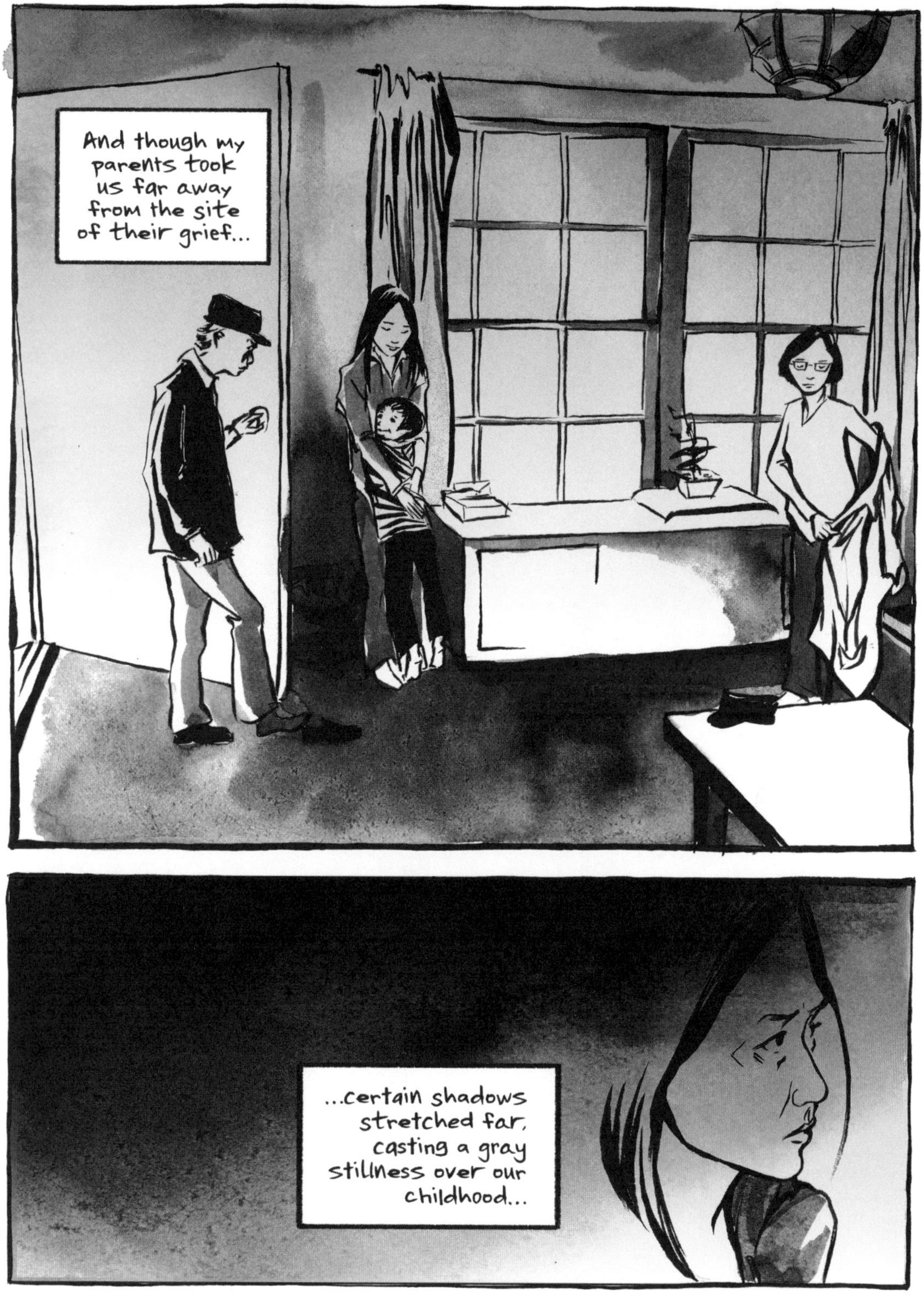
And though my parents took us far away from the site of their grief...
...certain shadows stretched far, casting a gray stillness over our childhood...

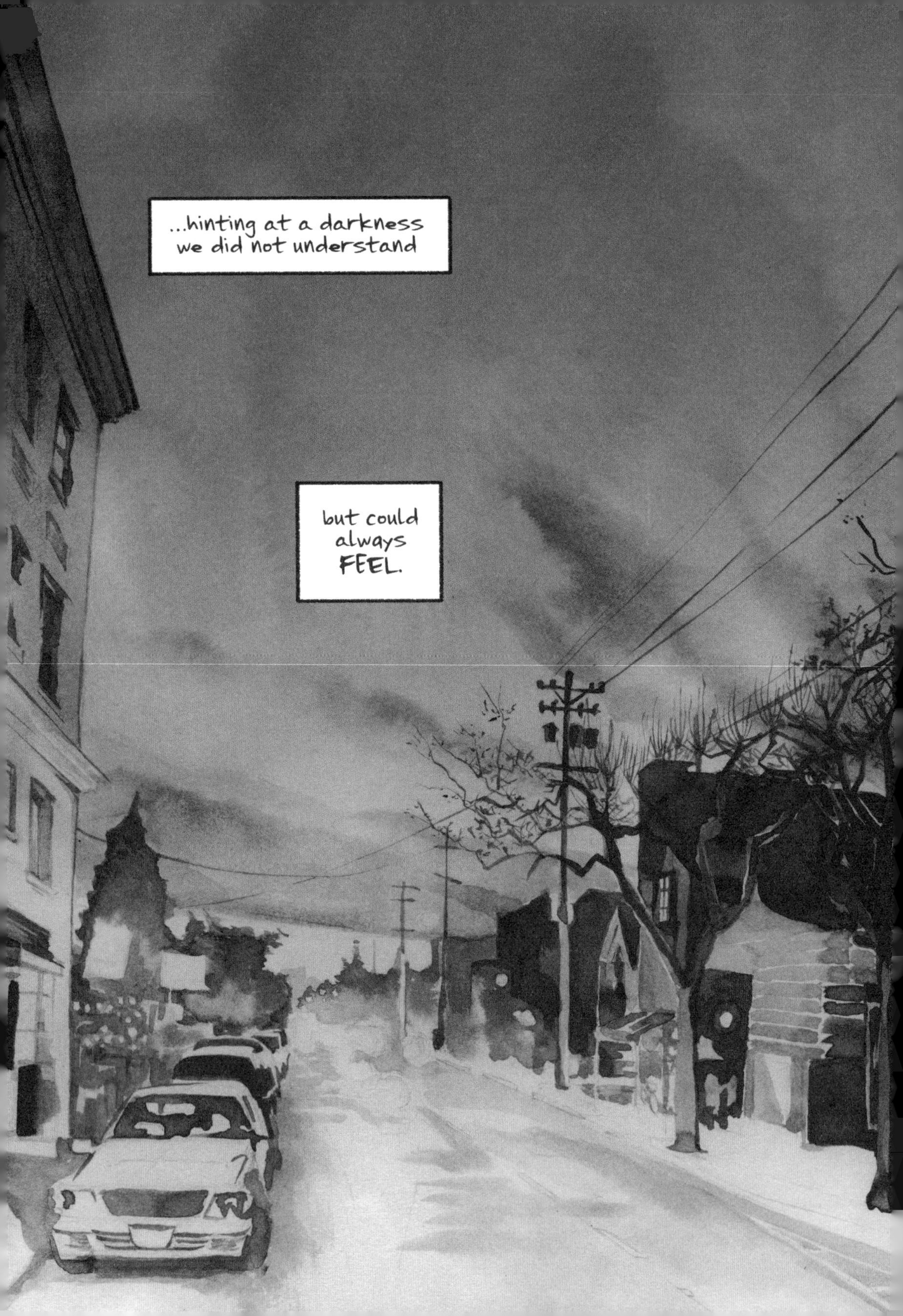
...hinting at a darkness we did not understand
but could always FEEL.

CHAPTER 3
HOME, THE HOLDING PEN

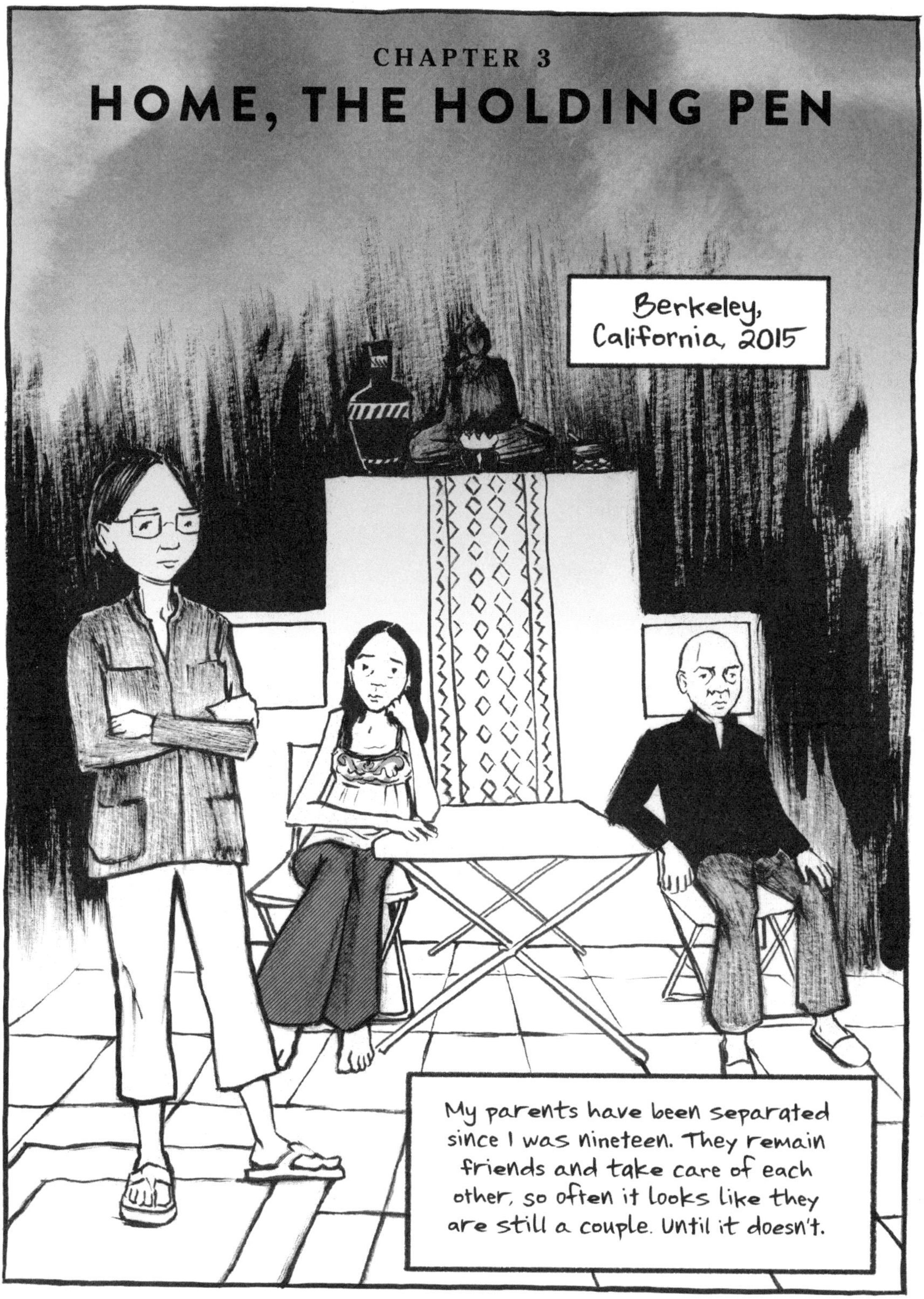
Berkeley, California, 2015
My parents have been separated since I was nineteen. They remain friends and take care of each other, so often it looks like they are still a couple. Until it doesn't.

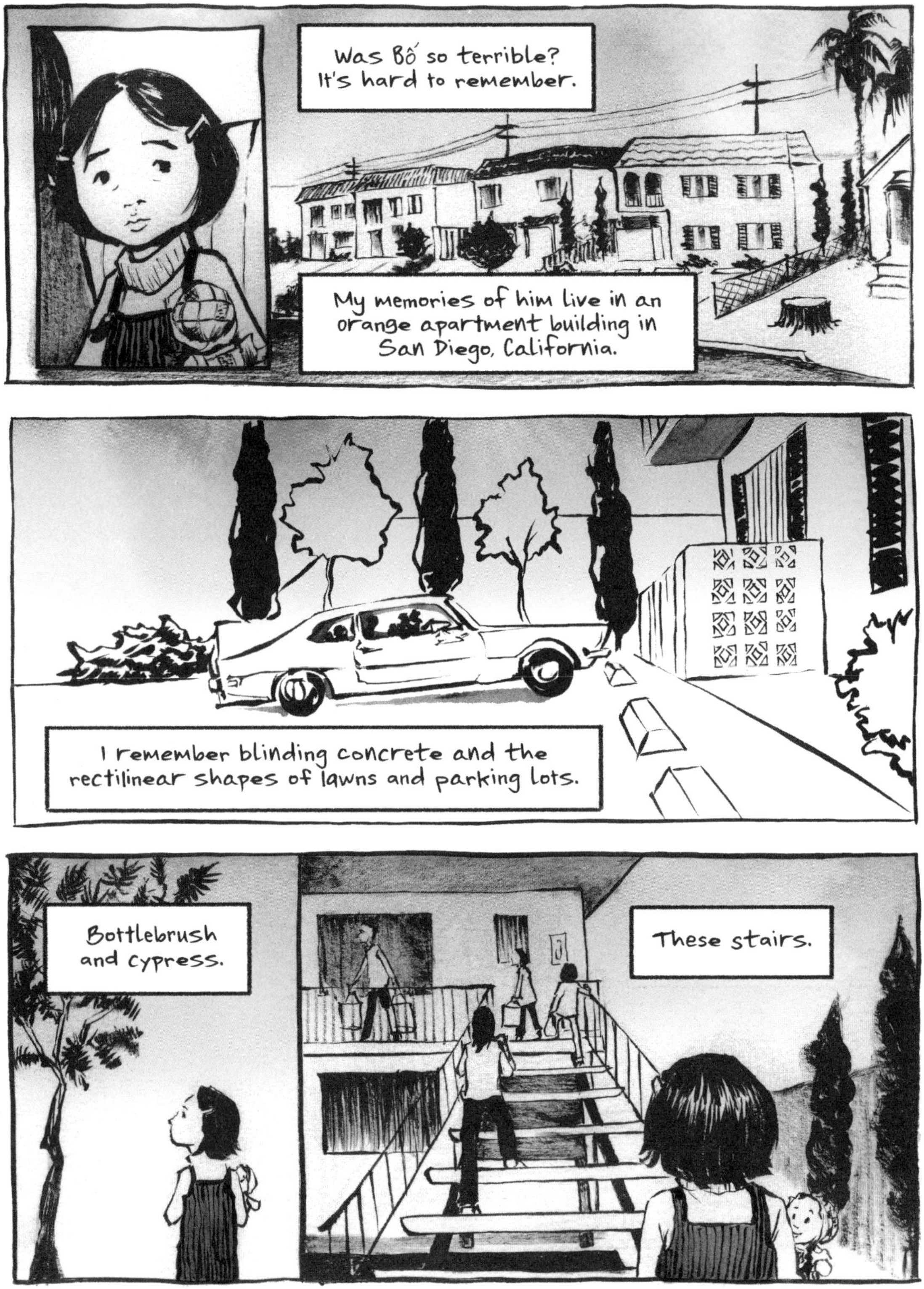
Was Bố so terrible? It's hard to remember.
My memories of him live in an orange apartment building in San Diego, California.
I remember blinding concrete and the rectilinear shapes of lawns and parking lots.
Bottlebrush and cypress.
These stairs.

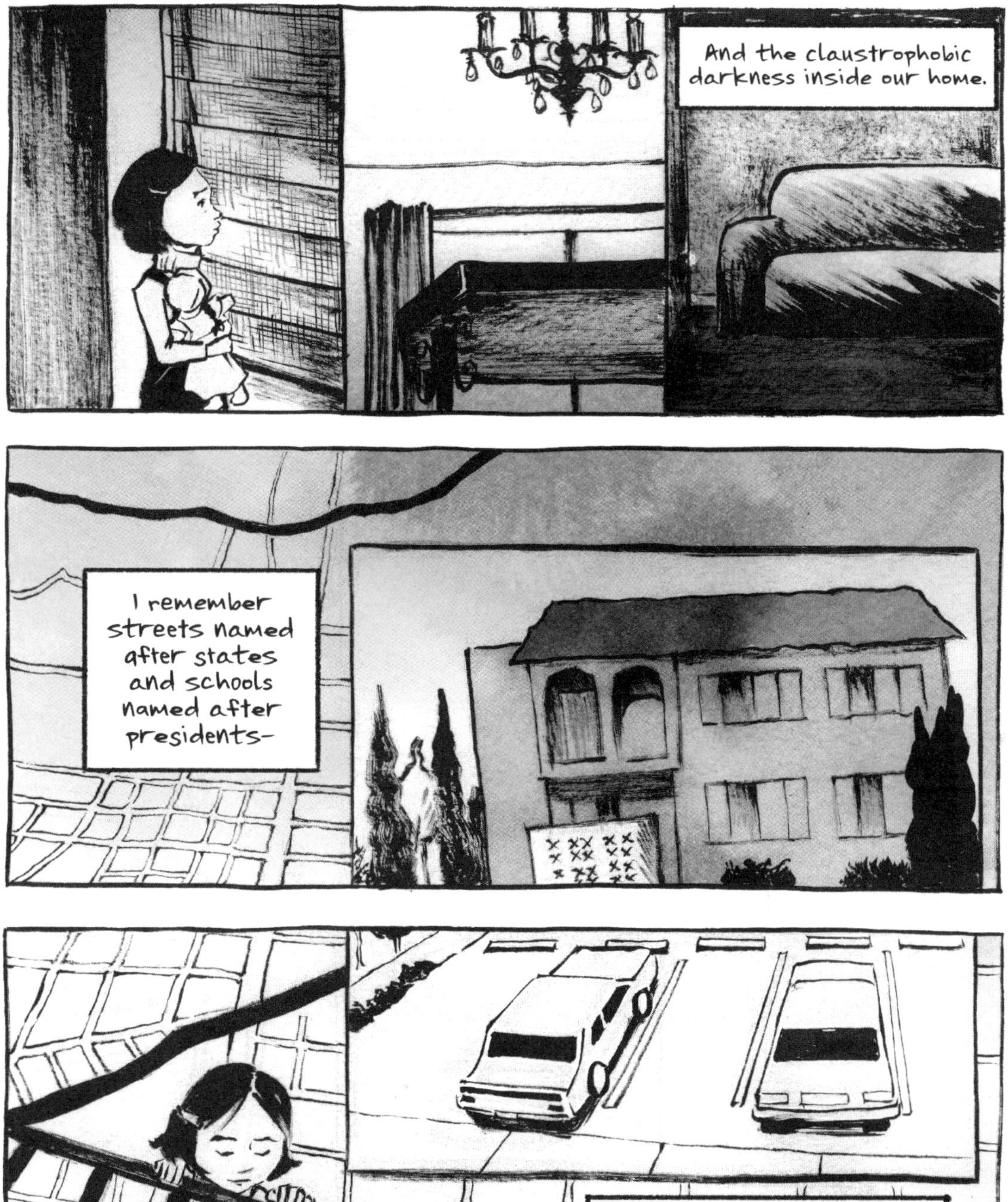
And the claustrophobic darkness inside our home.
I remember streets named after states and schools named after presidents-
-and imagine each block, each day turned us a little more American.

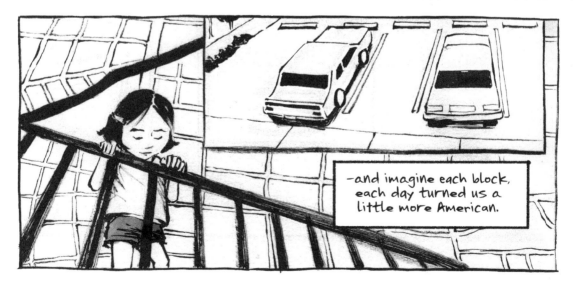

The same month we moved into the orange building, a sixteen-year-old girl in San Diego aimed her rifle

at the elementary school children across the street from her house, killing two people and injuring nine.

The mayor at the time was PETE WILSON,

the same California governor I would hate many years later

for backing one of the most anti-immigrant laws in history.

ILLEGALS GO HOME

CAUTION

NO MORE HAND OUTS

SAVE OUR STATE

San Diego was a naval and marine corps base, where the wounds of the Vietnam War were still fresh,

and not everyone welcomed our presence.

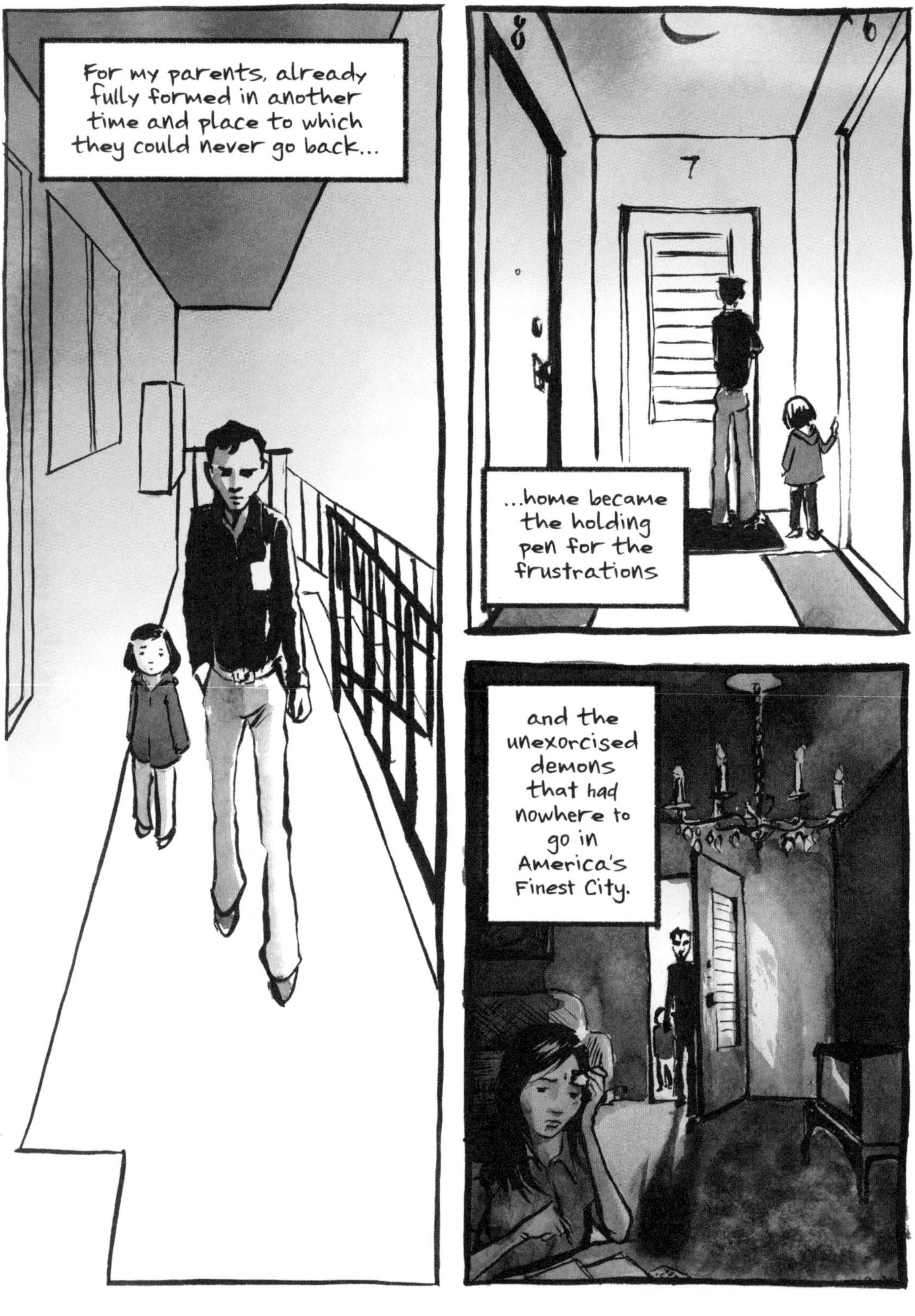
For my parents, already fully formed in another time and place to which they could never go back...
7
...home became the holding pen for the frustrations
and the unexorcised demons that had nowhere to go in America's Finest City.

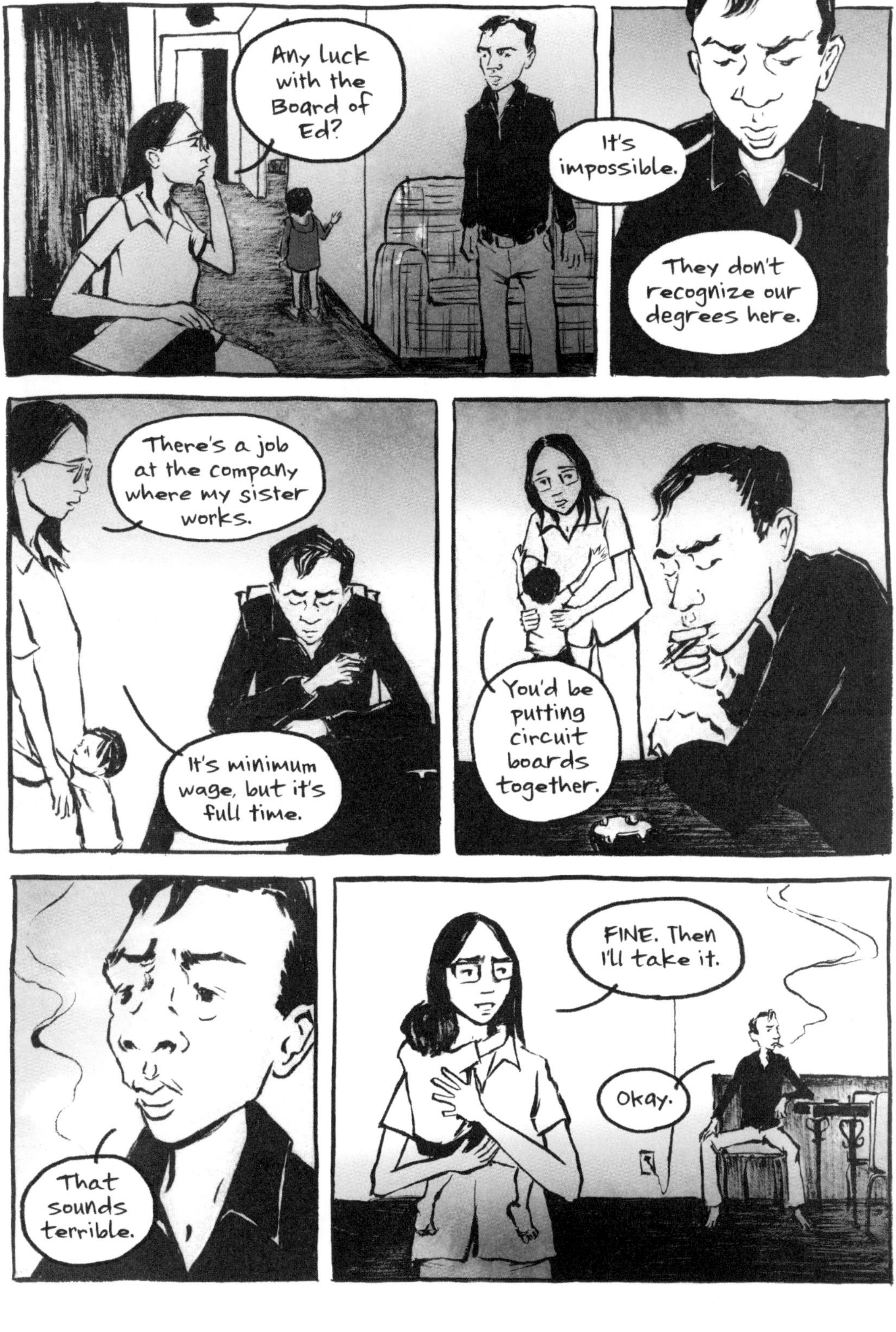
Any luck with the Board of Ed?
It's impossible.
They don't recognize our degrees here.
There's a job at the company where my sister works.
It's minimum wage, but it's full time.
You'd be putting circuit boards together.
That sounds terrible.
FINE. Then I'll take it.
Okay.

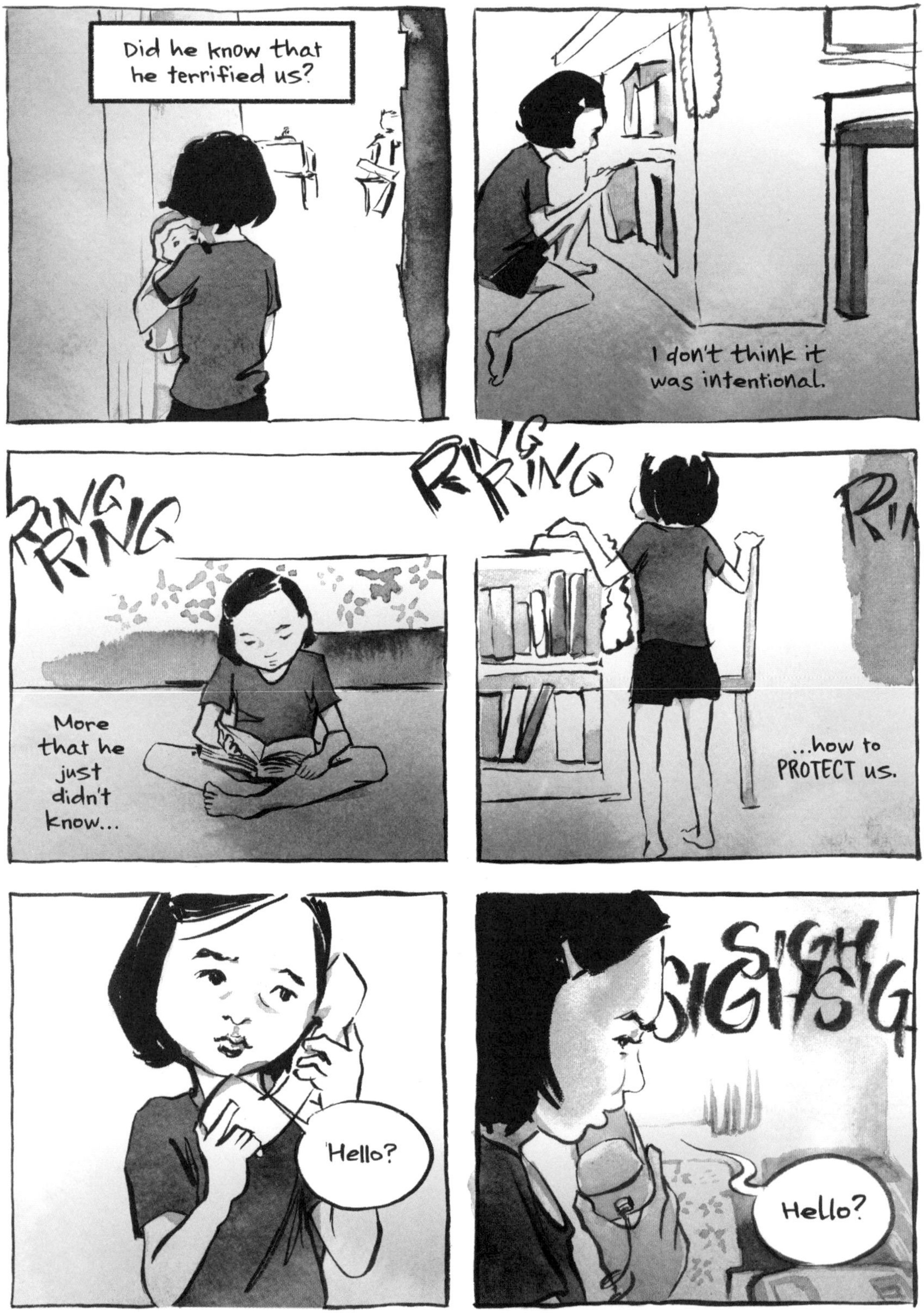

Did he know that he terrified us?
I don't think it was intentional.
RING RING
RING RING
More that he just didn't know...
...how to PROTECT us.
Hello?
Hello?

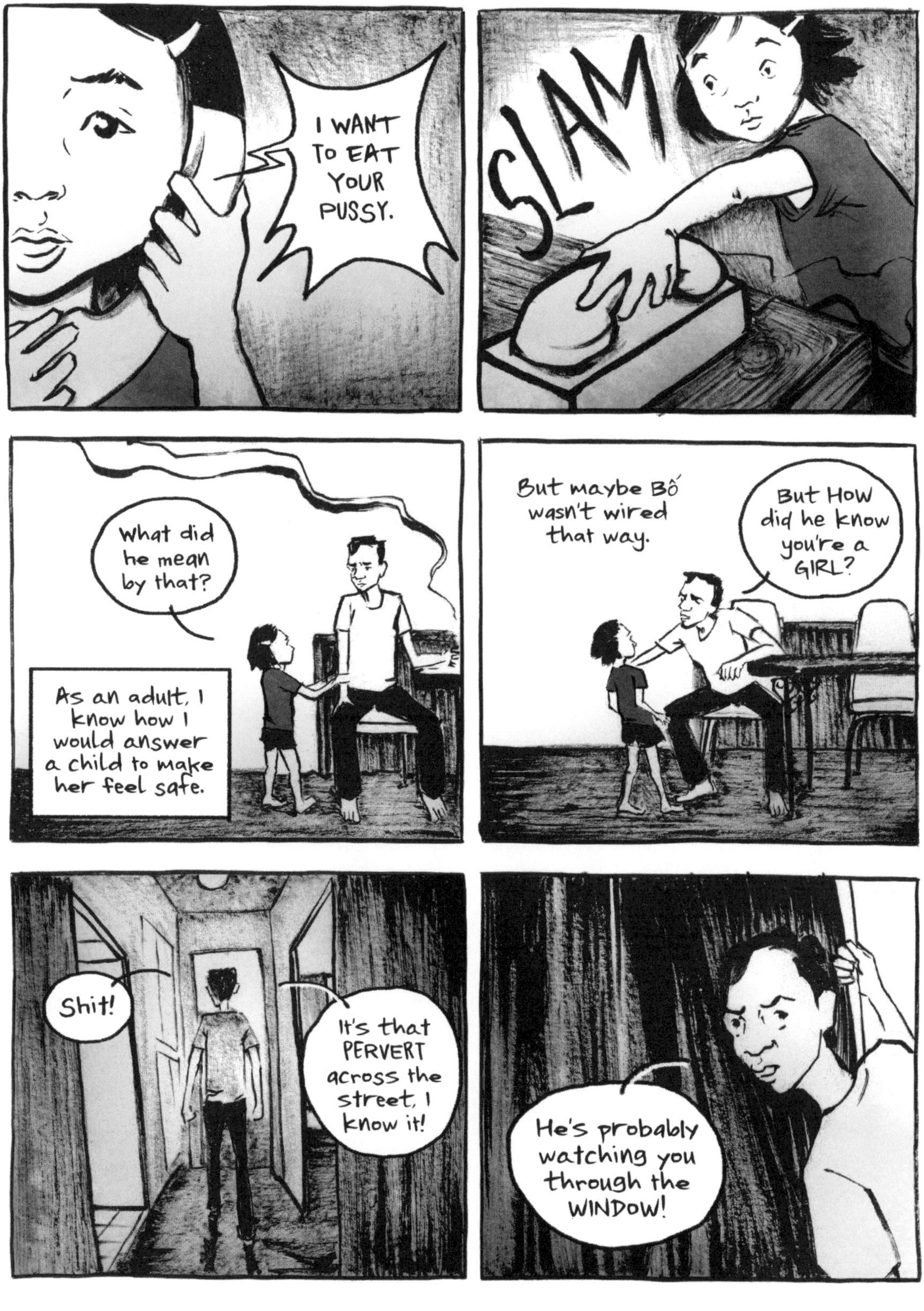
I WANT TO EAT YOUR PUSSY.
SLAM
What did he mean by that?
As an adult, I know how I would answer a child to make her feel safe.
But maybe Bố wasn't wired that way.
But HOW did he know you're a GIRL?
Shit!
It's that PERVERT across the street, I know it!
He's probably watching you through the WINDOW!

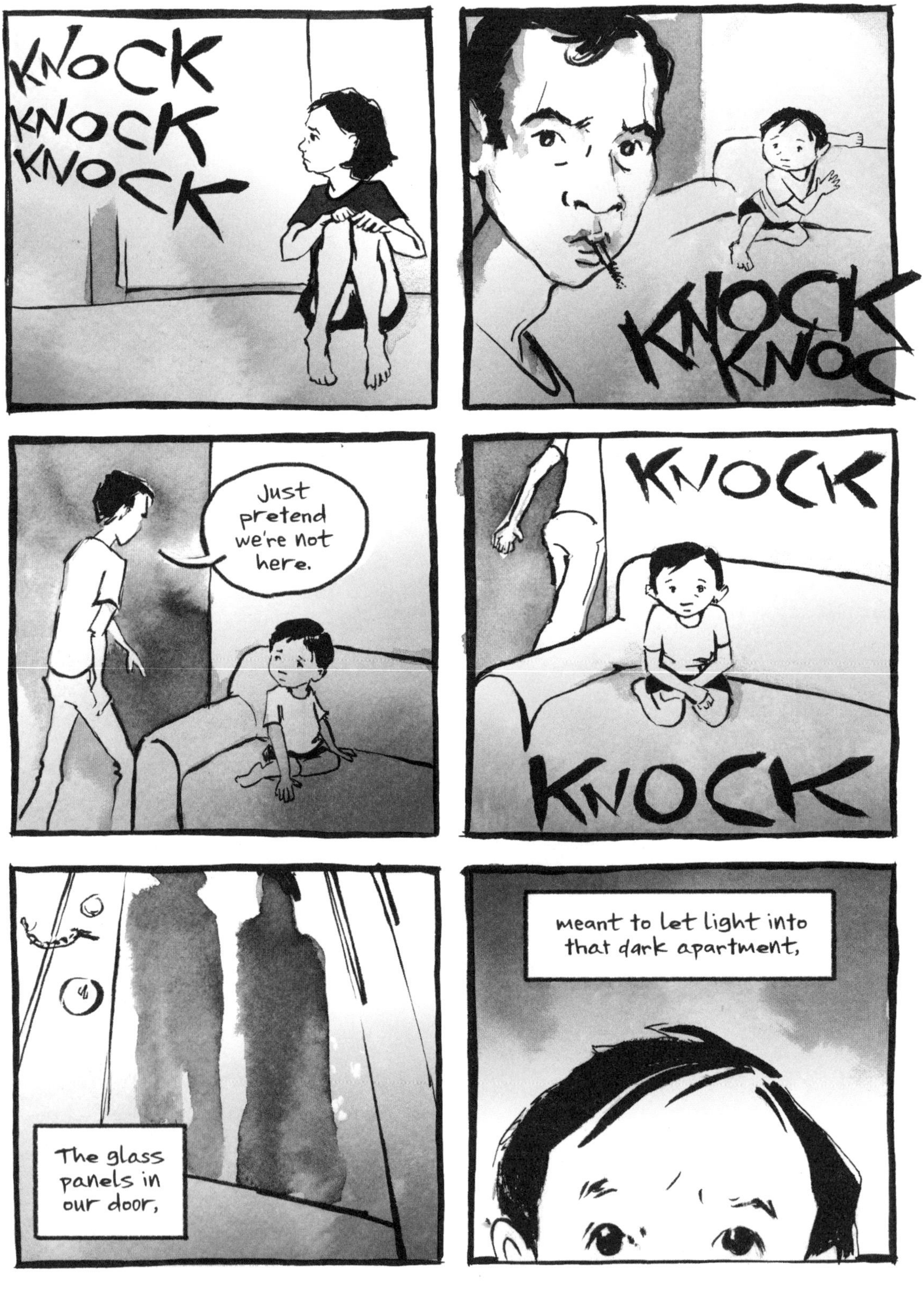
KNOCK
KNOCK
KNOCK
KNOCK
KNOC
Just pretend we're not here.
KNOCK
KNOCK
The glass panels in our door,
meant to let light into that dark apartment,

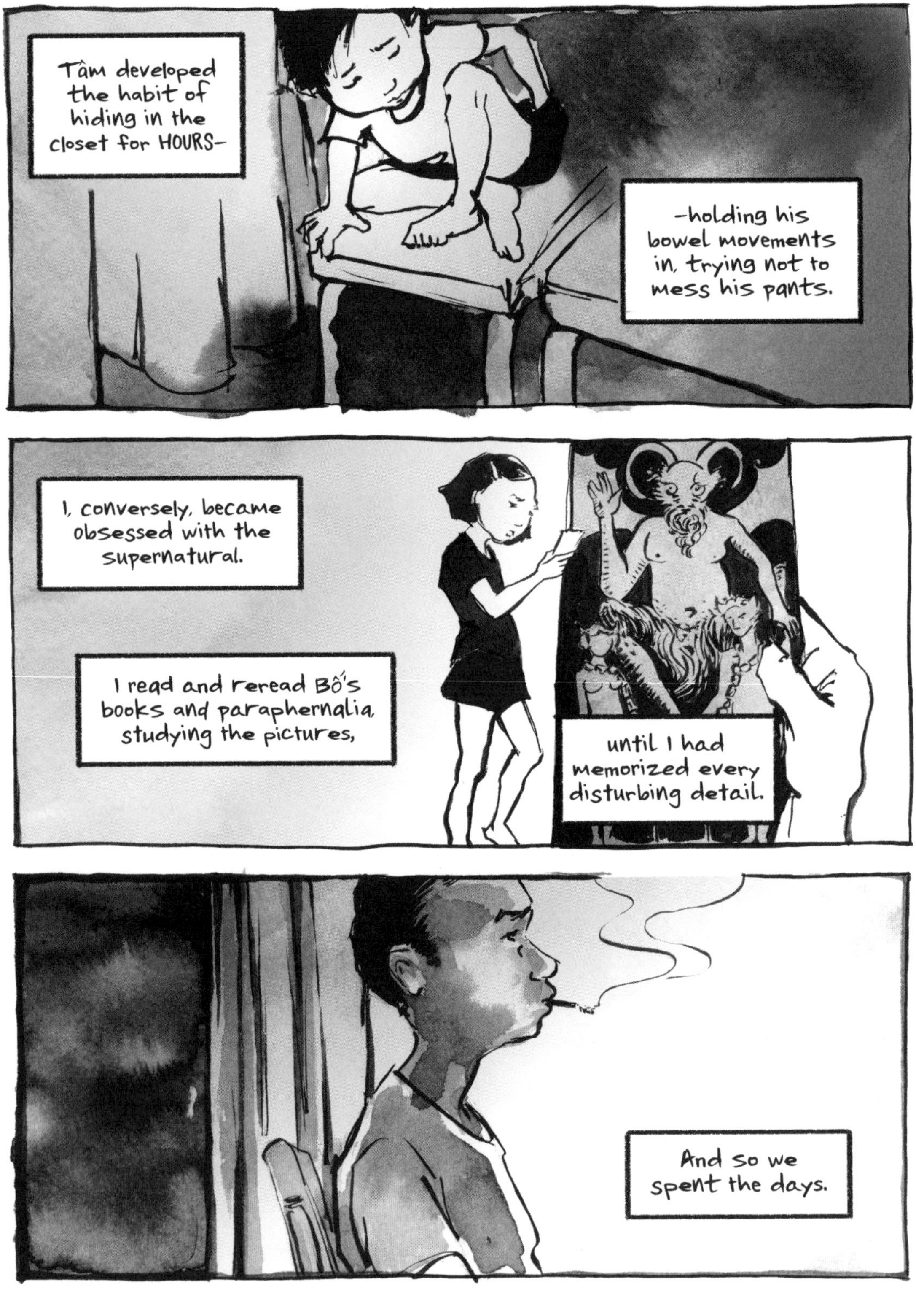

Tâm developed the habit of hiding in the closet for HOURS–
–holding his bowel movements in, trying not to mess his pants.
I, conversely, became obsessed with the supernatural.
I read and reread Bố's books and paraphernalia, studying the pictures,
until I had memorized every disturbing detail.
And so we spent the days.

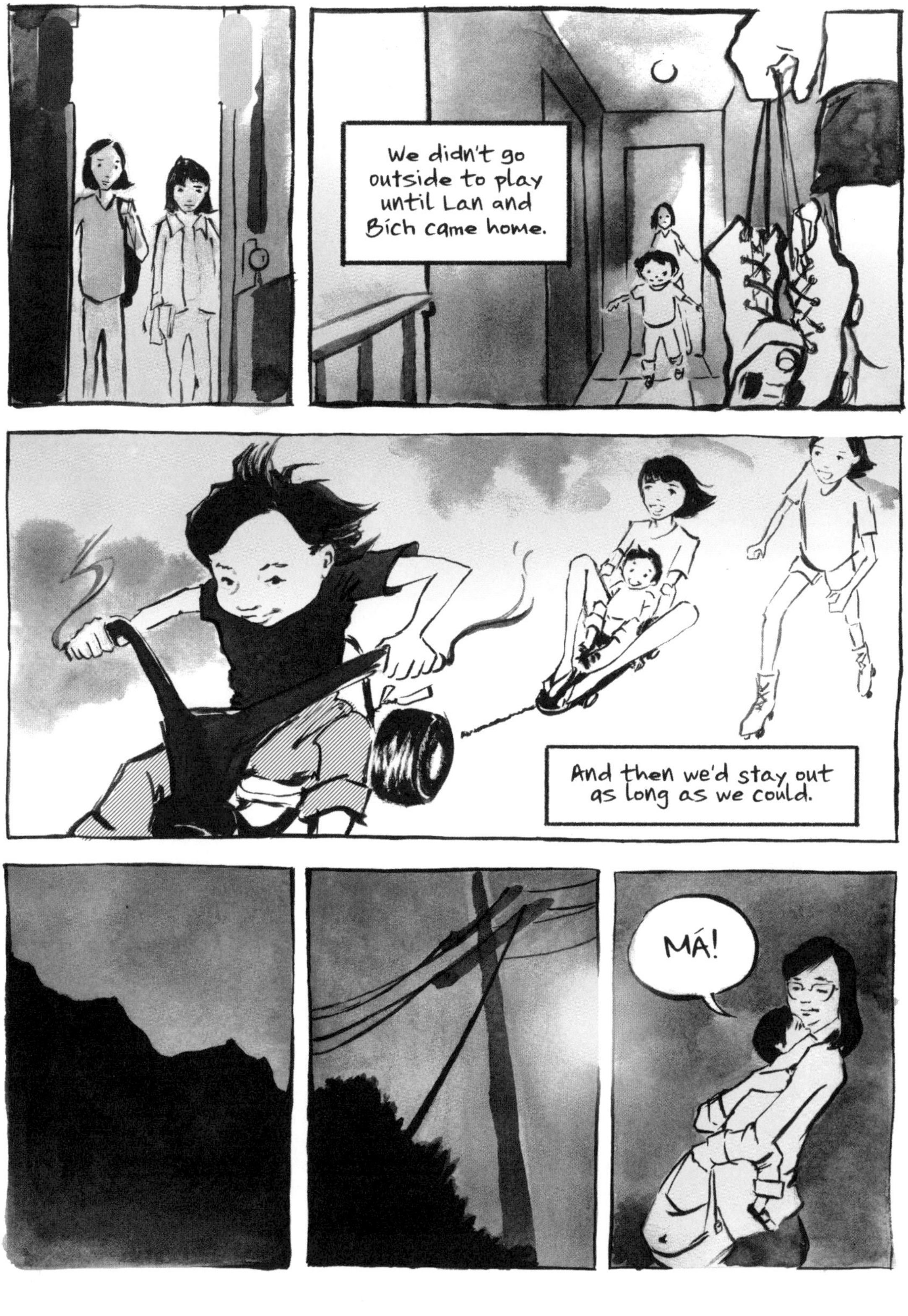

We didn't go outside to play until Lan and Bich came home.
And then we'd stay out as long as we could.
MÁ!

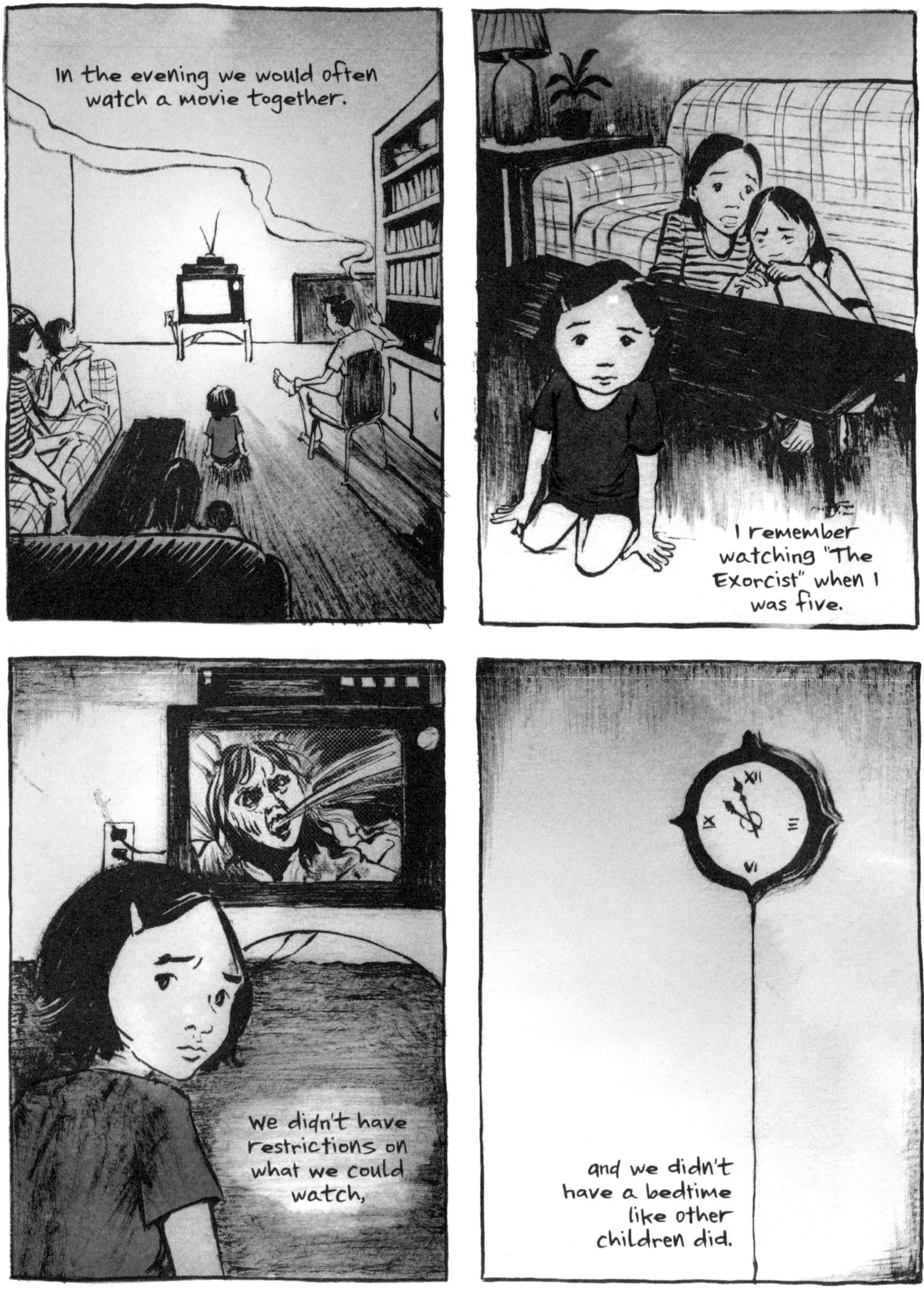
In the evening we would often watch a movie together.
I remember watching "The Exorcist" when I was five.
We didn't have restrictions on what we could watch,
and we didn't have a bedtime like other children did.

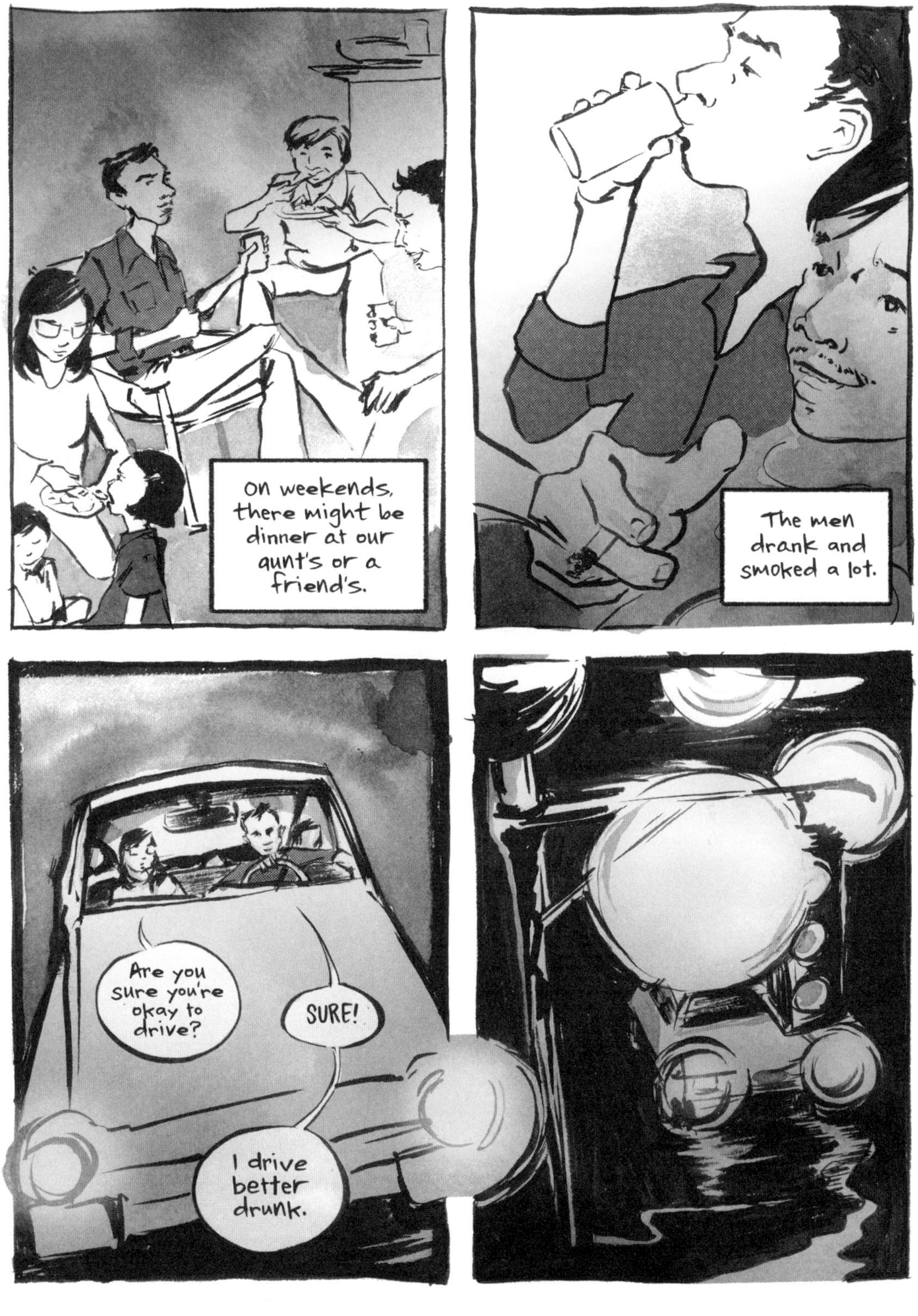
On weekends, there might be dinner at our aunt's or a friend's.
The men drank and smoked a lot.
Are you sure you're okay to drive?
SURE!
I drive better drunk.

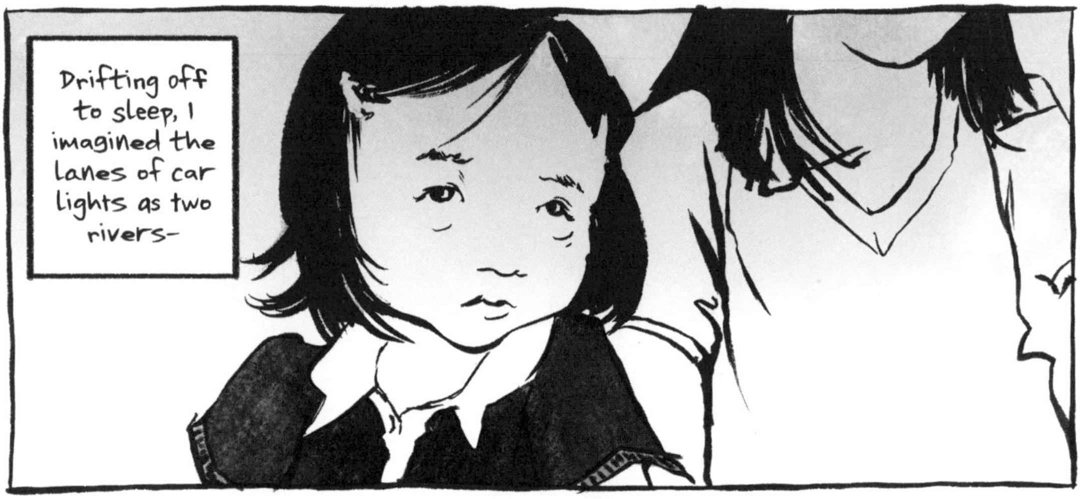
Drifting off to sleep, I imagined the lanes of car lights as two rivers-

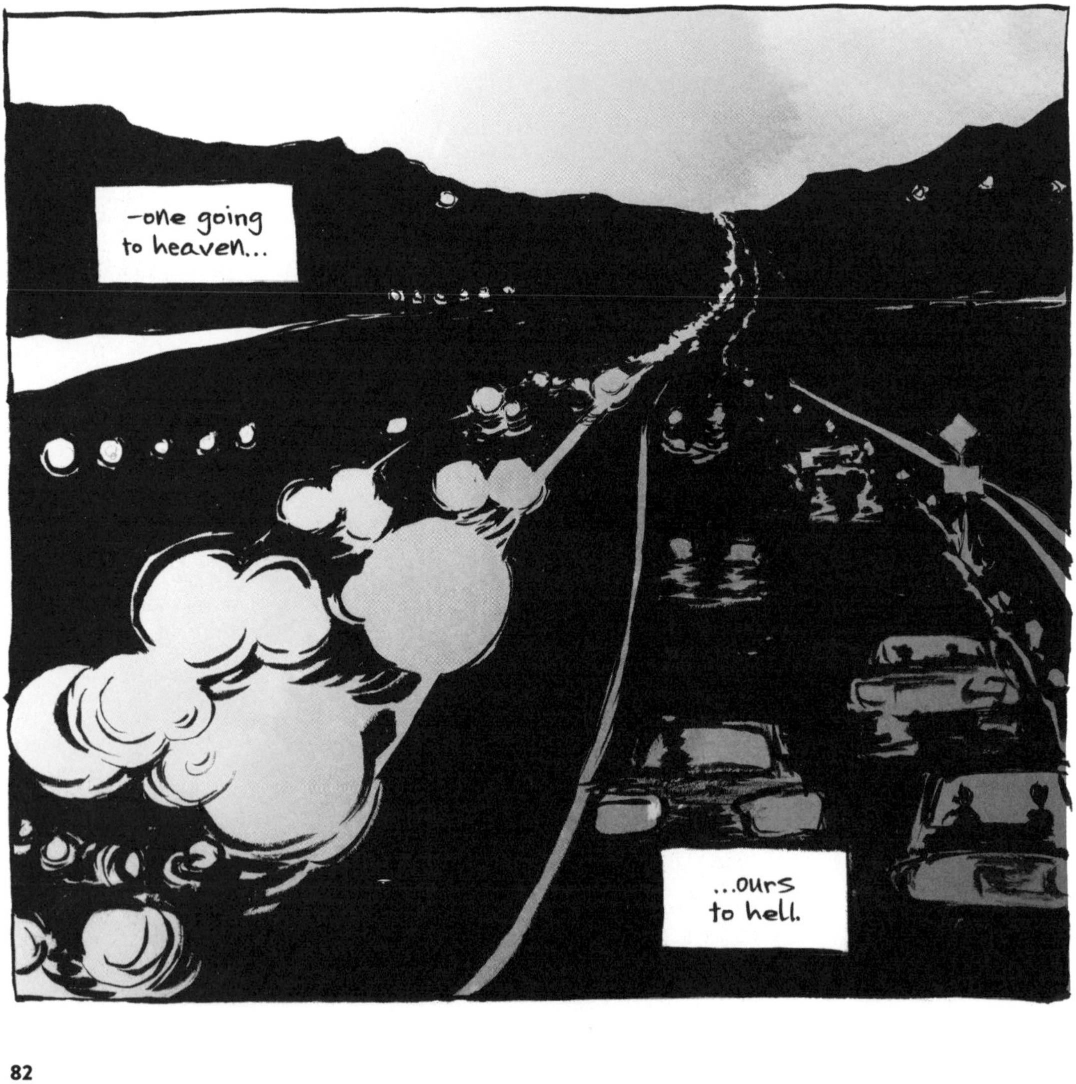
-one going to heaven...
...ours to hell.

In my sleep,
I dreamt of
how terrible
it would be to
not find my
way home.

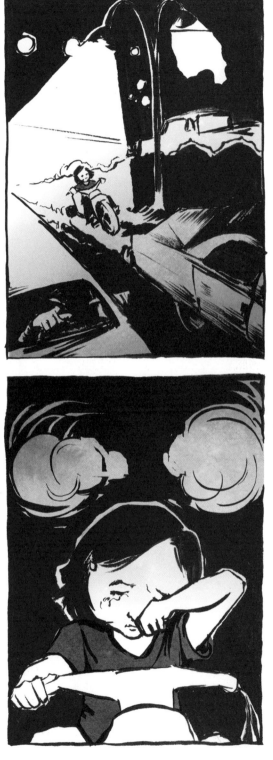

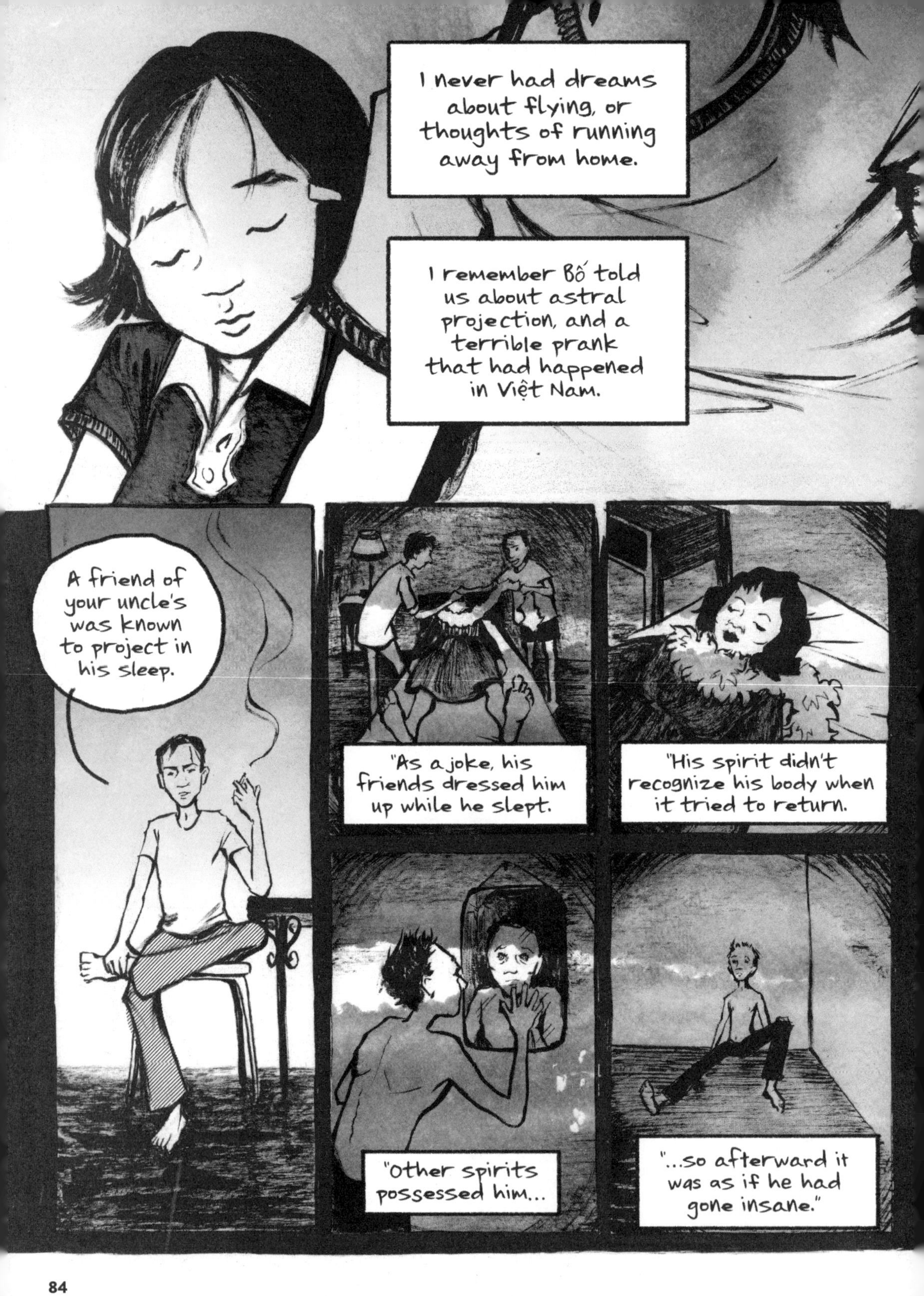
I never had dreams about flying, or thoughts of running away from home.
I remember Bố told us about astral projection, and a terrible prank that had happened in Việt Nam.
A friend of your uncle's was known to project in his sleep.
"As a joke, his friends dressed him up while he slept.
"His spirit didn't recognize his body when it tried to return.
"Other spirits possessed him...
"...so afterward it was as if he had gone insane."

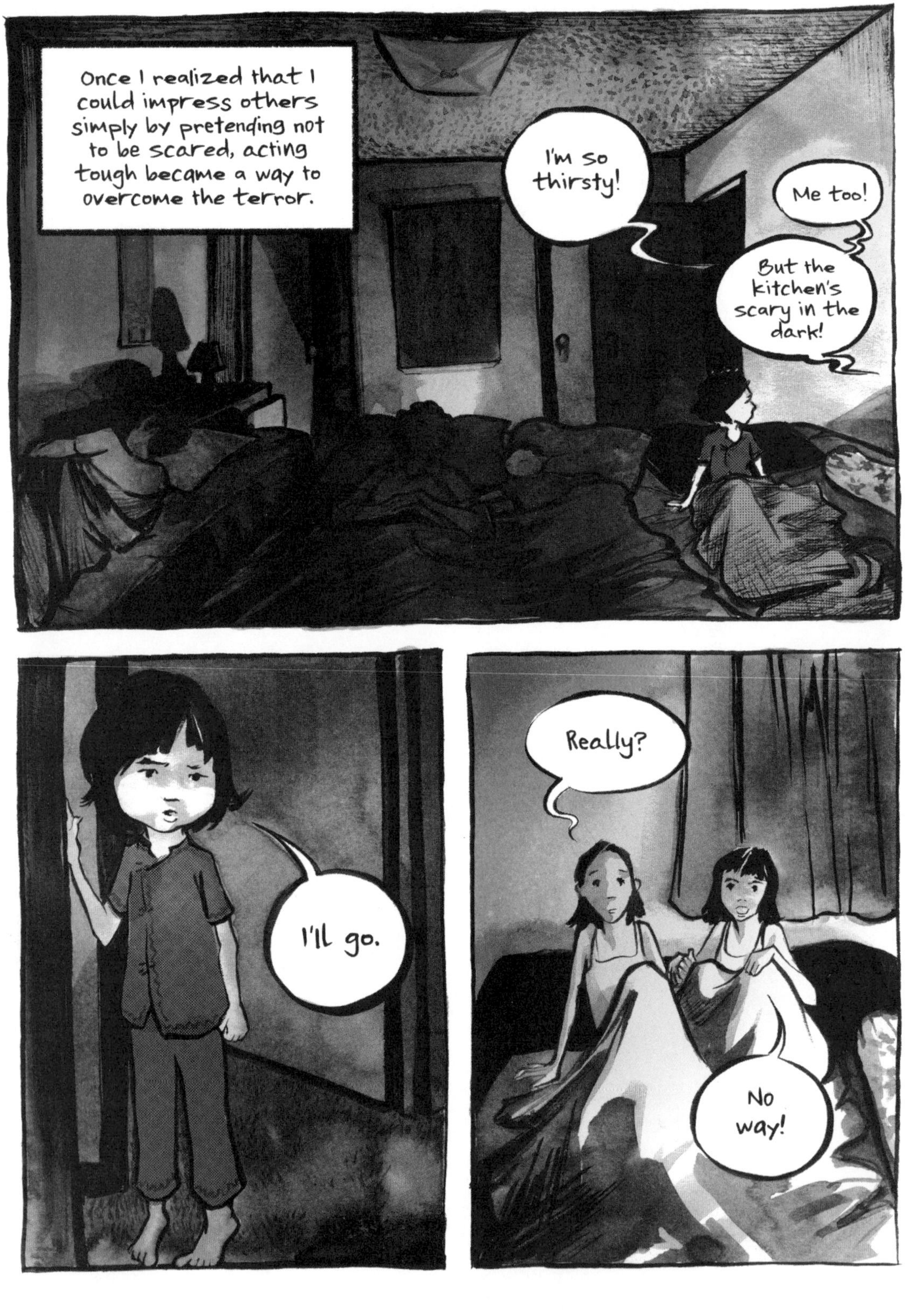
Once I realized that I could impress others simply by pretending not to be scared, acting tough became a way to overcome the terror.
I'm so thirsty!
Me too!
But the kitchen's scary in the dark!
I'll go.
Really?
No way!

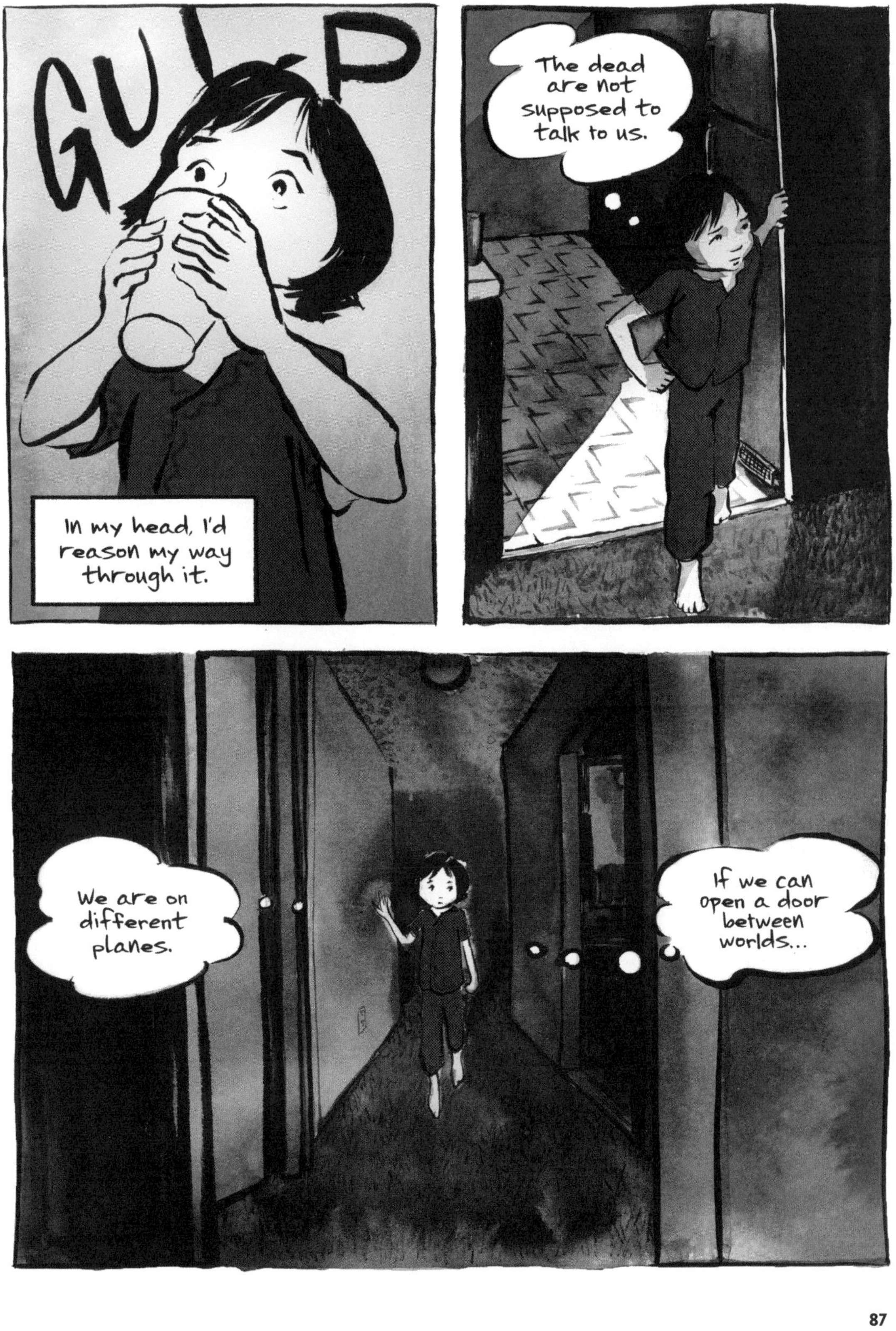
GULP
In my head, I'd reason my way through it.
The dead are not supposed to talk to us.
We are on different planes.
If we can open a door between worlds...

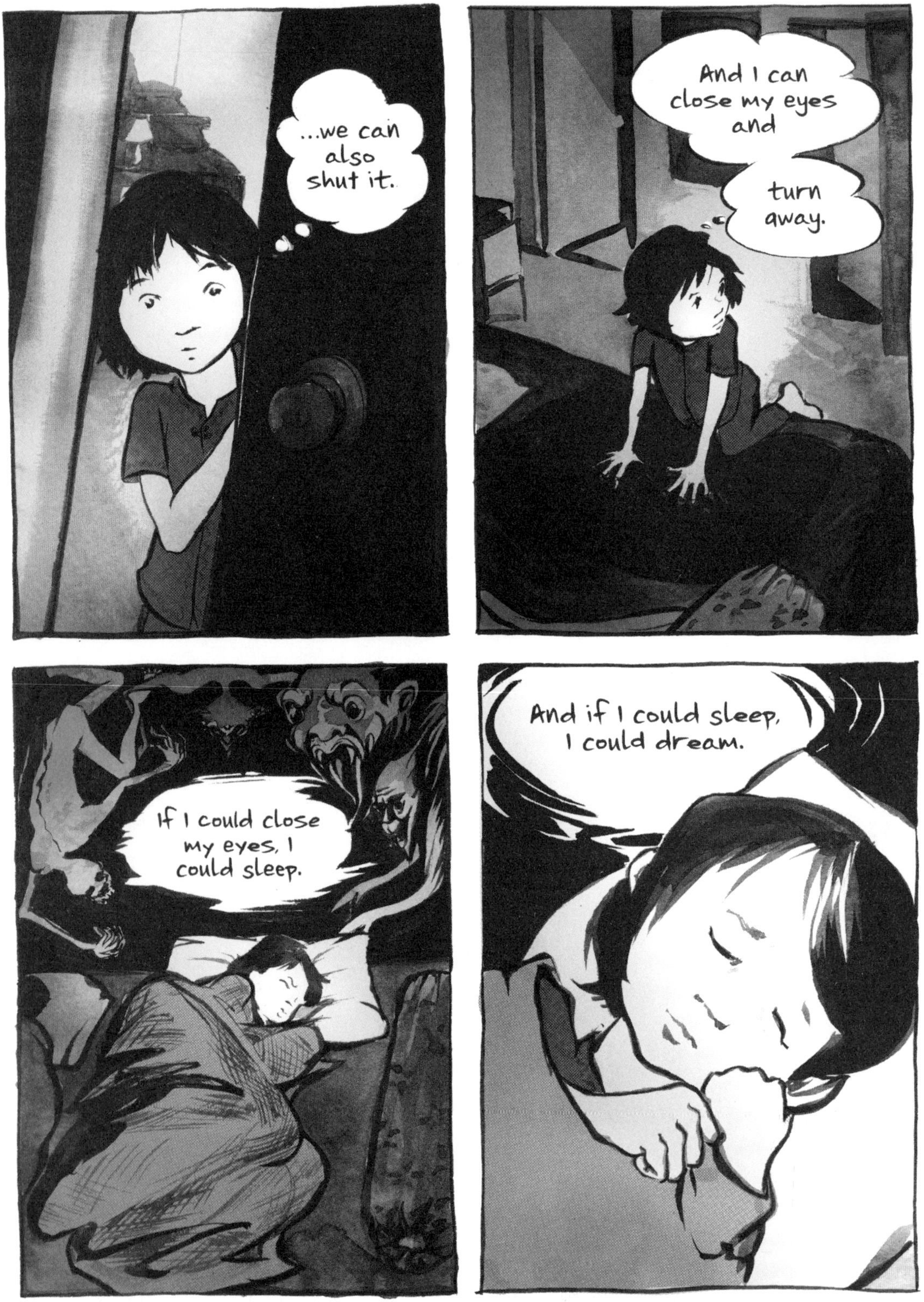
...we can also shut it.
And I can close my eyes and
turn away.
If I could close my eyes, I could sleep.
And if I could sleep, I could dream.

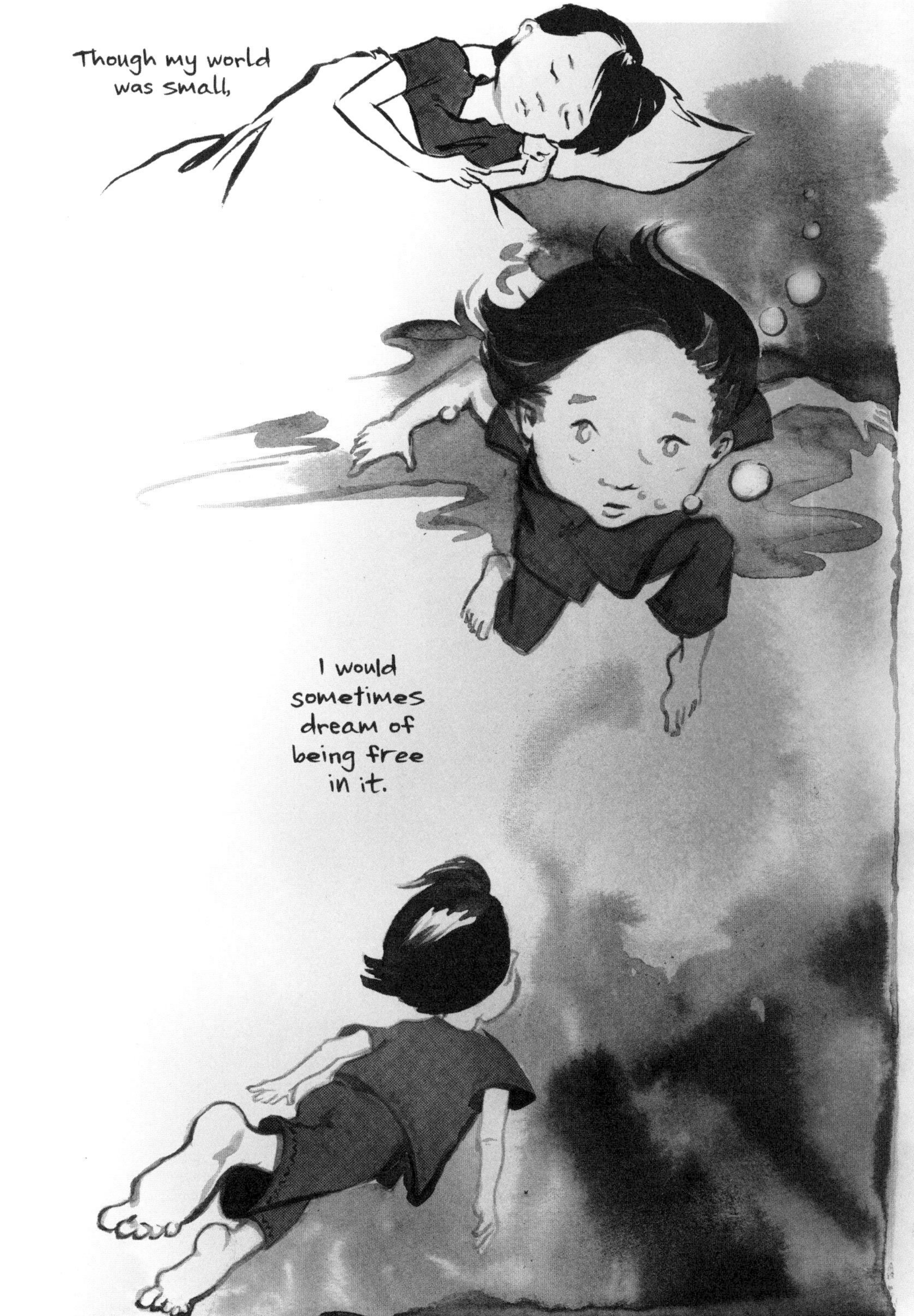
Though my world
was small,
I would
sometimes
dream of
being free
in it.

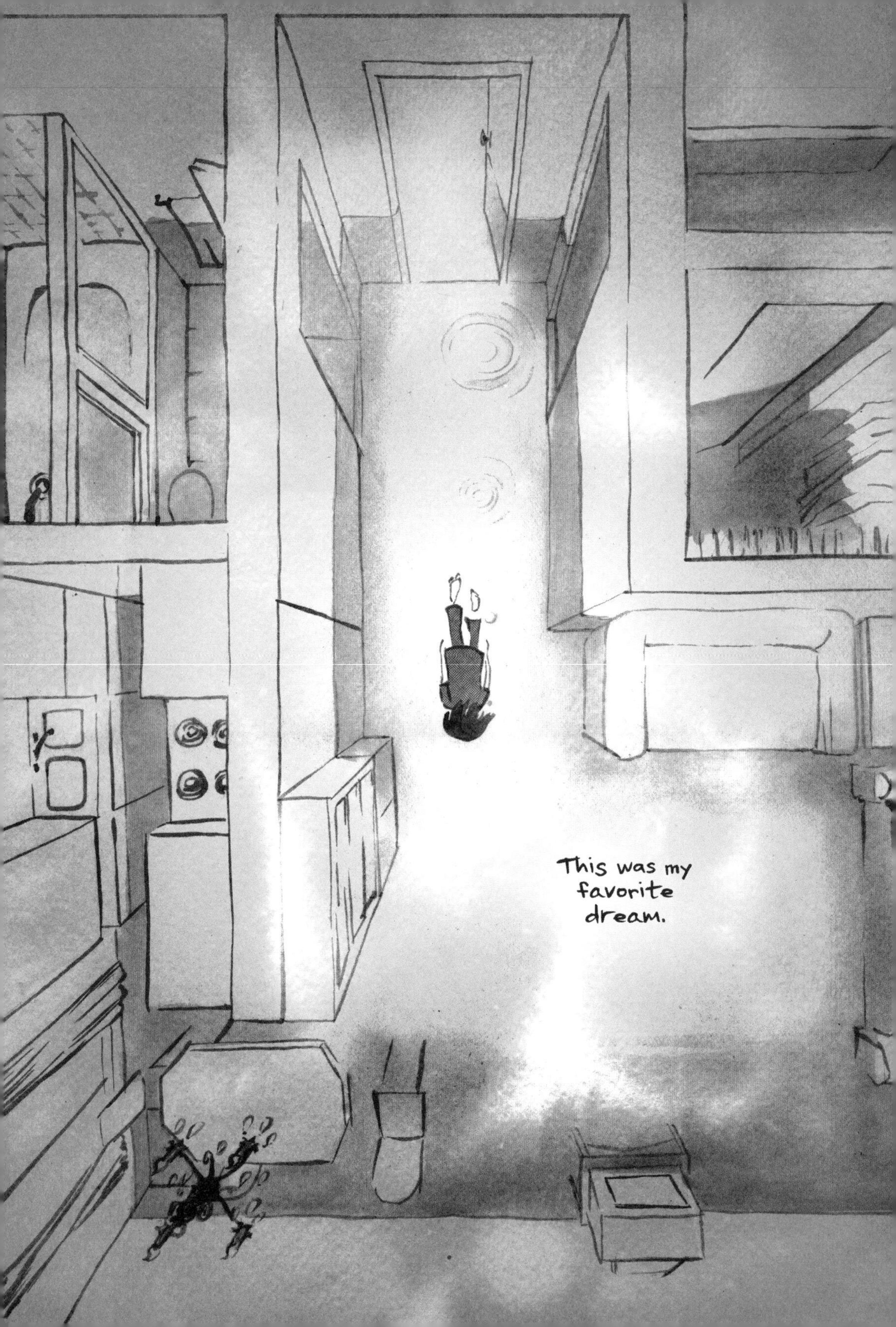
This was my favorite dream.

CHAPTER 4

BLOOD AND RICE

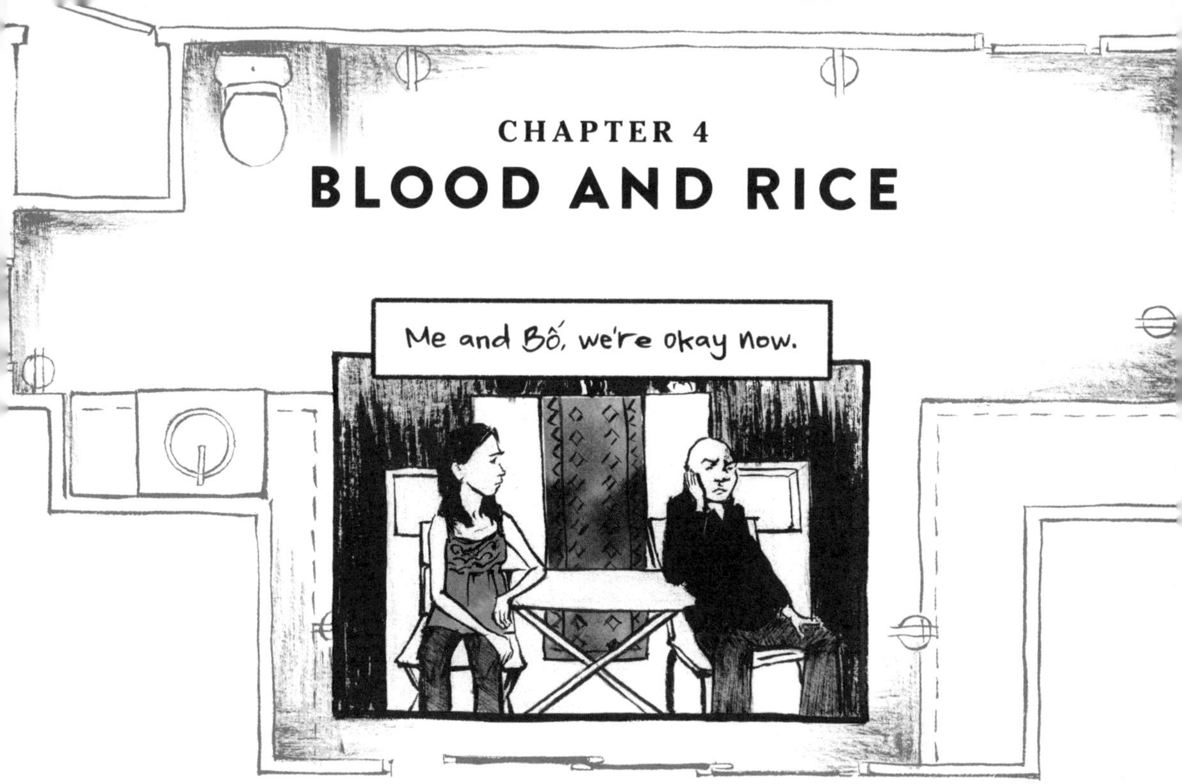
Me and Bố, we're okay now.

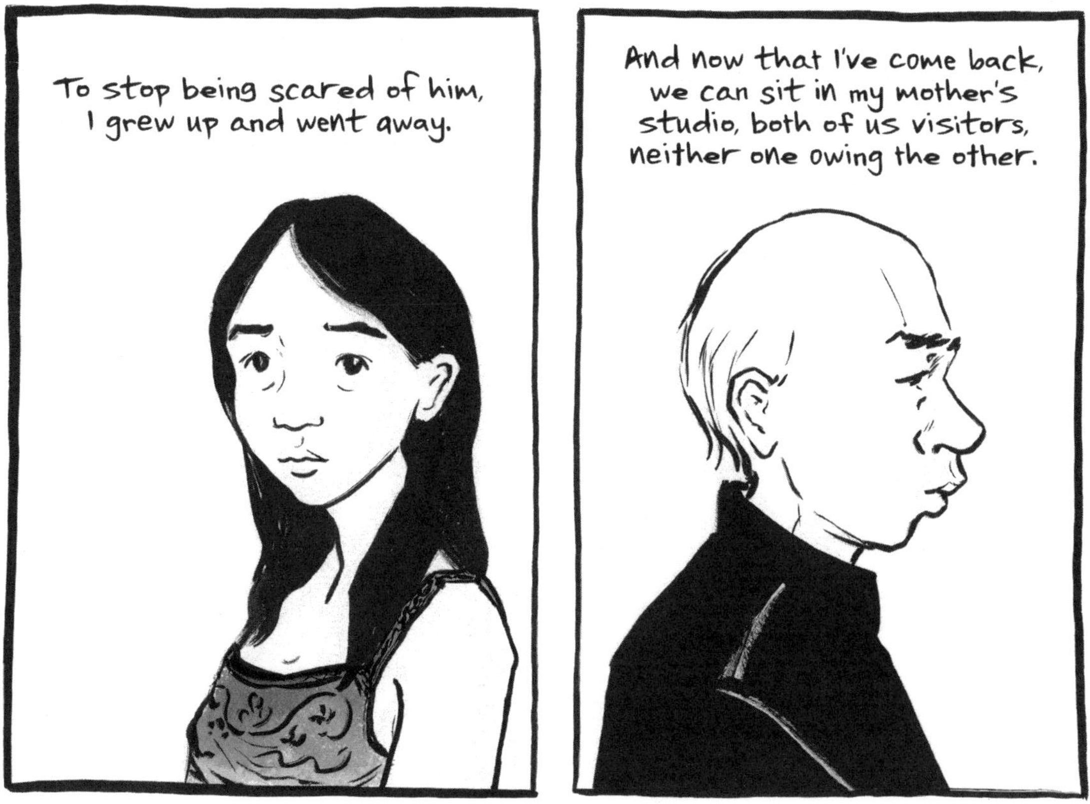
To stop being scared of him, I grew up and went away.
And now that I've come back, we can sit in my mother's studio, both of us visitors, neither one owing the other.

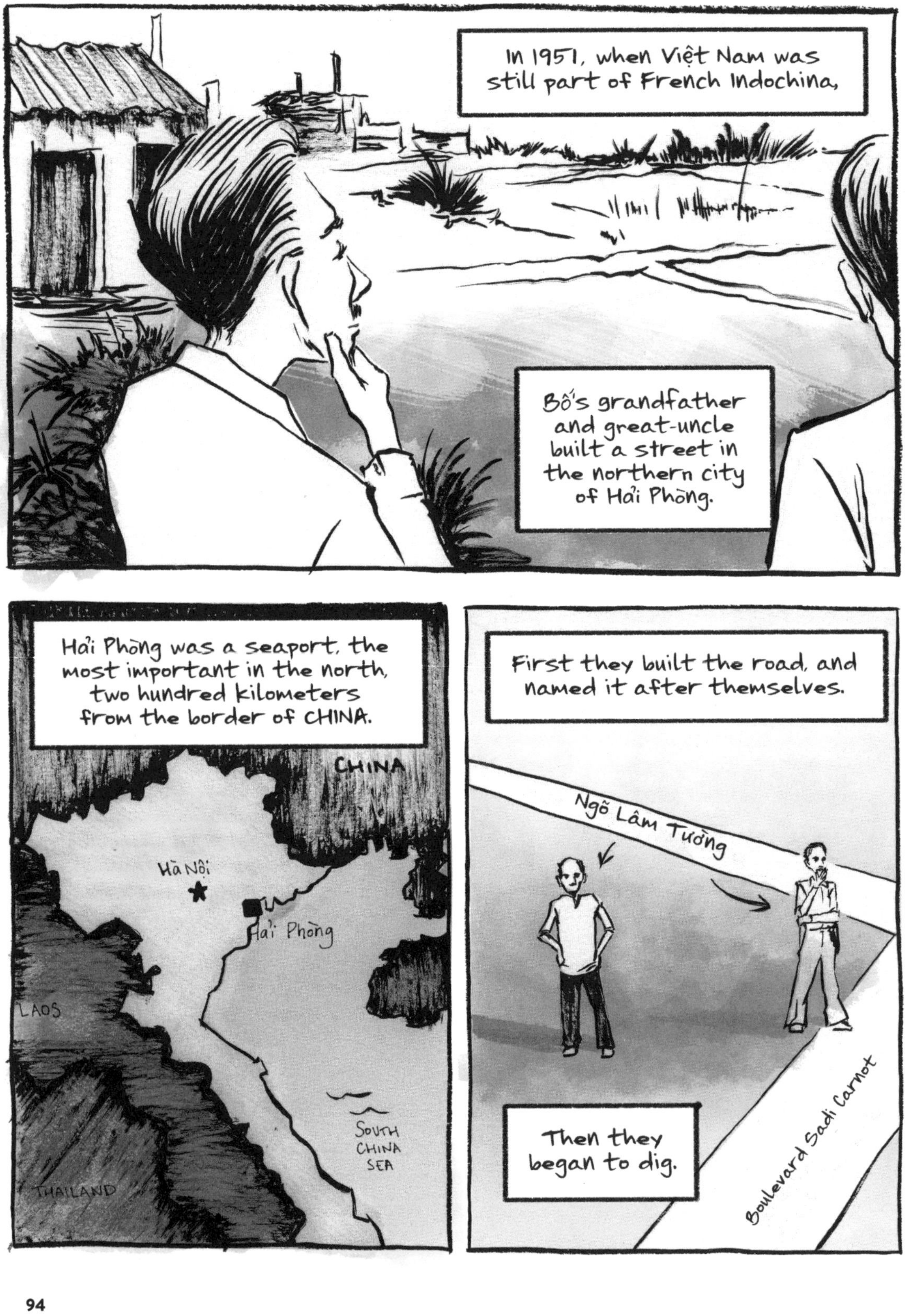
In 1951, when Việt Nam was still part of French Indochina,
Bố's grandfather and great-uncle built a street in the northern city of Hải Phòng.
Hải Phòng was a seaport, the most important in the north, two hundred kilometers from the border of CHINA.
CHINA
Hà Nội
Hải Phòng
LAOS
SOUTH CHINA SEA
THAILAND
First they built the road, and named it after themselves.
Ngô Lâm Tường
Then they began to dig.
Boulevard Sadi Carnot

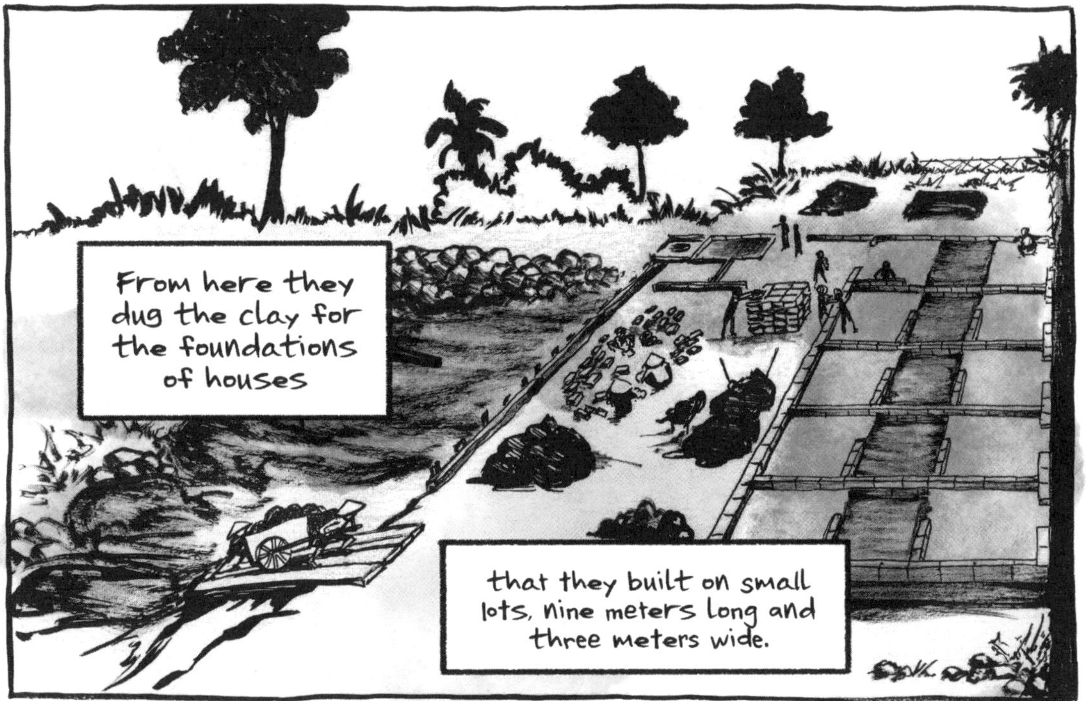
From here they dug the clay for the foundations of houses
that they built on small lots, nine meters long and three meters wide.

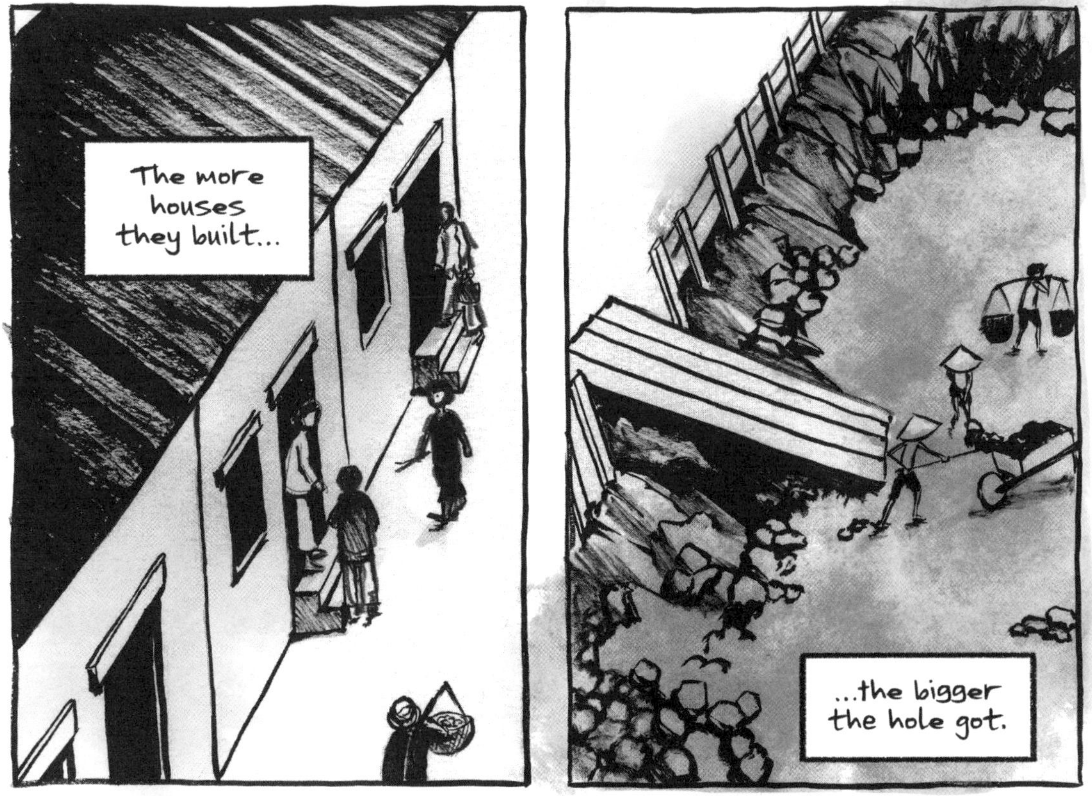
The more houses they built...
...the bigger the hole got.

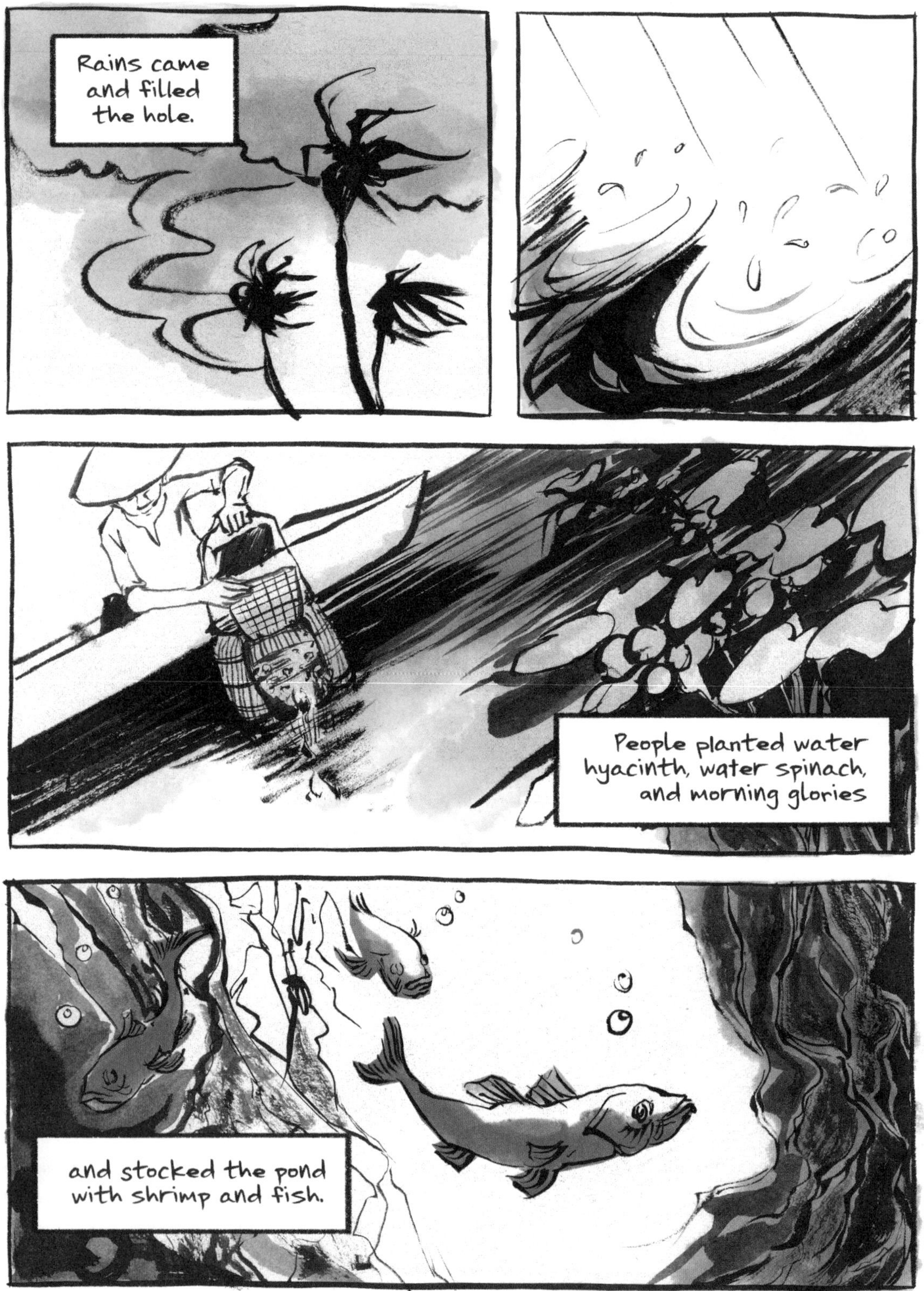
Rains came and filled the hole.
People planted water hyacinth, water spinach, and morning glories
and stocked the pond with shrimp and fish.

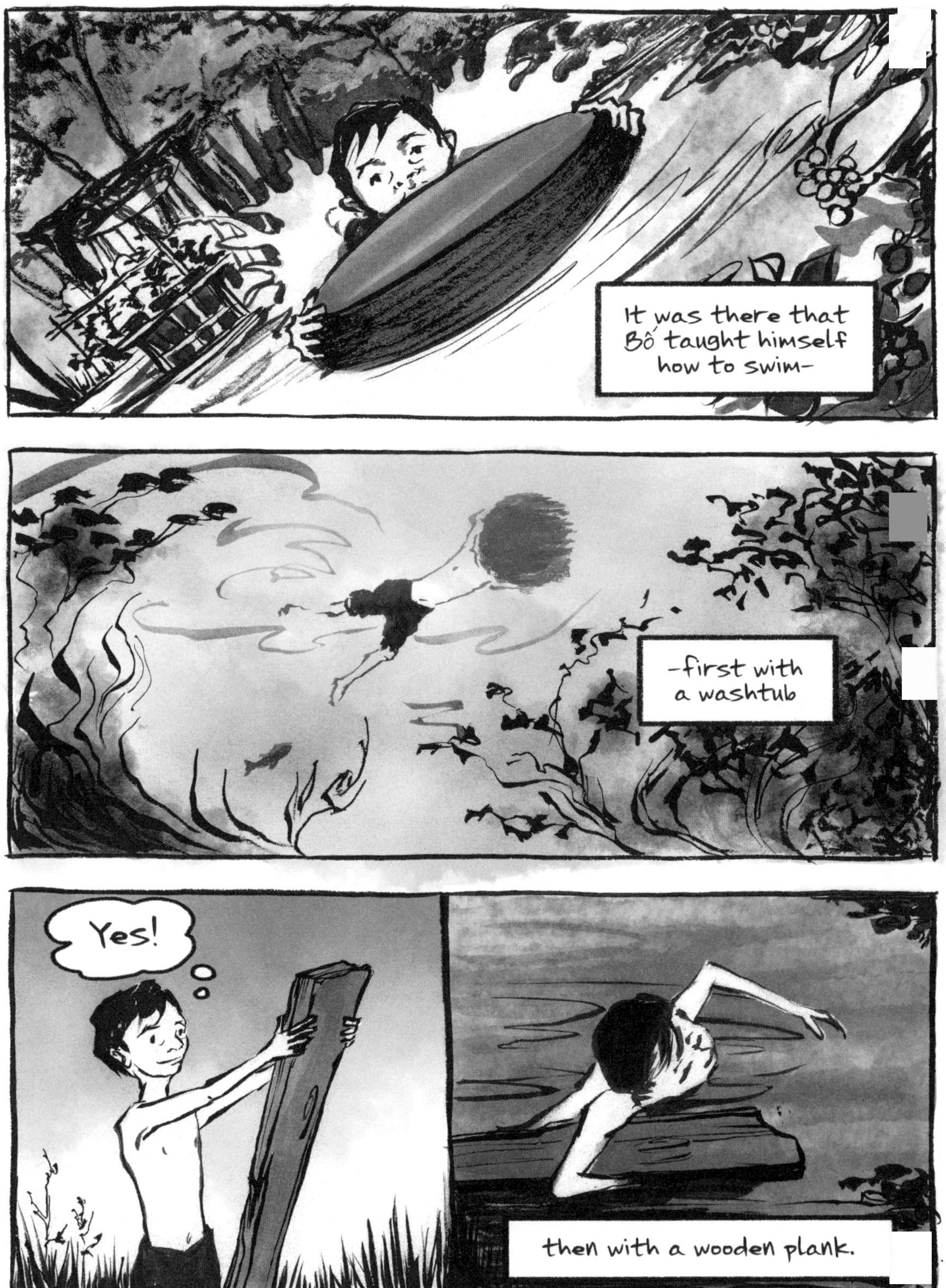
It was there that Bố taught himself how to swim-
-first with a washtub
Yes!
then with a wooden plank.

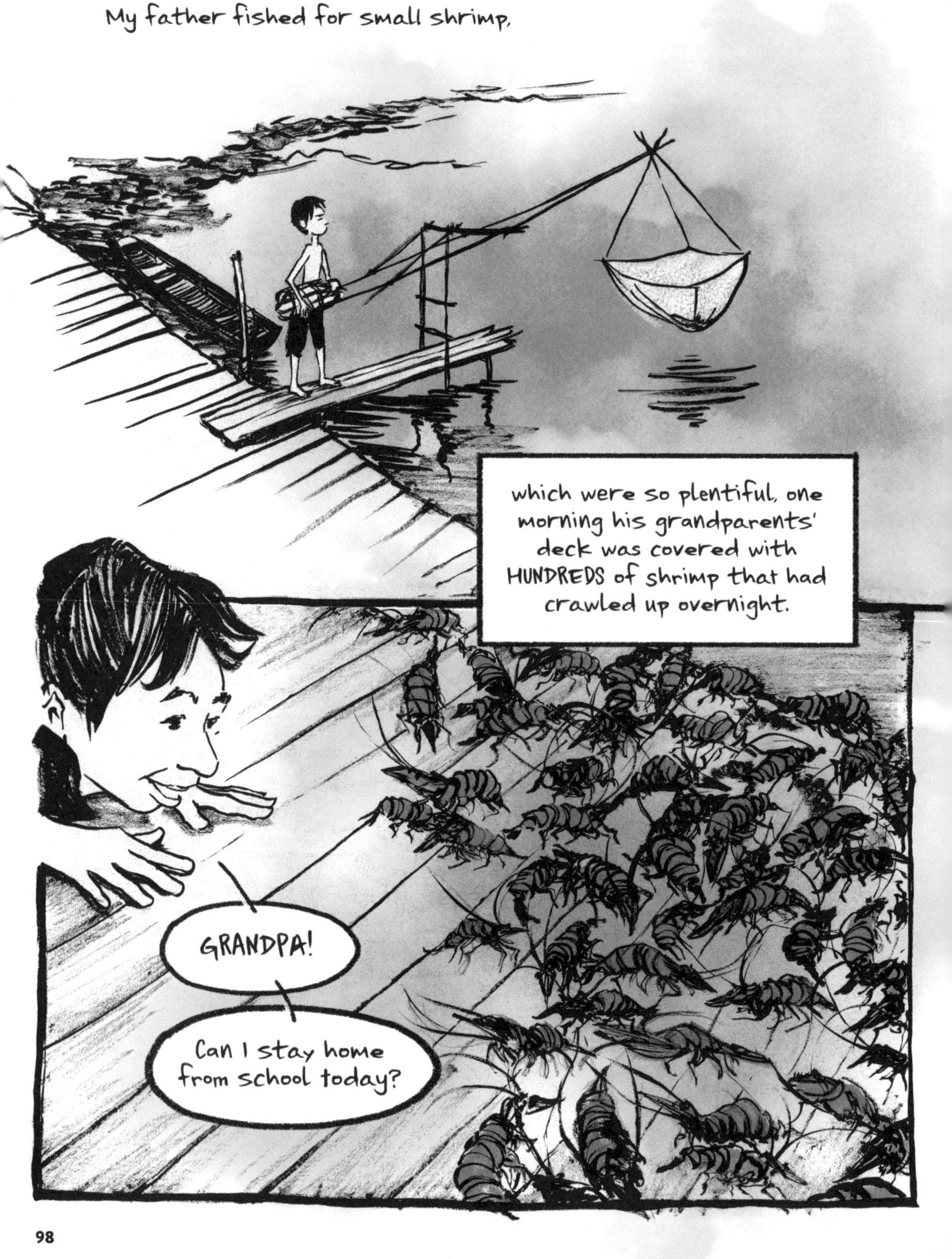
My father fished for small shrimp,
which were so plentiful, one morning his grandparents' deck was covered with HUNDREDS of shrimp that had crawled up overnight.
GRANDPA!
Can I stay home from school today?

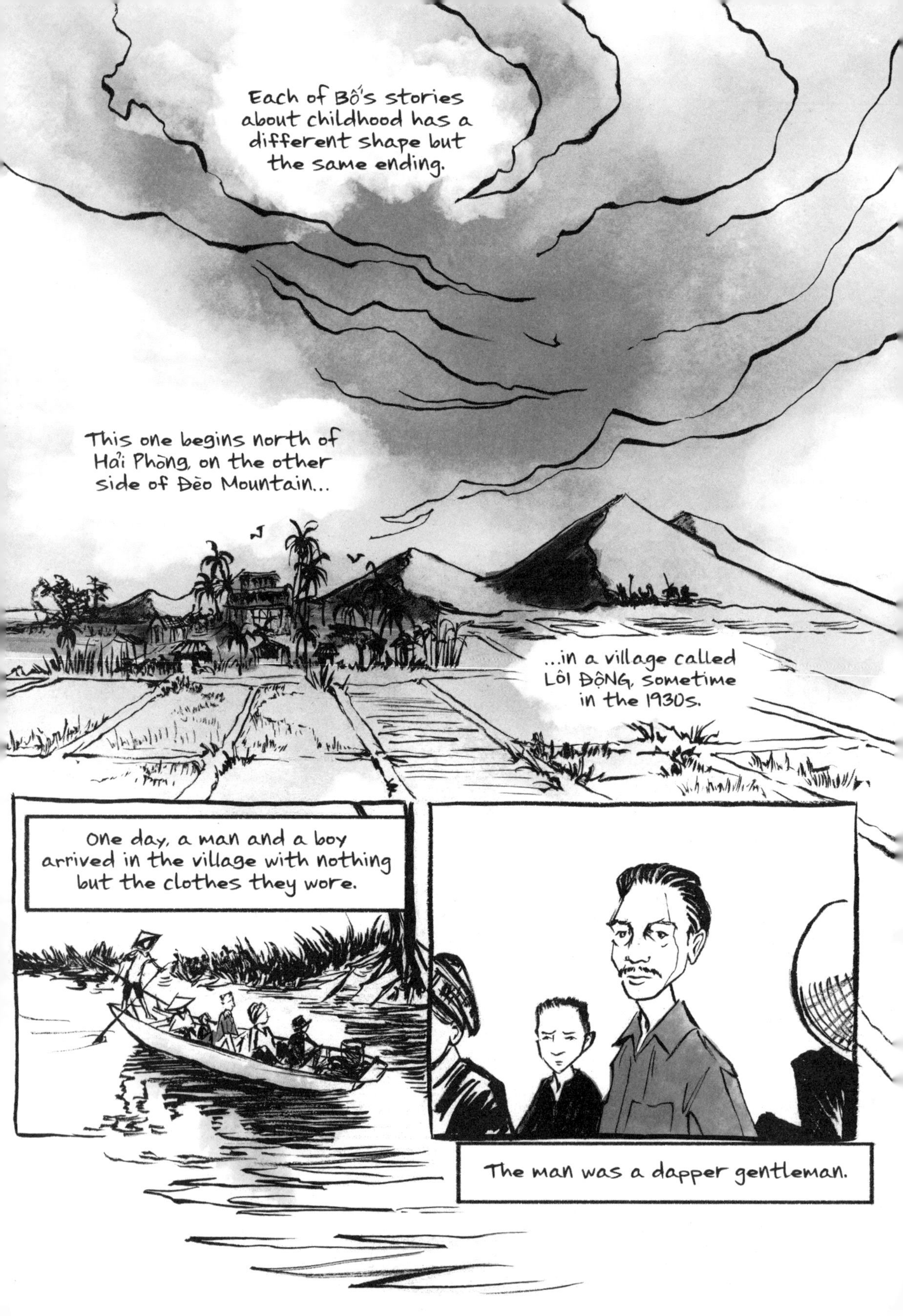

Each of Bố's stories about childhood has a different shape but the same ending.
This one begins north of Hải Phòng, on the other side of Đèo Mountain...
...in a village called LÔI ĐỘNG, sometime in the 1930s.
One day, a man and a boy arrived in the village with nothing but the clothes they wore.
The man was a dapper gentleman.

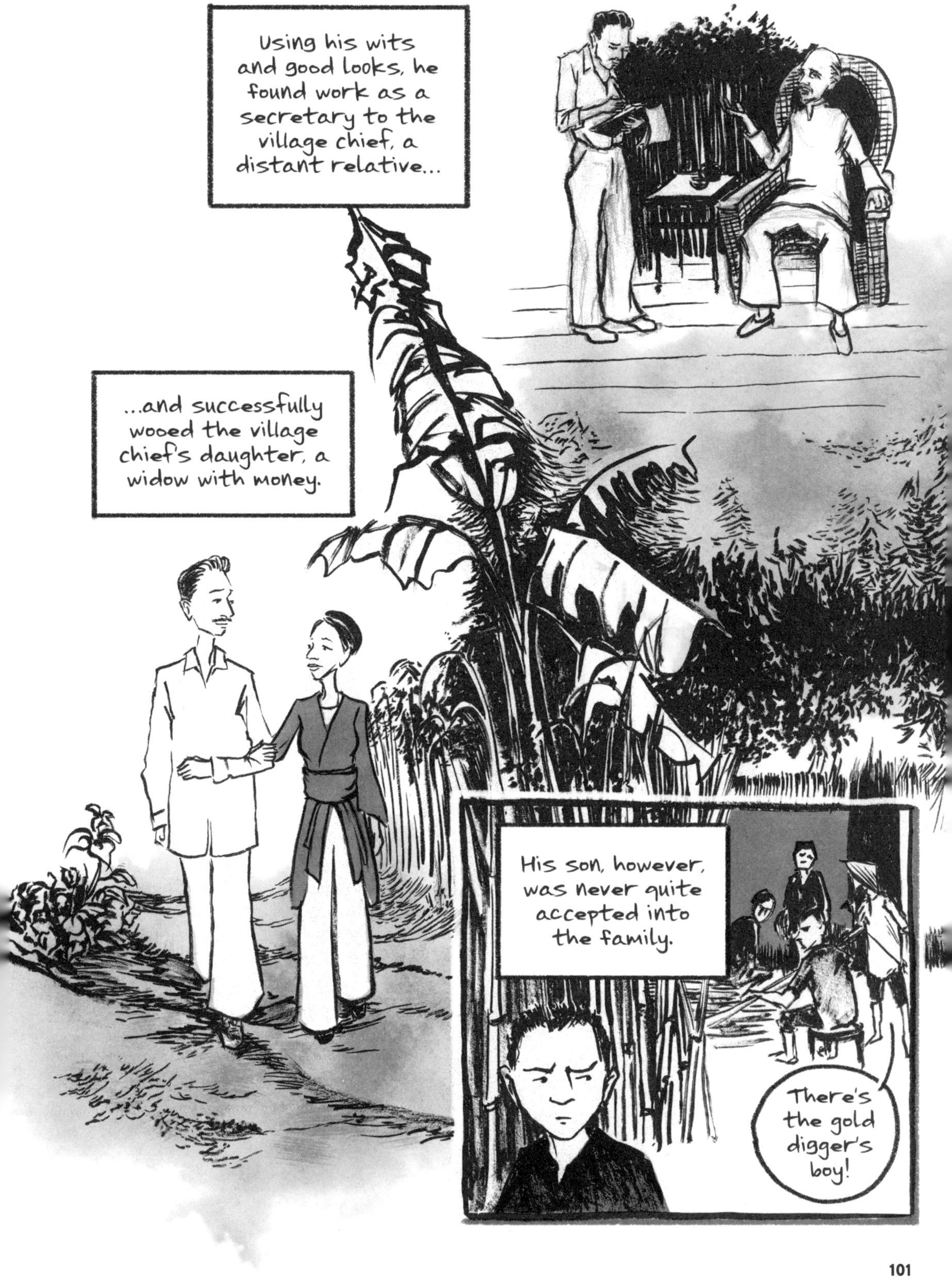
Using his wits and good looks, he found work as a secretary to the village chief, a distant relative...
...and successfully wooed the village chief's daughter, a widow with money.
His son, however, was never quite accepted into the family.
There's the gold digger's boy!

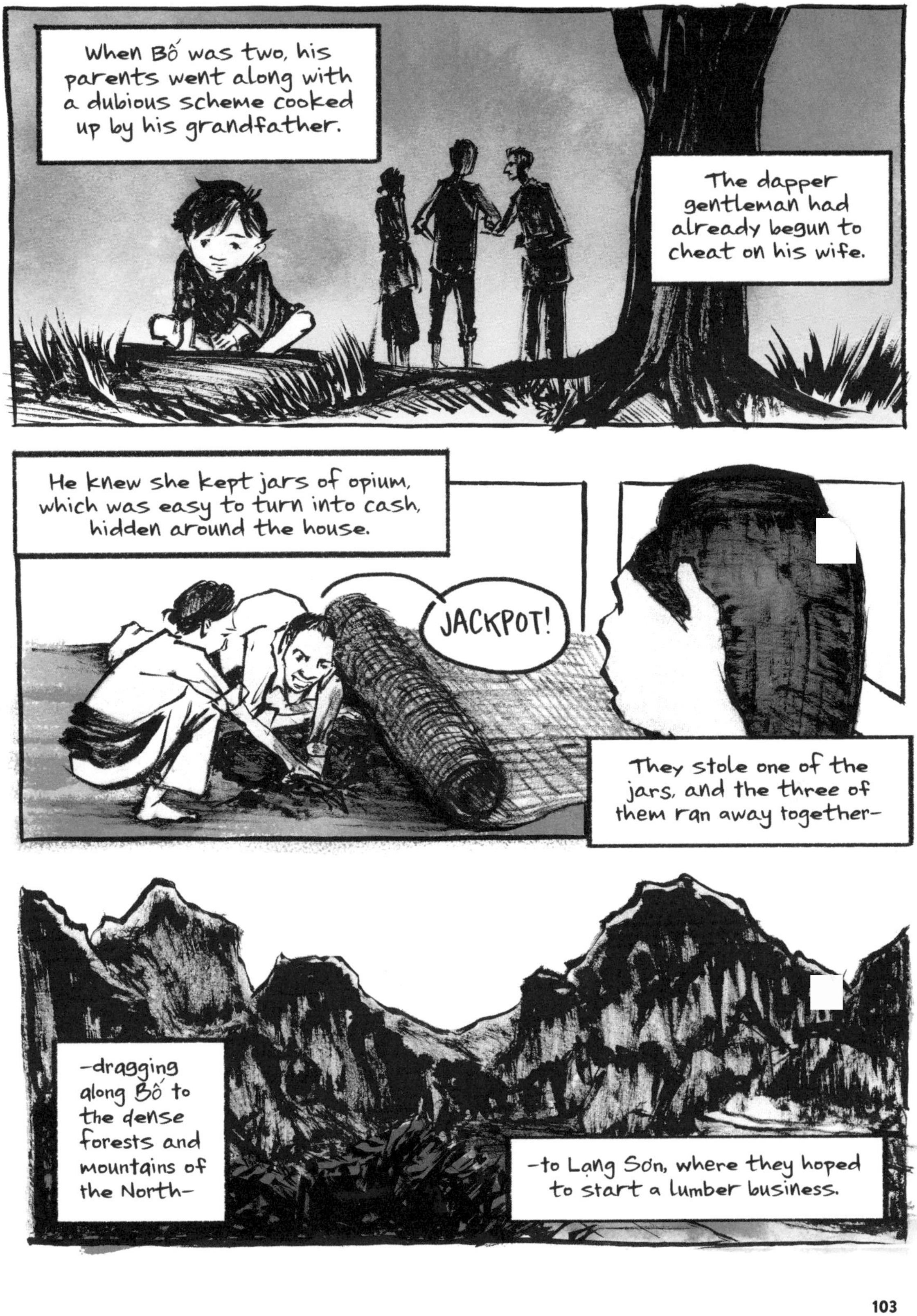
When Bố was two, his parents went along with a dubious scheme cooked up by his grandfather.
The dapper gentleman had already begun to cheat on his wife.
He knew she kept jars of opium, which was easy to turn into cash, hidden around the house.
JACKPOT!
They stole one of the jars, and the three of them ran away together–
–dragging along Bố to the dense forests and mountains of the North–
–to Lạng Sơn, where they hoped to start a lumber business.

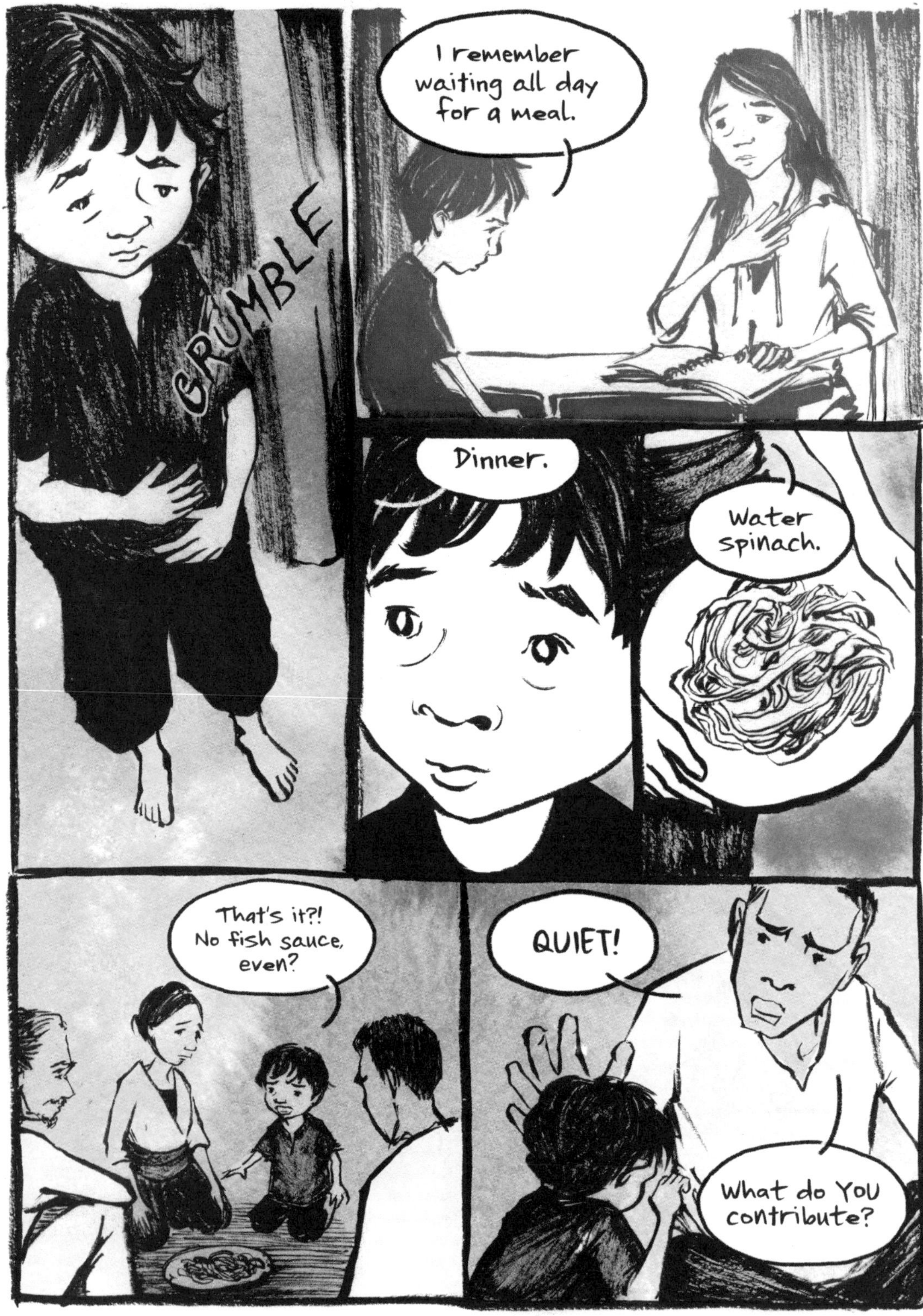
GRUMBLE
I remember waiting all day for a meal.
Dinner.
Water spinach.
That's it?! No fish sauce, even?
QUIET!
What do YOU contribute?

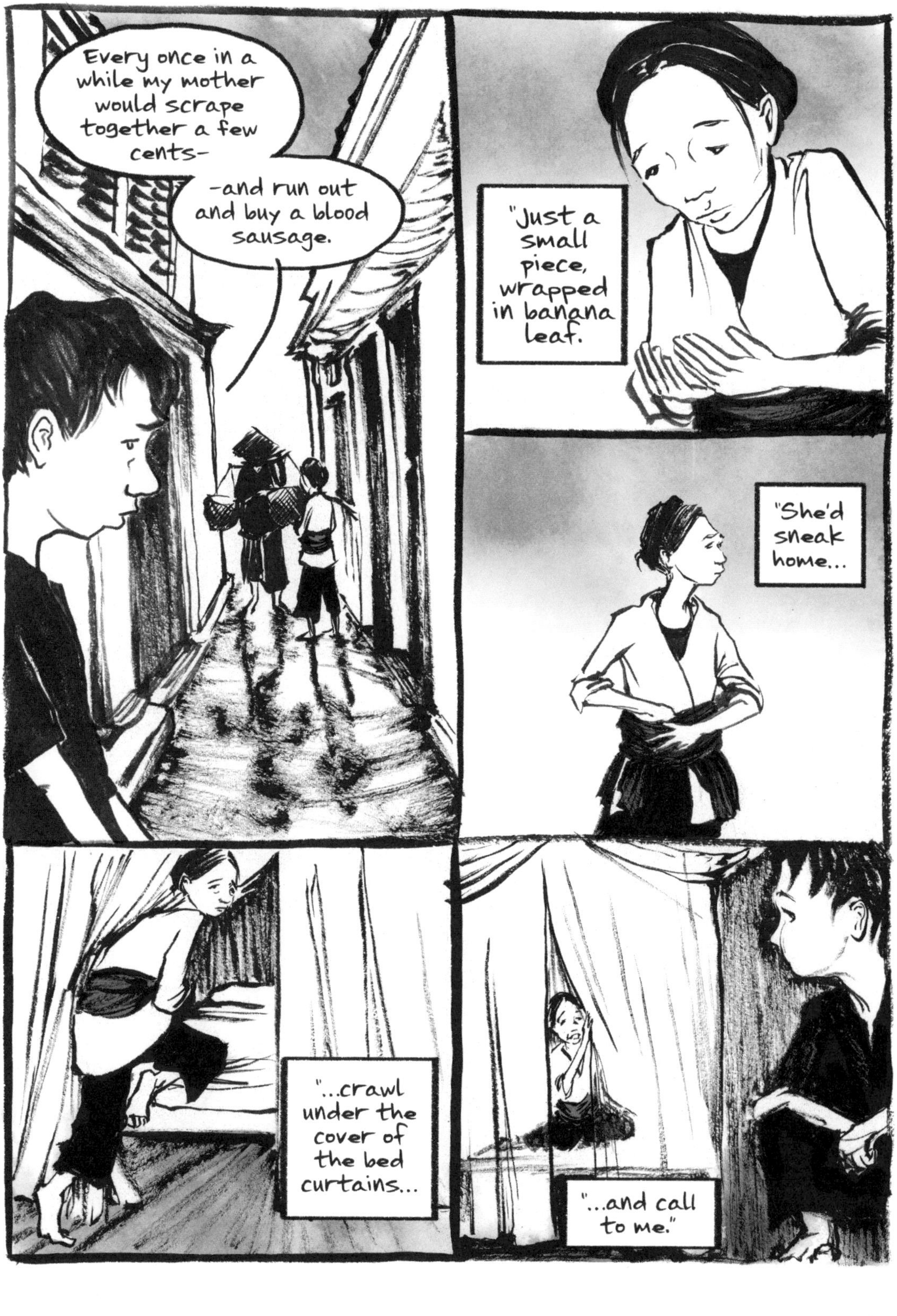
Every once in a while my mother would scrape together a few cents-
-and run out and buy a blood sausage.
"Just a small piece, wrapped in banana leaf.
"She'd sneak home...
"...crawl under the cover of the bed curtains...
"...and call to me."

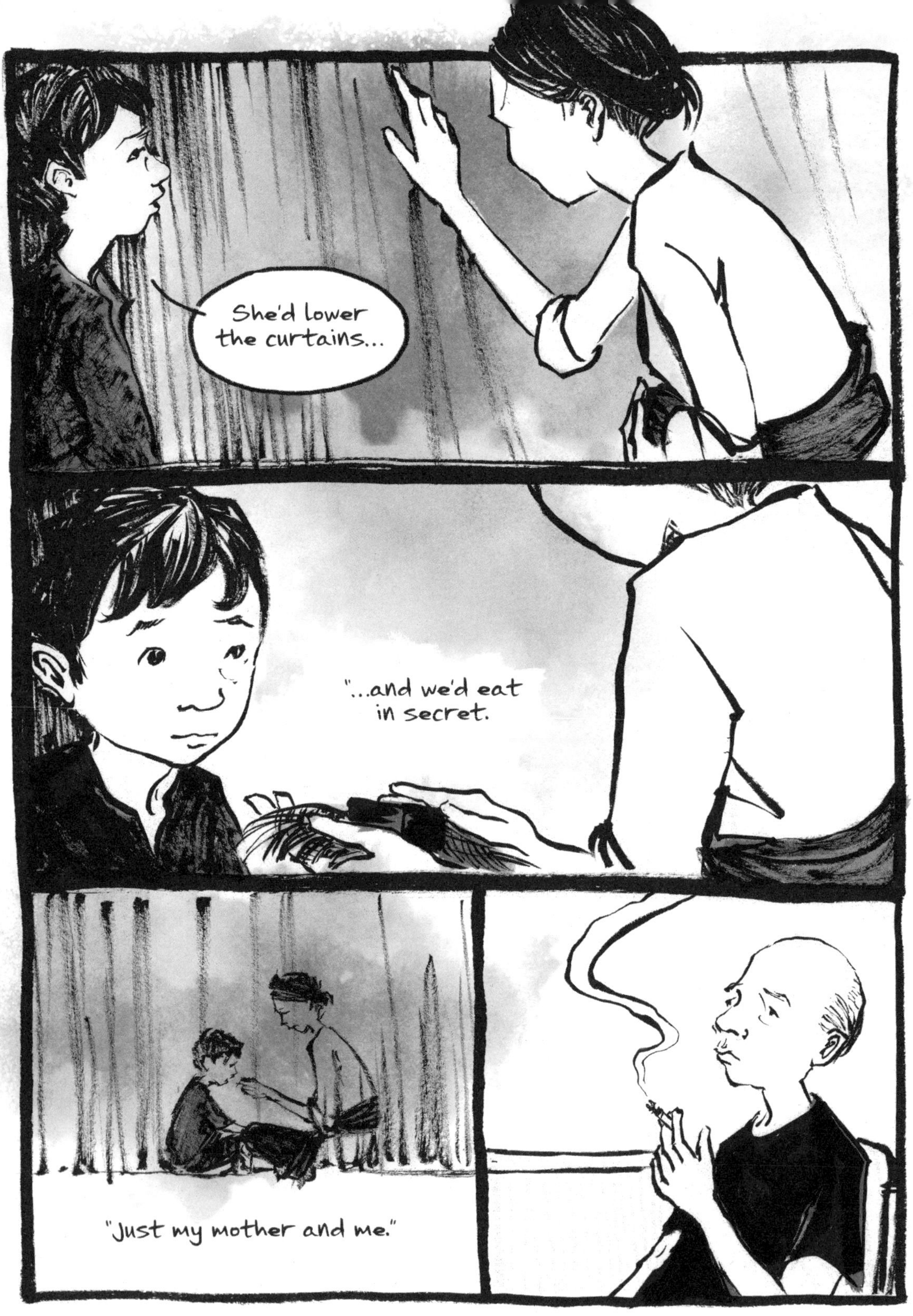
She'd lower the curtains...
"...and we'd eat in secret.
"Just my mother and me."

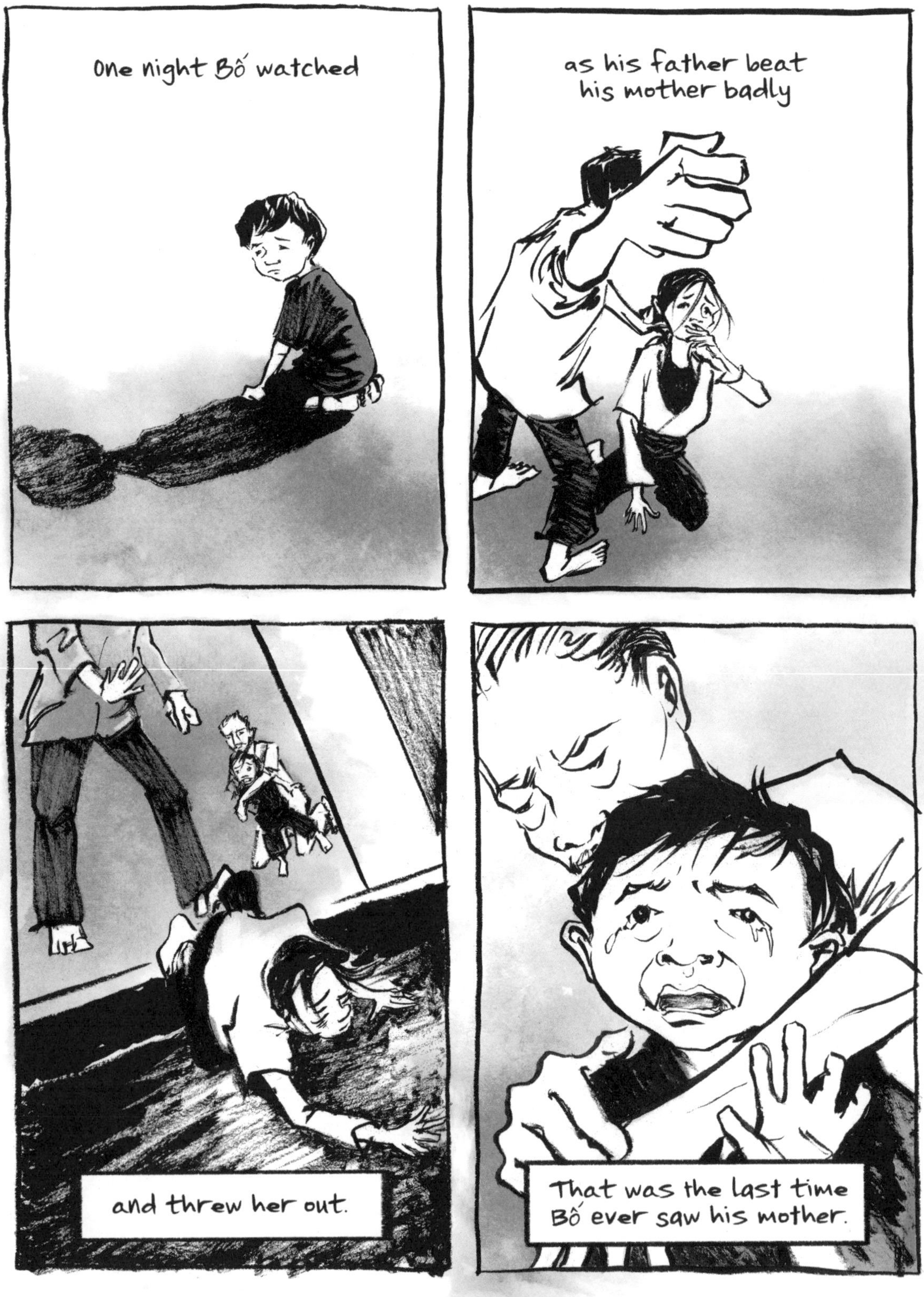
One night Bố watched
as his father beat
his mother badly
and threw her out.
That was the last time
Bố ever saw his mother.

The family disbanded. Bố's father and grandfather, each focused on his own survival, went separate ways.

Bố's father joined the Việt Minh, partly because his paramour, the pretty neighbor, was a recruiter for them, and partly because they would feed him.

Bố's grandfather went to Lôi Đông to make amends with his wife—

—hoping that a hungry, helpless grandchild would help her forgive his lying, cheating, and stealing.

For the sake of the boy?

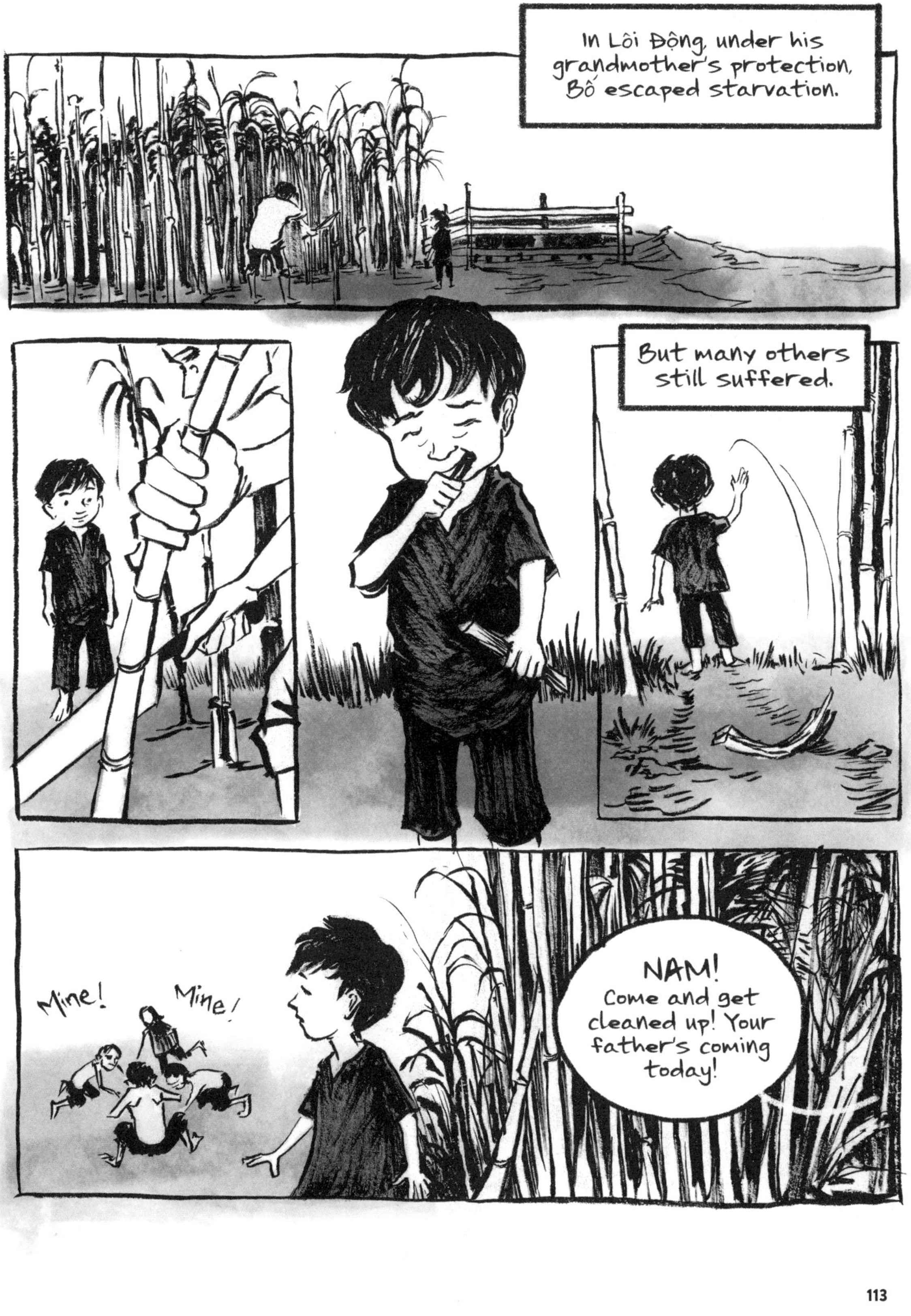
In Lôi Động, under his grandmother's protection, Bố escaped starvation.
But many others still suffered.
Mine!
Mine!
NAM!
Come and get cleaned up! Your father's coming today!

114

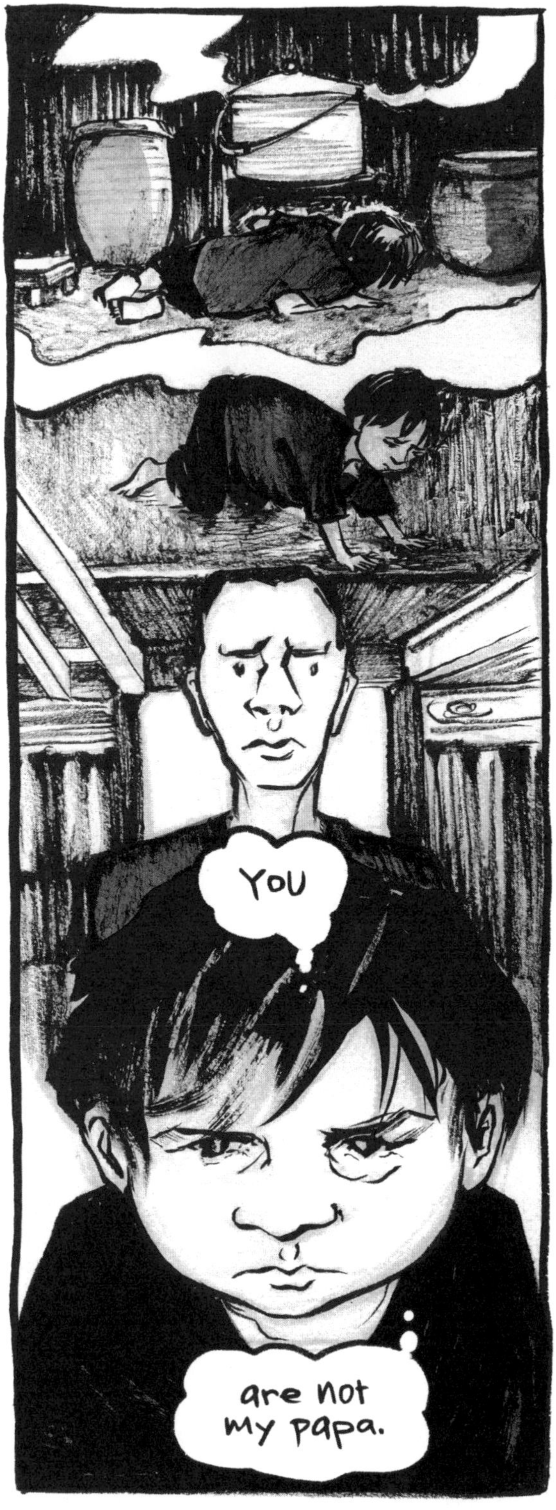
YOU
are not my papa.

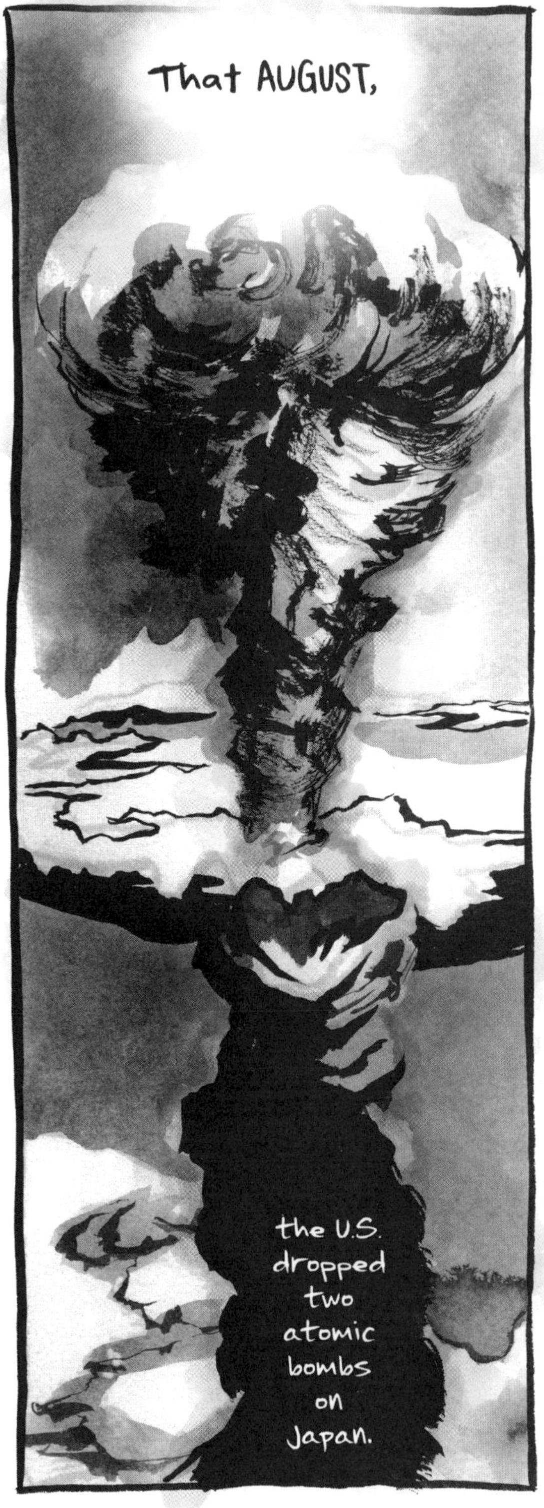
That AUGUST,
the U.S. dropped two atomic bombs on Japan.

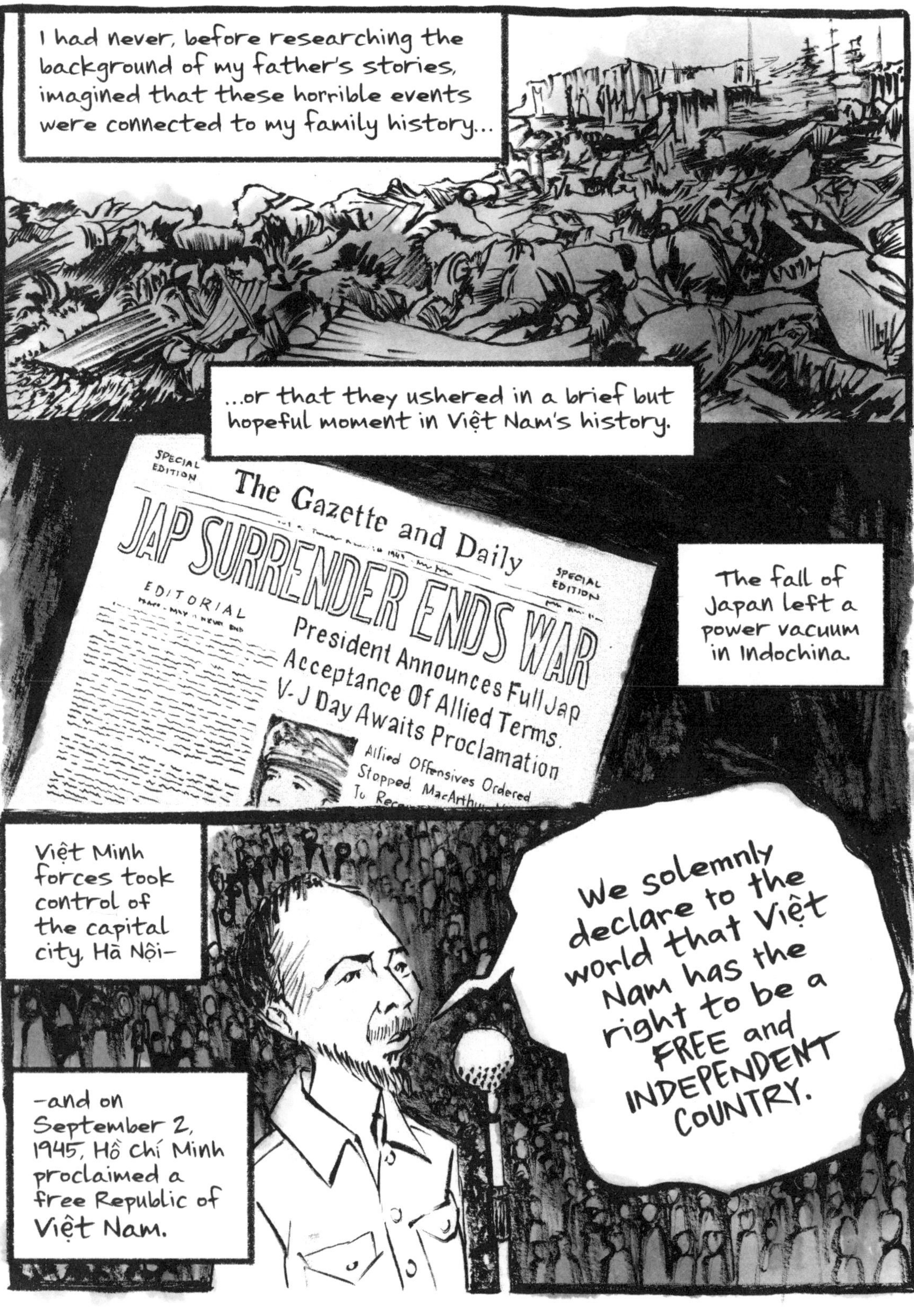
I had never, before researching the background of my father's stories, imagined that these horrible events were connected to my family history...
...or that they ushered in a brief but hopeful moment in Việt Nam's history.
SPECIAL EDITION
The Gazette and Daily
SPECIAL EDITION
JAP SURRENDER ENDS WAR
EDITORIAL
President Announces Full Jap Acceptance Of Allied Terms.
V-J Day Awaits Proclamation
Allied Offensives Ordered Stopped.
The fall of Japan left a power vacuum in Indochina.
Việt Minh forces took control of the capital city, Hà Nội–
–and on September 2, 1945, Hồ Chí Minh proclaimed a free Republic of Việt Nam.
We solemnly declare to the world that Việt Nam has the right to be a FREE and INDEPENDENT COUNTRY.

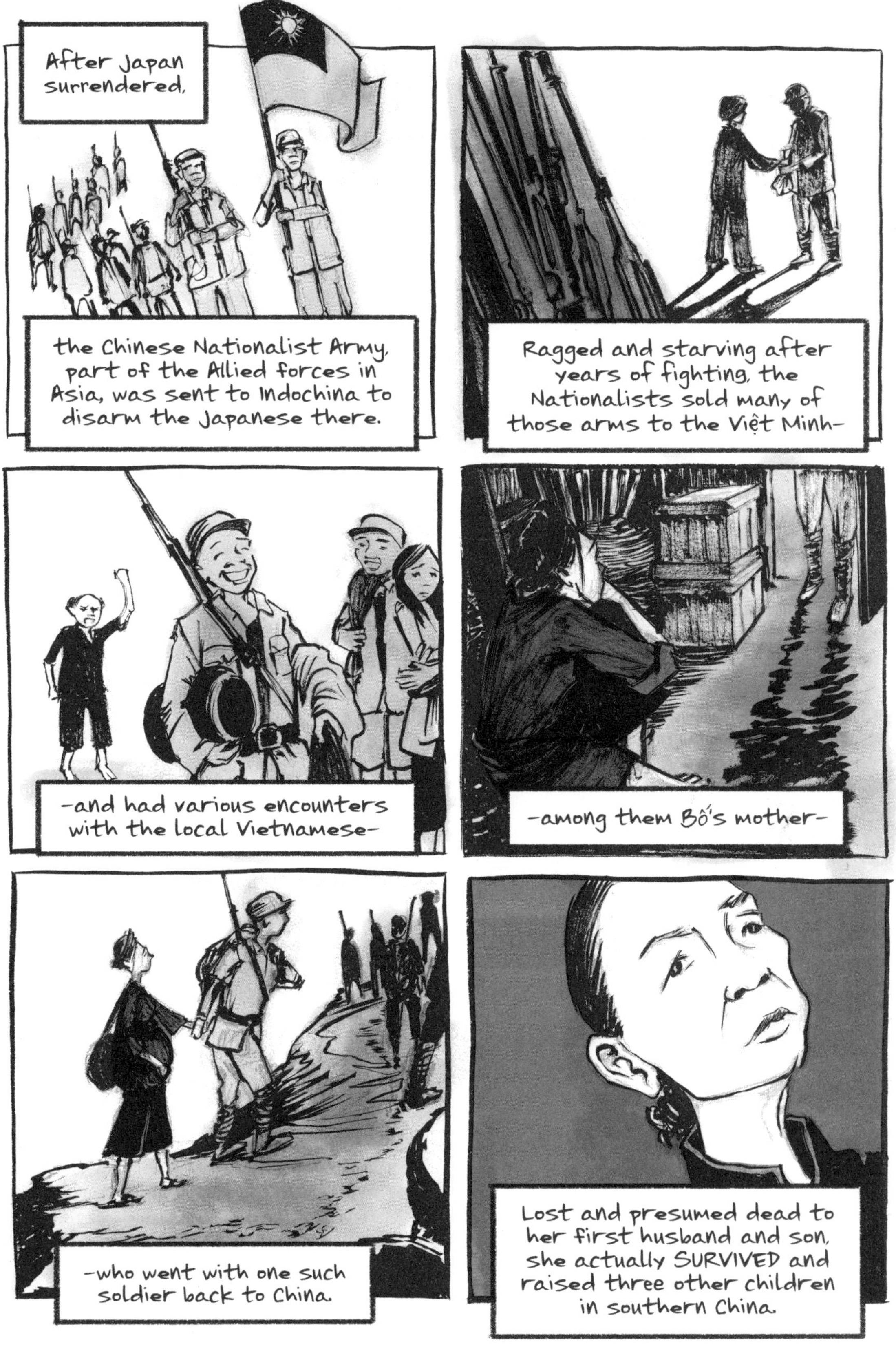

After Japan surrendered,
the Chinese Nationalist Army, part of the Allied forces in Asia, was sent to Indochina to disarm the Japanese there.
Ragged and starving after years of fighting, the Nationalists sold many of those arms to the Việt Minh-
-and had various encounters with the local Vietnamese-
-among them Bố's mother-
-who went with one such soldier back to China.
Lost and presumed dead to her first husband and son, she actually SURVIVED and raised three other children in southern China.

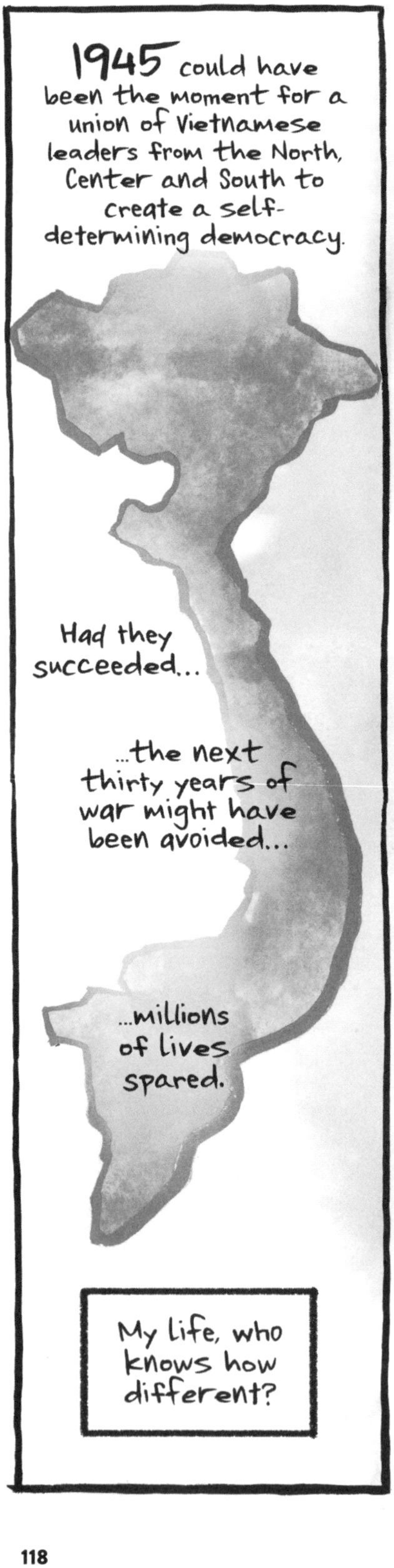
1945 could have been the moment for a union of Vietnamese leaders from the North, Center and South to create a self-determining democracy.
Had they succeeded...
...the next thirty years of war might have been avoided...
...millions of lives spared.
My life, who knows how different?

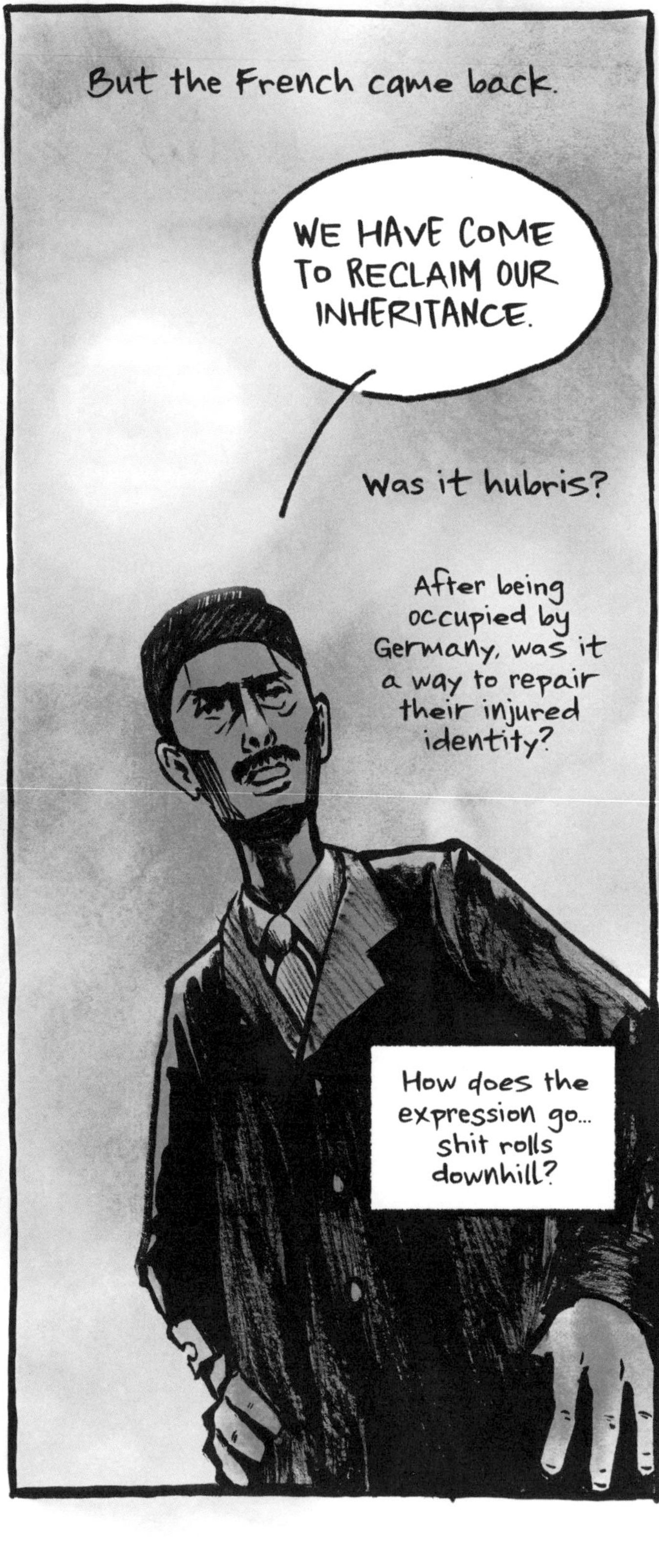
But the French came back.
WE HAVE COME TO RECLAIM OUR INHERITANCE.
Was it hubris?
After being occupied by Germany, was it a way to repair their injured identity?
How does the expression go... shit rolls downhill?

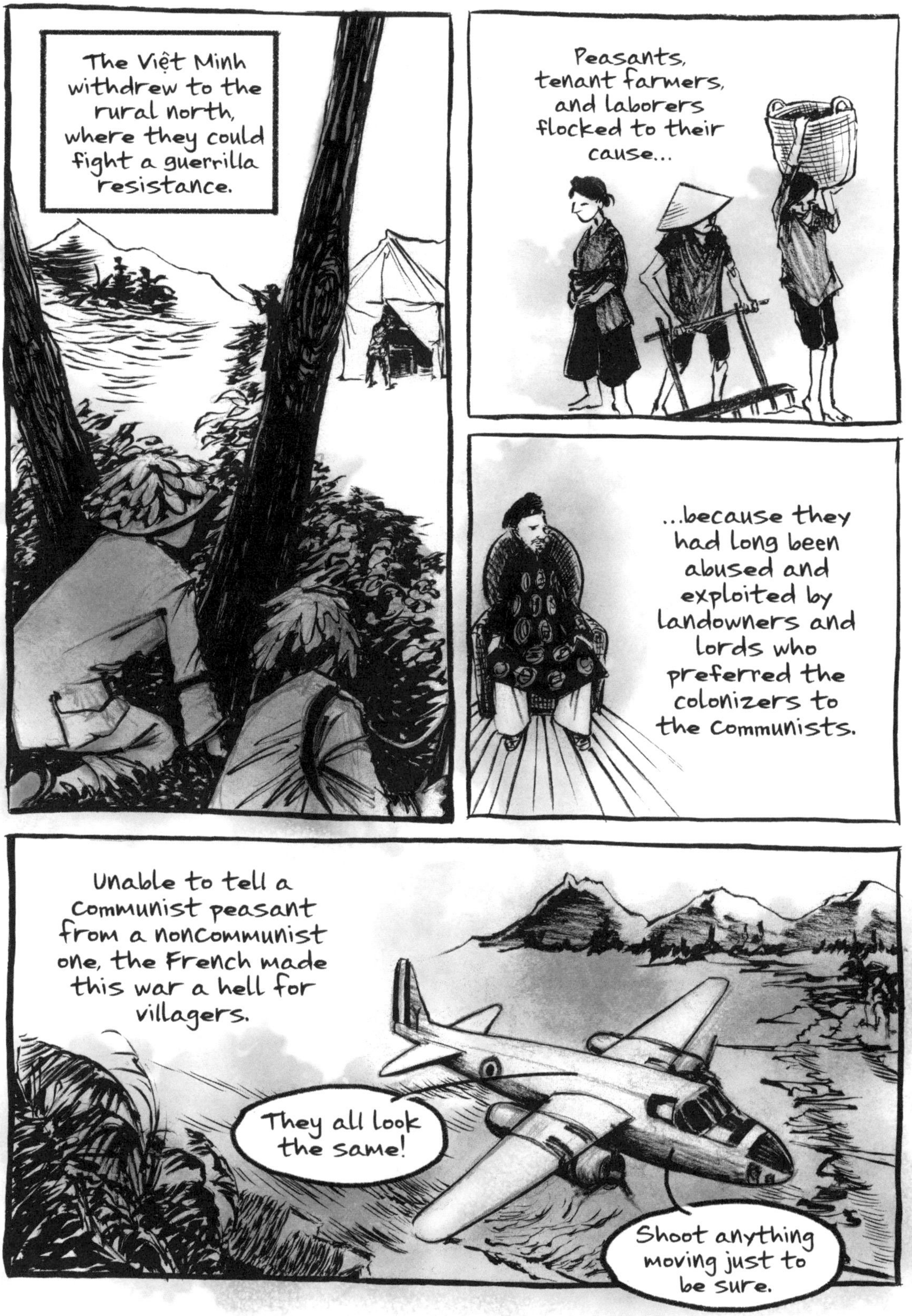
The Việt Minh withdrew to the rural north, where they could fight a guerrilla resistance.
Peasants, tenant farmers, and laborers flocked to their cause...
...because they had long been abused and exploited by landowners and lords who preferred the colonizers to the communists.
Unable to tell a communist peasant from a noncommunist one, the French made this war a hell for villagers.
They all look the same!
Shoot anything moving just to be sure.

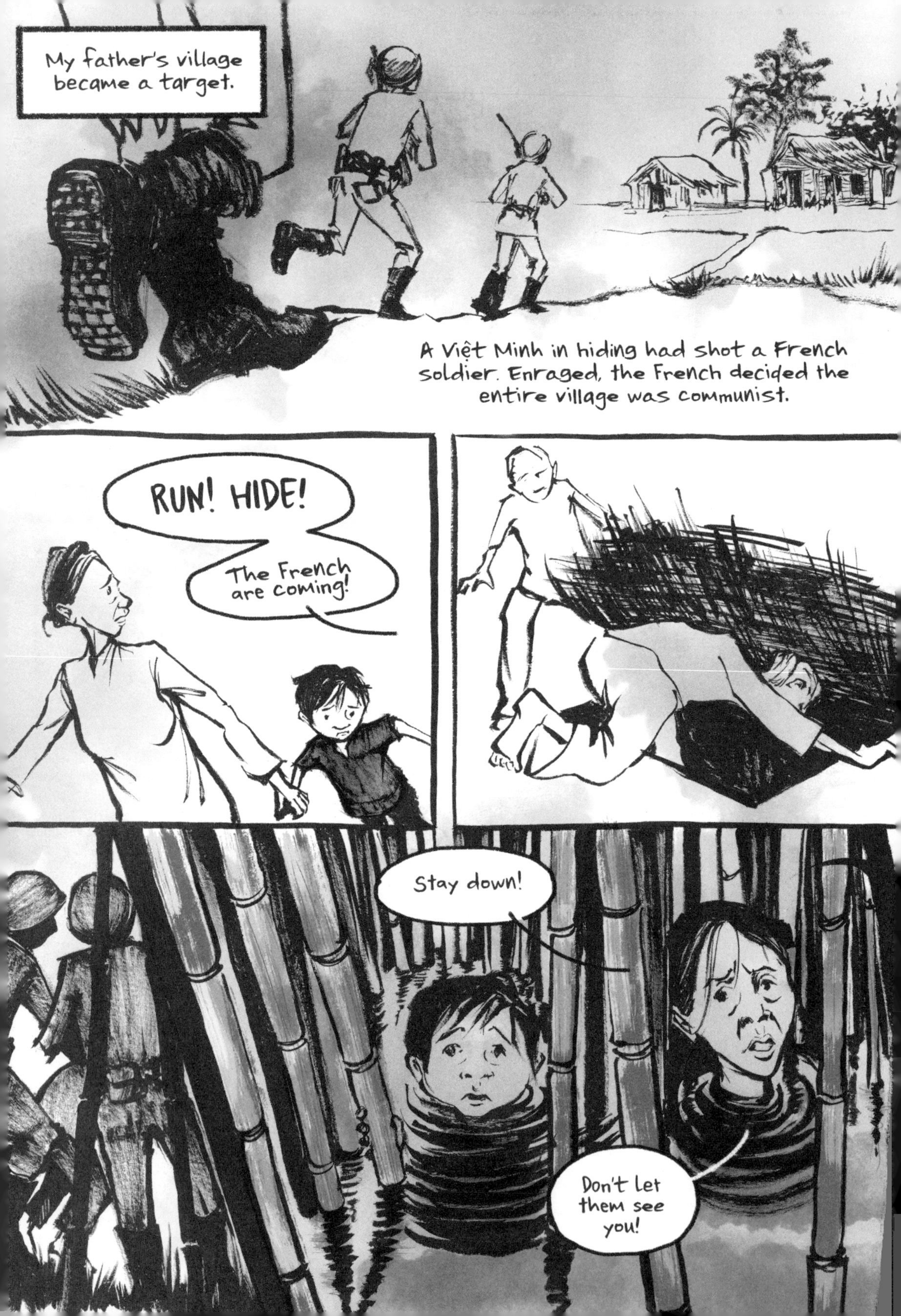
My father's village became a target.
A Việt Minh in hiding had shot a French soldier. Enraged, the French decided the entire village was communist.
RUN! HIDE!
The French are coming!
Stay down!
Don't let them see you!

121

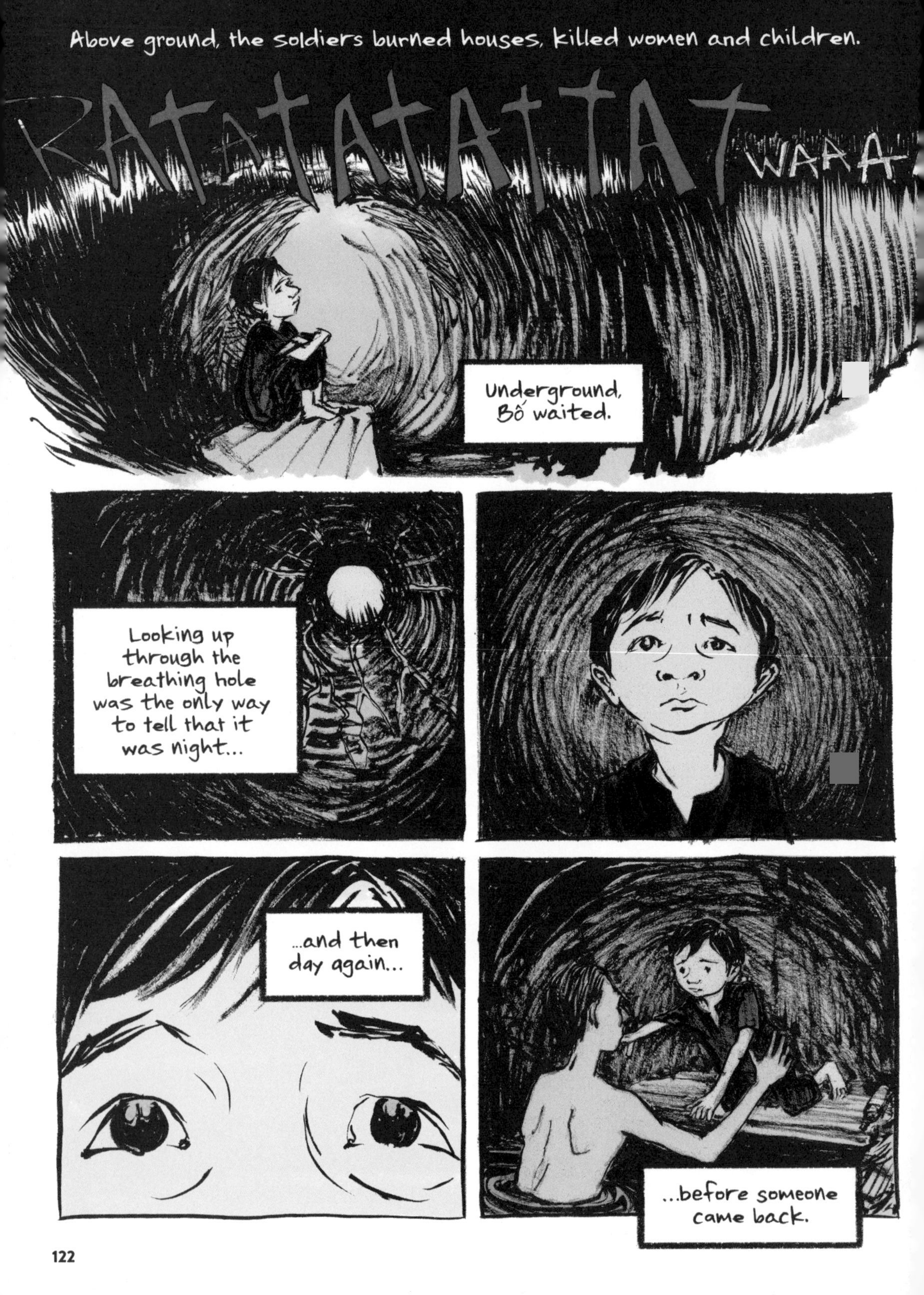
Above ground, the soldiers burned houses, killed women and children.
RATATATATTAT
WAAA
Underground, Bố waited.
Looking up through the breathing hole was the only way to tell that it was night...
...and then day again...
...before someone came back.

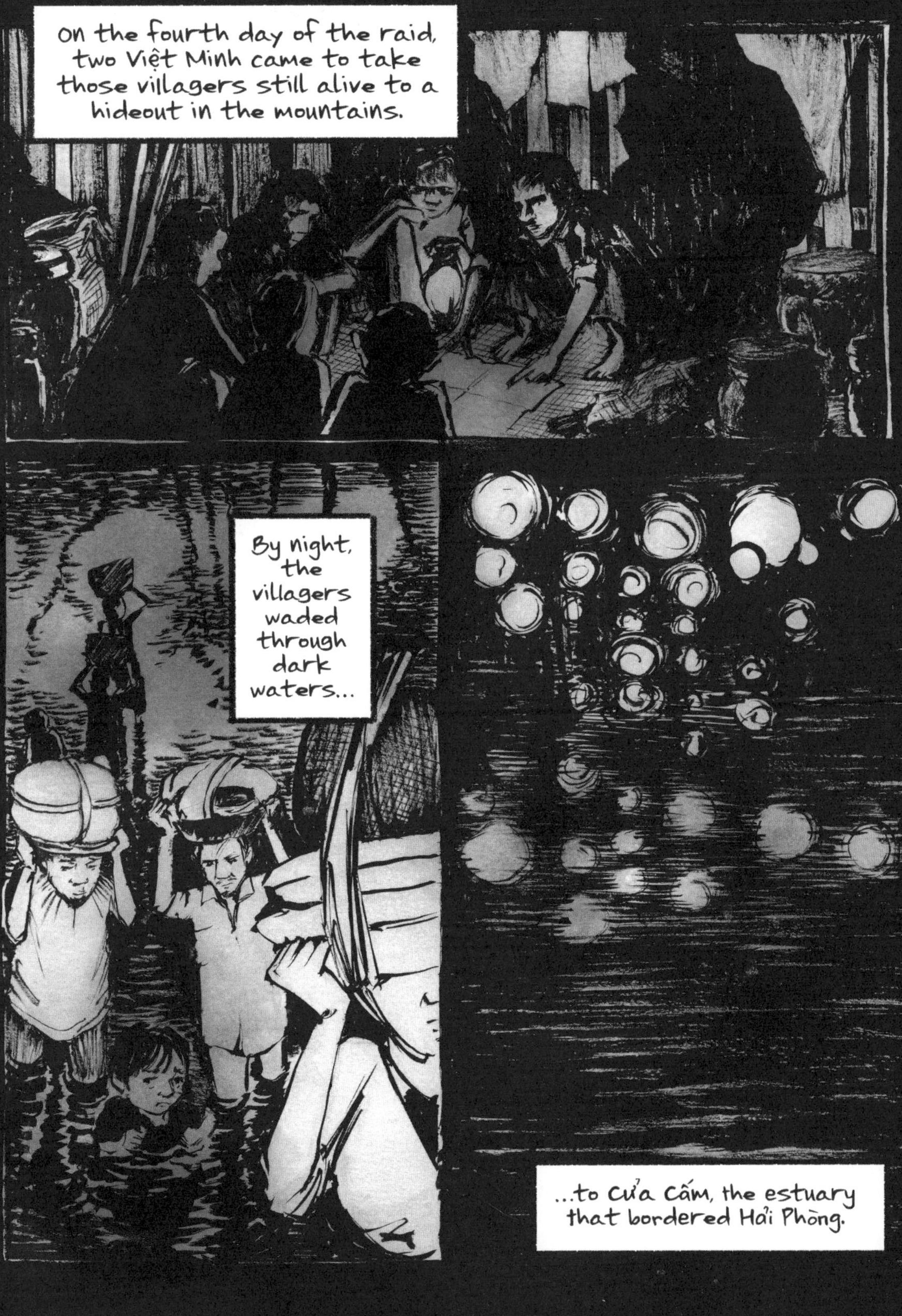
On the fourth day of the raid, two Việt Minh came to take those villagers still alive to a hideout in the mountains.
By night, the villagers waded through dark waters...
...to Cửa Cấm, the estuary that bordered Hải Phòng.

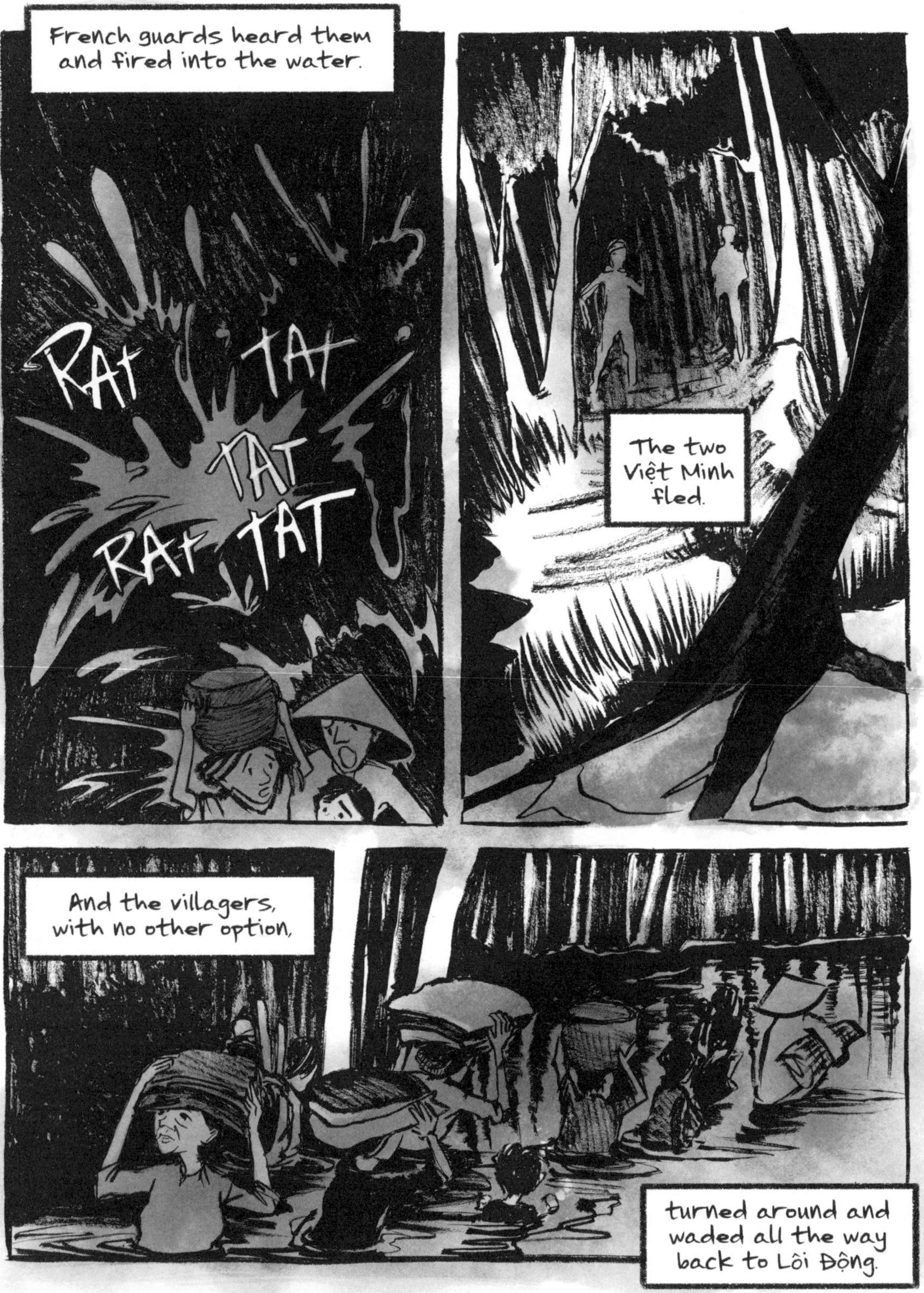
French guards heard them and fired into the water.
RAT TAT
TAT
RAT TAT
The two Việt Minh fled.
And the villagers, with no other option,
turned around and waded all the way back to Lôi Động.

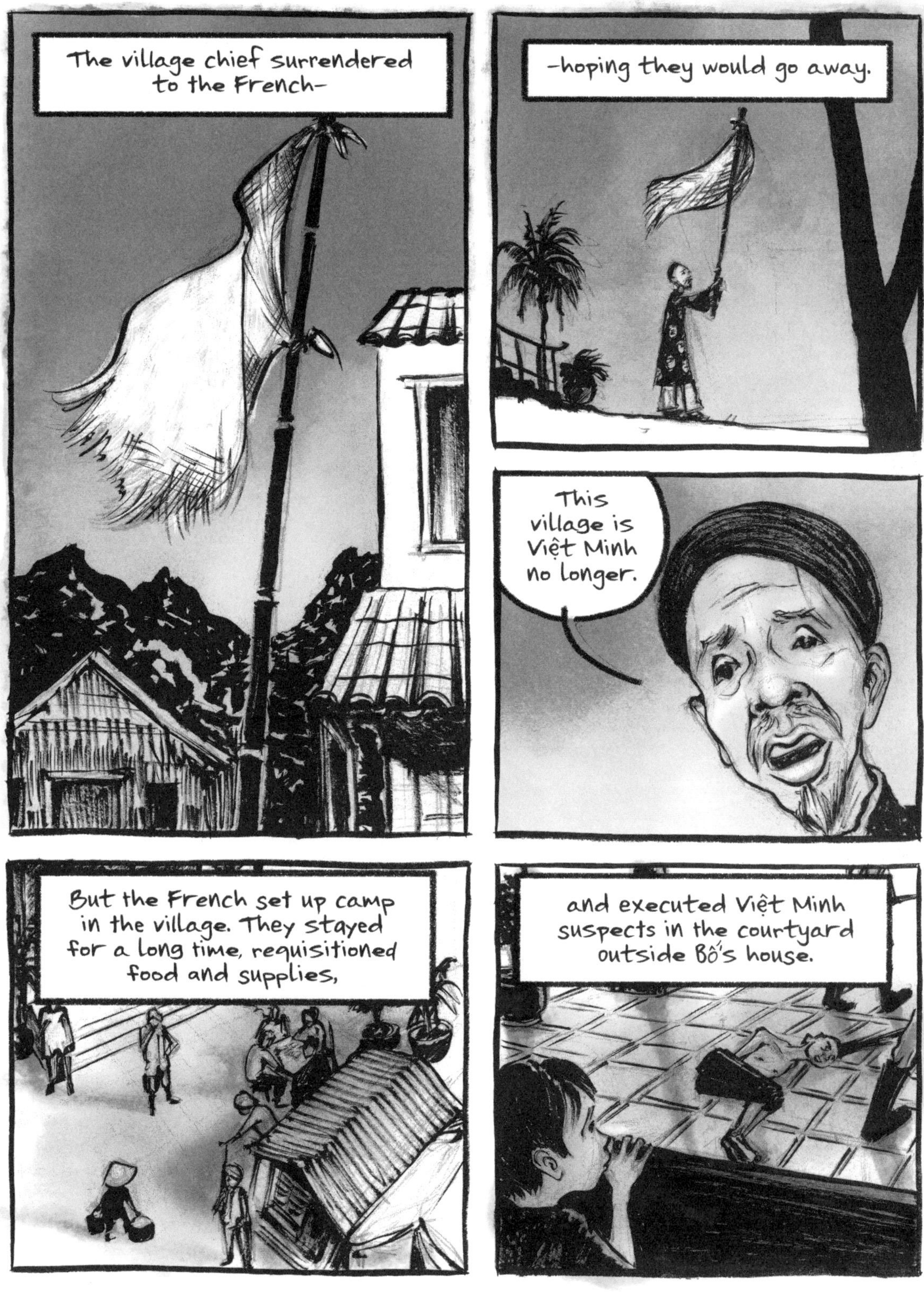
The village chief surrendered to the French-
-hoping they would go away.
This village is Việt Minh no longer.
But the French set up camp in the village. They stayed for a long time, requisitioned food and supplies,
and executed Việt Minh suspects in the courtyard outside Bố's house.

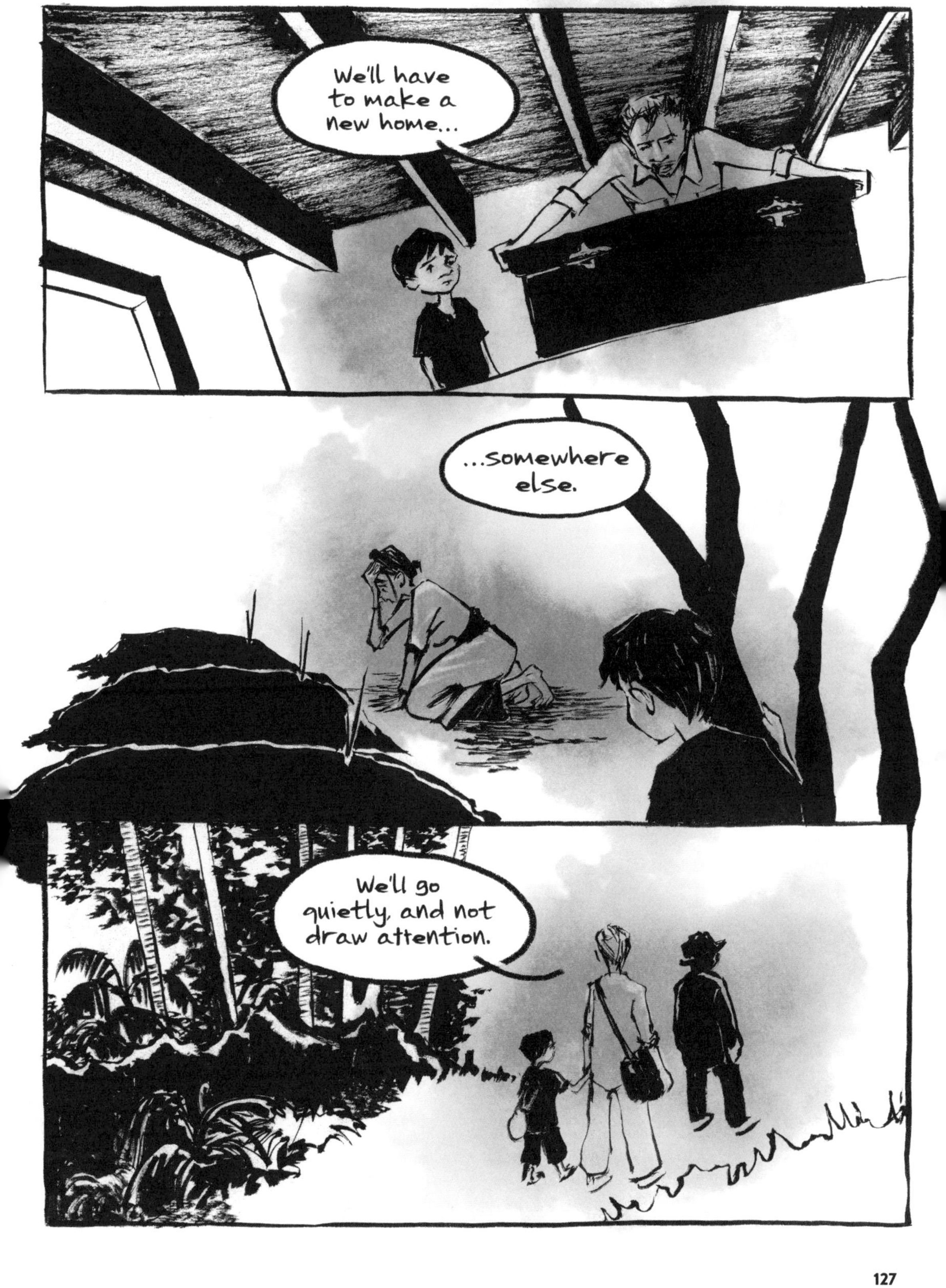
We'll have to make a new home...
...somewhere else.
We'll go quietly, and not draw attention.

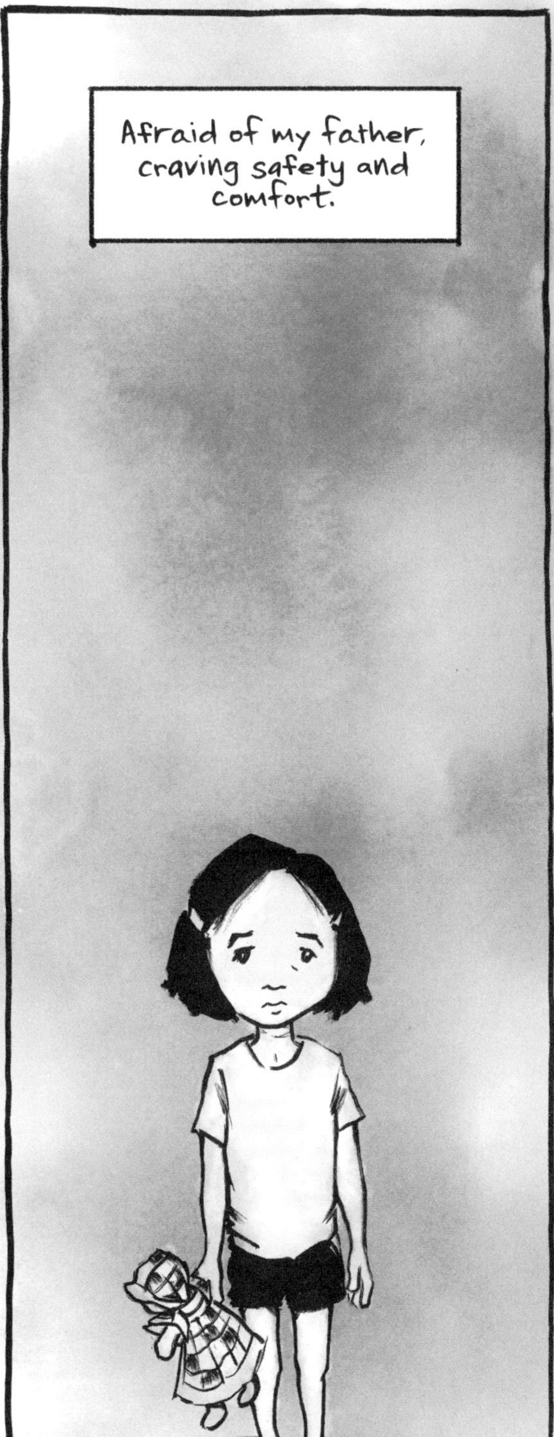
Afraid of my father, craving safety and comfort.

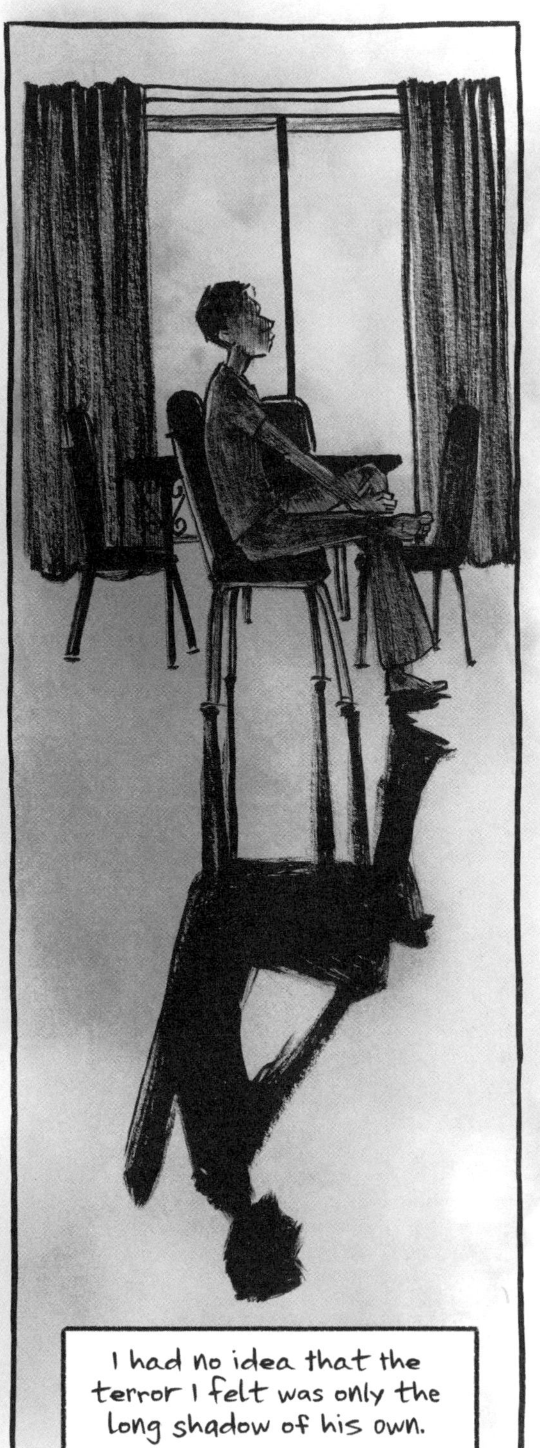
I had no idea that the terror I felt was only the long shadow of his own.

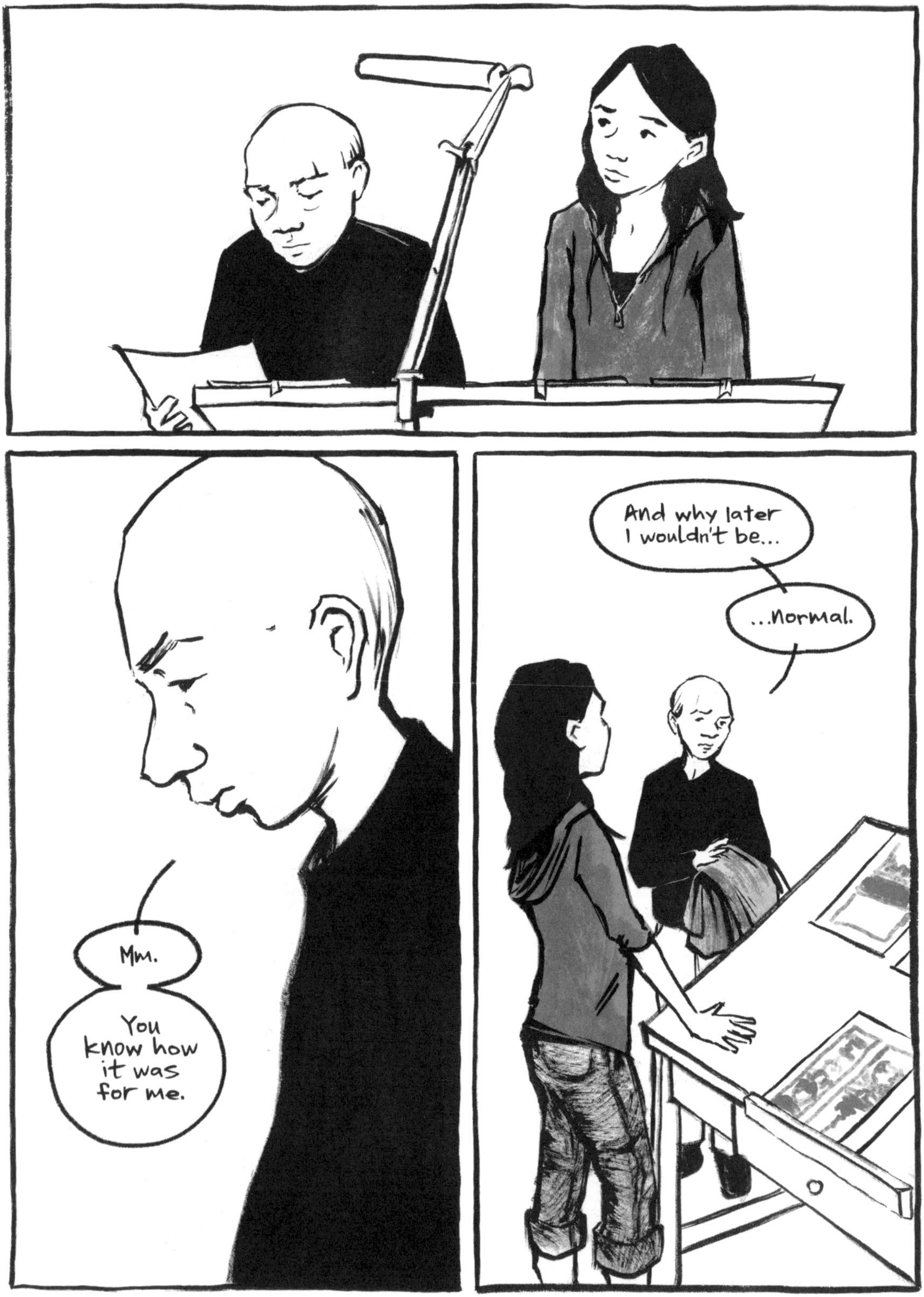
Mm.
You know how it was for me.
And why later I wouldn't be...
...normal.

CHAPTER 5

EITHER, OR

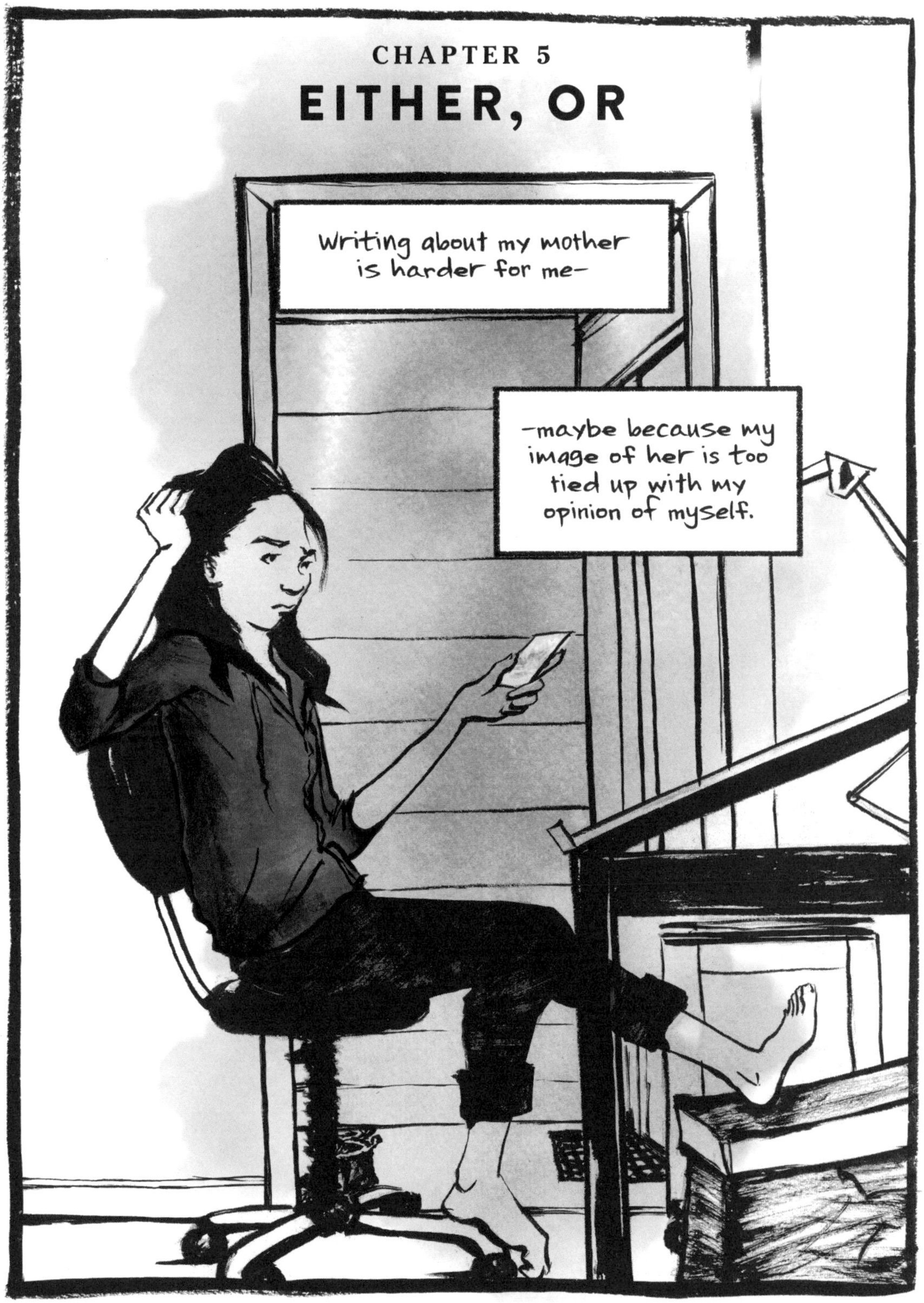
Writing about my mother is harder for me–
–maybe because my image of her is too tied up with my opinion of myself.

I never looked this good.

To be honest, Má didn't look that good by the time I was aware of things like good looks.

This is a portrait I drew of my mother when I was ten. I remember her mostly in work clothes, frowning and rushing to get dinner for six on the table.

When Má relaxed, which was less common, she looked like this to me.

She was soft and smelled like Oil of Olay.

She peeled all of our fruit for us, even the grapes.

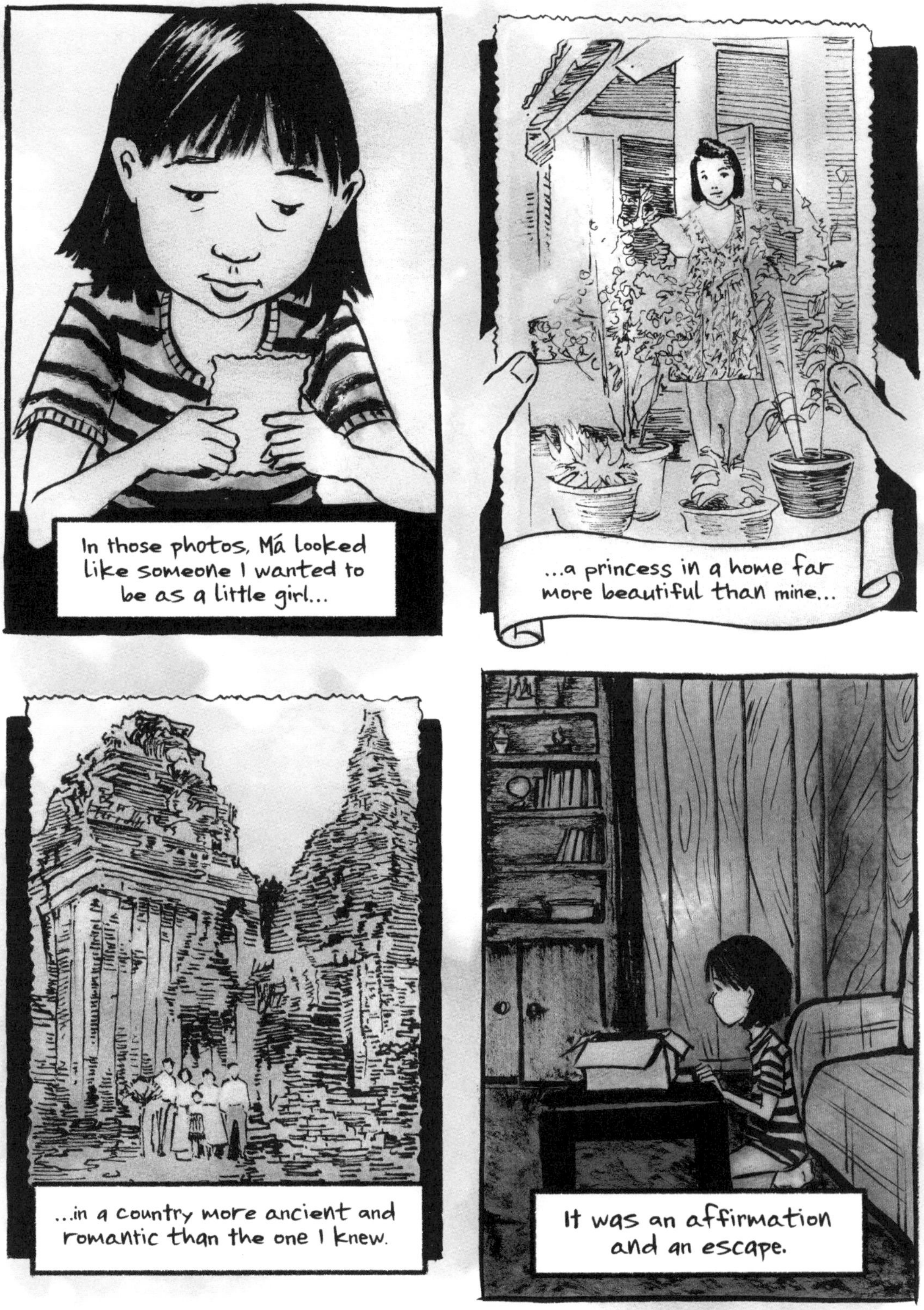
In those photos, Má looked like someone I wanted to be as a little girl...
...a princess in a home far more beautiful than mine...
...in a country more ancient and romantic than the one I knew.
It was an affirmation and an escape.

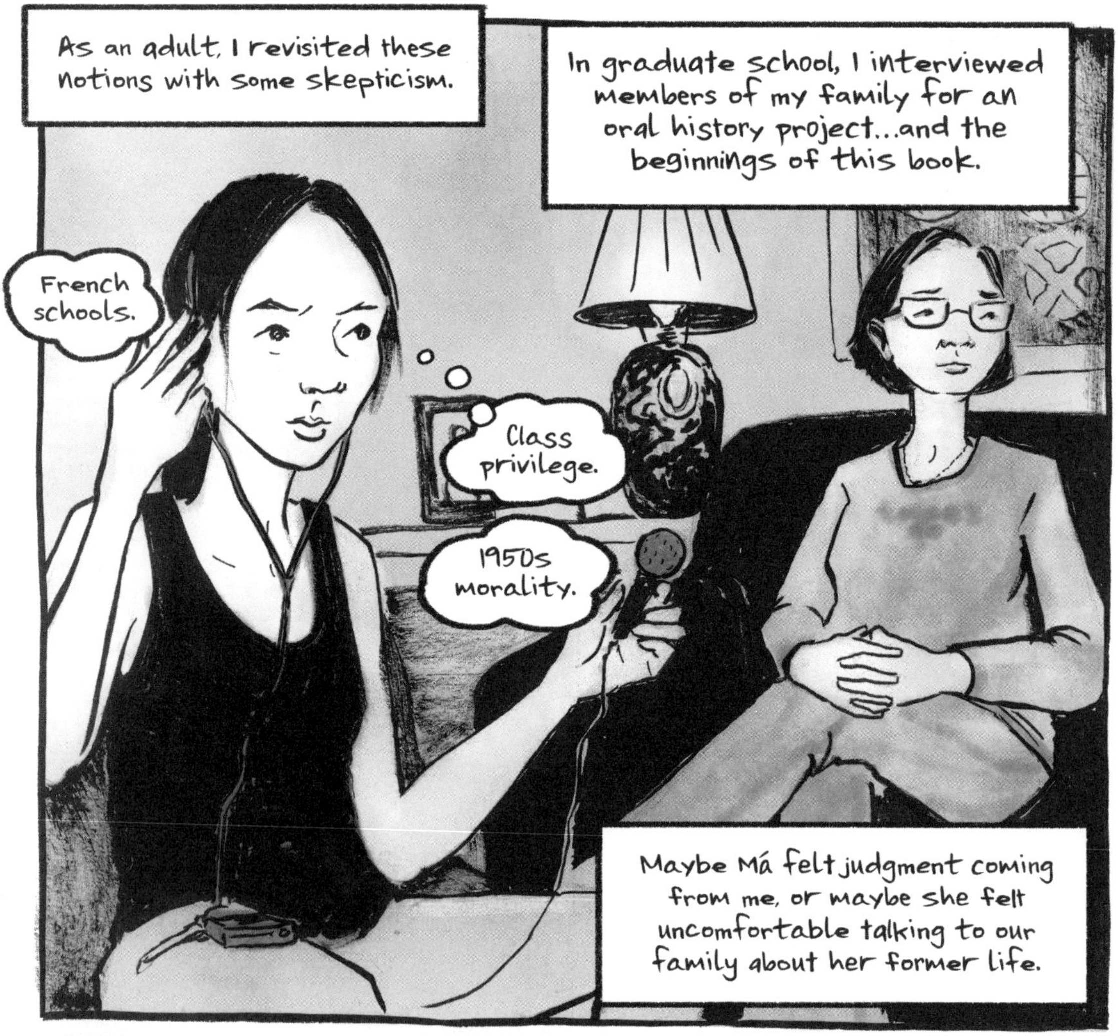
As an adult, I revisited these notions with some skepticism.
In graduate school, I interviewed members of my family for an oral history project...and the beginnings of this book.
French schools.
Class privilege.
1950s morality.
Maybe Má felt judgment coming from me, or maybe she felt uncomfortable talking to our family about her former life.

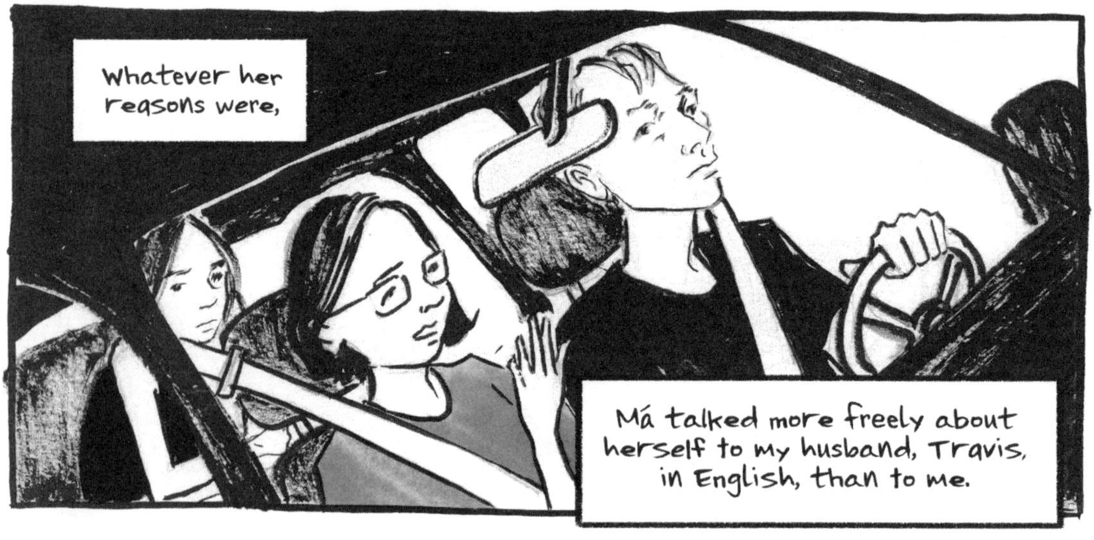
Whatever her reasons were,
Má talked more freely about herself to my husband, Travis, in English, than to me.

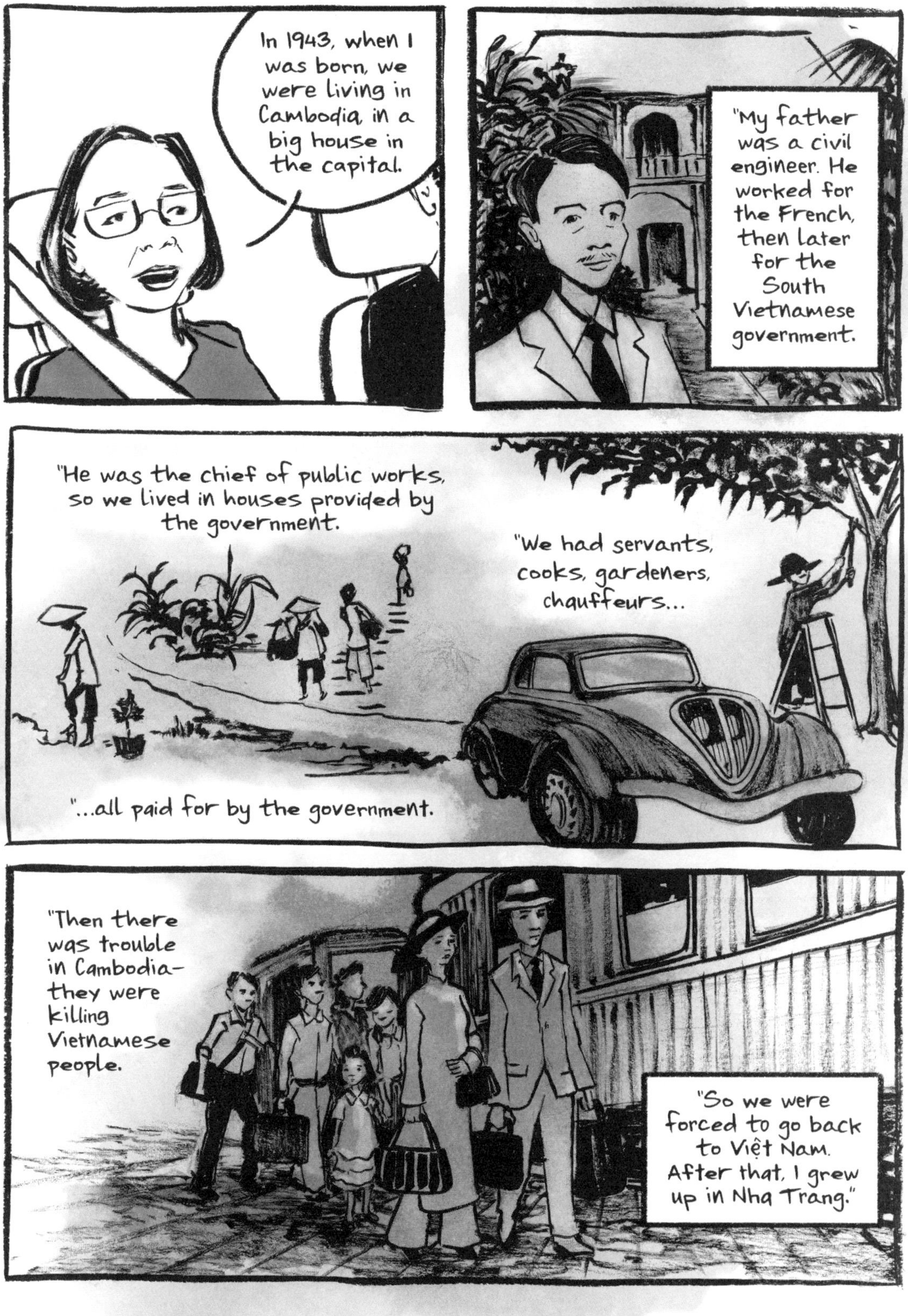
In 1943, when I was born, we were living in Cambodia, in a big house in the capital.
"My father was a civil engineer. He worked for the French, then later for the South Vietnamese government.
"He was the chief of public works, so we lived in houses provided by the government.
"We had servants, cooks, gardeners, chauffeurs...
"...all paid for by the government.
"Then there was trouble in Cambodia–they were killing Vietnamese people.
"So we were forced to go back to Việt Nam. After that, I grew up in Nha Trang."

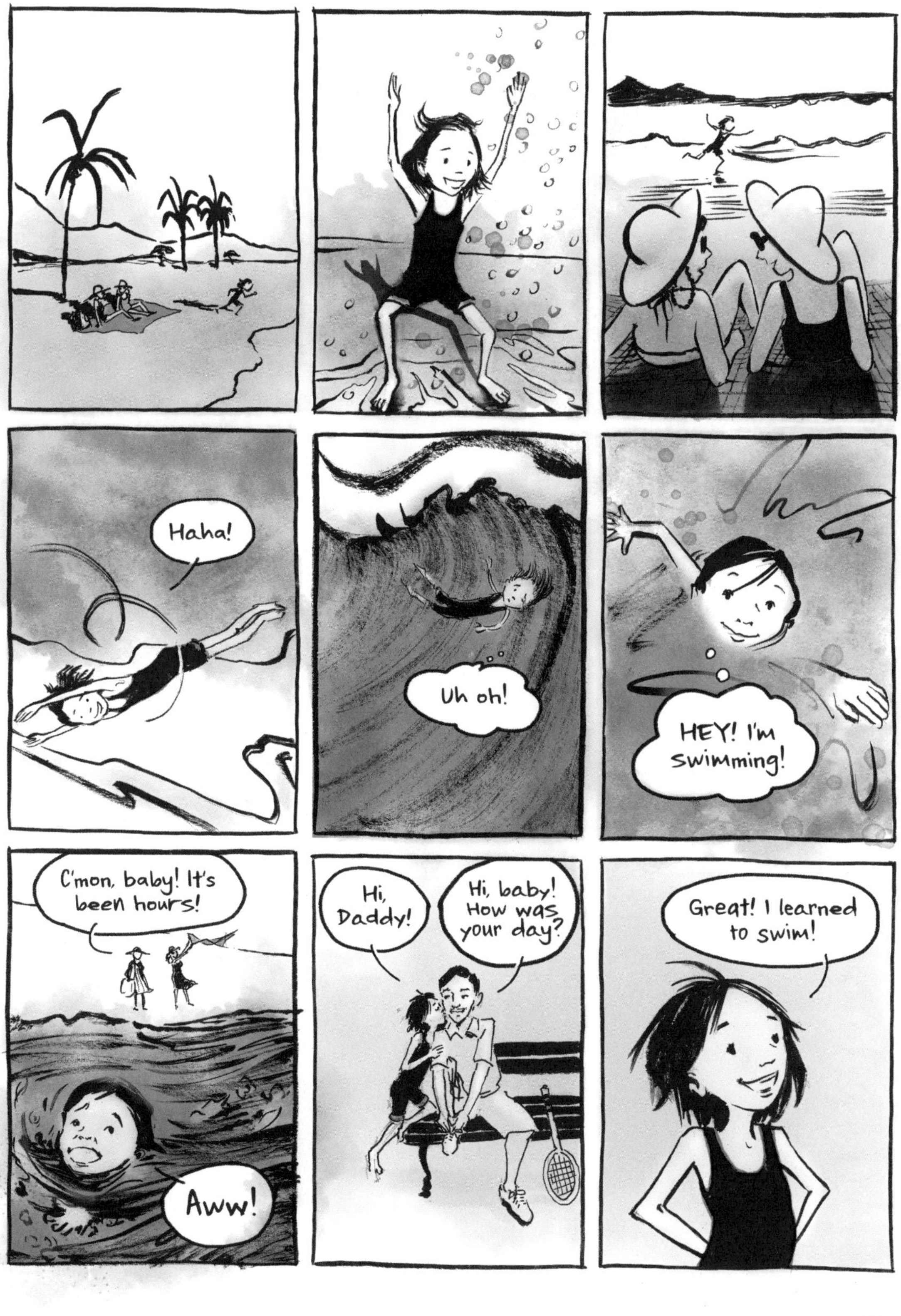
Haha!
Uh oh!
HEY! I'm swimming!
C'mon, baby! It's been hours!
Aww!
Hi, Daddy!
Hi, baby! How was your day?
Great! I learned to swim!

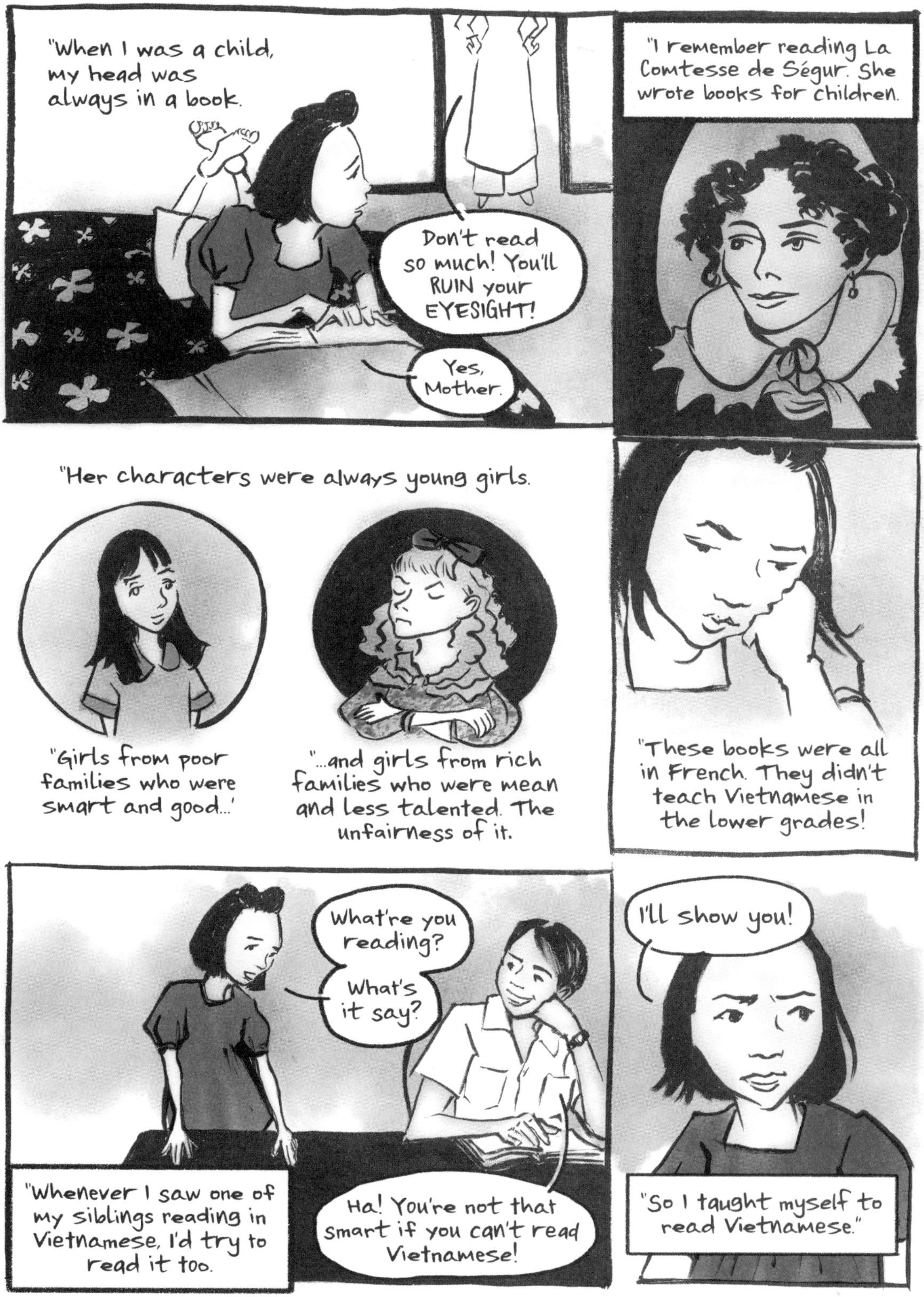
"When I was a child, my head was always in a book.
Don't read so much! You'll RUIN your EYESIGHT!
Yes, Mother.
"I remember reading La Comtesse de Ségur. She wrote books for children.
"Her characters were always young girls.
"Girls from poor families who were smart and good...'
"...and girls from rich families who were mean and less talented. The unfairness of it.
"These books were all in French. They didn't teach Vietnamese in the lower grades!
What're you reading?
What's it say?
"Whenever I saw one of my siblings reading in Vietnamese, I'd try to read it too.
Ha! You're not that smart if you can't read Vietnamese!
I'll show you!
"So I taught myself to read Vietnamese."

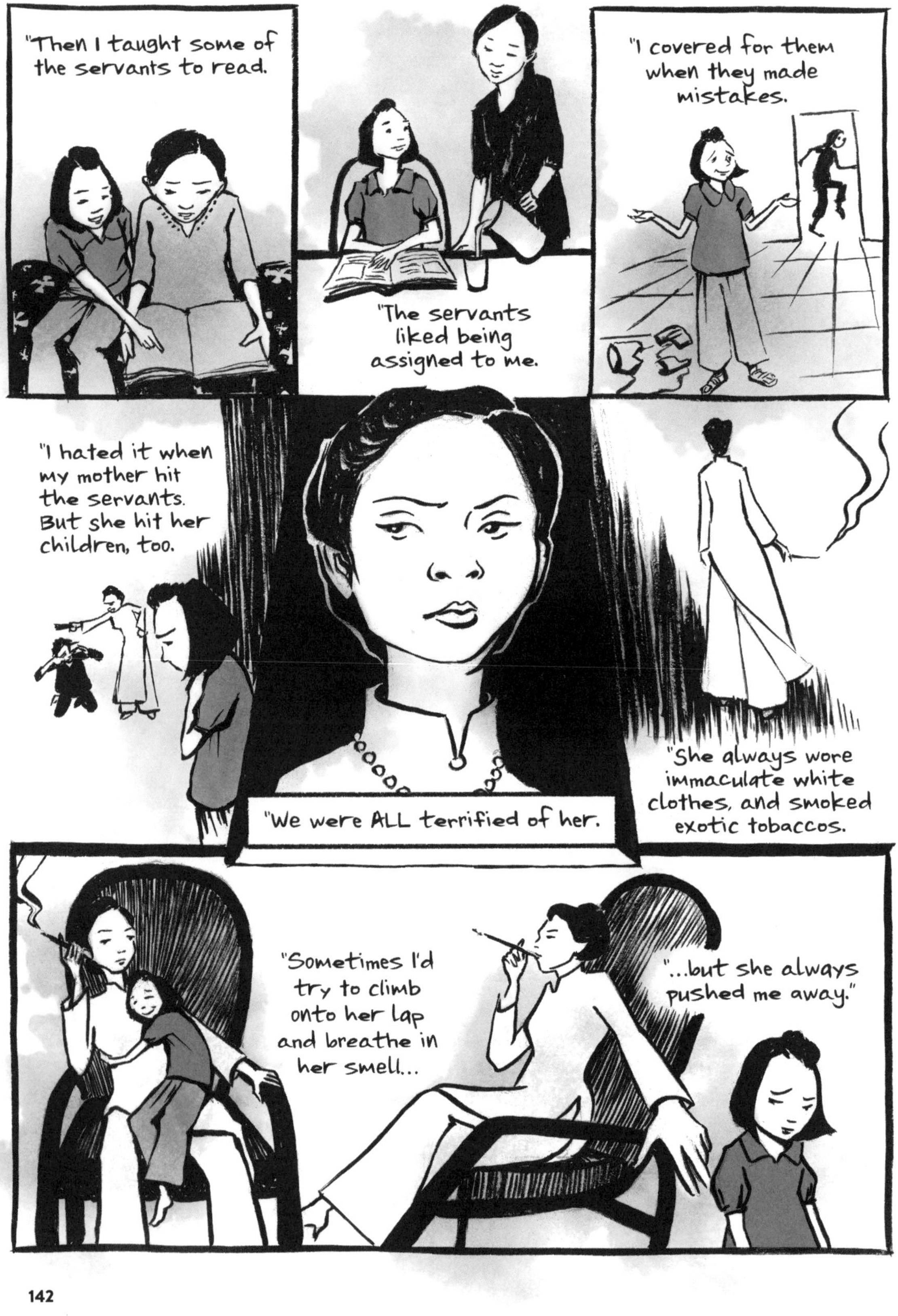
"Then I taught some of the servants to read.
"The servants liked being assigned to me.
"I covered for them when they made mistakes.
"I hated it when my mother hit the servants. But she hit her children, too.
"We were ALL terrified of her.
"She always wore immaculate white clothes, and smoked exotic tobaccos.
"Sometimes I'd try to climb onto her lap and breathe in her smell...
"...but she always pushed me away."

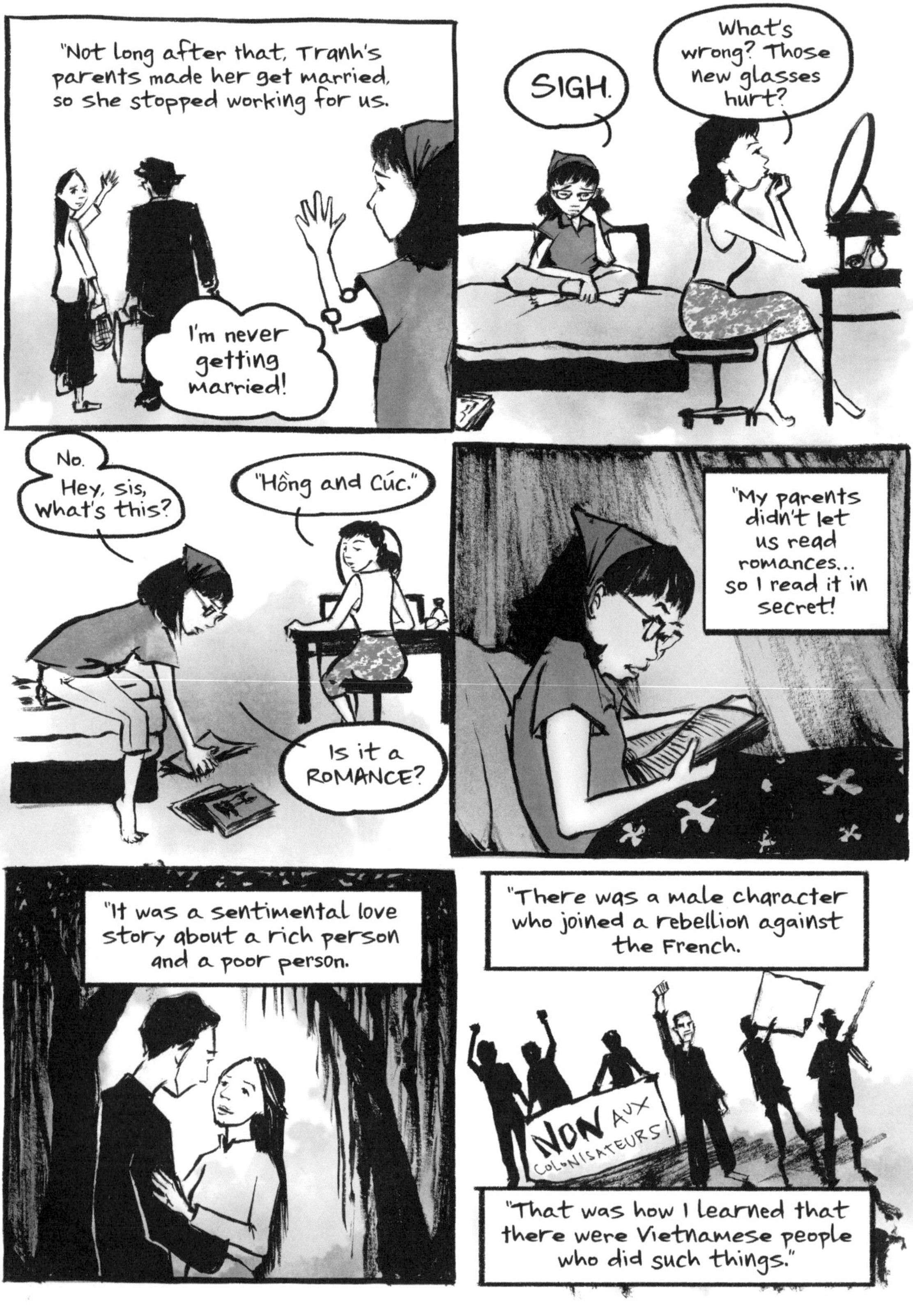
"Not long after that, Tranh's parents made her get married, so she stopped working for us.
I'm never getting married!
SIGH.
What's wrong? Those new glasses hurt?
No. Hey, sis, what's this?
"Hồng and Cúc."
Is it a ROMANCE?
"My parents didn't let us read romances... so I read it in secret!
"It was a sentimental love story about a rich person and a poor person.
"There was a male character who joined a rebellion against the French.
NON AUX COLONISATEURS!
"That was how I learned that there were Vietnamese people who did such things."

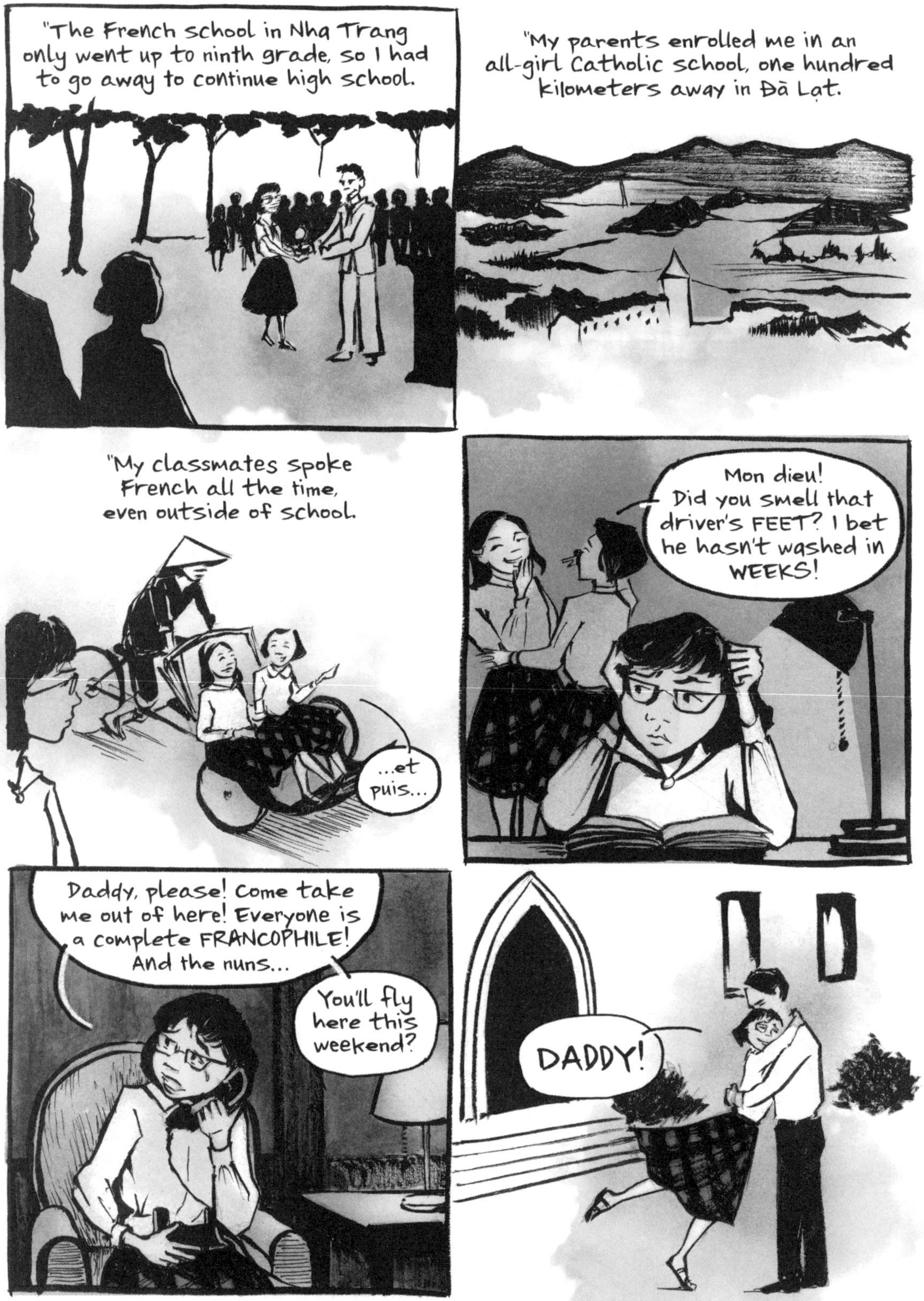
"The French school in Nha Trang only went up to ninth grade, so I had to go away to continue high school.
"My parents enrolled me in an all-girl Catholic school, one hundred kilometers away in Đà Lạt.
"My classmates spoke French all the time, even outside of school.
...et puis...
Mon dieu! Did you smell that driver's FEET? I bet he hasn't washed in WEEKS!
Daddy, please! Come take me out of here! Everyone is a complete FRANCOPHILE! And the nuns...
You'll fly here this weekend?
DADDY!

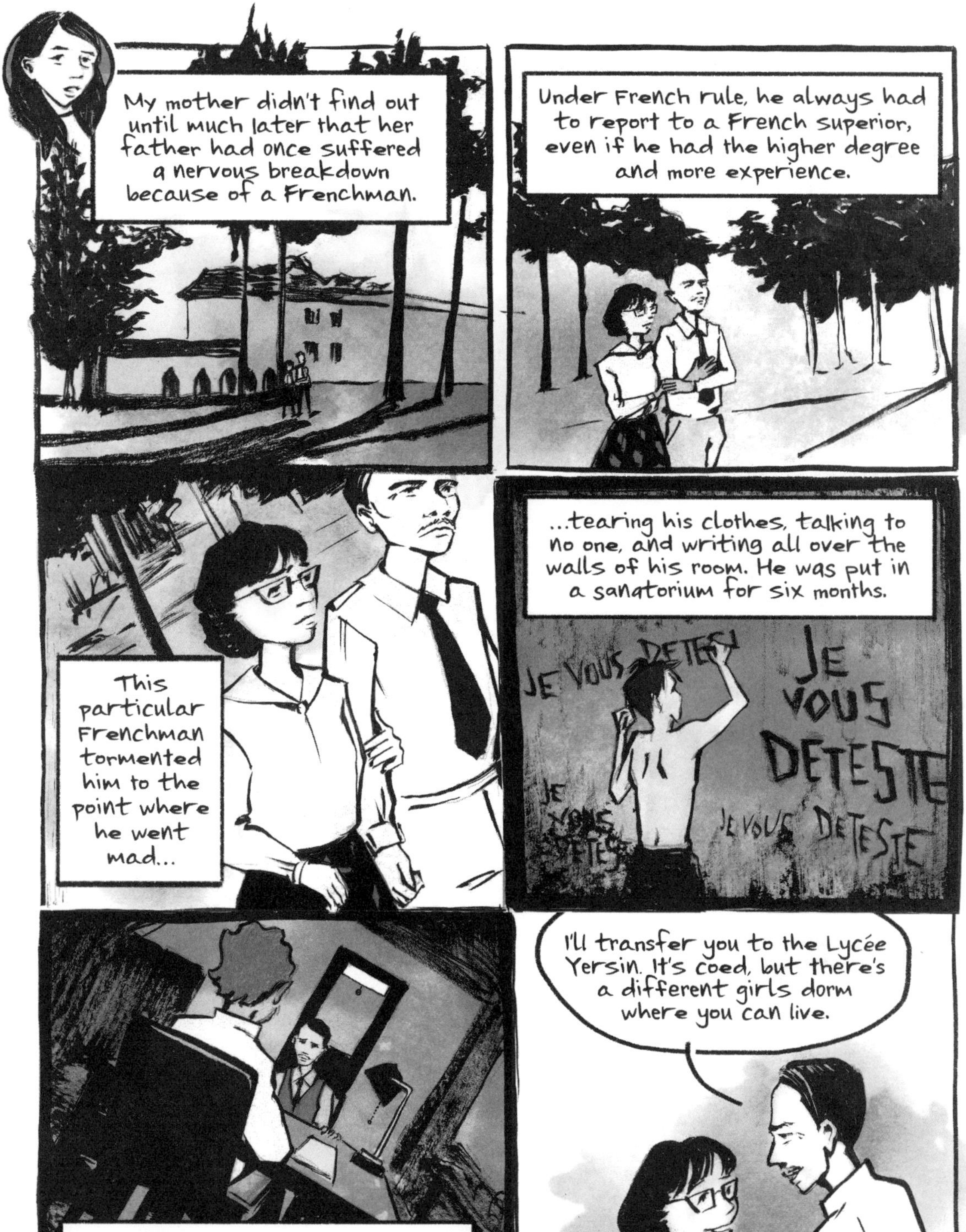

My mother didn't find out until much later that her father had once suffered a nervous breakdown because of a Frenchman.
Under French rule, he always had to report to a French superior, even if he had the higher degree and more experience.
This particular Frenchman tormented him to the point where he went mad...
...tearing his clothes, talking to no one, and writing all over the walls of his room. He was put in a sanatorium for six months.
JE VOUS DETESTE
JE VOUS DETESTE
JE VOUS DETESTE
My mother guesses this was why, afterward, he was transferred to Cambodia, away from his boss.
I'll transfer you to the Lycée Yersin. It's coed, but there's a different girls dorm where you can live.

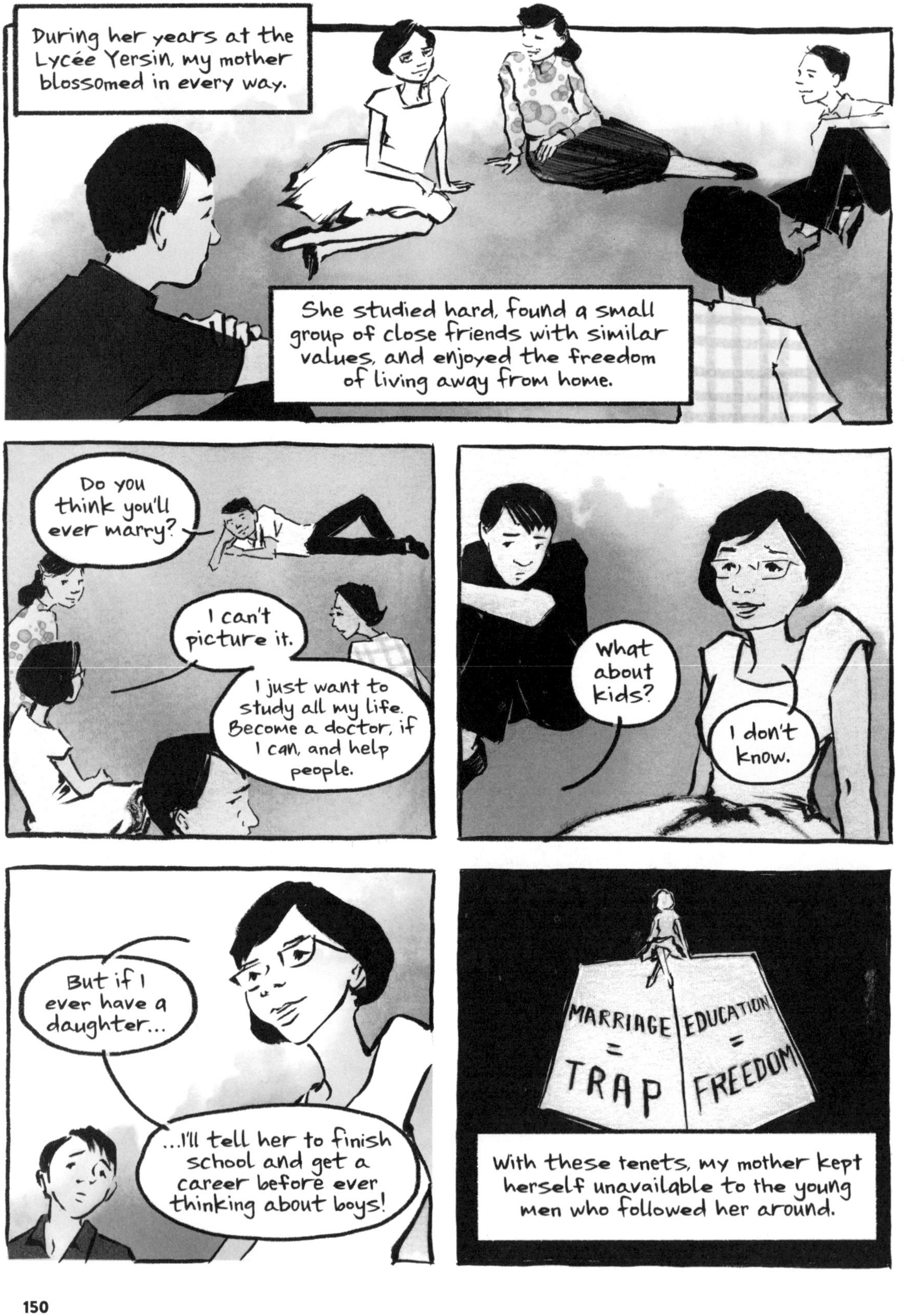
During her years at the Lycée Yersin, my mother blossomed in every way.
She studied hard, found a small group of close friends with similar values, and enjoyed the freedom of living away from home.
Do you think you'll ever marry?
I can't picture it.
I just want to study all my life. Become a doctor, if I can, and help people.
What about kids?
I don't know.
But if I ever have a daughter...
...I'll tell her to finish school and get a career before ever thinking about boys!
MARRIAGE = TRAP
EDUCATION = FREEDOM
With these tenets, my mother kept herself unavailable to the young men who followed her around.

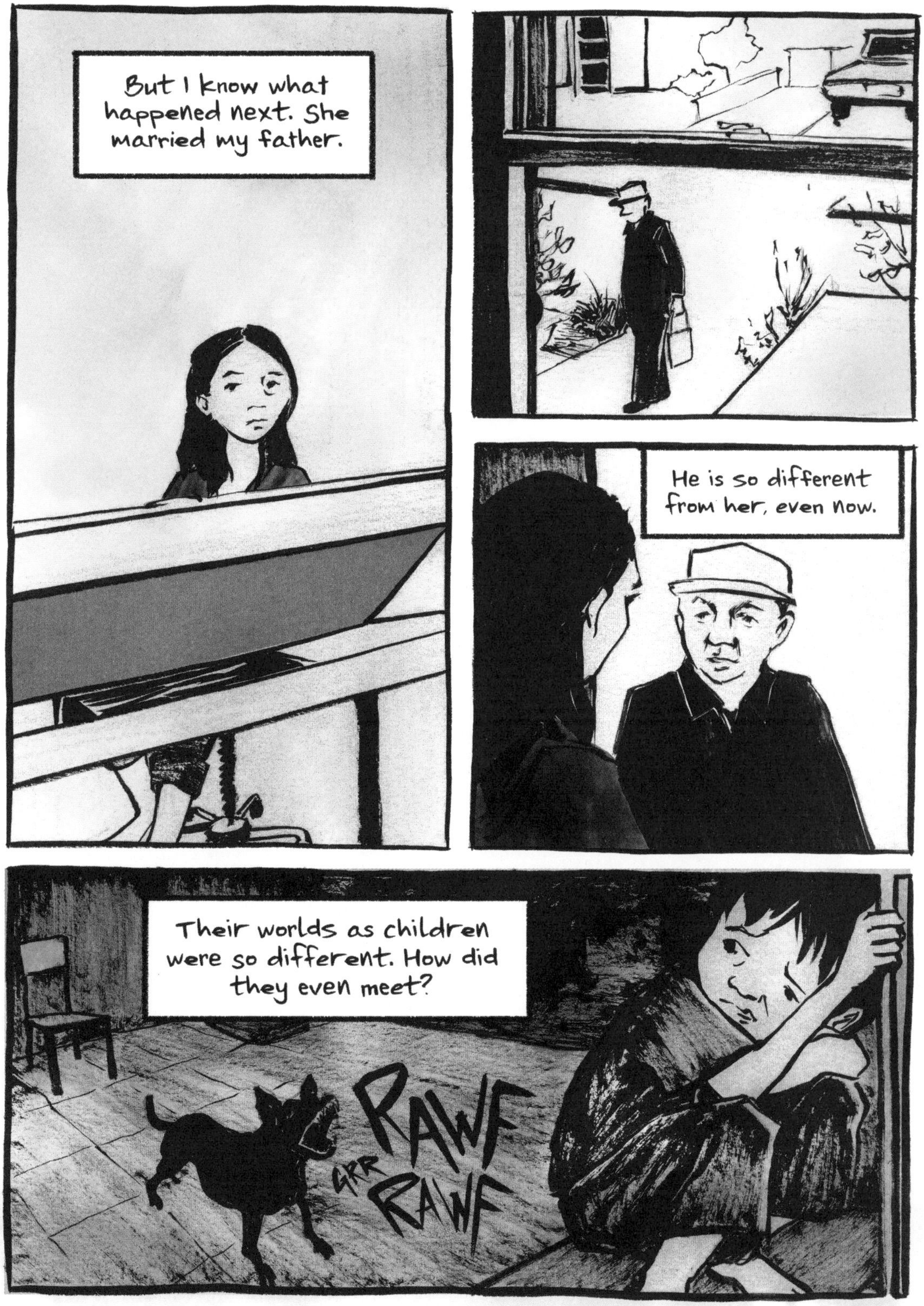
But I know what happened next. She married my father.
He is so different from her, even now.
Their worlds as children were so different. How did they even meet?
RAWF
GRR
RAWF

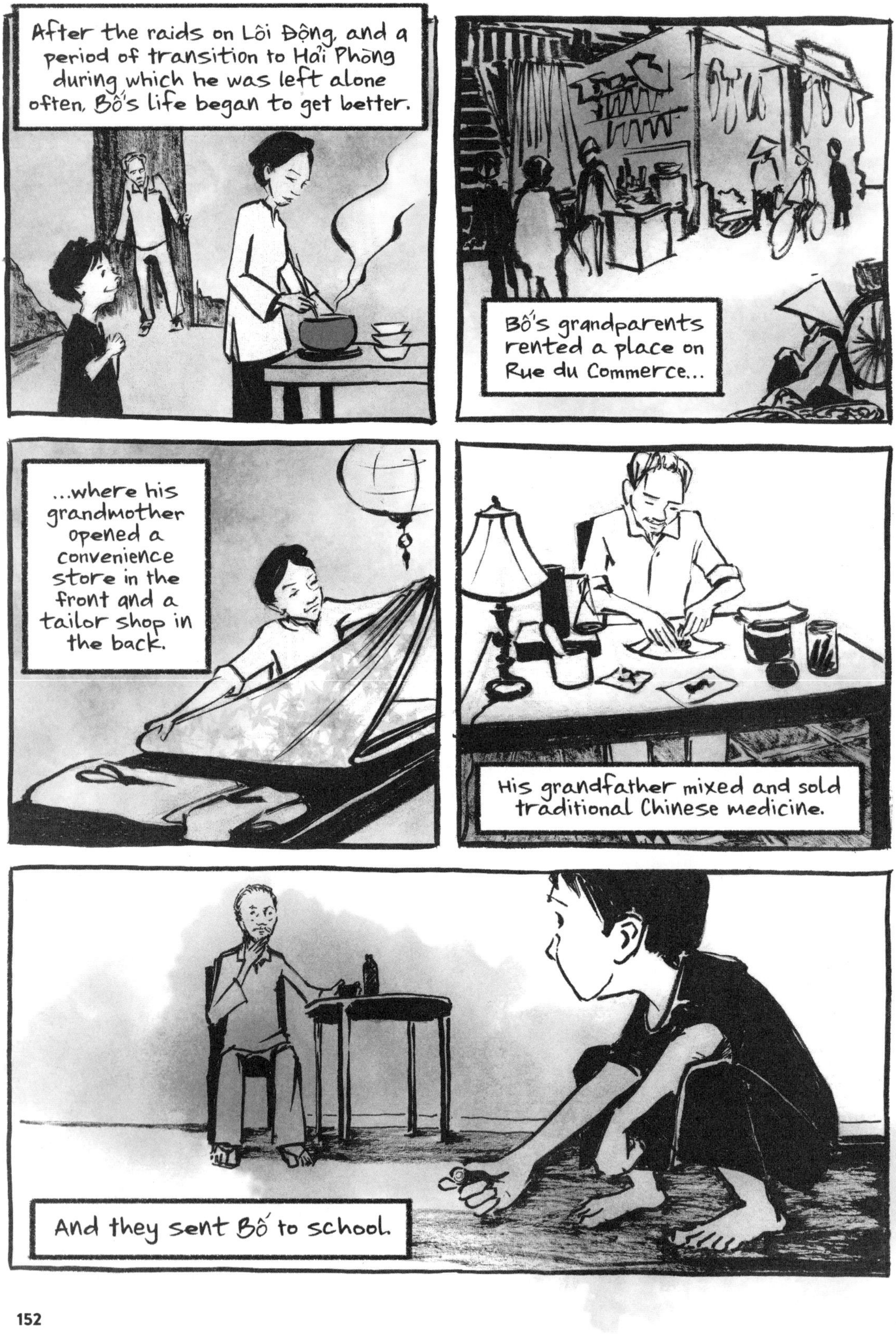
After the raids on Lôi Động, and a period of transition to Hải Phòng during which he was left alone often, Bố's life began to get better.
Bố's grandparents rented a place on Rue du Commerce...
...where his grandmother opened a convenience store in the front and a tailor shop in the back.
His grandfather mixed and sold traditional Chinese medicine.
And they sent Bố to school.

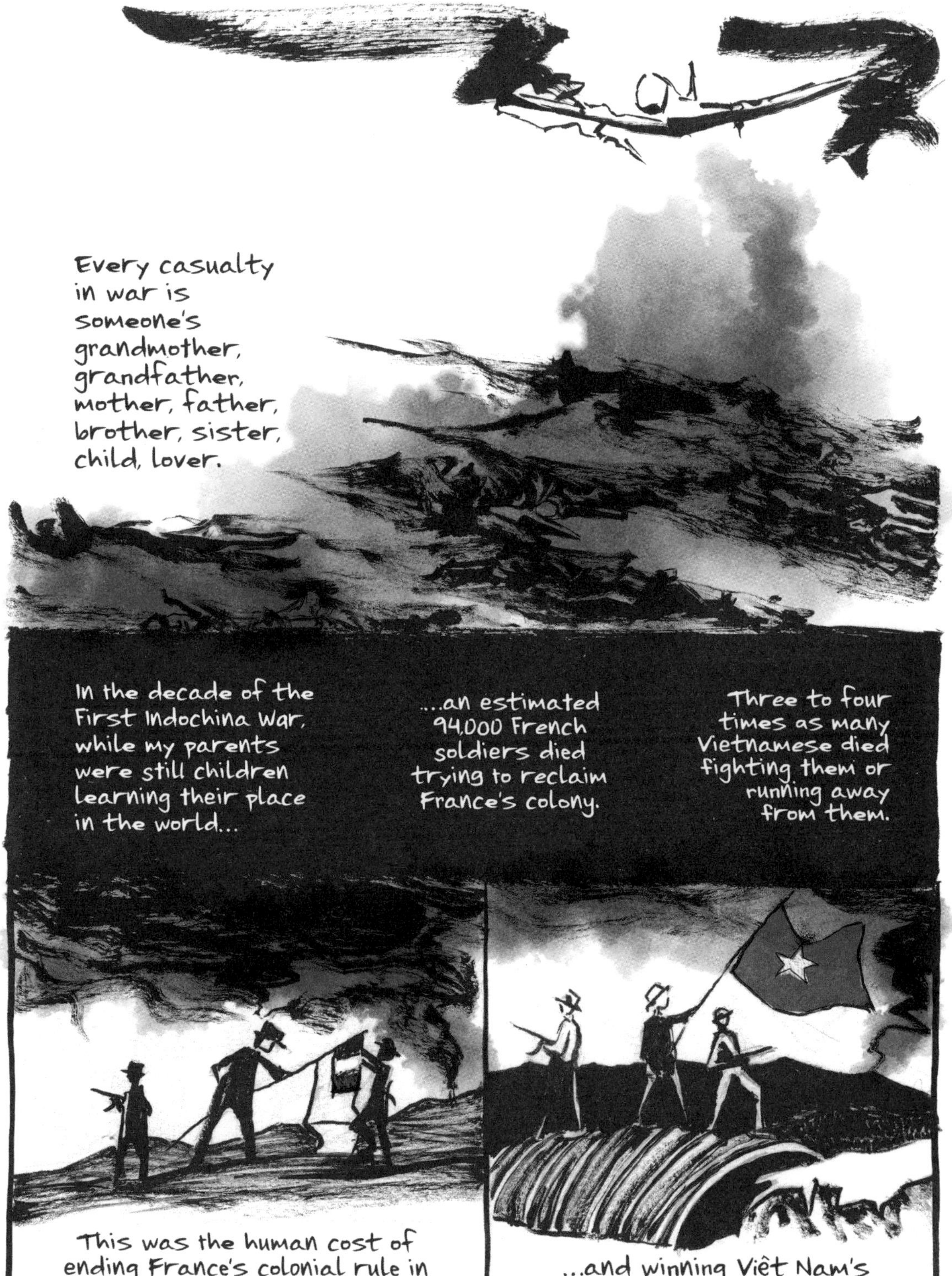
Every casualty in war is someone's grandmother, grandfather, mother, father, brother, sister, child, lover.
In the decade of the First Indochina War, while my parents were still children learning their place in the world...
...an estimated 94,000 French soldiers died trying to reclaim France's colony.
Three to four times as many Vietnamese died fighting them or running away from them.
This was the human cost of ending France's colonial rule in Southeast Asia...
...and winning Việt Nam's independence.

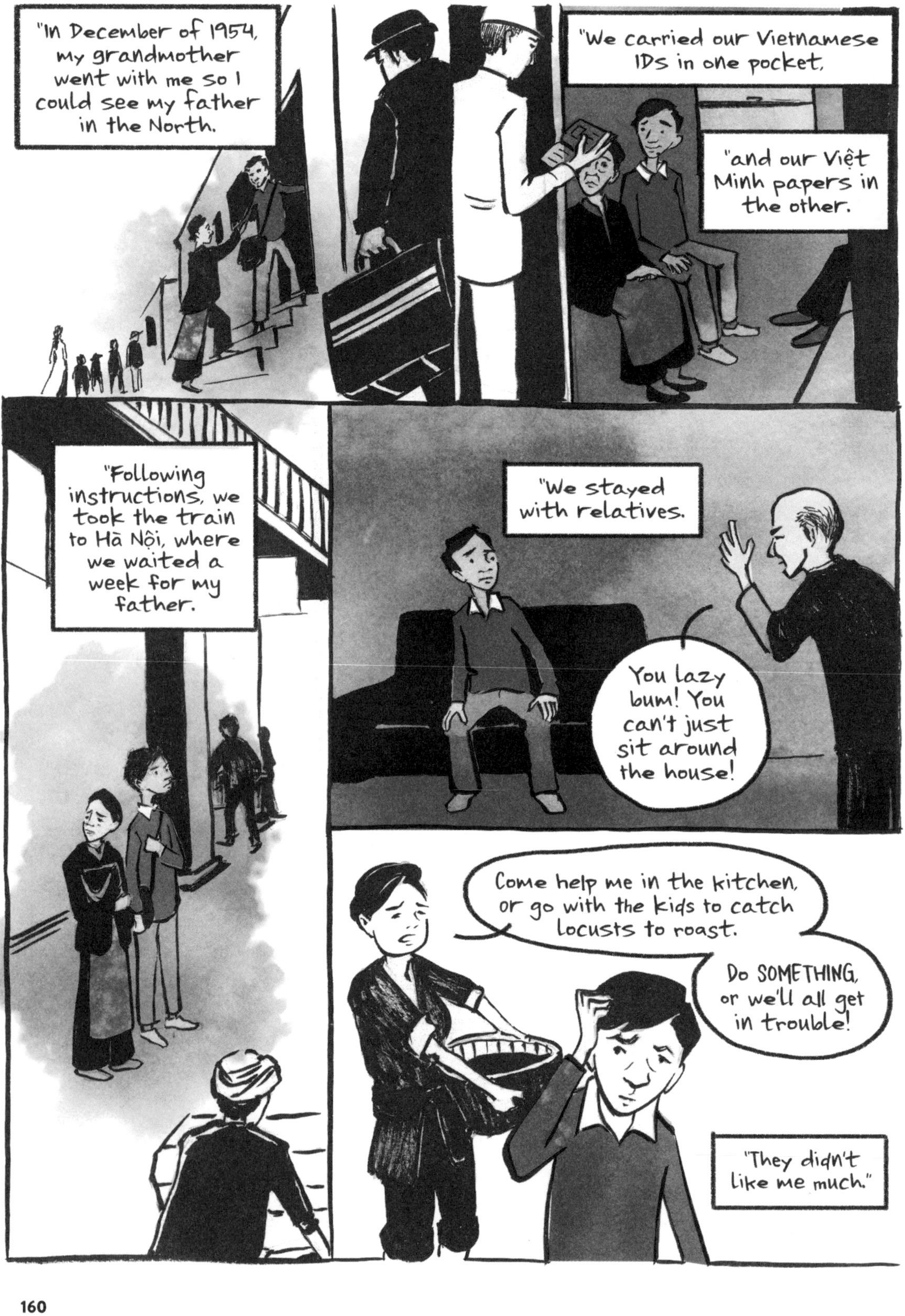
"In December of 1954, my grandmother went with me so I could see my father in the North.
"We carried our Vietnamese IDs in one pocket,
"and our Việt Minh papers in the other.
"Following instructions, we took the train to Hà Nội, where we waited a week for my father.
"We stayed with relatives.
You lazy bum! You can't just sit around the house!
Come help me in the kitchen, or go with the kids to catch locusts to roast.
Do SOMETHING, or we'll all get in trouble!
"They didn't like me much."

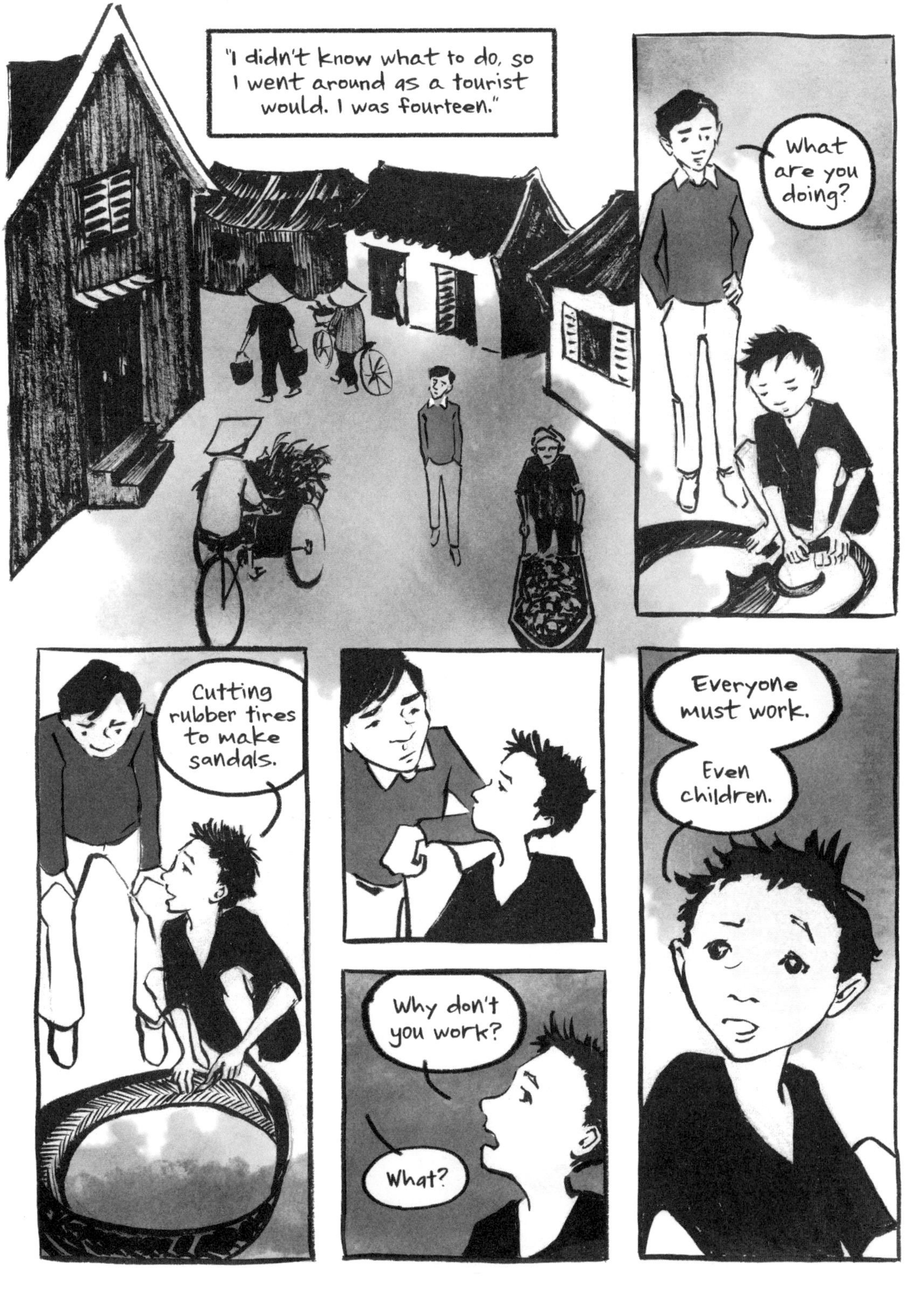
"I didn't know what to do, so I went around as a tourist would. I was fourteen."
What are you doing?
Cutting rubber tires to make sandals.
Why don't you work?
What?
Everyone must work.
Even children.

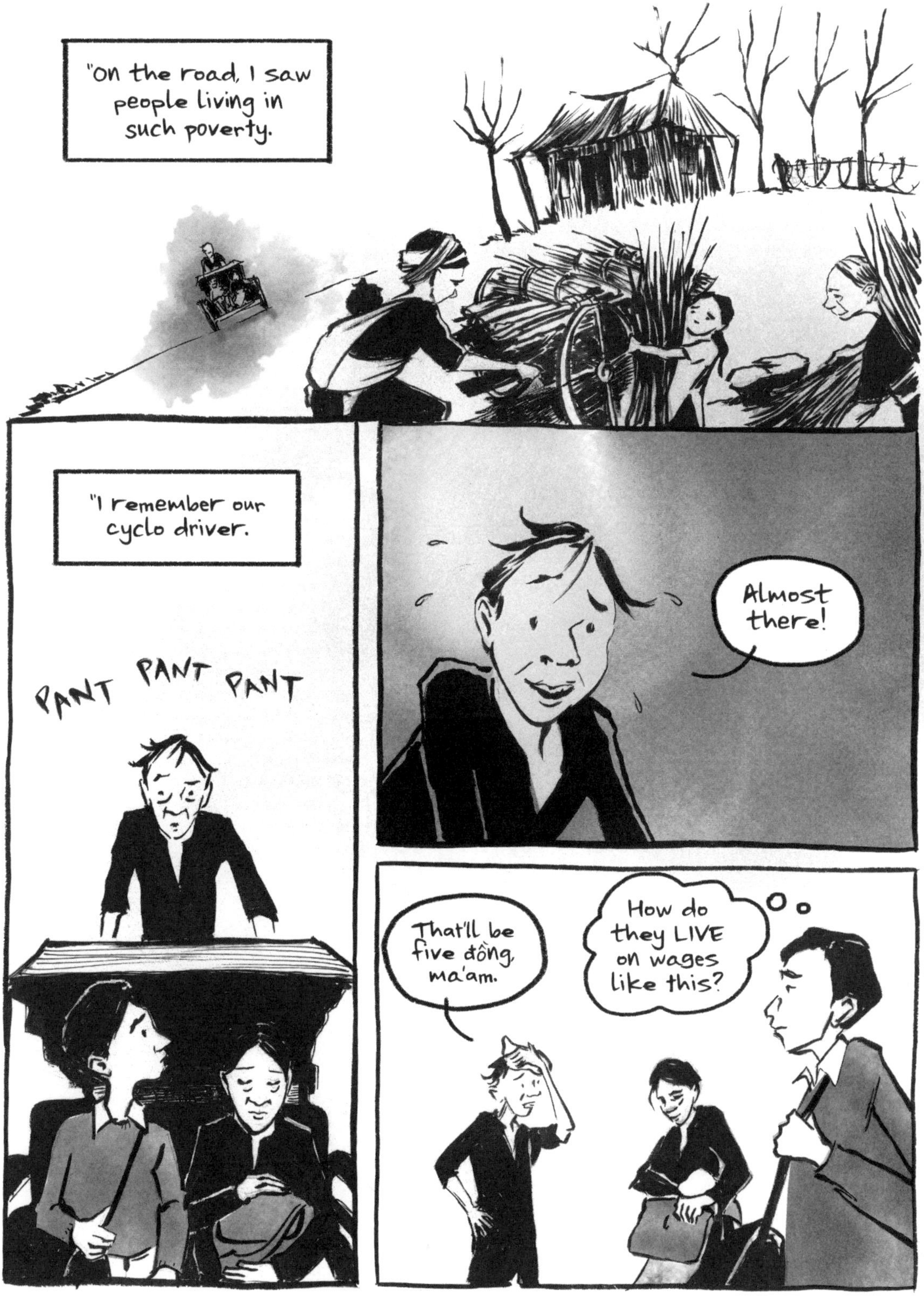
"On the road, I saw people living in such poverty.
"I remember our cyclo driver.
PANT PANT PANT
Almost there!
That'll be five đồng, ma'am.
How do they LIVE on wages like this?

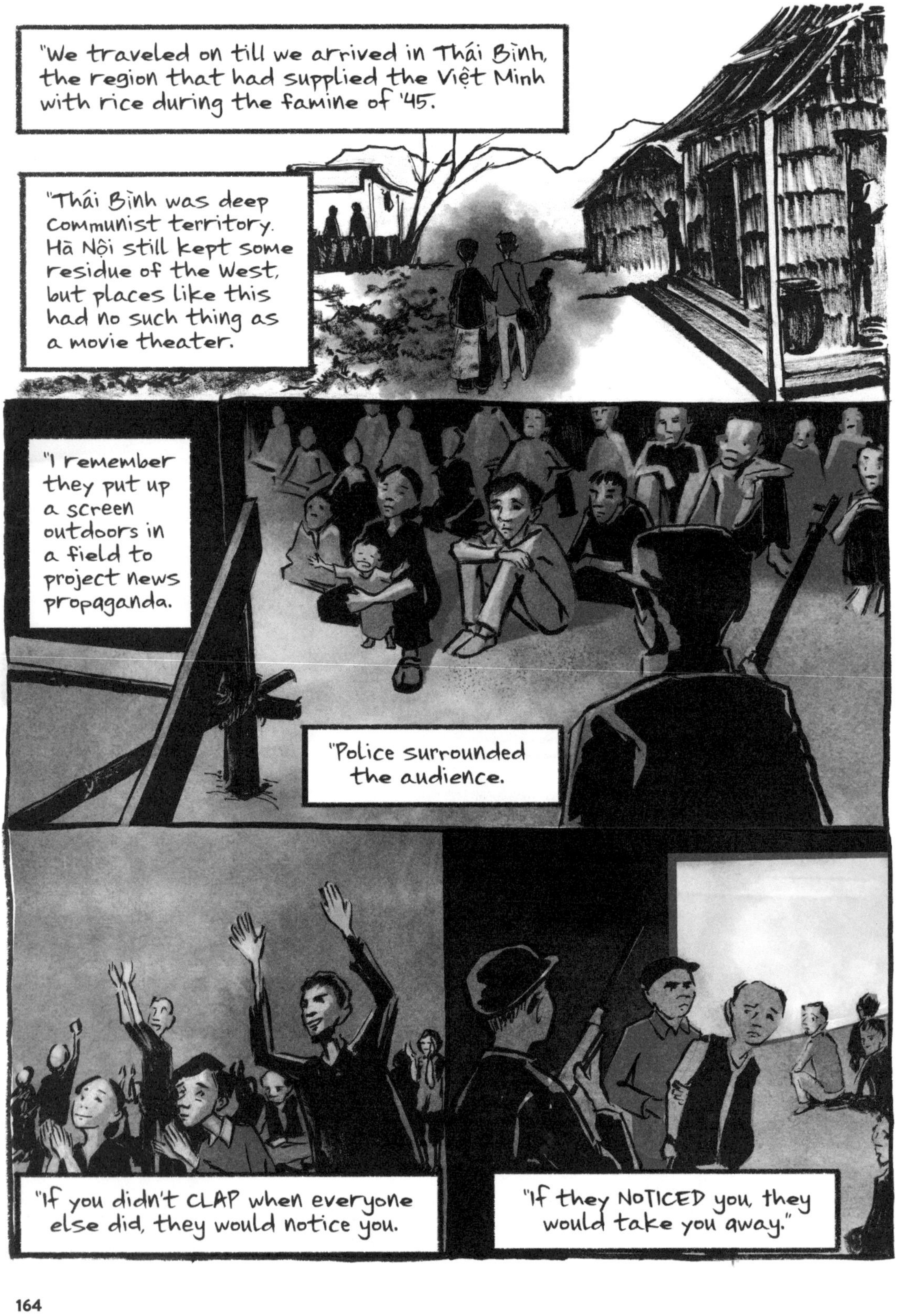

"We traveled on till we arrived in Thái Bình, the region that had supplied the Việt Minh with rice during the famine of '45.
"Thái Bình was deep communist territory. Hà Nội still kept some residue of the West, but places like this had no such thing as a movie theater.
"I remember they put up a screen outdoors in a field to project news propaganda.
"Police surrounded the audience.
"If you didn't CLAP when everyone else did, they would notice you.
"If they NOTICED you, they would take you away."

166

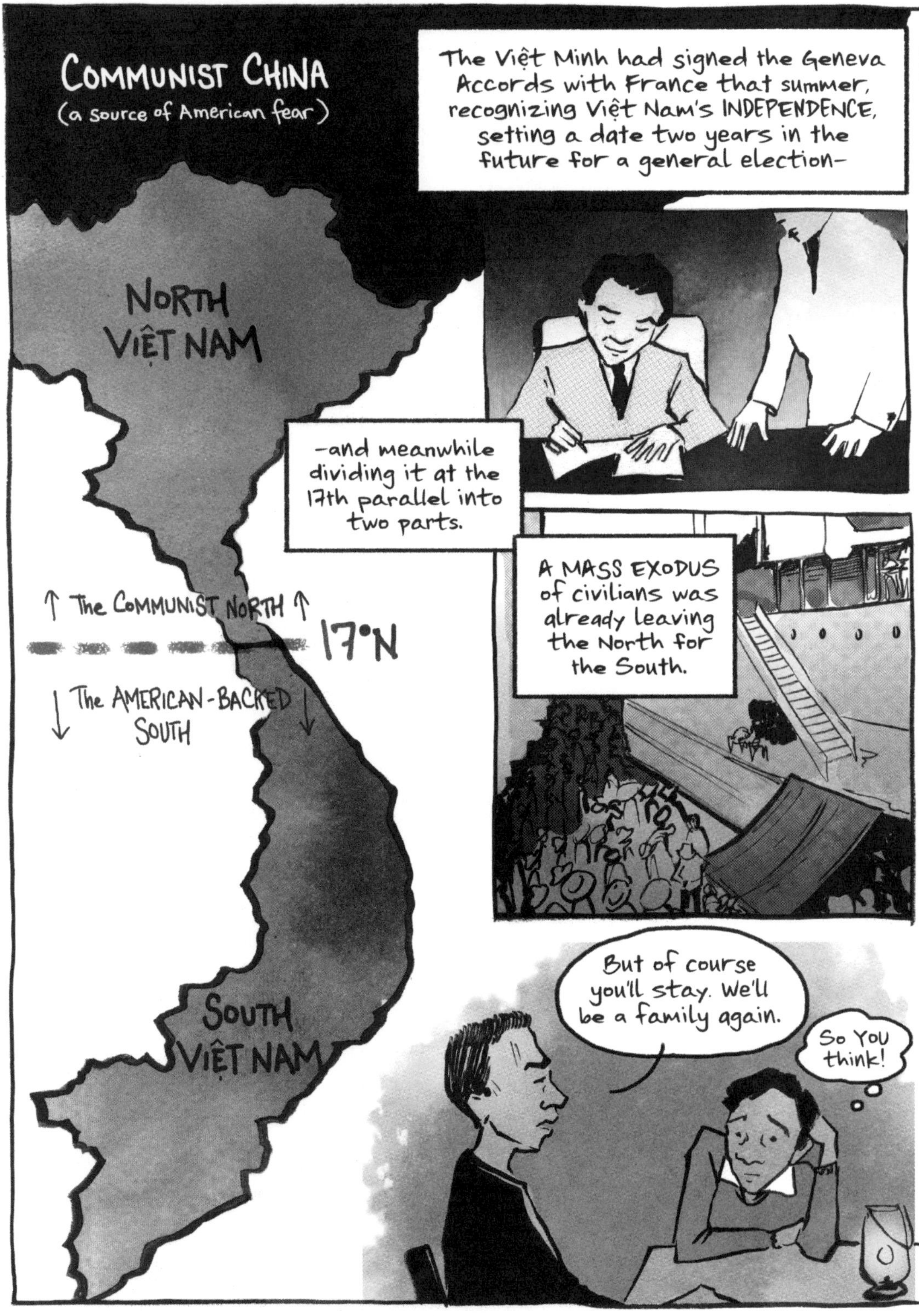

COMMUNIST CHINA
(a source of American fear)
The Việt Minh had signed the Geneva Accords with France that summer, recognizing Việt Nam's INDEPENDENCE, setting a date two years in the future for a general election-
NORTH VIỆT NAM
-and meanwhile dividing it at the 17th parallel into two parts.
↑ The COMMUNIST NORTH ↑
17°N
↓ The AMERICAN-BACKED SOUTH ↓
A MASS EXODUS of civilians was already leaving the North for the South.
SOUTH VIỆT NAM
But of course you'll stay. We'll be a family again.
So YOU think!

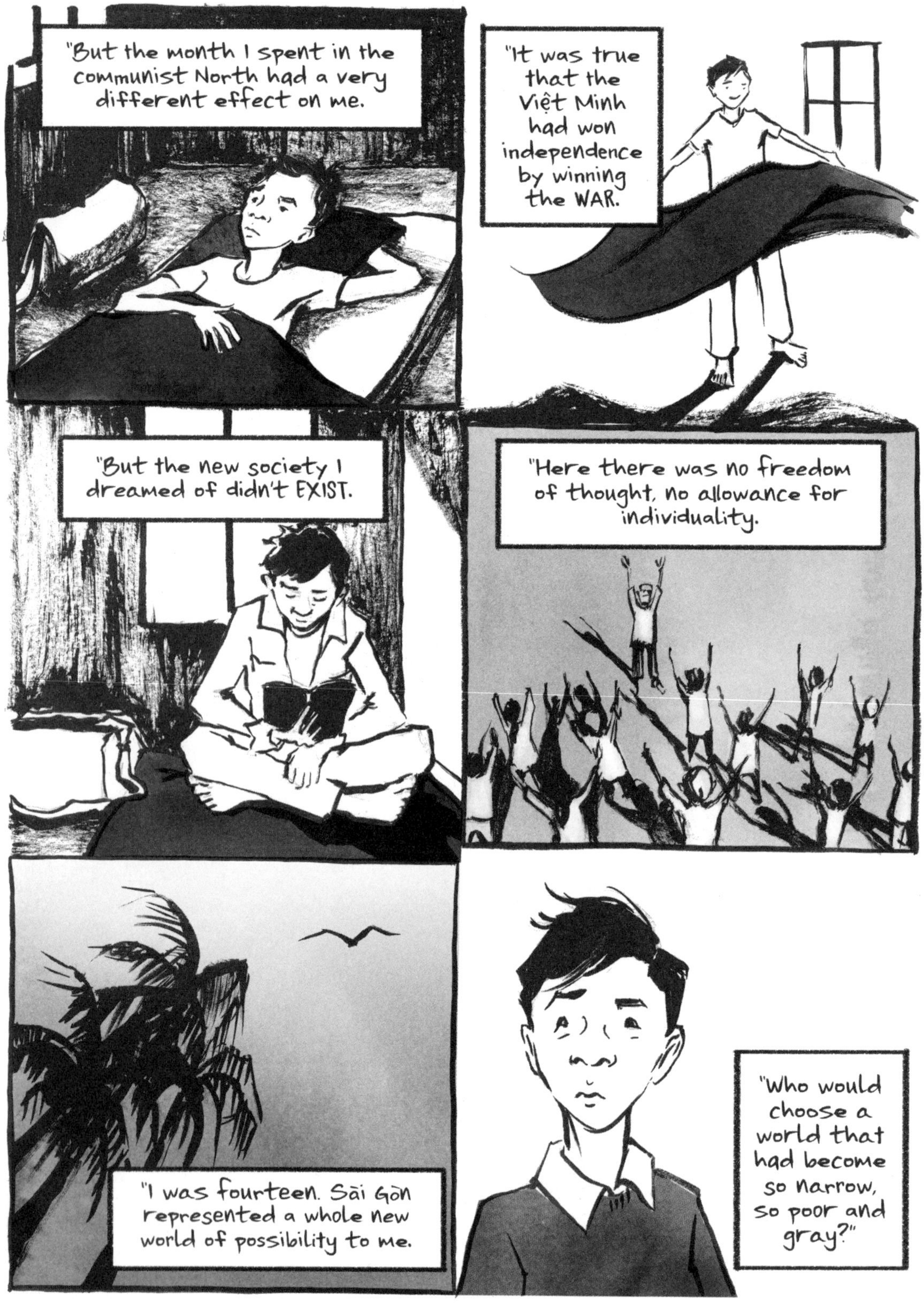
"But the month I spent in the communist North had a very different effect on me.
"It was true that the Việt Minh had won independence by winning the WAR.
"But the new society I dreamed of didn't EXIST.
"Here there was no freedom of thought, no allowance for individuality.
"I was fourteen. Sài Gòn represented a whole new world of possibility to me.
"Who would choose a world that had become so narrow, so poor and gray?"

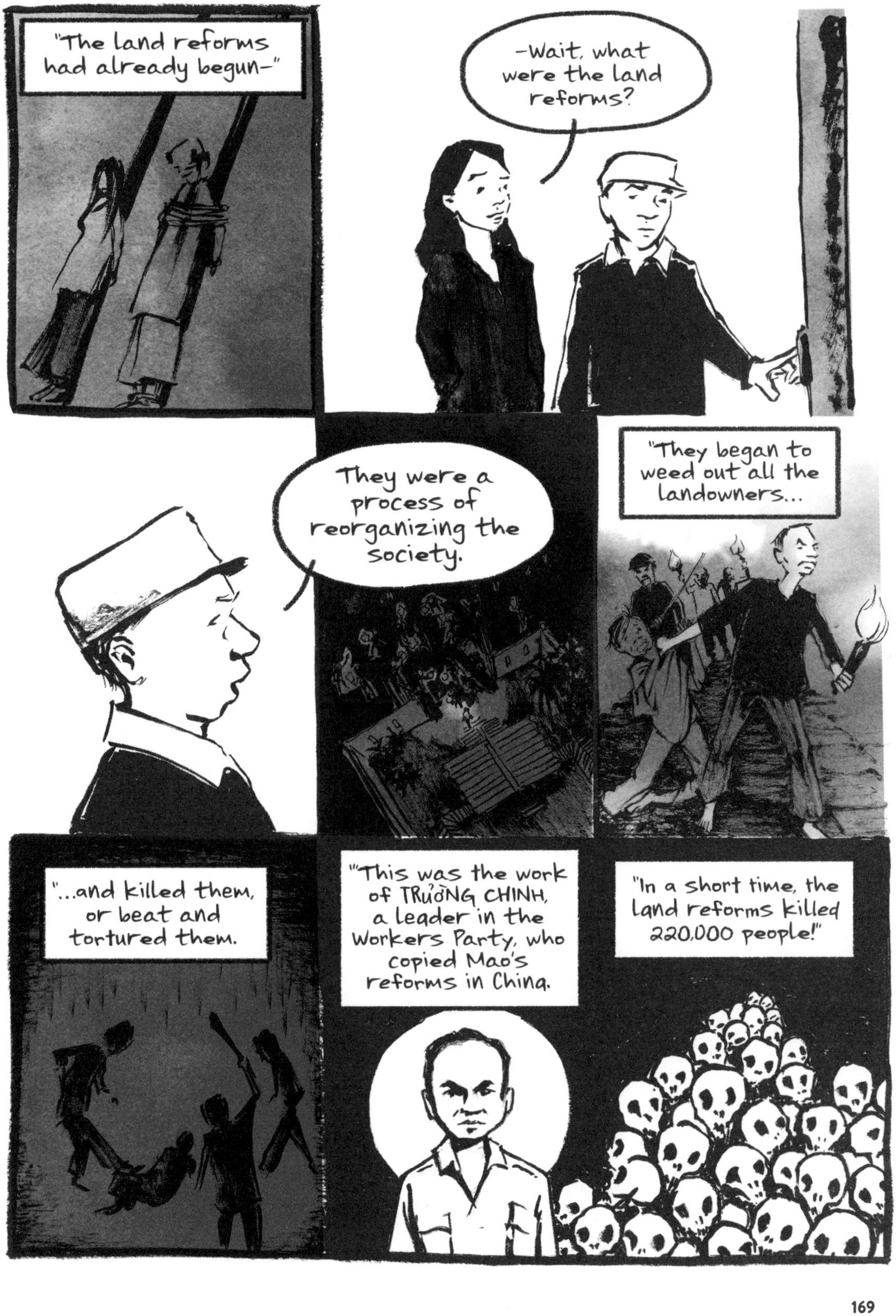

"The land reforms had already begun-"
-Wait, what were the land reforms?
They were a process of reorganizing the society.
"They began to weed out all the landowners...
"...and killed them, or beat and tortured them.
"This was the work of TRƯỜNG CHINH, a leader in the Workers Party, who copied Mao's reforms in China.
"In a short time, the land reforms killed 220,000 people!"

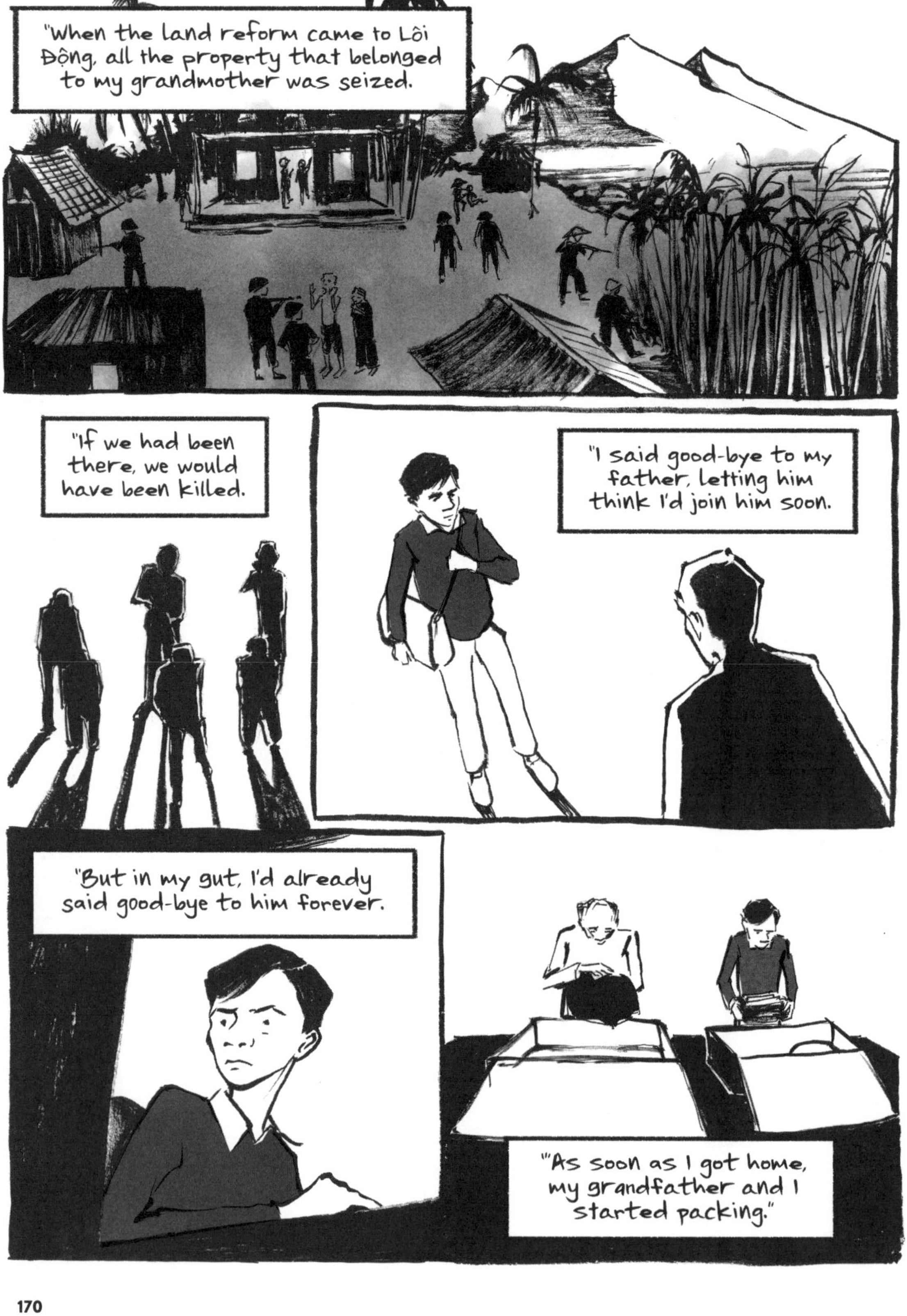
"When the land reform came to Lôi Động, all the property that belonged to my grandmother was seized.
"If we had been there, we would have been killed.
"I said good-bye to my father, letting him think I'd join him soon.
"But in my gut, I'd already said good-bye to him forever.
"As soon as I got home, my grandfather and I started packing."

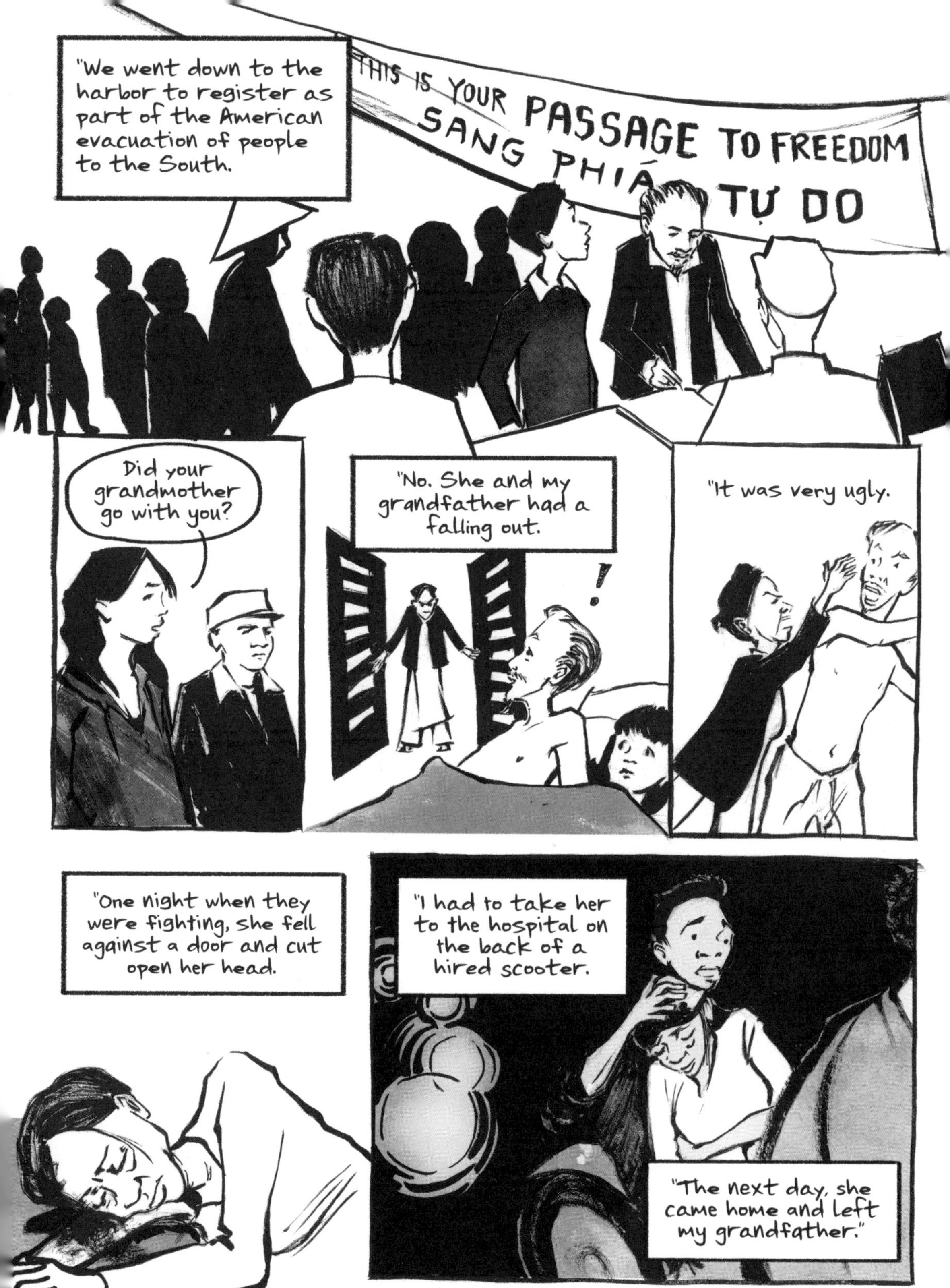
"We went down to the harbor to register as part of the American evacuation of people to the South.
THIS IS YOUR PASSAGE TO FREEDOM
SANG PHÍA TỰ DO
Did your grandmother go with you?
"No. She and my grandfather had a falling out.
!
"It was very ugly.
"One night when they were fighting, she fell against a door and cut open her head.
"I had to take her to the hospital on the back of a hired scooter.
"The next day, she came home and left my grandfather."

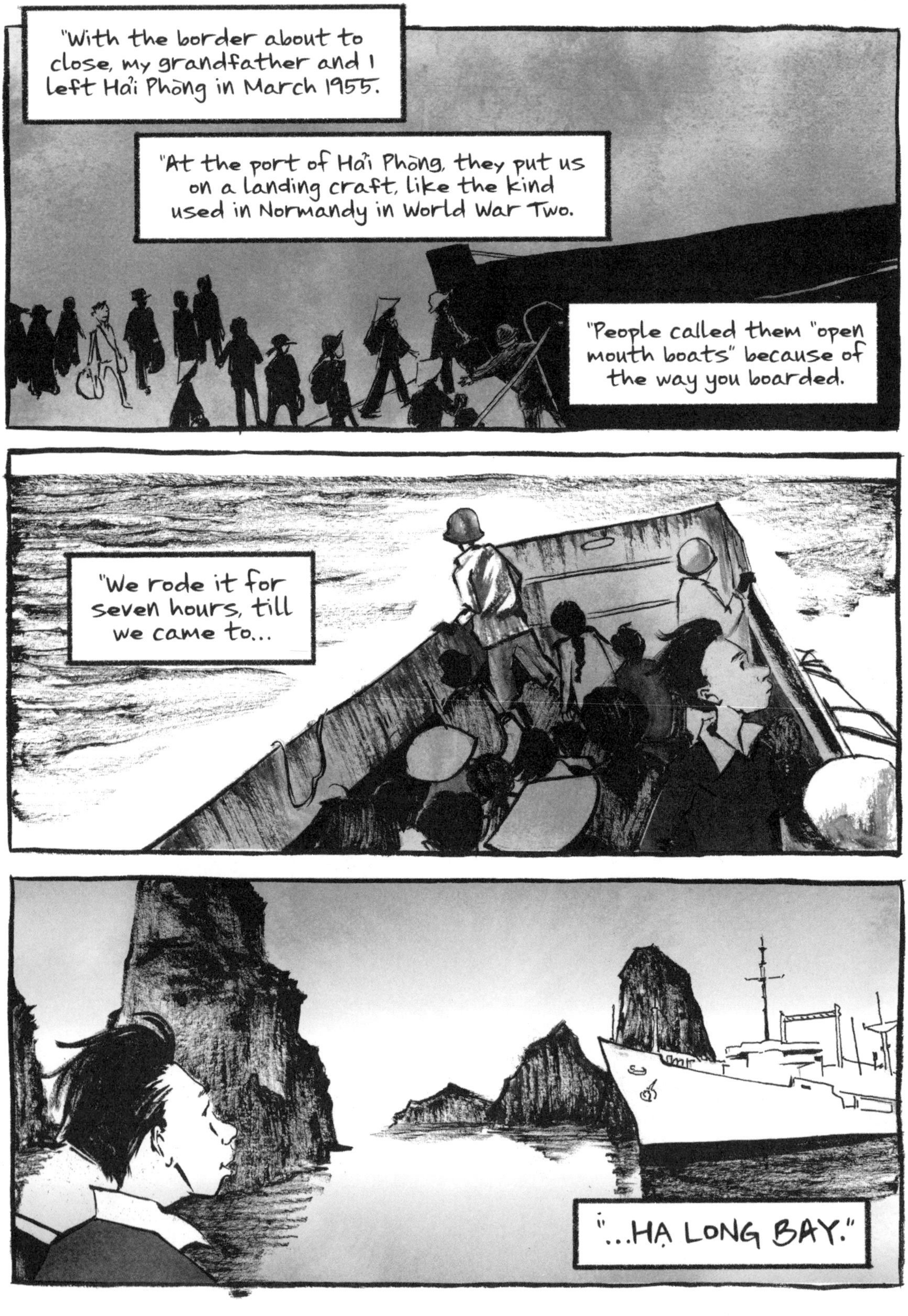
"With the border about to close, my grandfather and I left Hải Phòng in March 1955.
"At the port of Hải Phòng, they put us on a landing craft, like the kind used in Normandy in World War Two.
"People called them "open mouth boats" because of the way you boarded.
"We rode it for seven hours, till we came to...
"...HẠ LONG BAY."

CHAPTER 6

THE CHESSBOARD

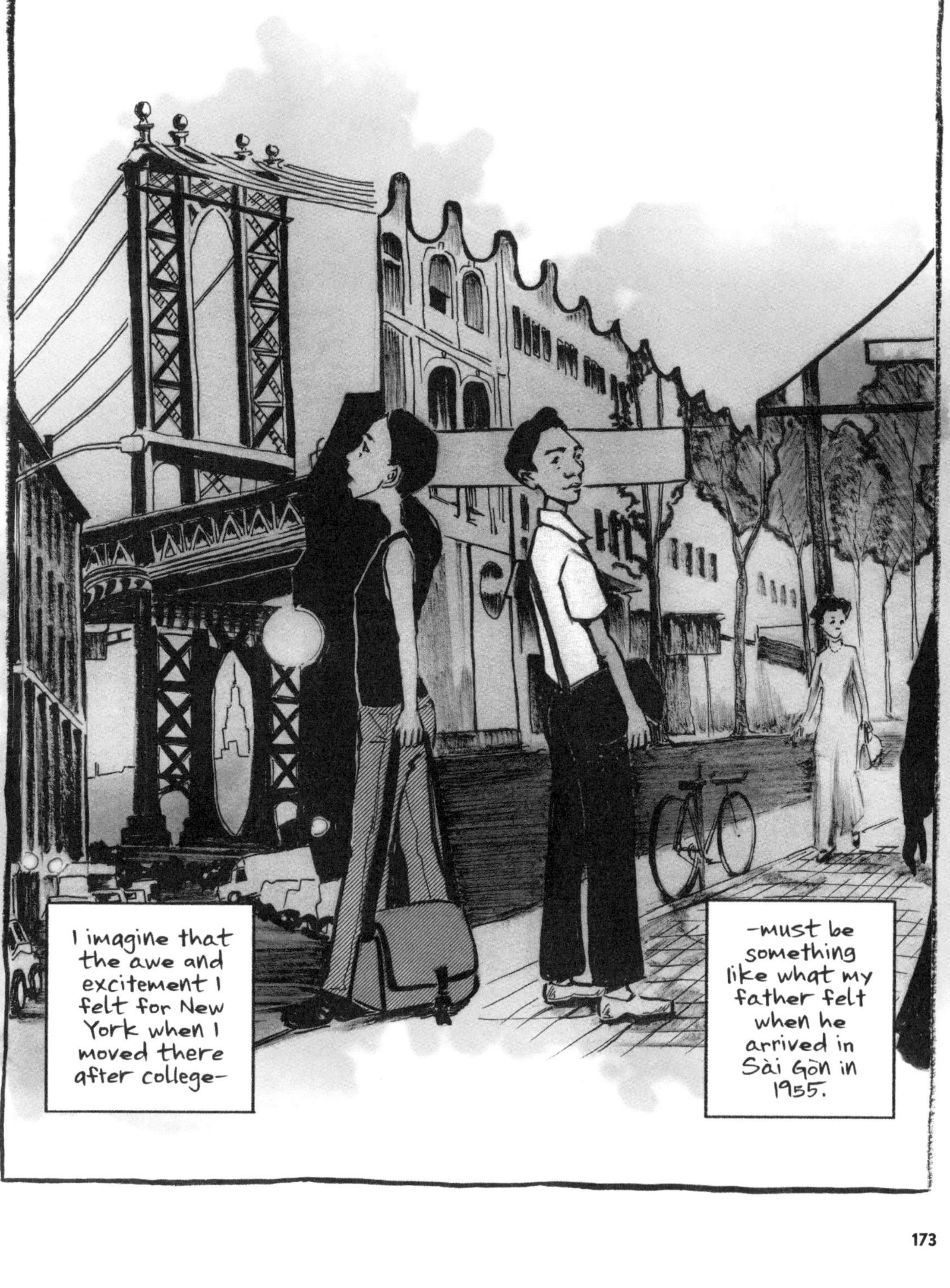
I imagine that the awe and excitement I felt for New York when I moved there after college-
-must be something like what my father felt when he arrived in Sài Gòn in 1955.

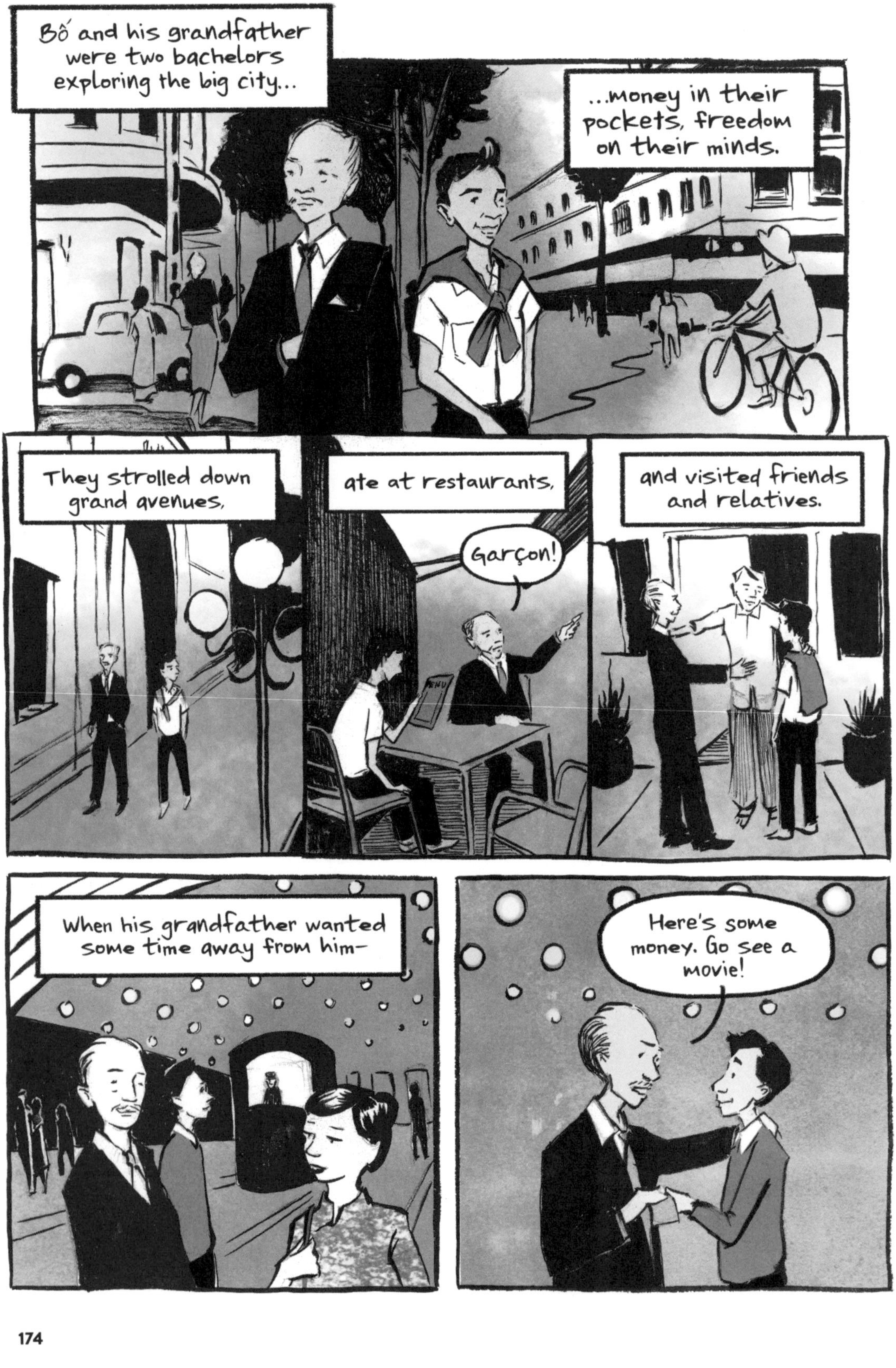
Bố and his grandfather were two bachelors exploring the big city...
...money in their pockets, freedom on their minds.
They strolled down grand avenues,
ate at restaurants,
Garçon!
MENU
and visited friends and relatives.
When his grandfather wanted some time away from him–
Here's some money. Go see a movie!

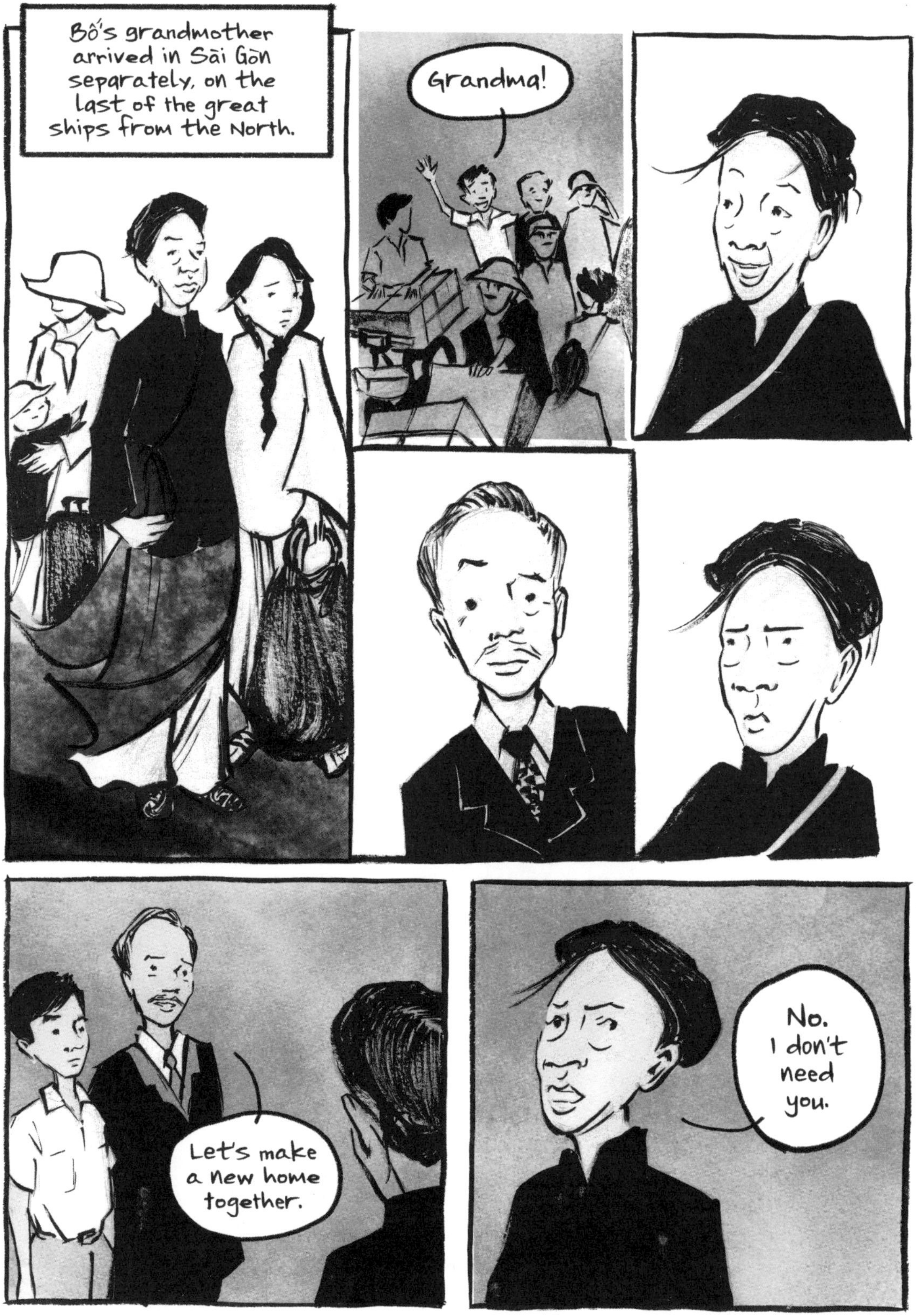
Bố's grandmother arrived in Sài Gòn separately, on the last of the great ships from the North.
Grandma!
Let's make a new home together.
No. I don't need you.

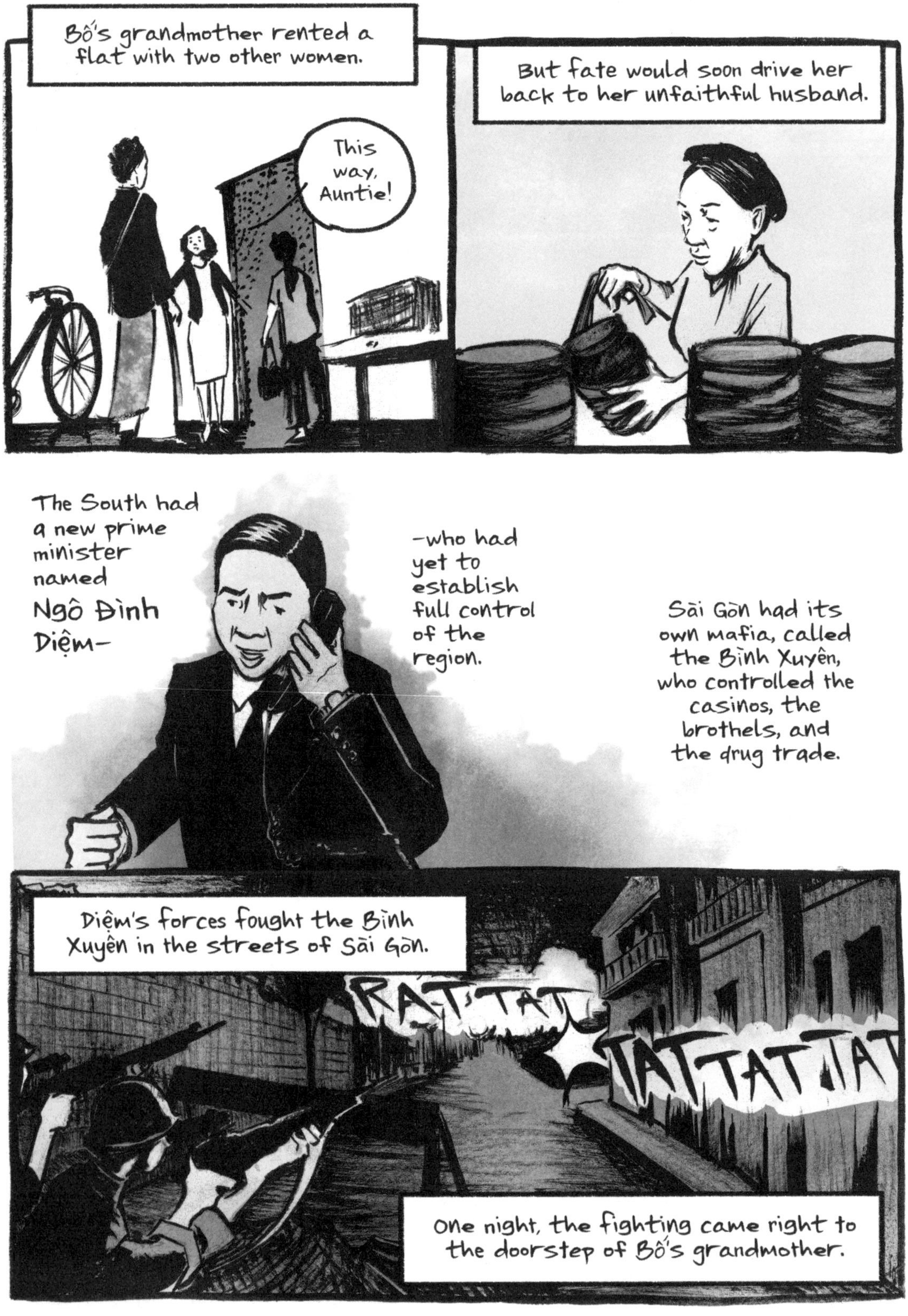
Bố's grandmother rented a flat with two other women.
This way, Auntie!
But fate would soon drive her back to her unfaithful husband.
The South had a new prime minister named Ngô Đình Diệm–
–who had yet to establish full control of the region.
Sài Gòn had its own mafia, called the Bình Xuyên, who controlled the casinos, the brothels, and the drug trade.
Diệm's forces fought the Bình Xuyên in the streets of Sài Gòn.
RAT TAT
TAT TAT TAT
One night, the fighting came right to the doorstep of Bố's grandmother.

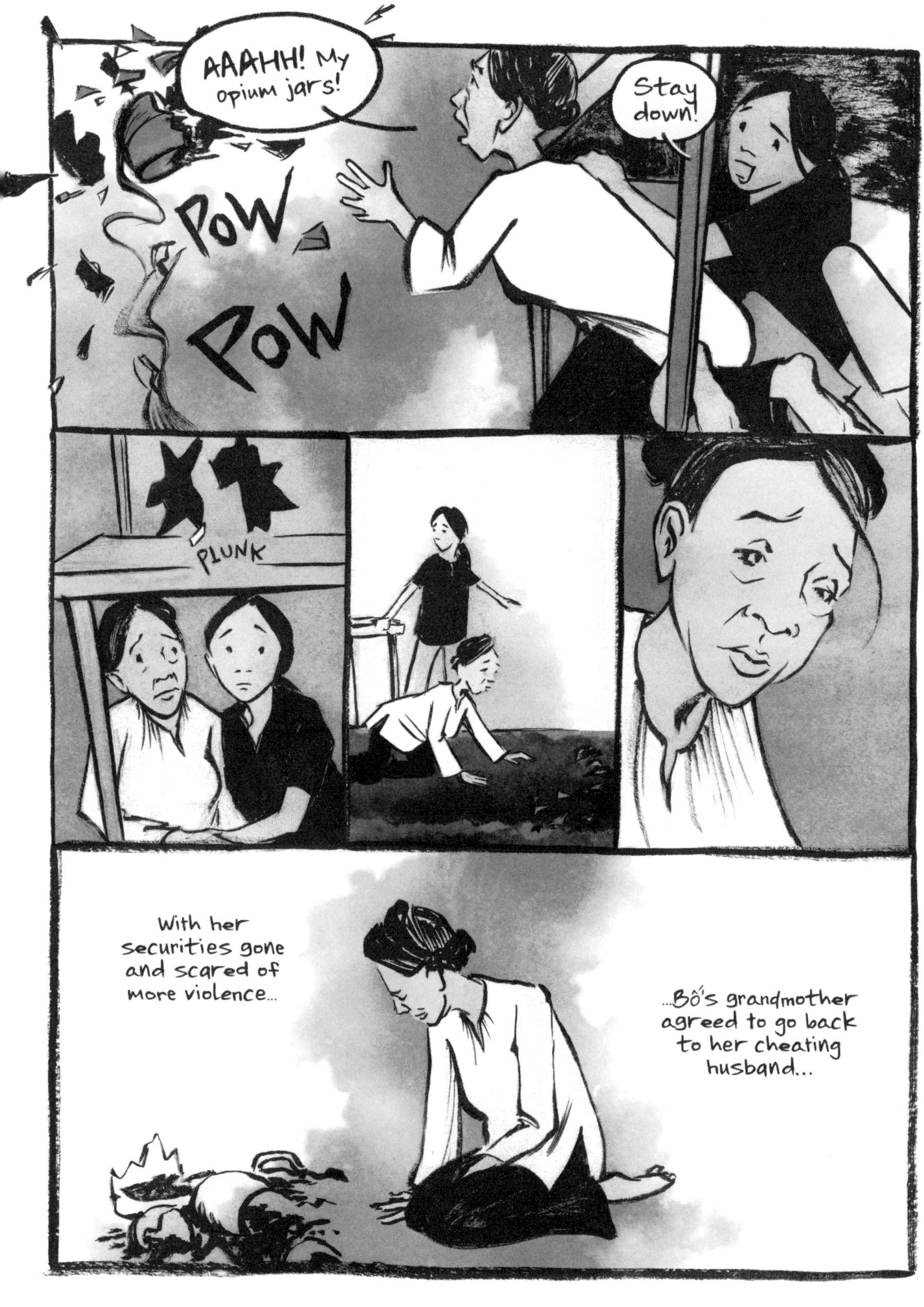
AAAHH! My opium jars!
Stay down!
POW
POW
PLUNK
With her securities gone and scared of more violence...
...Bố's grandmother agreed to go back to her cheating husband...

179

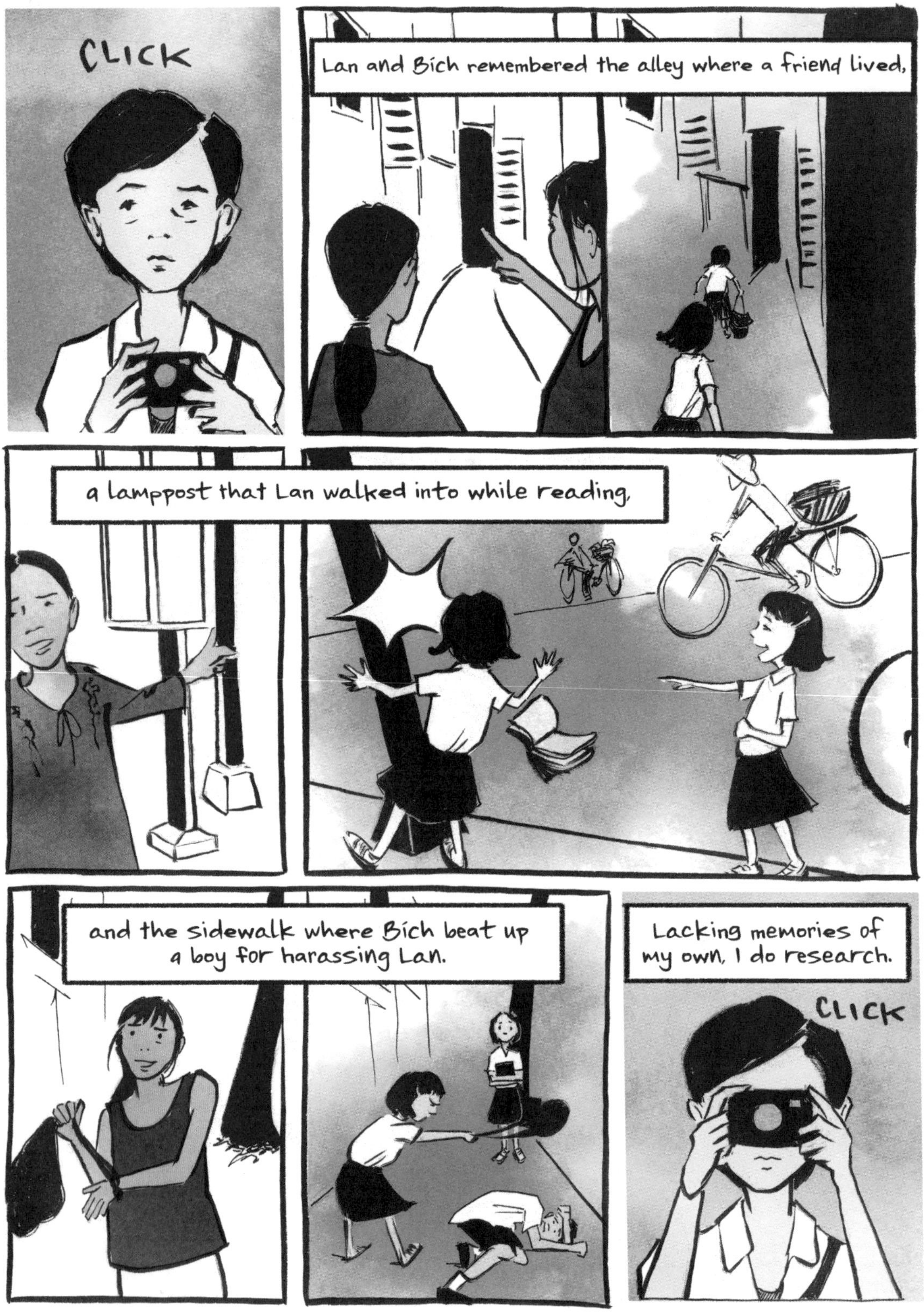
CLICK
Lan and Bích remembered the alley where a friend lived,
a lamppost that Lan walked into while reading,
and the sidewalk where Bích beat up a boy for harassing Lan.
Lacking memories of my own, I do research.
CLICK

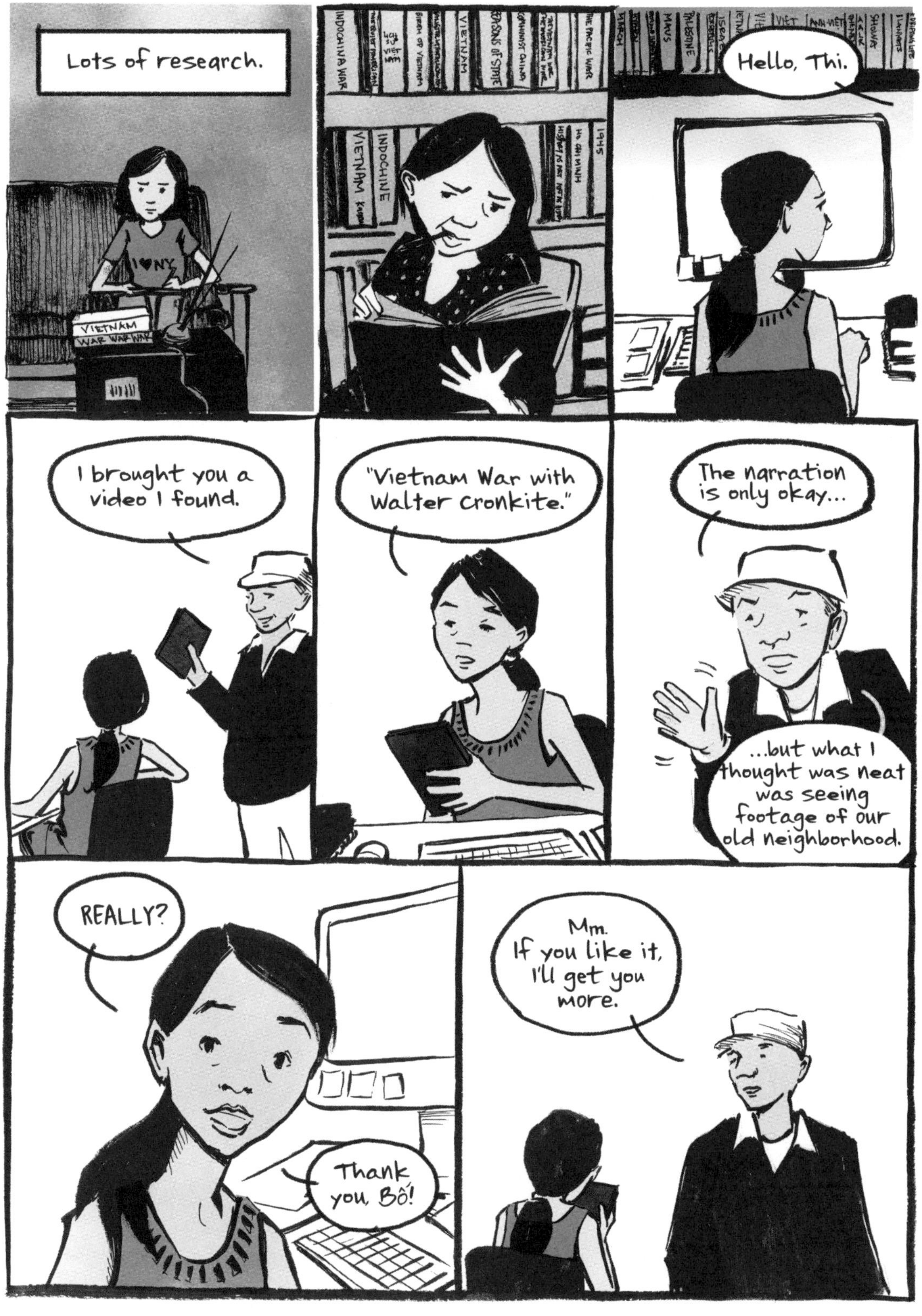
Lots of research.
VIETNAM
WAR WAR WAR
INDOCHINA WAR
VIETNAM
SEASONS OF STATE
THE PACIFIC WAR
VIETNAM
INDOCHINE
HO CHI MINH
1945
Hello, Thi.
I brought you a video I found.
"Vietnam War with Walter Cronkite."
The narration is only okay...
...but what I thought was neat was seeing footage of our old neighborhood.
REALLY?
Thank you, Bố!
Mm. If you like it, I'll get you more.

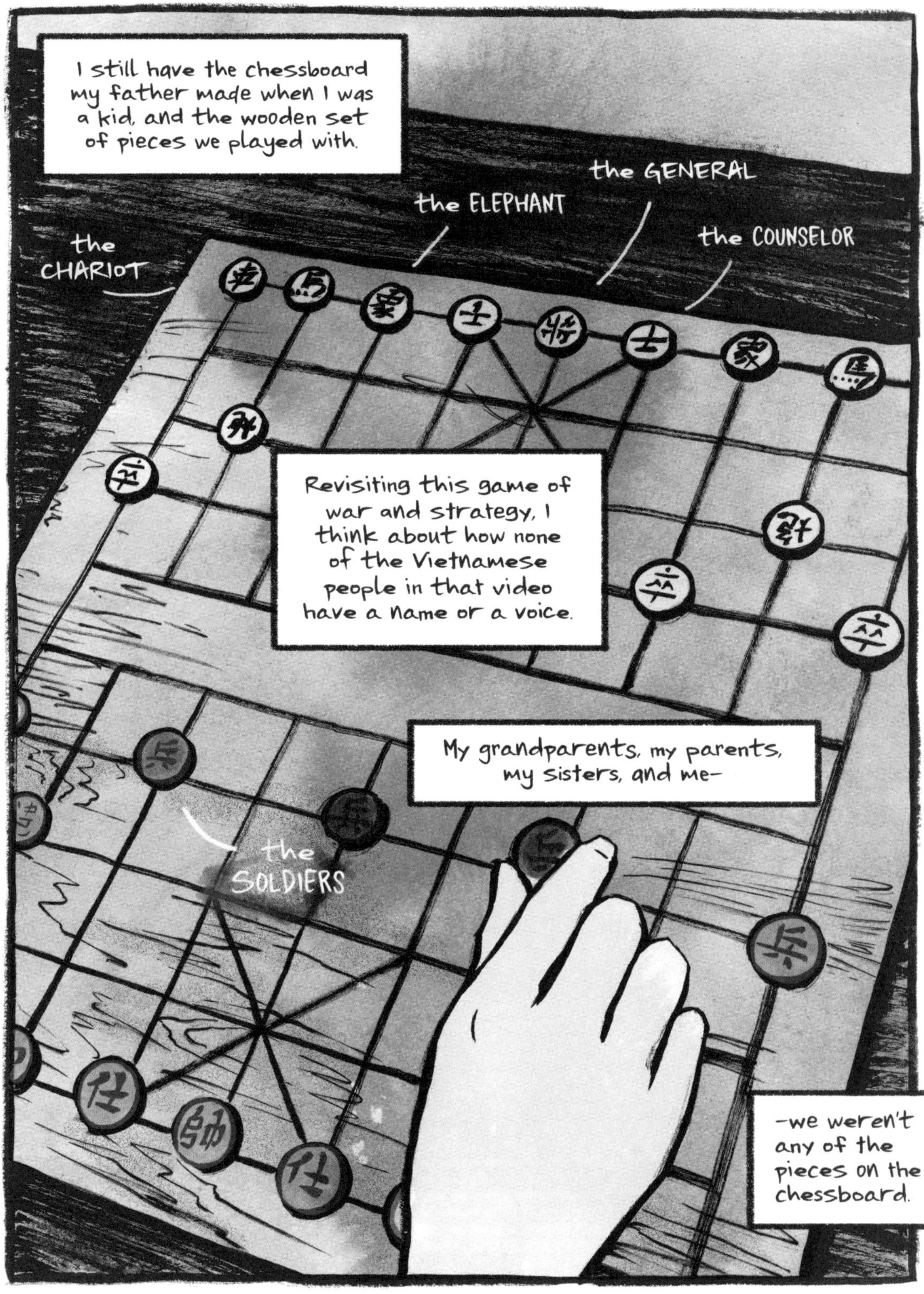
I still have the chessboard my father made when I was a kid, and the wooden set of pieces we played with.
the CHARIOT
the ELEPHANT
the GENERAL
the COUNSELOR
Revisiting this game of war and strategy, I think about how none of the Vietnamese people in that video have a name or a voice.
My grandparents, my parents, my sisters, and me-
the SOLDIERS
-we weren't any of the pieces on the chessboard.

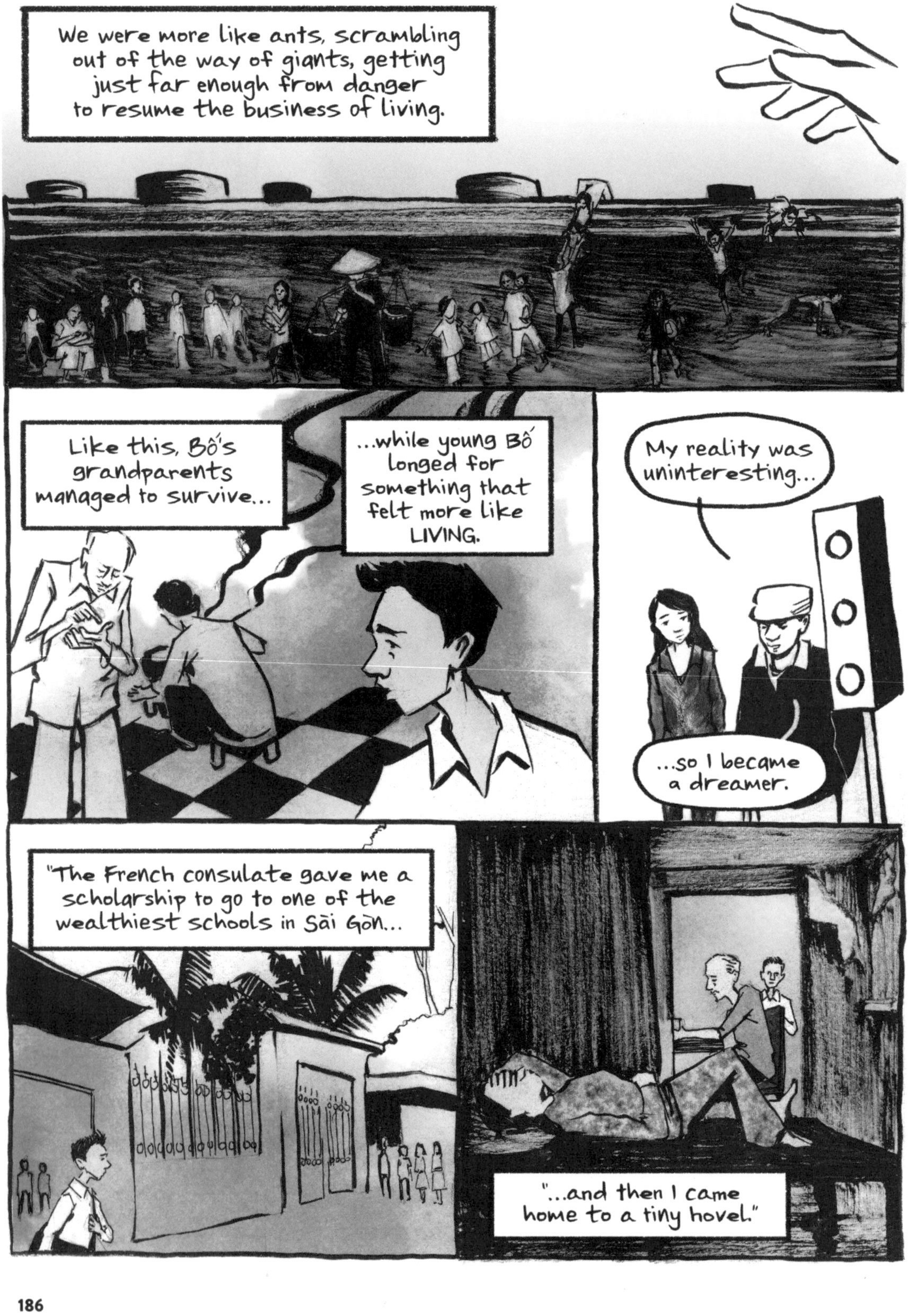
We were more like ants, scrambling out of the way of giants, getting just far enough from danger to resume the business of living.
Like this, Bố's grandparents managed to survive...
...while young Bố longed for something that felt more like LIVING.
My reality was uninteresting...
...so I became a dreamer.
"The French consulate gave me a scholarship to go to one of the wealthiest schools in Sài Gòn...
"...and then I came home to a tiny hovel."

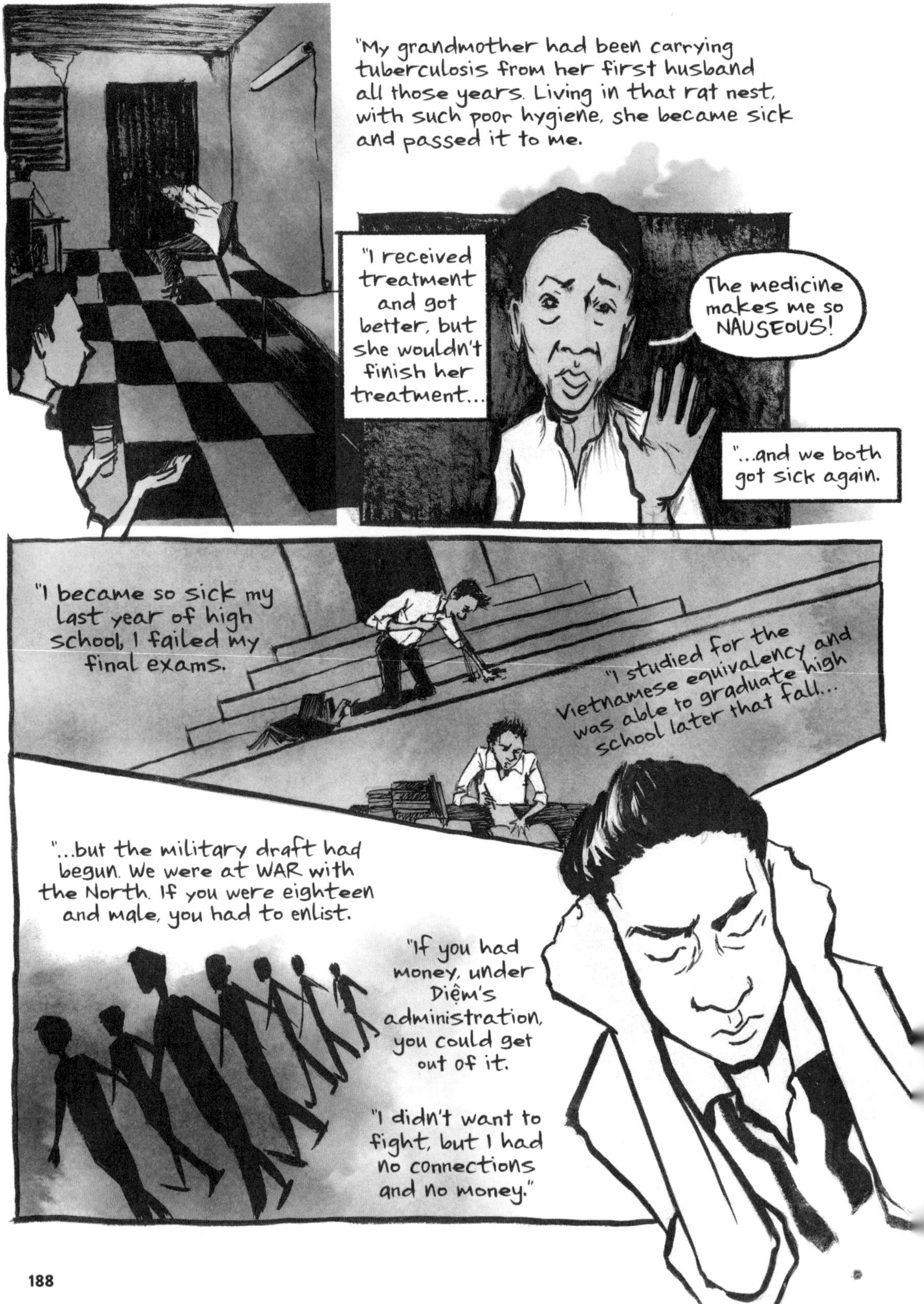
"My grandmother had been carrying tuberculosis from her first husband all those years. Living in that rat nest, with such poor hygiene, she became sick and passed it to me.
"I received treatment and got better, but she wouldn't finish her treatment...
The medicine makes me so NAUSEOUS!
"...and we both got sick again.
"I became so sick my last year of high school, I failed my final exams.
"I studied for the Vietnamese equivalency and was able to graduate high school later that fall...
"...but the military draft had begun. We were at WAR with the North. If you were eighteen and male, you had to enlist.
"If you had money, under Diệm's administration, you could get out of it.
"I didn't want to fight, but I had no connections and no money."

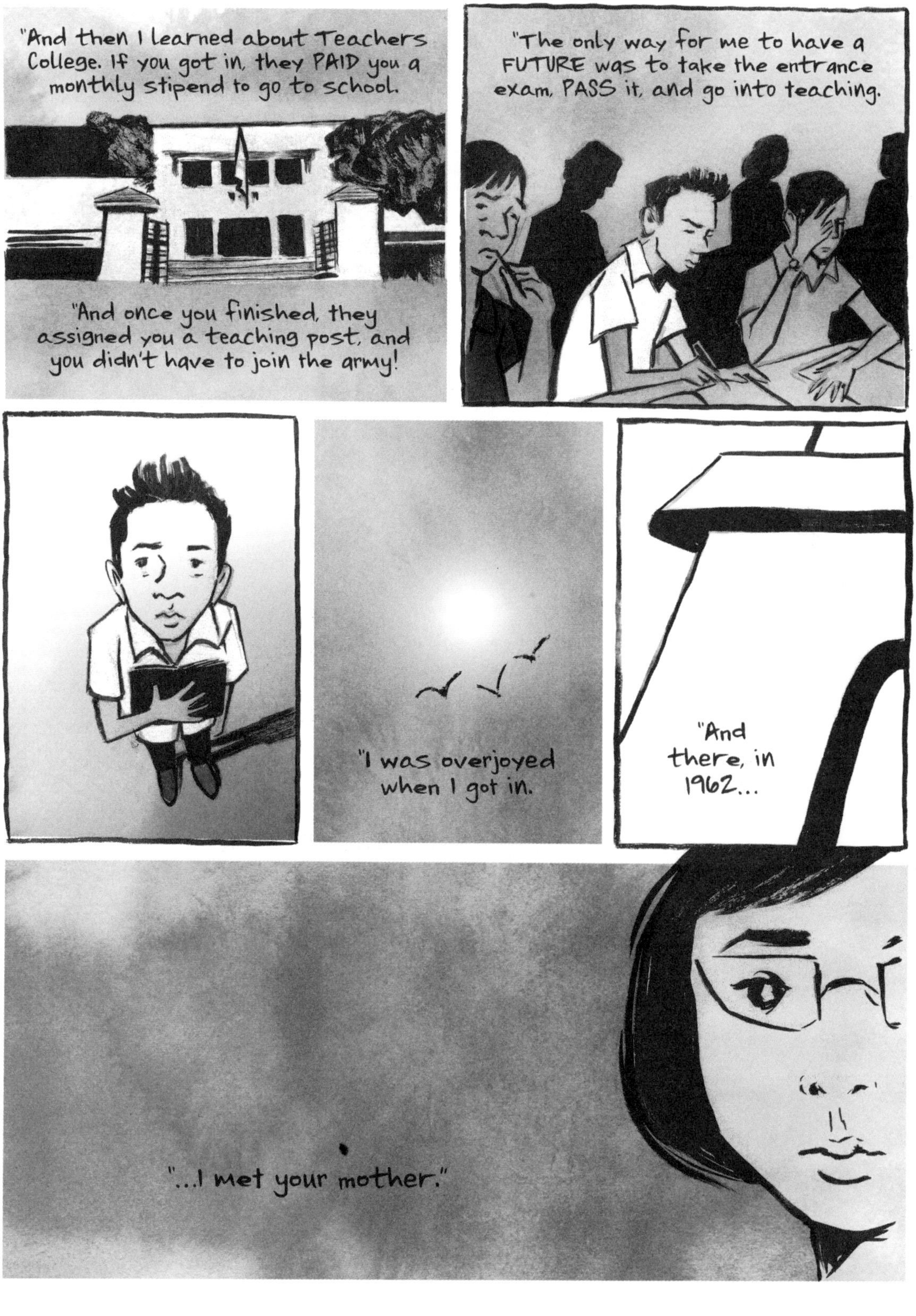
"And then I learned about Teachers College. If you got in, they PAID you a monthly stipend to go to school.
"And once you finished, they assigned you a teaching post, and you didn't have to join the army!
"The only way for me to have a FUTURE was to take the entrance exam, PASS it, and go into teaching.
"I was overjoyed when I got in.
"And there, in 1962...
"...I met your mother."

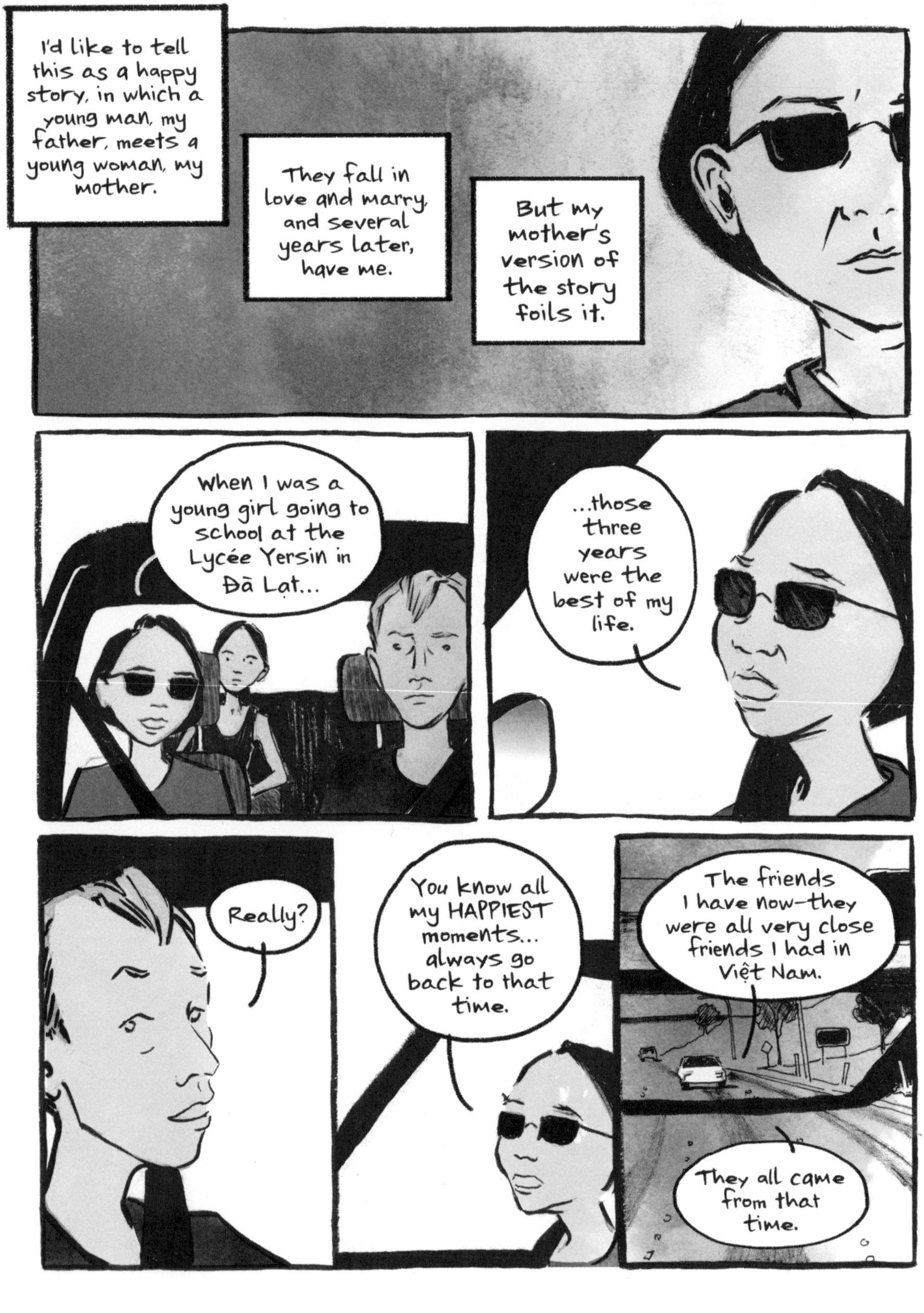
I'd like to tell this as a happy story, in which a young man, my father, meets a young woman, my mother.
They fall in love and marry, and several years later, have me.
But my mother's version of the story foils it.
When I was a young girl going to school at the Lycée Yersin in Đà Lạt...
...those three years were the best of my life.
Really?
You know all my HAPPIEST moments... always go back to that time.
The friends I have now—they were all very close friends I had in Việt Nam.
They all came from that time.

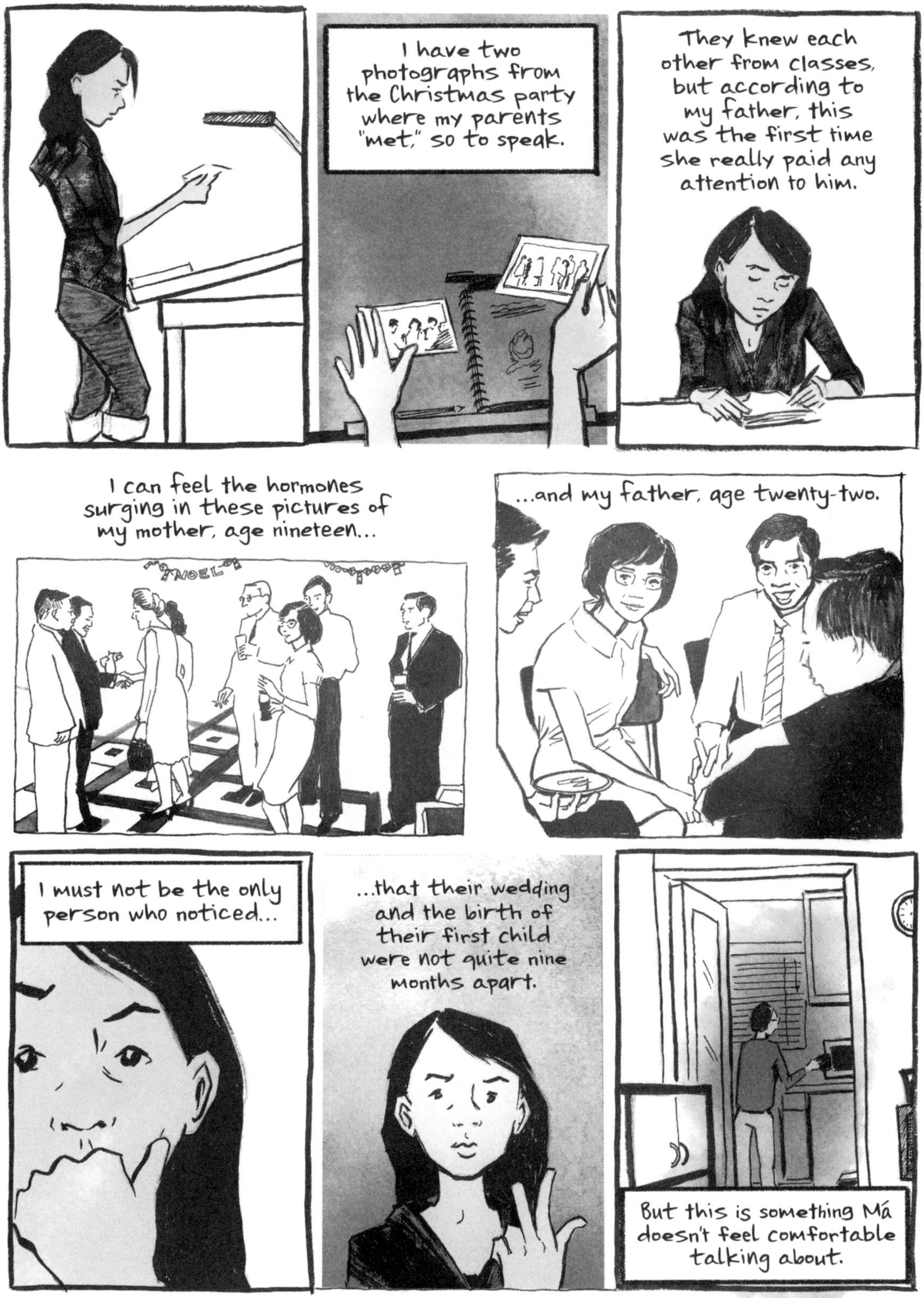
I have two photographs from the Christmas party where my parents "met," so to speak.
They knew each other from classes, but according to my father, this was the first time she really paid any attention to him.
I can feel the hormones surging in these pictures of my mother, age nineteen...
NOEL
...and my father, age twenty-two.
I must not be the only person who noticed...
...that their wedding and the birth of their first child were not quite nine months apart.
But this is something Má doesn't feel comfortable talking about.

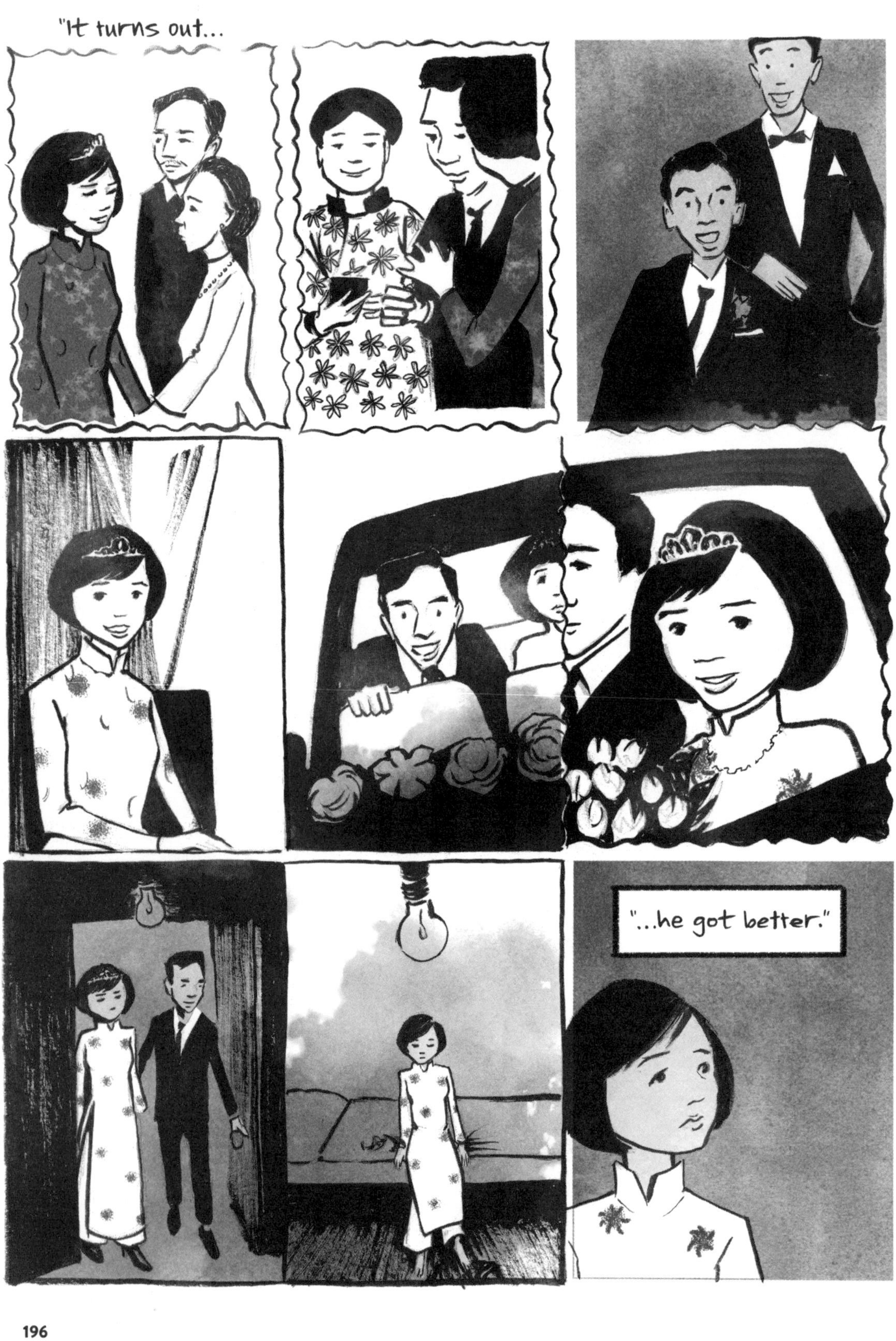
"It turns out...
"...he got better."

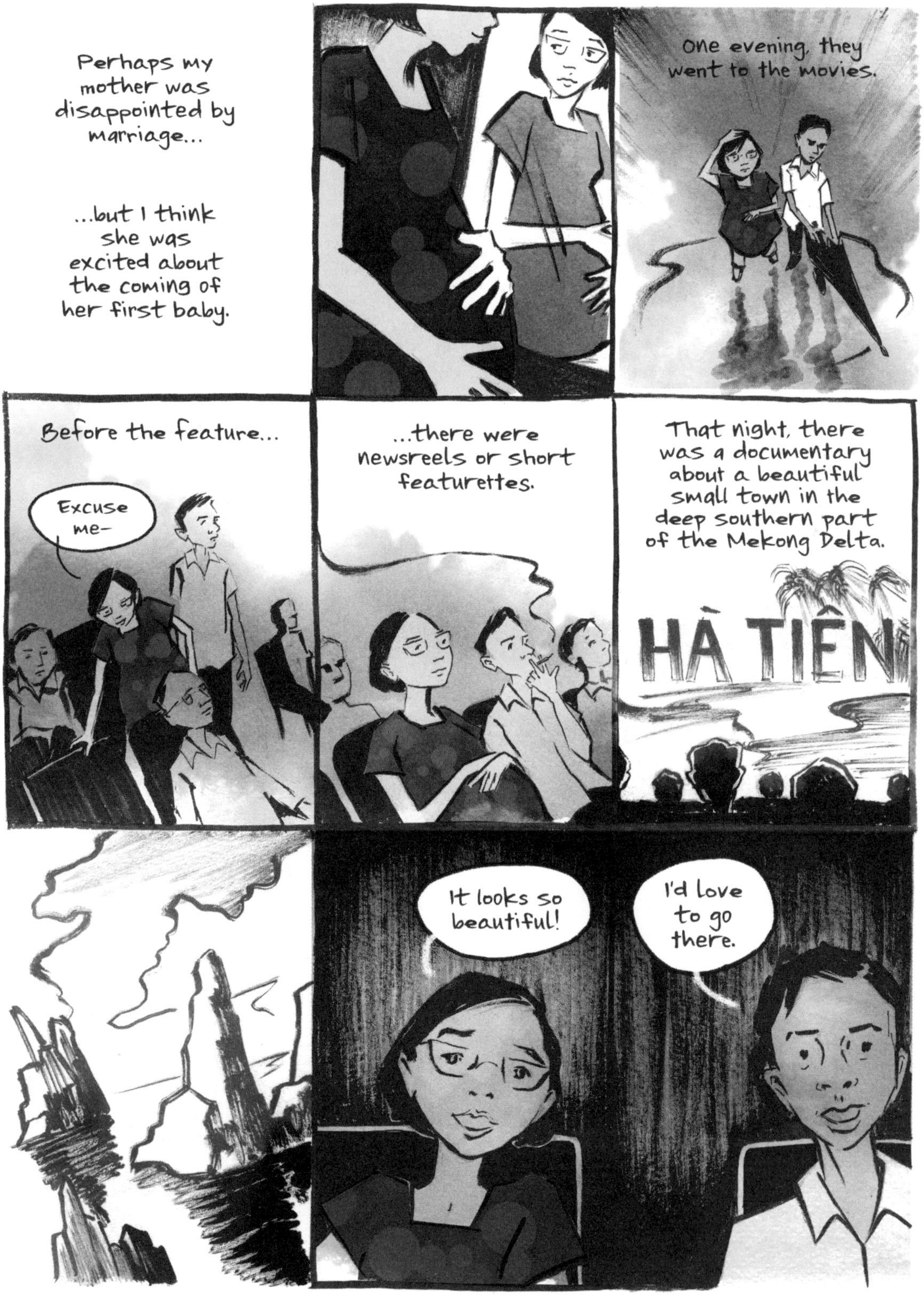
Perhaps my mother was disappointed by marriage...
...but I think she was excited about the coming of her first baby.
One evening, they went to the movies.
Before the feature...
Excuse me-
...there were newsreels or short featurettes.
That night, there was a documentary about a beautiful small town in the deep southern part of the Mekong Delta.
HÀ TIÊN
It looks so beautiful!
I'd love to go there.

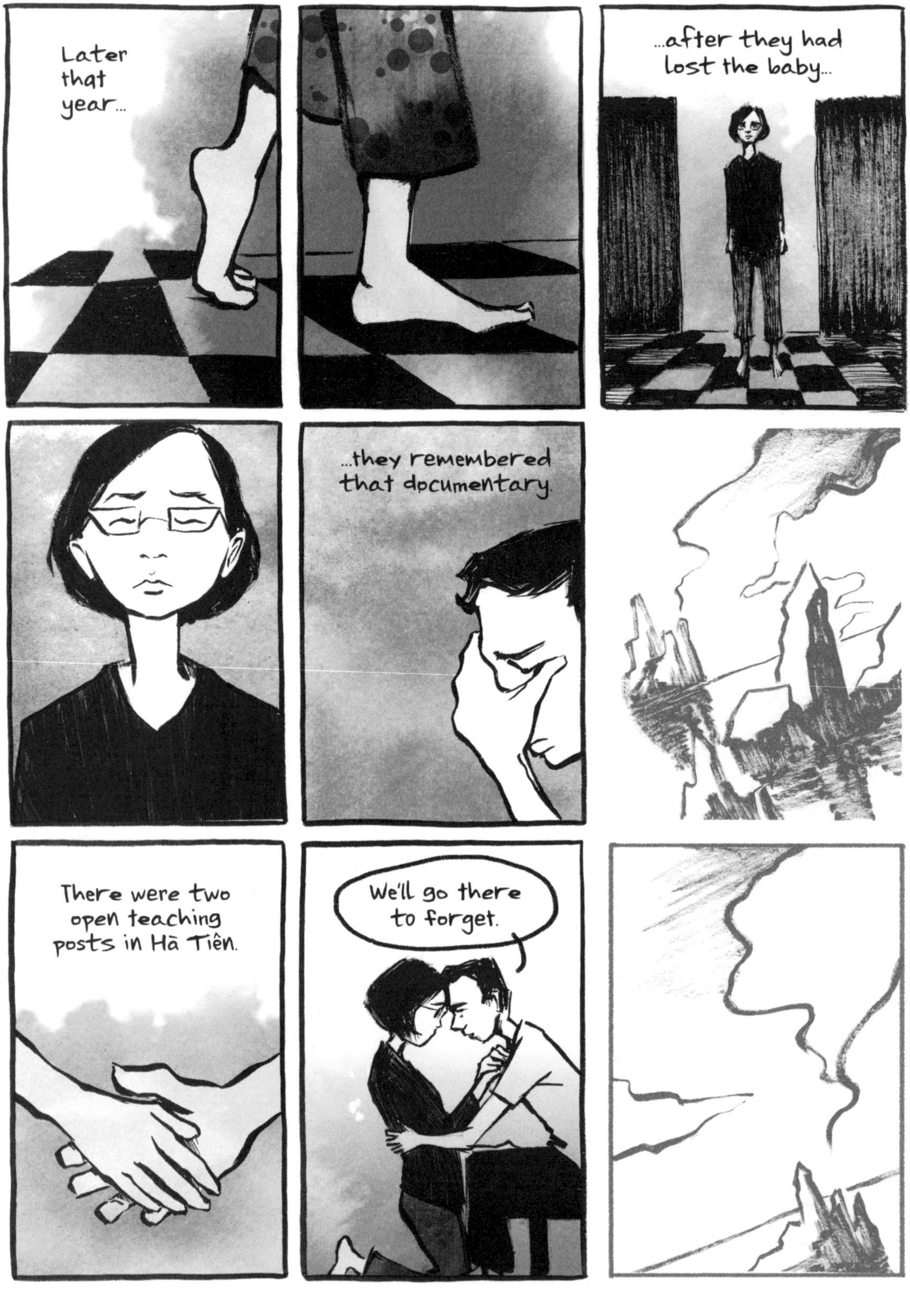
Later that year...
...after they had lost the baby...
...they remembered that documentary.
There were two open teaching posts in Hà Tiên.
We'll go there to forget.

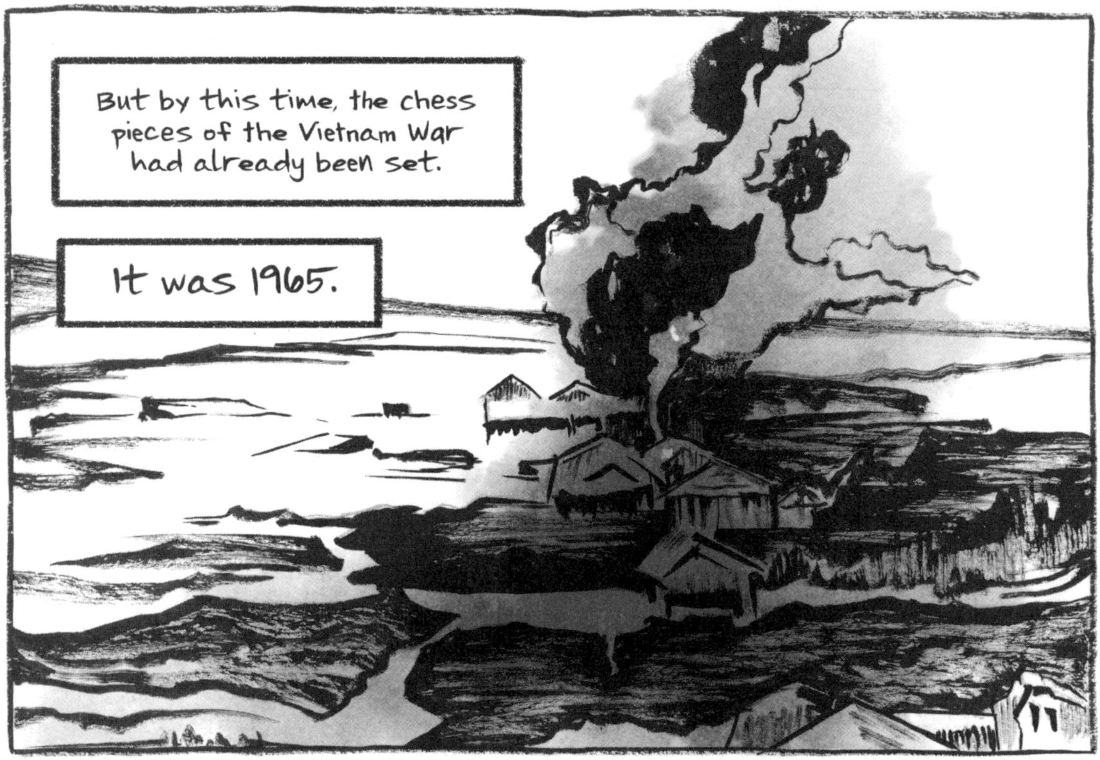
But by this time, the chess pieces of the Vietnam War had already been set.
It was 1965.

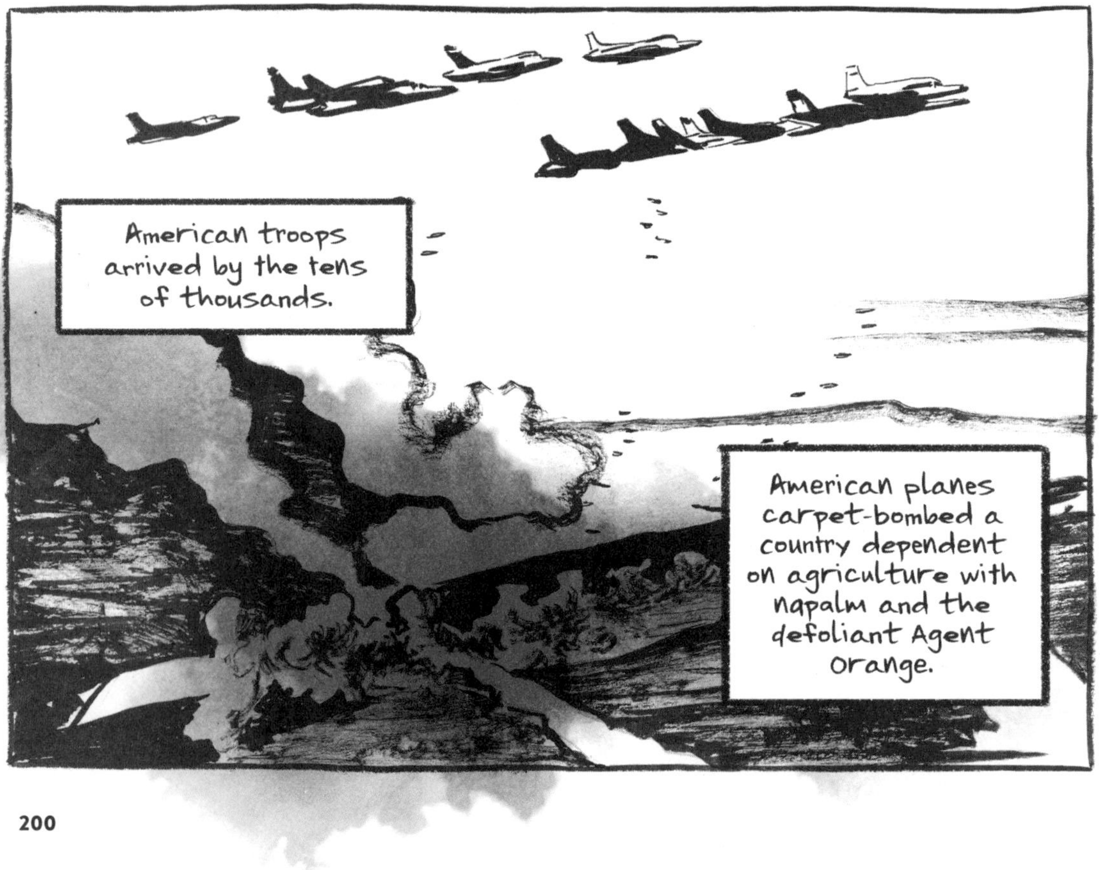
American troops arrived by the tens of thousands.
American planes carpet-bombed a country dependent on agriculture with napalm and the defoliant Agent Orange.

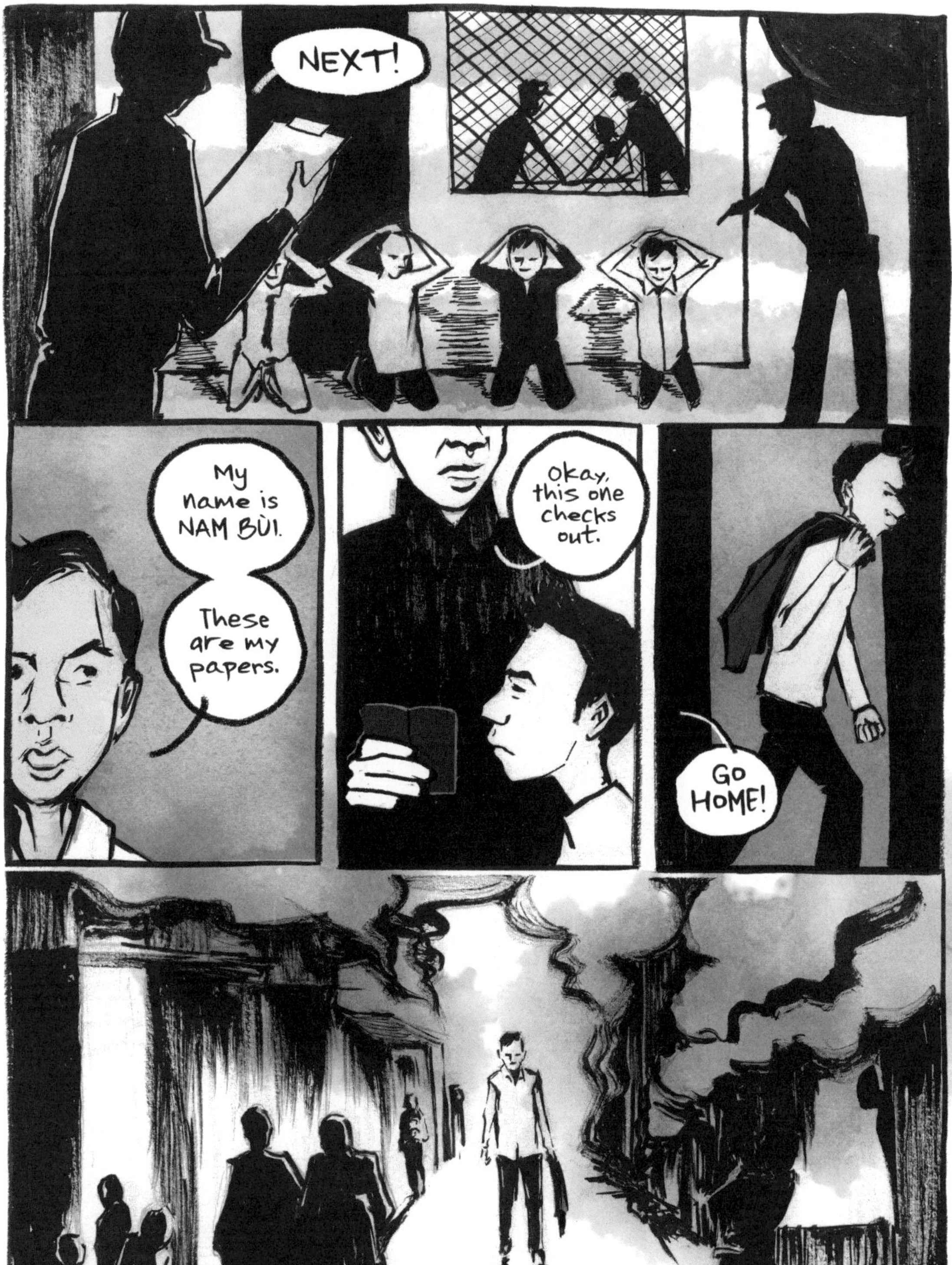
NEXT!
My name is NAM BÙI.
These are my papers.
Okay, this one checks out.
GO HOME!

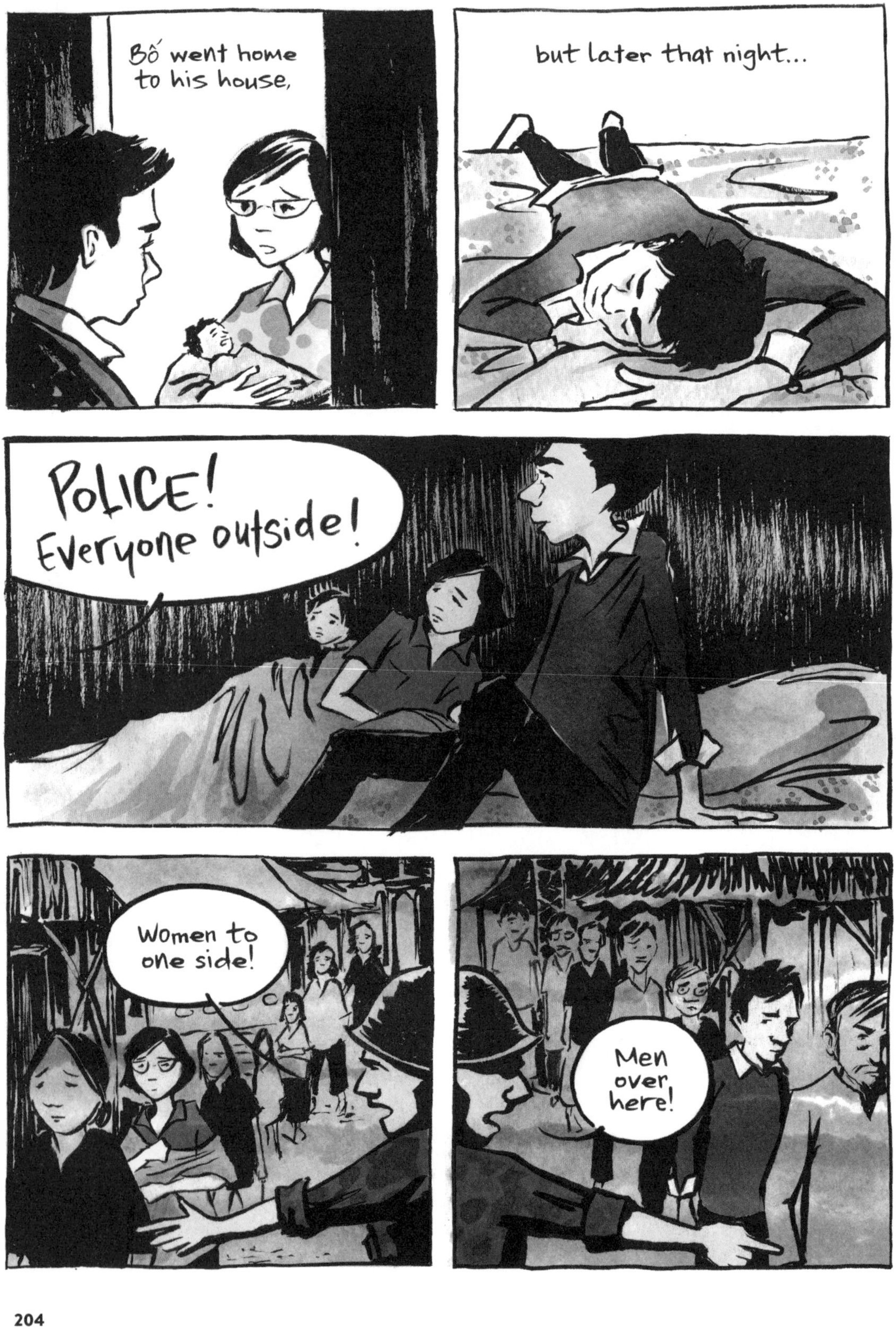
Bố went home to his house,
but later that night...
POLICE! Everyone outside!
Women to one side!
Men over here!

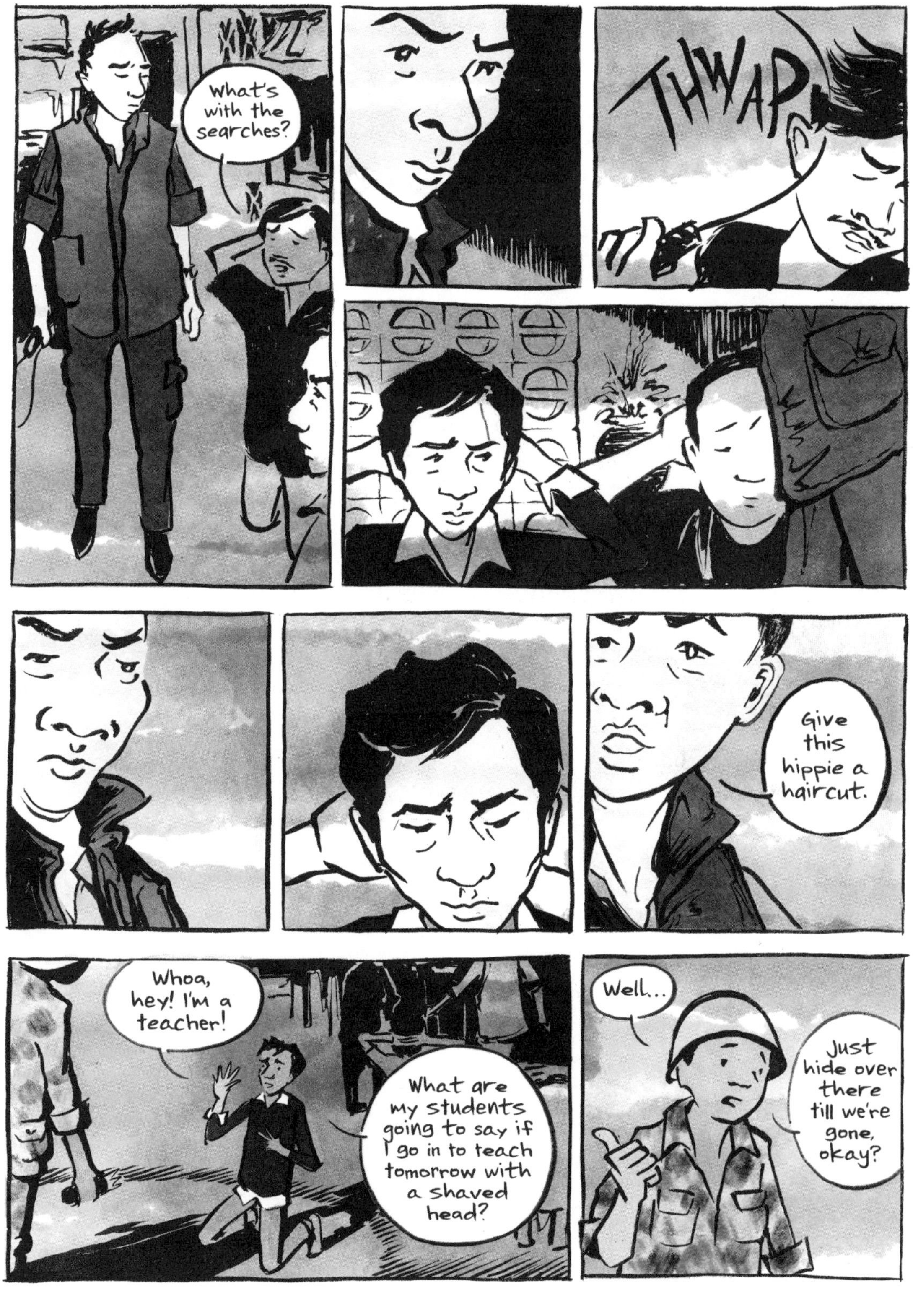
What's with the searches?
THWAP
Give this hippie a haircut.
Whoa, hey! I'm a teacher!
What are my students going to say if I go in to teach tomorrow with a shaved head?
Well...
Just hide over there till we're gone, okay?

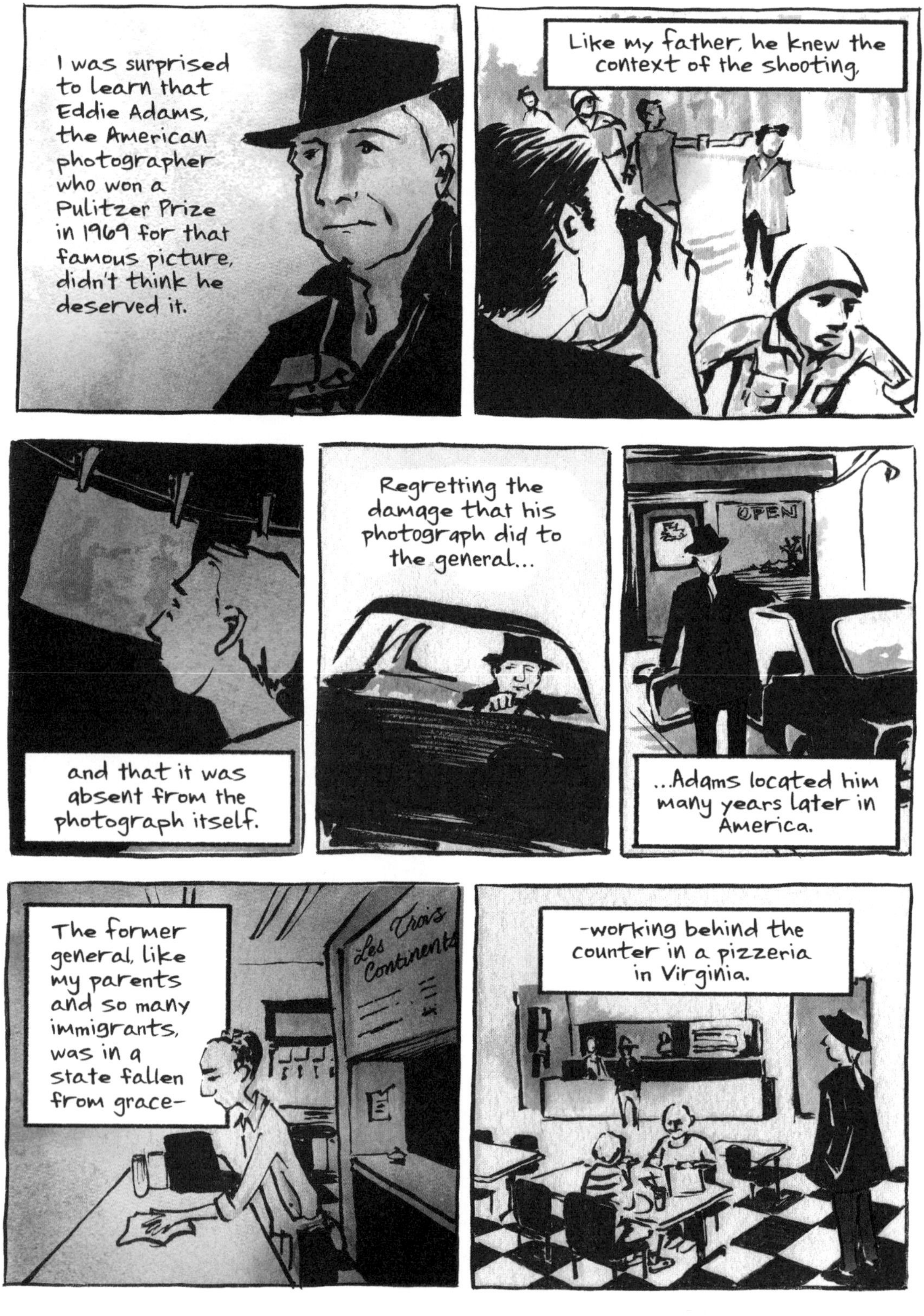
I was surprised to learn that Eddie Adams, the American photographer who won a Pulitzer Prize in 1969 for that famous picture, didn't think he deserved it.
Like my father, he knew the context of the shooting,
and that it was absent from the photograph itself.
Regretting the damage that his photograph did to the general...
OPEN
...Adams located him many years later in America.
The former general, like my parents and so many immigrants, was in a state fallen from grace-
Les Trois Continents
-working behind the counter in a pizzeria in Virginia.

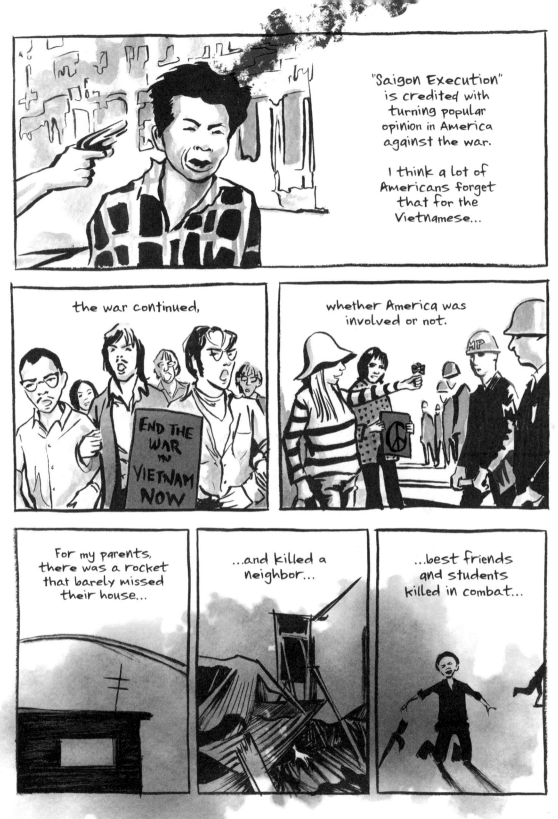

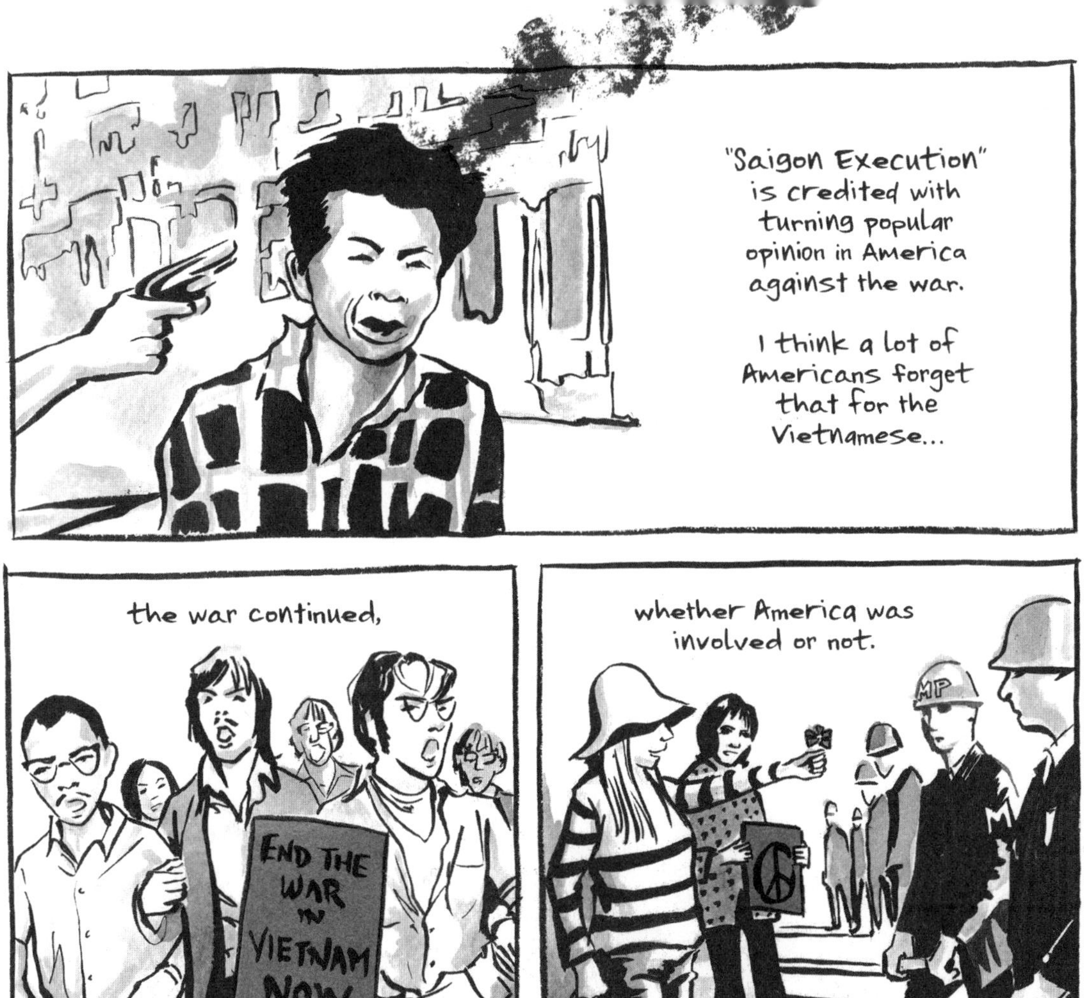
"Saigon Execution" is credited with turning popular opinion in America against the war.
I think a lot of Americans forget that for the Vietnamese...
the war continued,
END THE WAR IN VIETNAM NOW
whether America was involved or not.
MP
For my parents, there was a rocket that barely missed their house...
...and killed a neighbor...
...best friends and students killed in combat...

CHAPTER 7

HEROES AND LOSERS

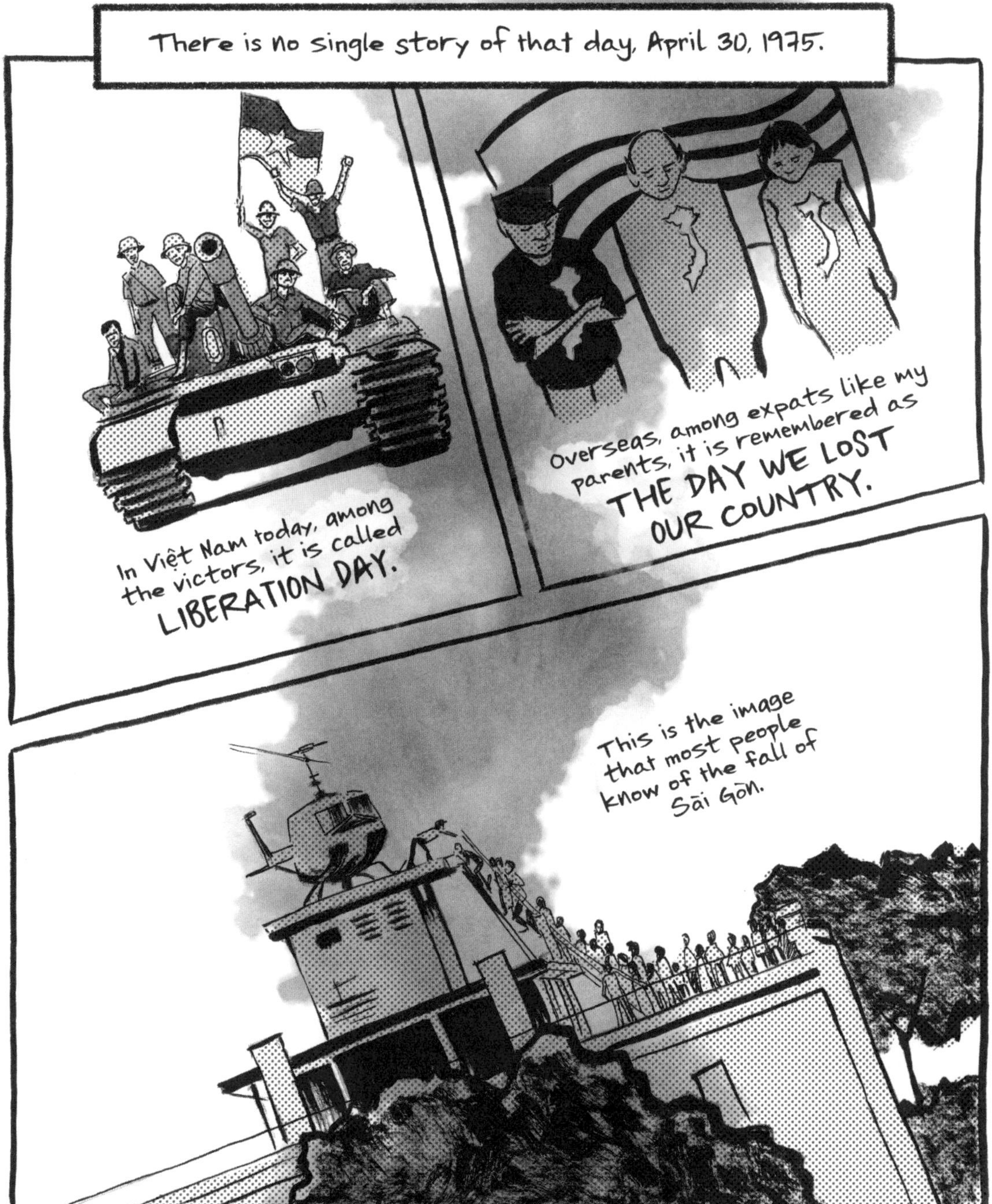
There is no single story of that day, April 30, 1975.
In Việt Nam today, among the victors, it is called LIBERATION DAY.
Overseas, among expats like my parents, it is remembered as THE DAY WE LOST OUR COUNTRY.
This is the image that most people know of the fall of Sài Gòn.

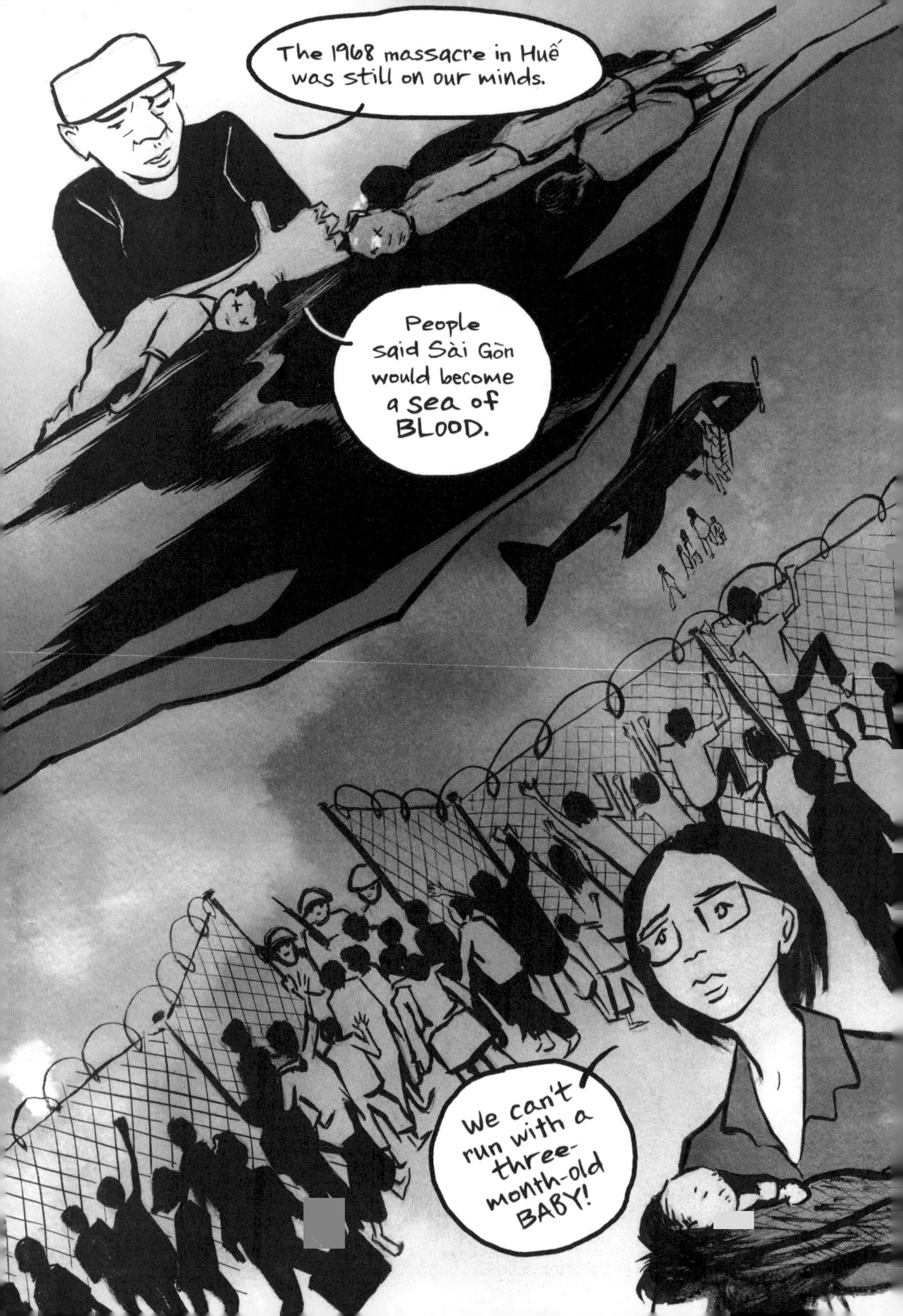
The 1968 massacre in Huế was still on our minds.
People said Sài Gòn would become a sea of BLOOD.
We can't run with a three-month-old BABY!

217

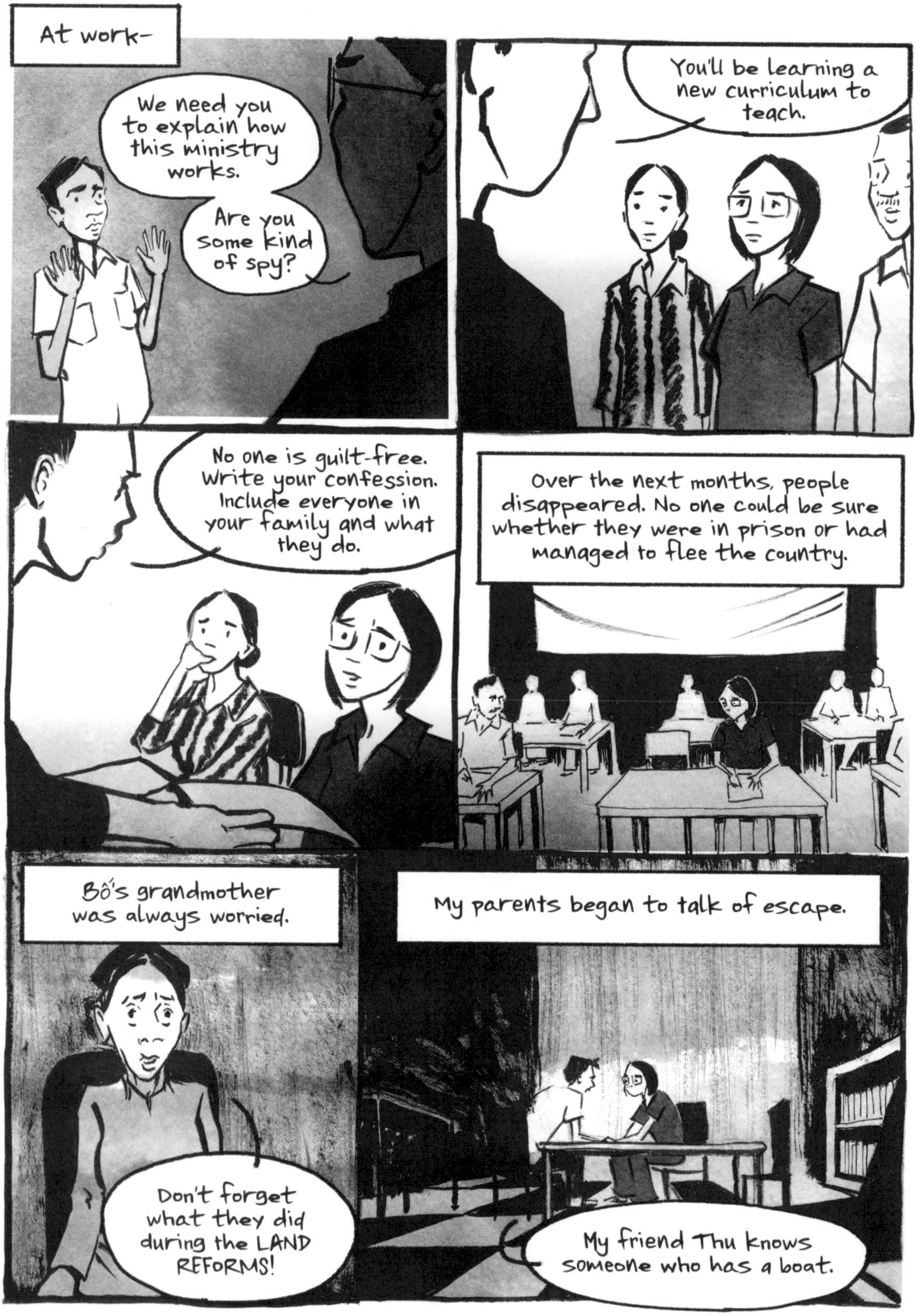
At work-
We need you to explain how this ministry works.
Are you some kind of spy?
You'll be learning a new curriculum to teach.
No one is guilt-free. Write your confession. Include everyone in your family and what they do.
Over the next months, people disappeared. No one could be sure whether they were in prison or had managed to flee the country.
Bố's grandmother was always worried.
Don't forget what they did during the LAND REFORMS!
My parents began to talk of escape.
My friend Thu knows someone who has a boat.

224

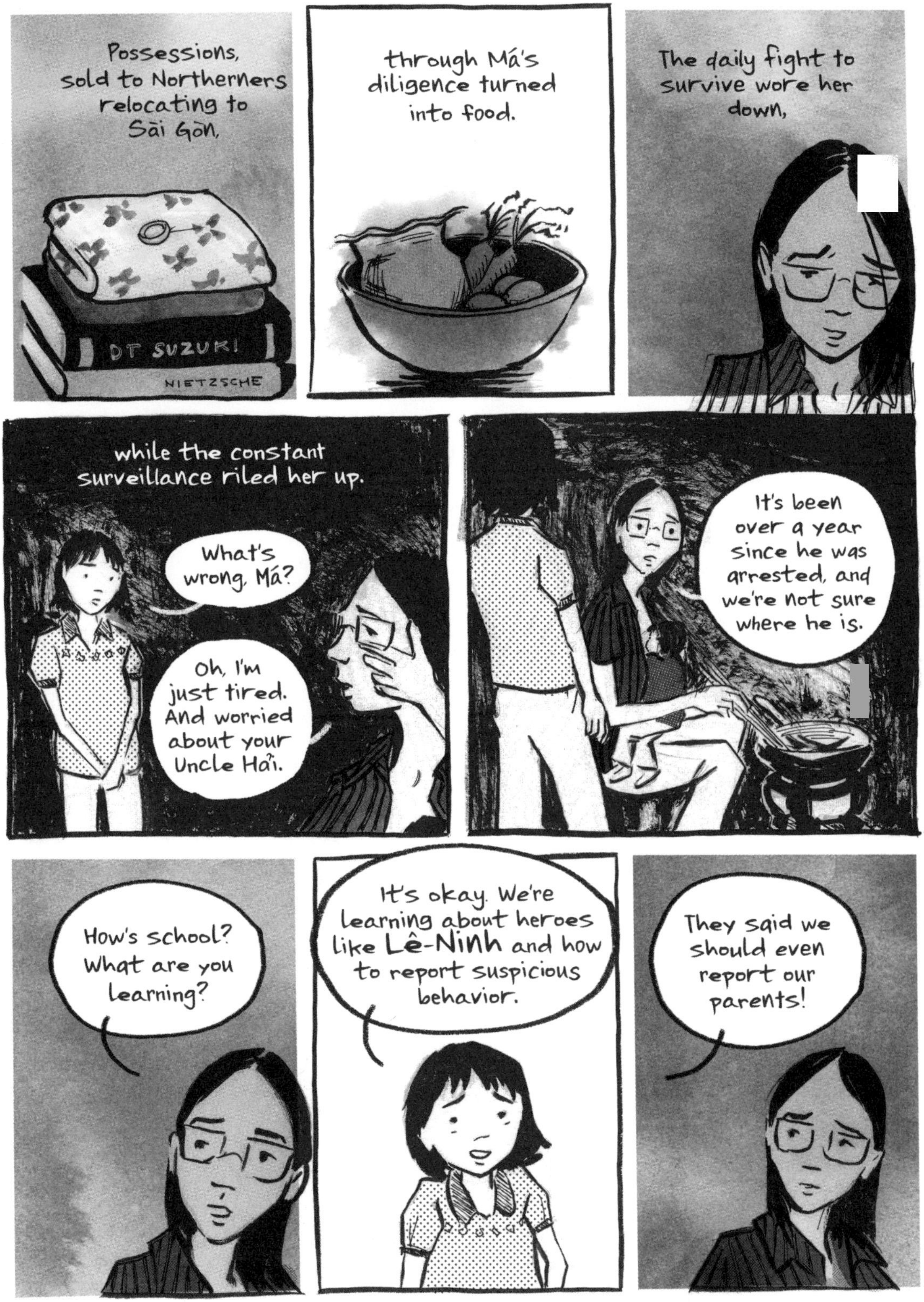

Possessions, sold to Northerners relocating to Sài Gòn,
DT SUZUKI
NIETZSCHE
through Má's diligence turned into food.
The daily fight to survive wore her down,
while the constant surveillance riled her up.
What's wrong, Má?
Oh, I'm just tired. And worried about your Uncle Hải.
It's been over a year since he was arrested, and we're not sure where he is.
How's school? What are you learning?
It's okay. We're learning about heroes like Lê-Ninh and how to report suspicious behavior.
They said we should even report our parents!

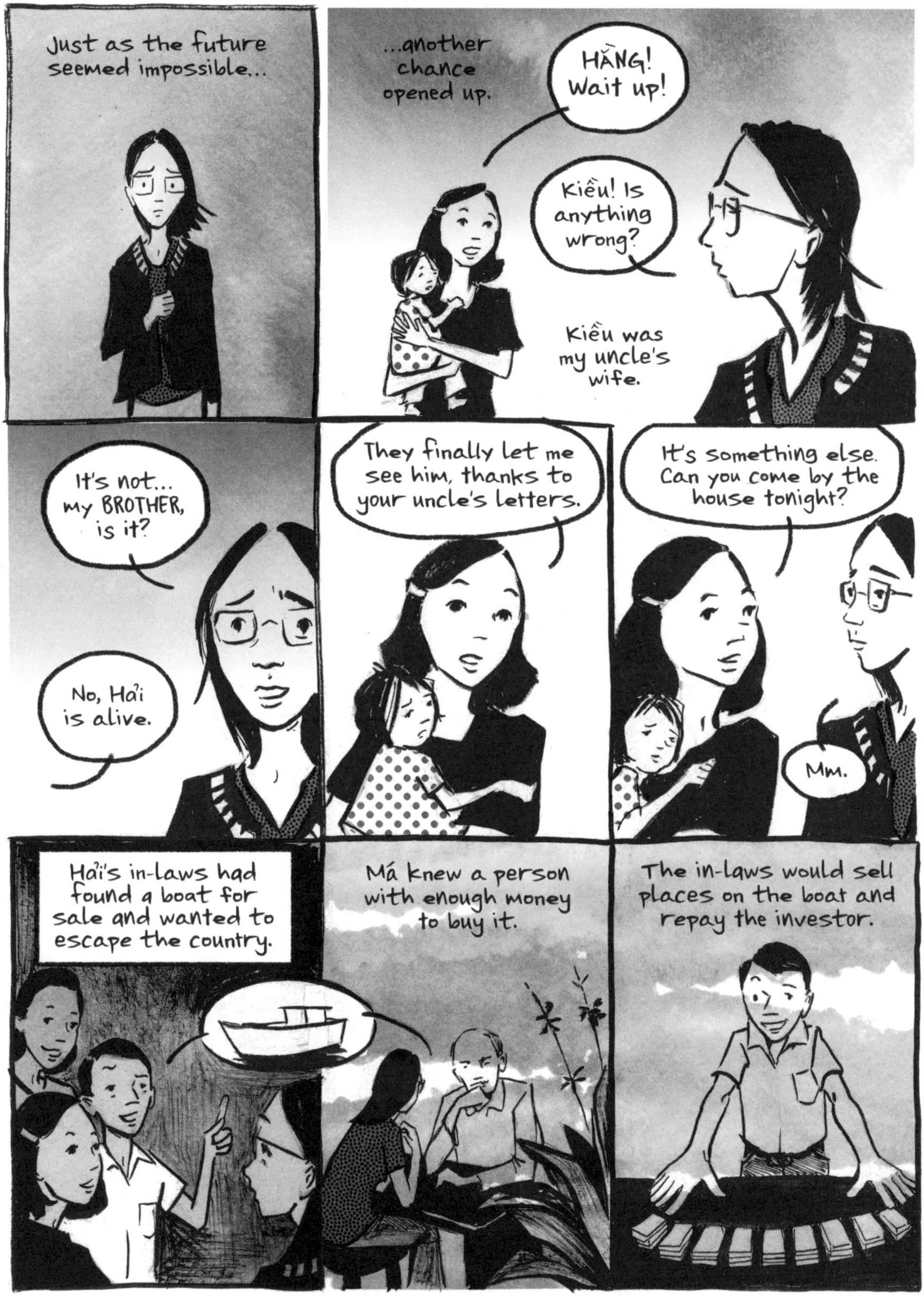

Just as the future seemed impossible...
...another chance opened up.
HẰNG! Wait up!
Kiều! Is anything wrong?
Kiều was my uncle's wife.
It's not... my BROTHER, is it?
No, Hải is alive.
They finally let me see him, thanks to your uncle's letters.
It's something else. Can you come by the house tonight?
Mm.
Hải's in-laws had found a boat for sale and wanted to escape the country.
Má knew a person with enough money to buy it.
The in-laws would sell places on the boat and repay the investor.

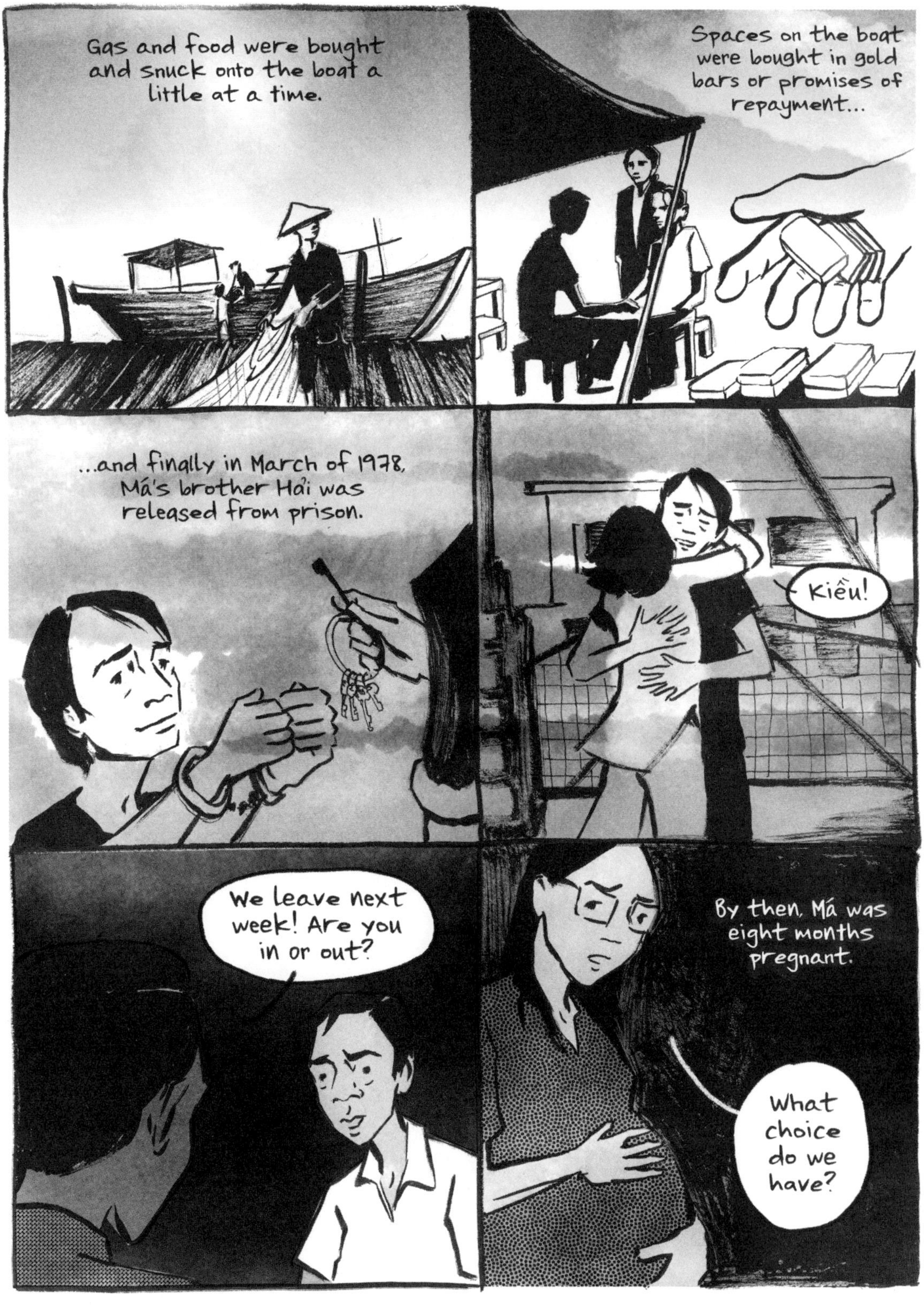
Gas and food were bought and snuck onto the boat a little at a time.
Spaces on the boat were bought in gold bars or promises of repayment...
...and finally in March of 1978, Má's brother Hải was released from prison.
Kiều!
We leave next week! Are you in or out?
By then, Má was eight months pregnant.
What choice do we have?

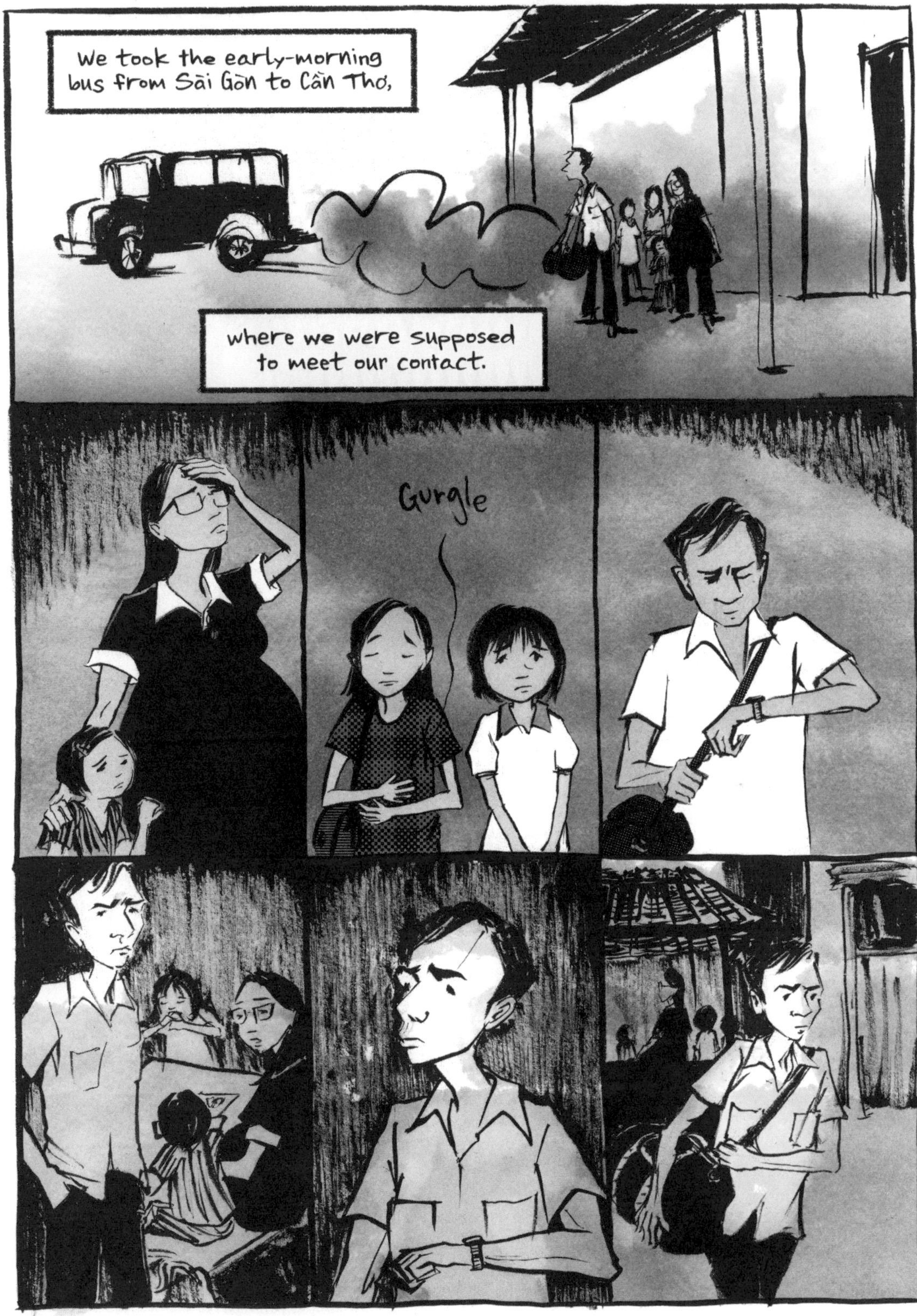
We took the early-morning bus from Sài Gòn to Cần Thơ,
where we were supposed to meet our contact.
Gurgle

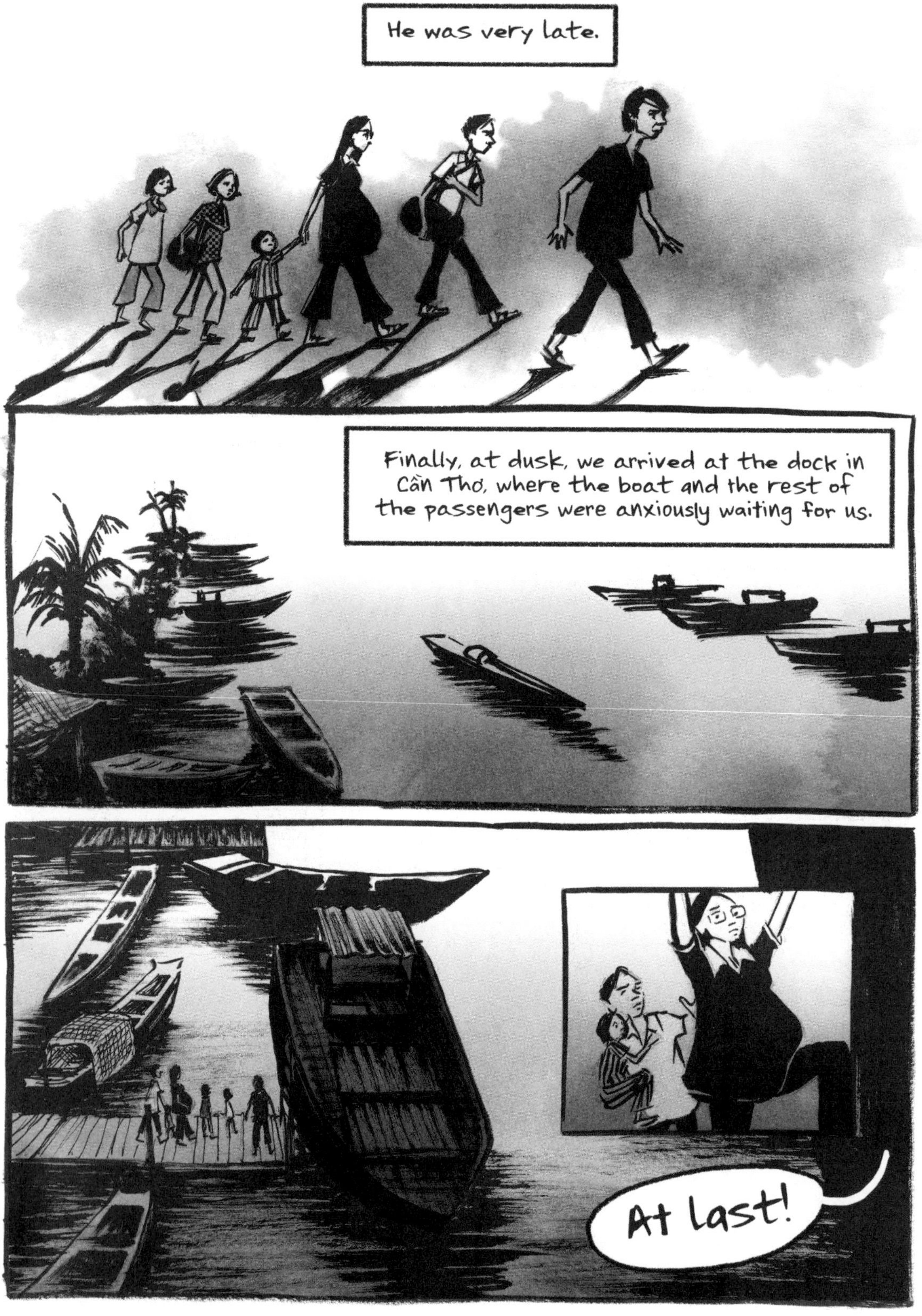
He was very late.
Finally, at dusk, we arrived at the dock in Cần Thơ, where the boat and the rest of the passengers were anxiously waiting for us.
At last!

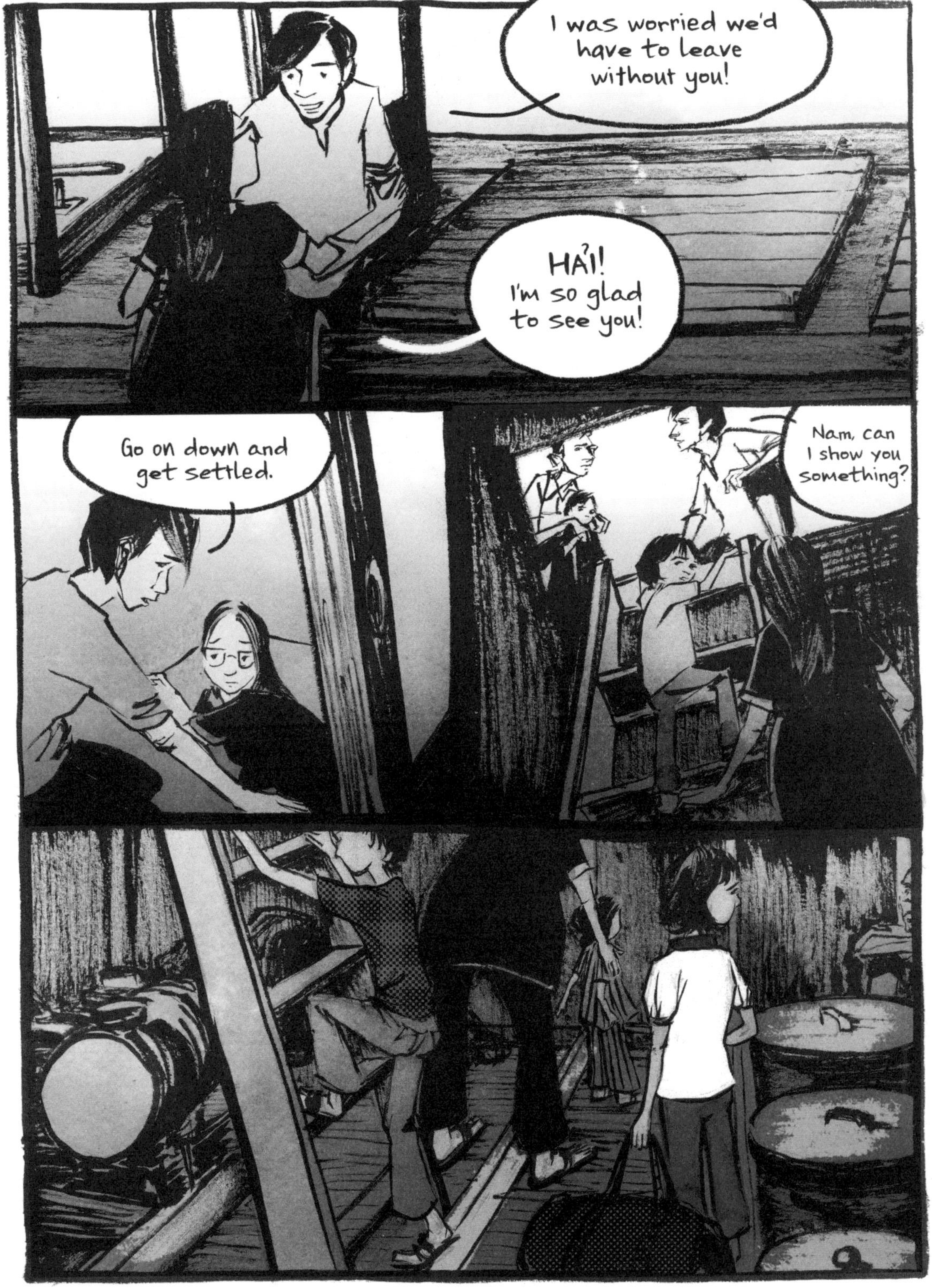
I was worried we'd have to leave without you!
HẢI! I'm so glad to see you!
Go on down and get settled.
Nam, can I show you something?

234

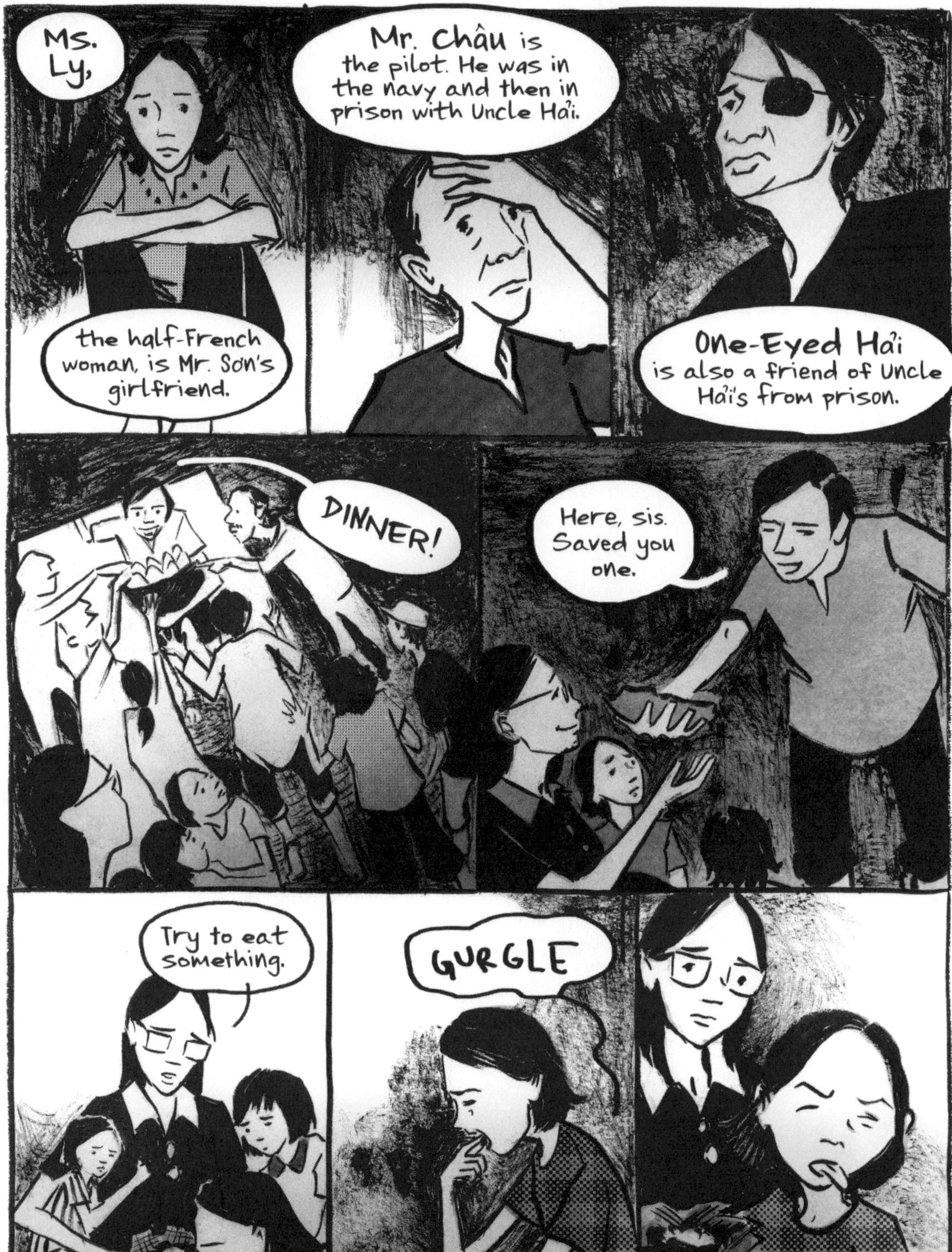
Ms. Ly,
the half-French woman, is Mr. Sơn's girlfriend.
Mr. Châu is the pilot. He was in the navy and then in prison with Uncle Hải.
One-Eyed Hải is also a friend of Uncle Hải's from prison.
DINNER!
Here, sis. Saved you one.
Try to eat something.
GURGLE
BLAK

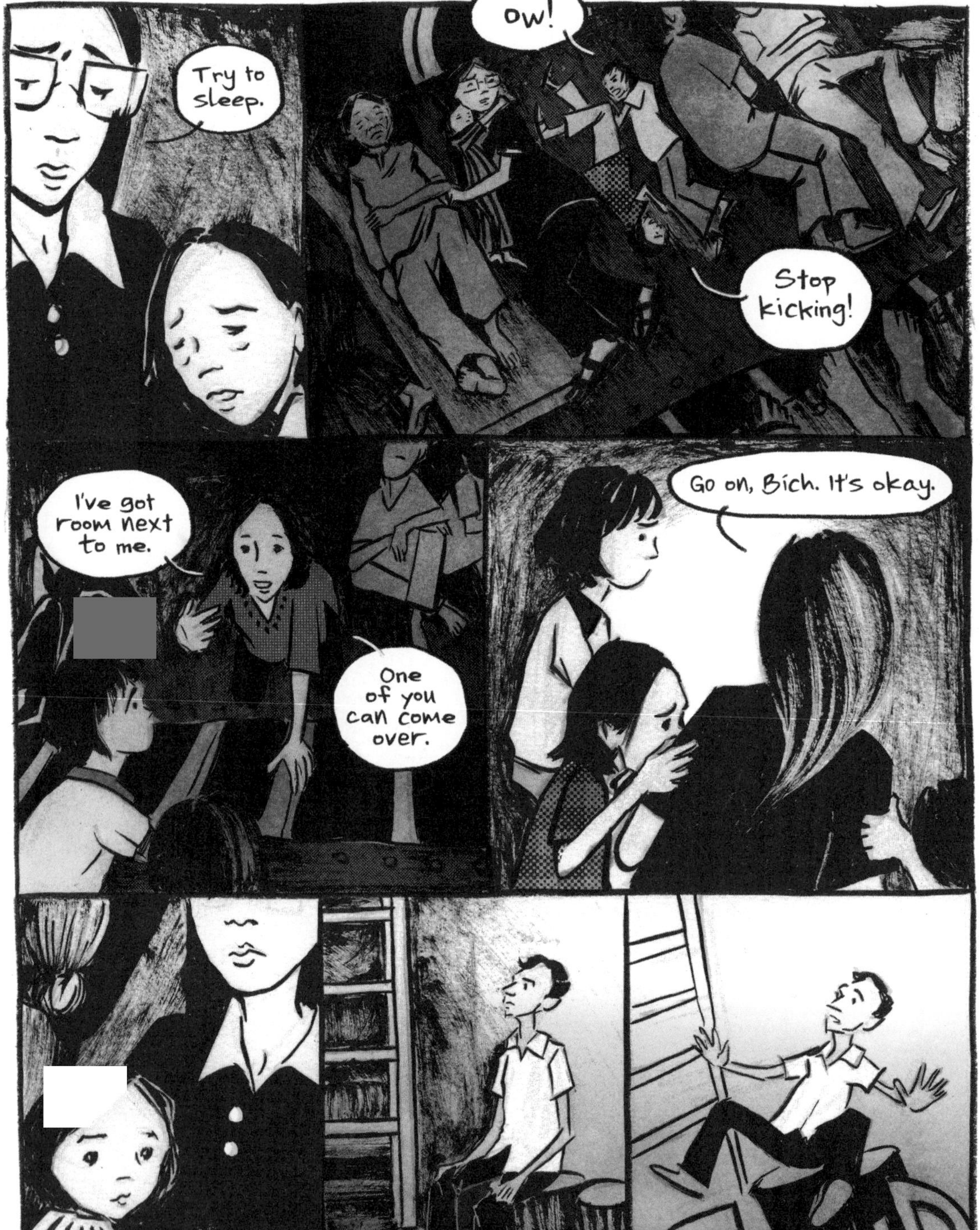

Try to sleep.
Ow!
Stop kicking!
I've got room next to me.
One of you can come over.
Go on, Bích. It's okay.
THUD

238

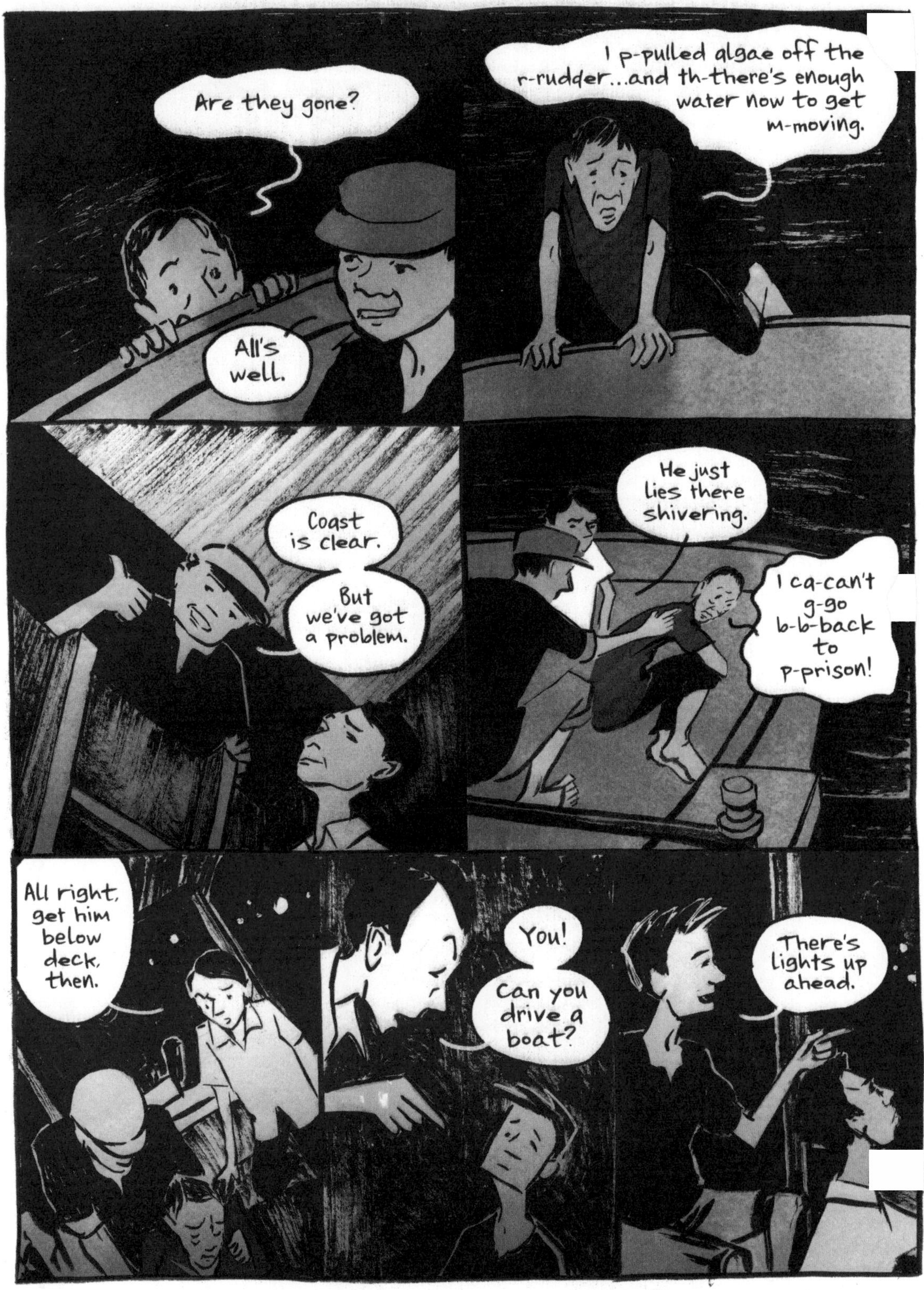

Are they gone?
All's well.
I p-pulled algae off the r-rudder...and th-there's enough water now to get m-moving.
Coast is clear.
But we've got a problem.
He just lies there shivering.
I ca-can't g-go b-b-back to p-prison!
All right, get him below deck, then.
You!
Can you drive a boat?
There's lights up ahead.

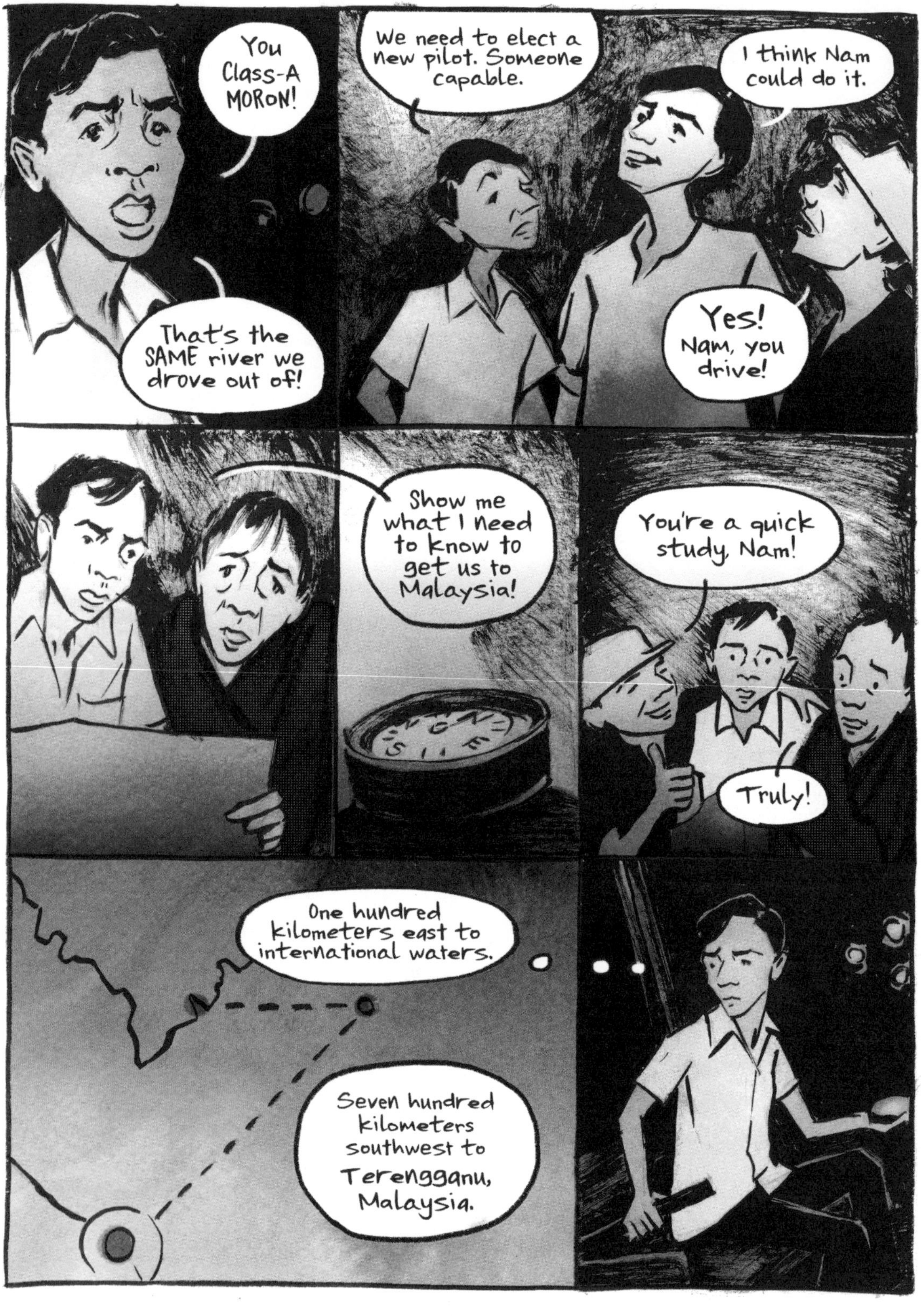
You Class-A MORON!
That's the SAME river we drove out of!
We need to elect a new pilot. Someone capable.
I think Nam could do it.
Yes! Nam, you drive!
Show me what I need to know to get us to Malaysia!
N
S
E
You're a quick study, Nam!
Truly!
One hundred kilometers east to international waters.
Seven hundred kilometers southwest to Terengganu, Malaysia.

241

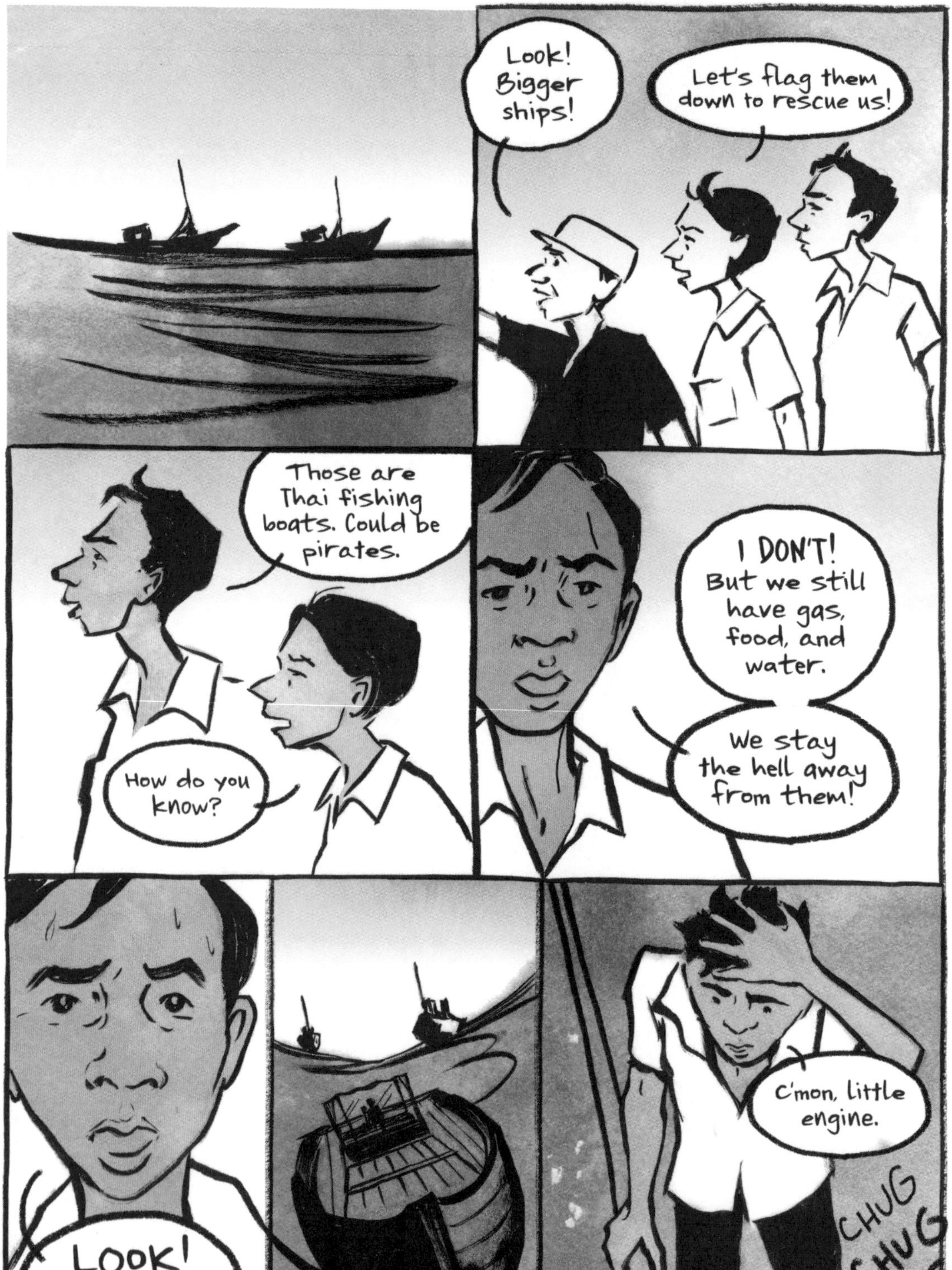
Look! Bigger ships!
Let's flag them down to rescue us!
Those are Thai fishing boats. Could be pirates.
How do you know?
I DON'T! But we still have gas, food, and water.
We stay the hell away from them!
LOOK! When I turn, they follow.
C'mon, little engine.
CHUG CHUG CHUG

243

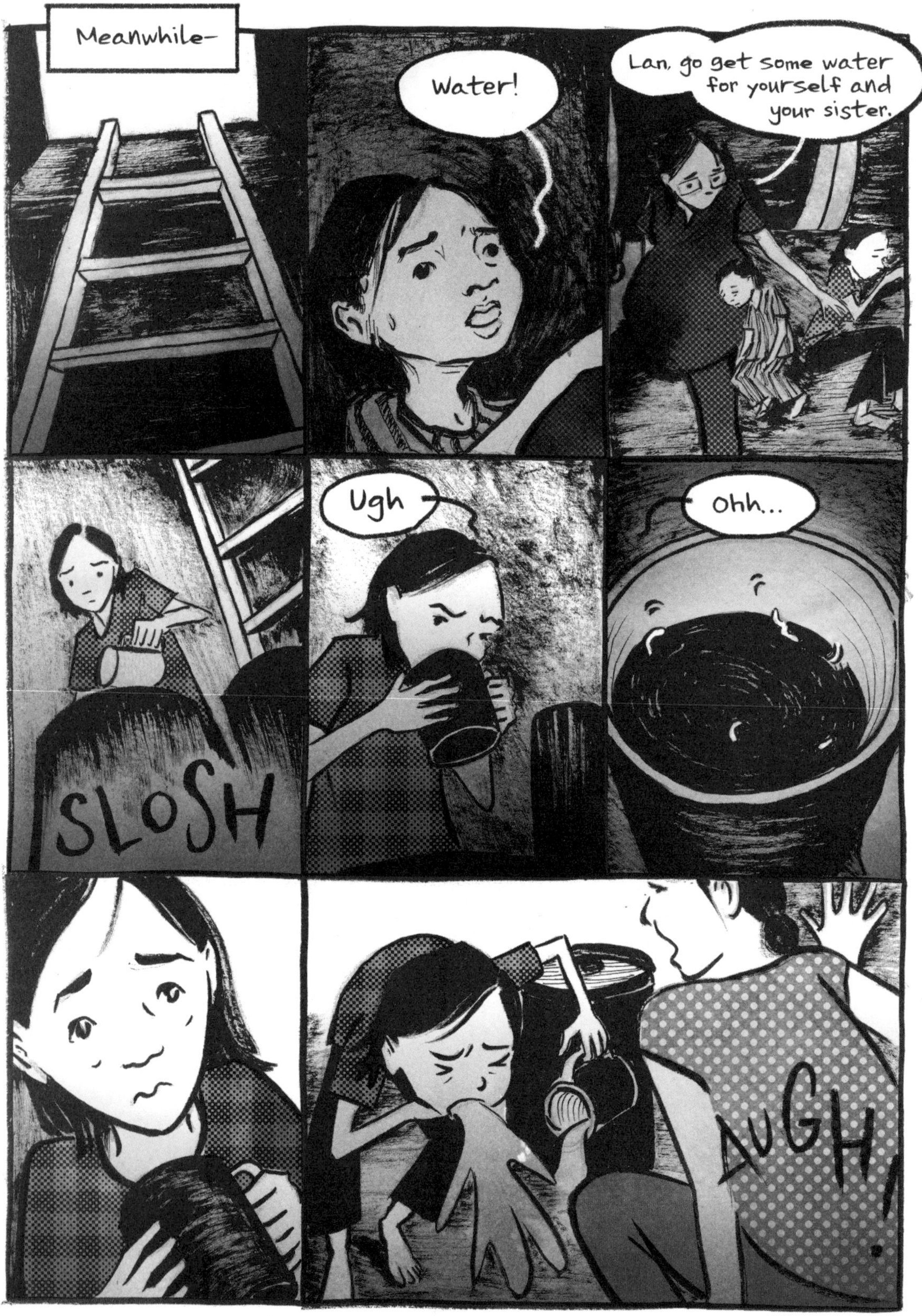
Meanwhile-
Water!
Lan, go get some water for yourself and your sister.
SLOSH
Ugh
Ohh...
AUGH!

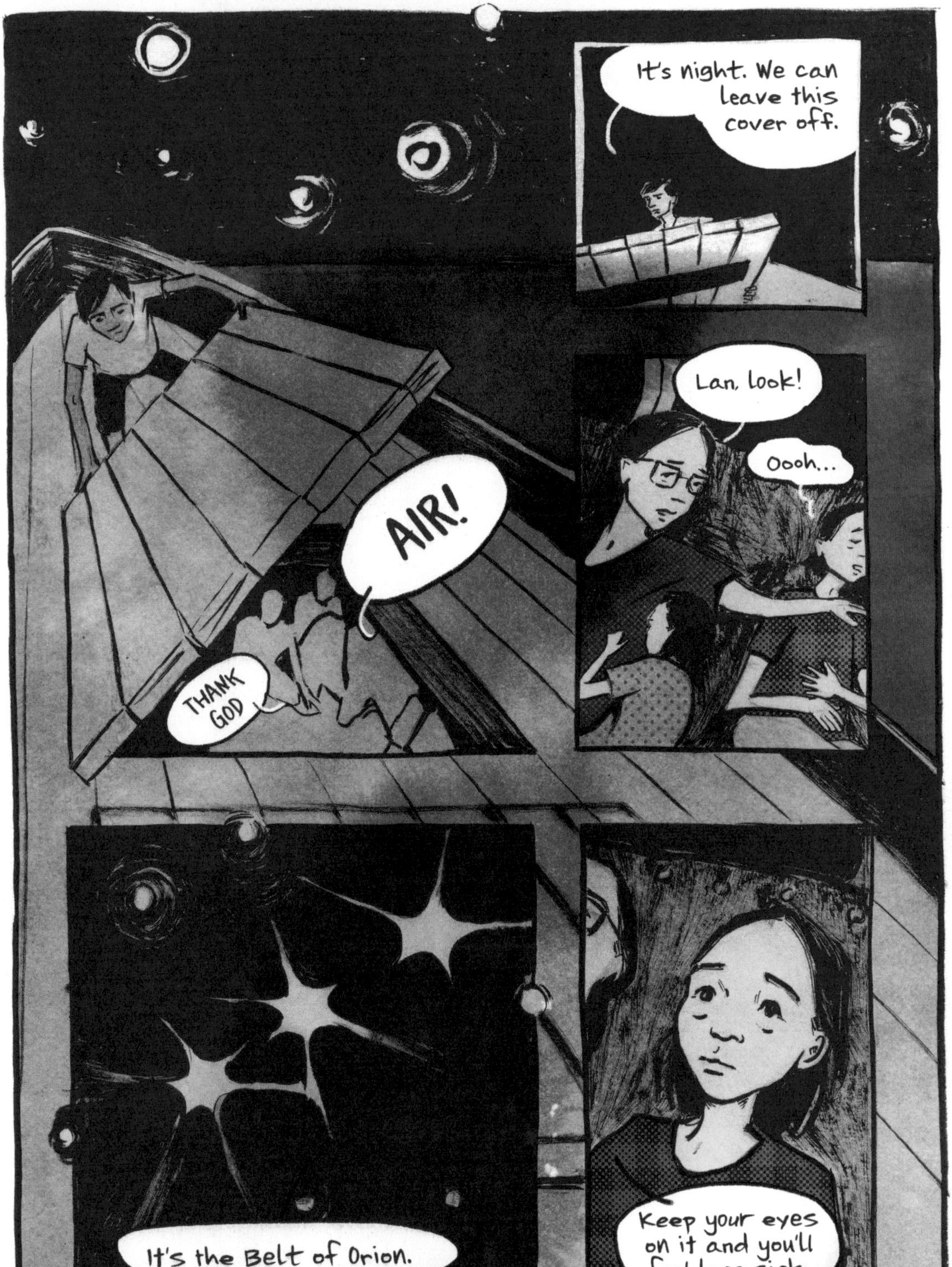
It's night. We can leave this cover off.
AIR!
THANK GOD
Lan, look!
Oooh...
It's the Belt of Orion.
Keep your eyes on it and you'll feel less sick.

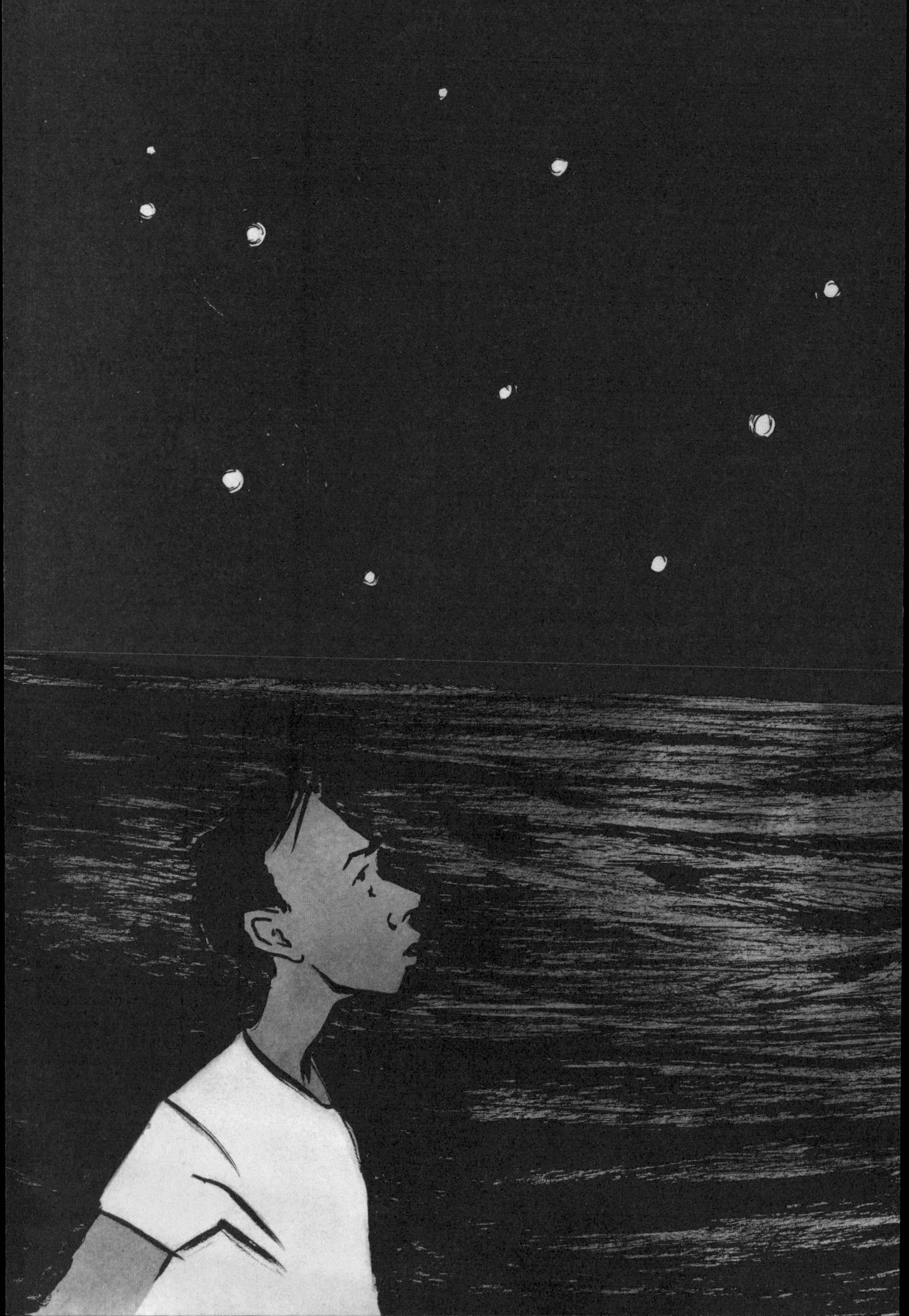

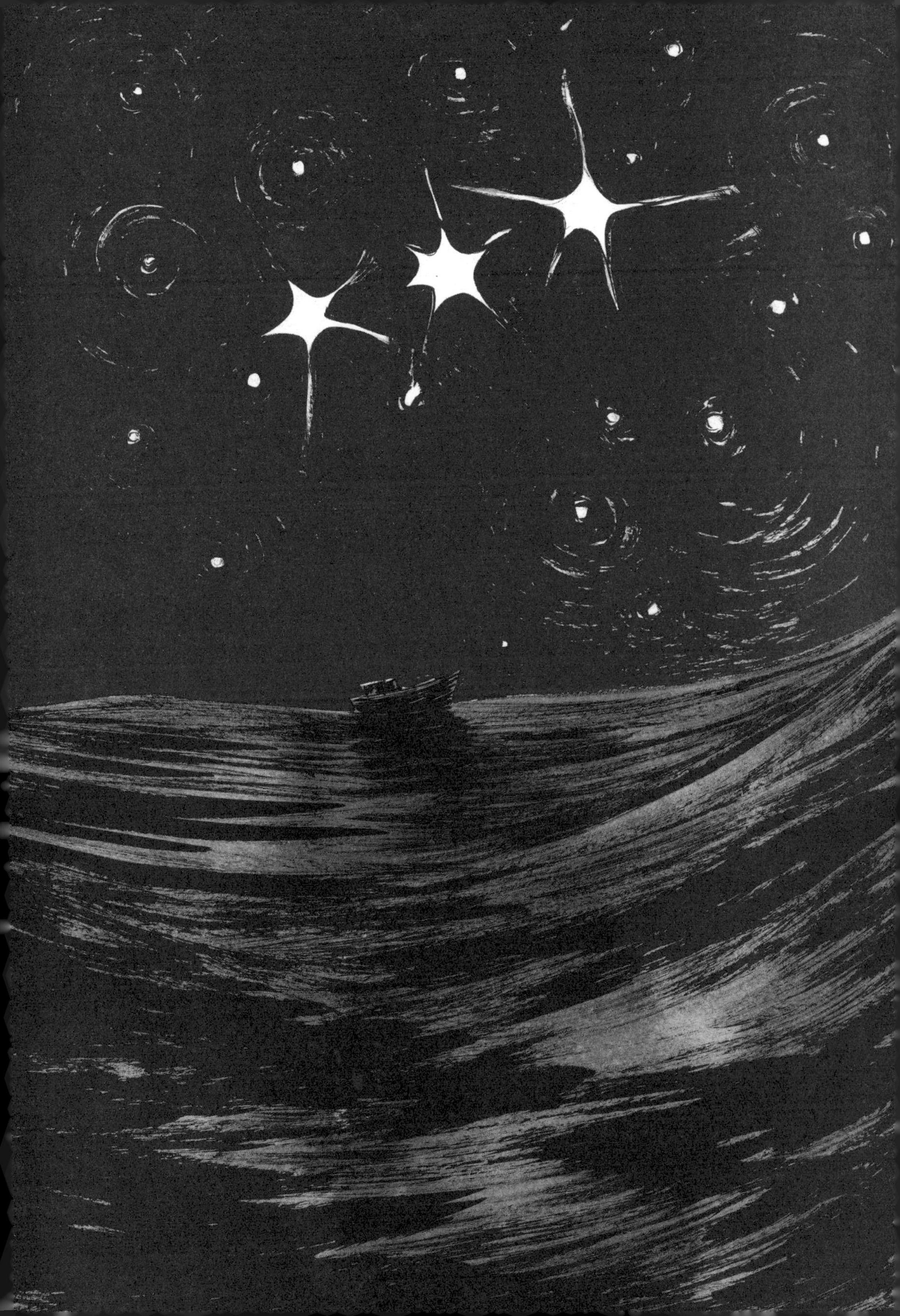

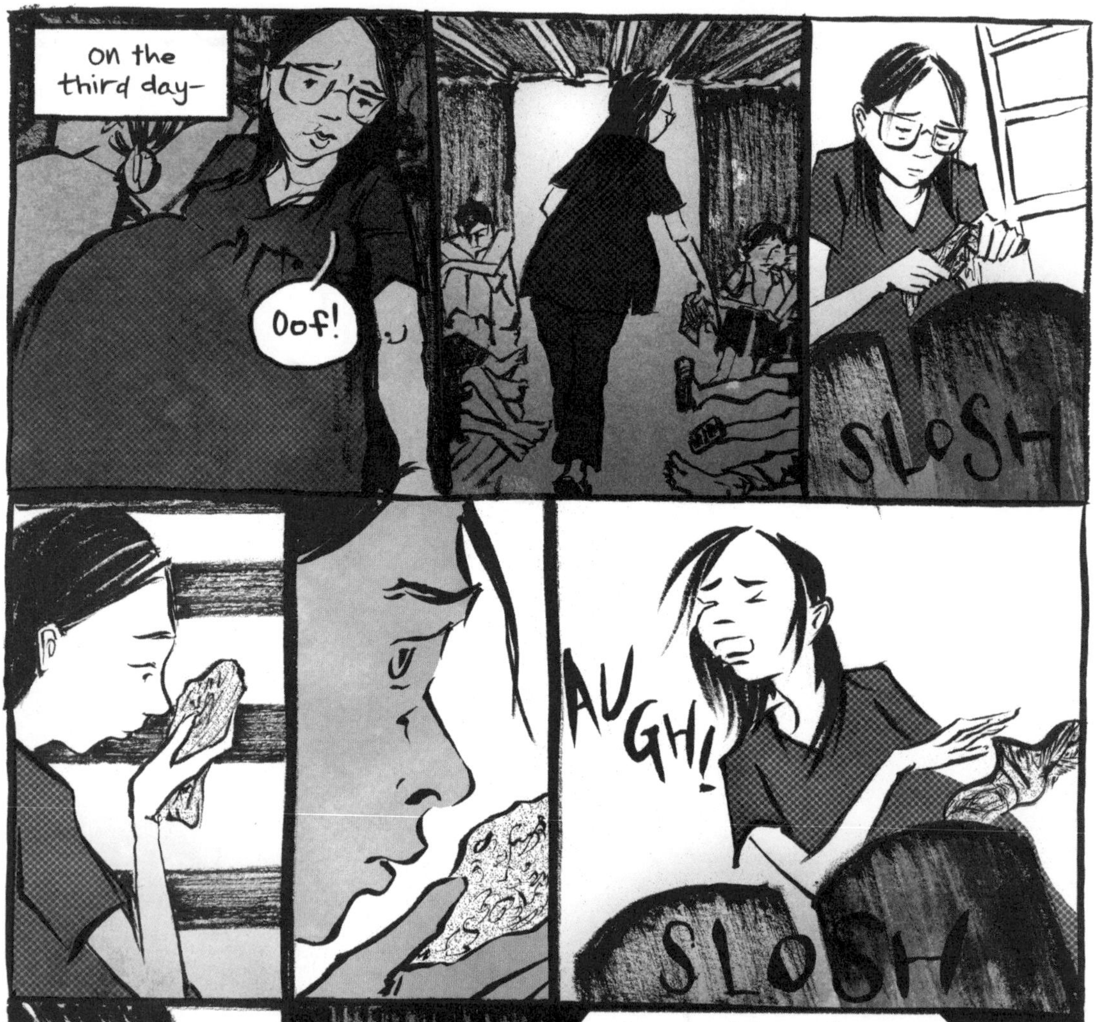
On the third day-
Oof!
SLOSH
AUGH!
SLOSH
!
How could you PISS in the washing water?!
It was dark! I was sleepy!

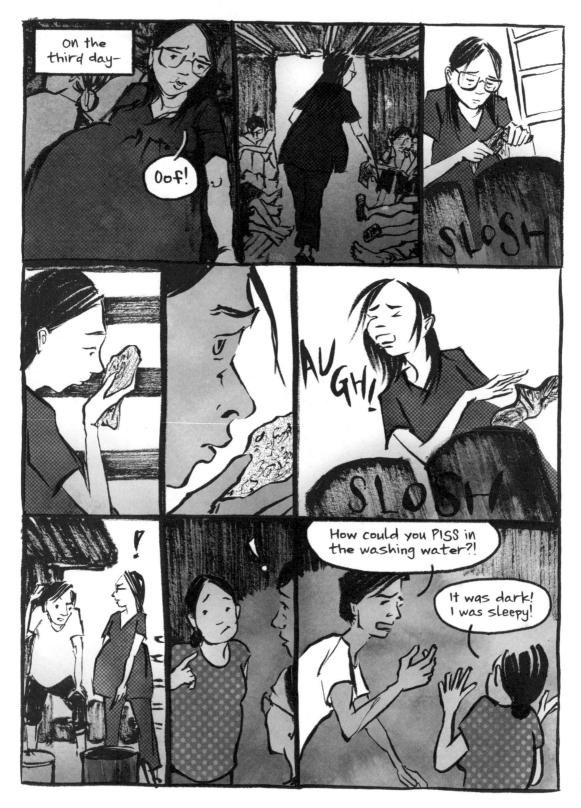

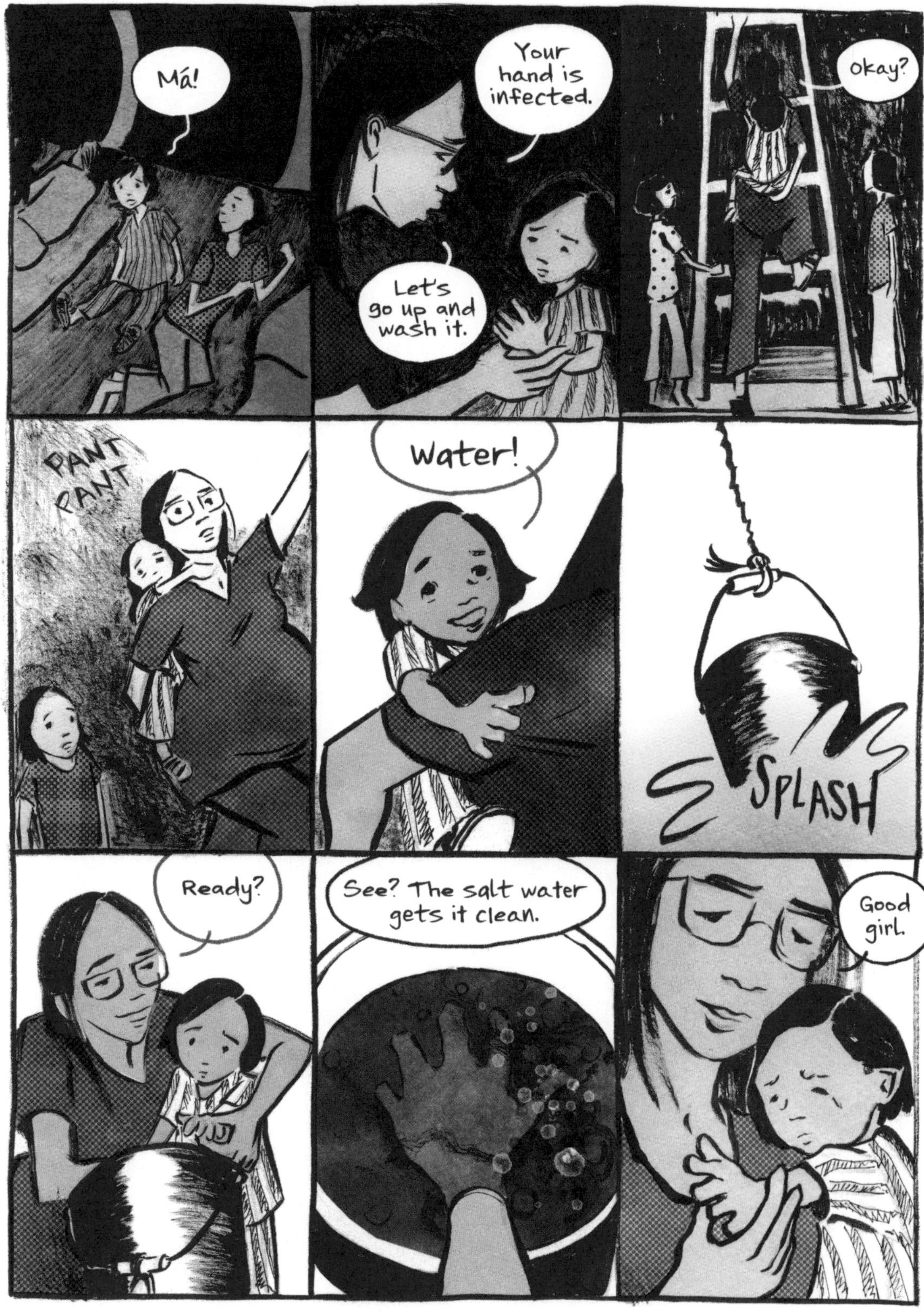
Má!
Your hand is infected.
Let's go up and wash it.
Okay?
PANT PANT
Water!
SPLASH
Ready?
See? The salt water gets it clean.
Good girl.

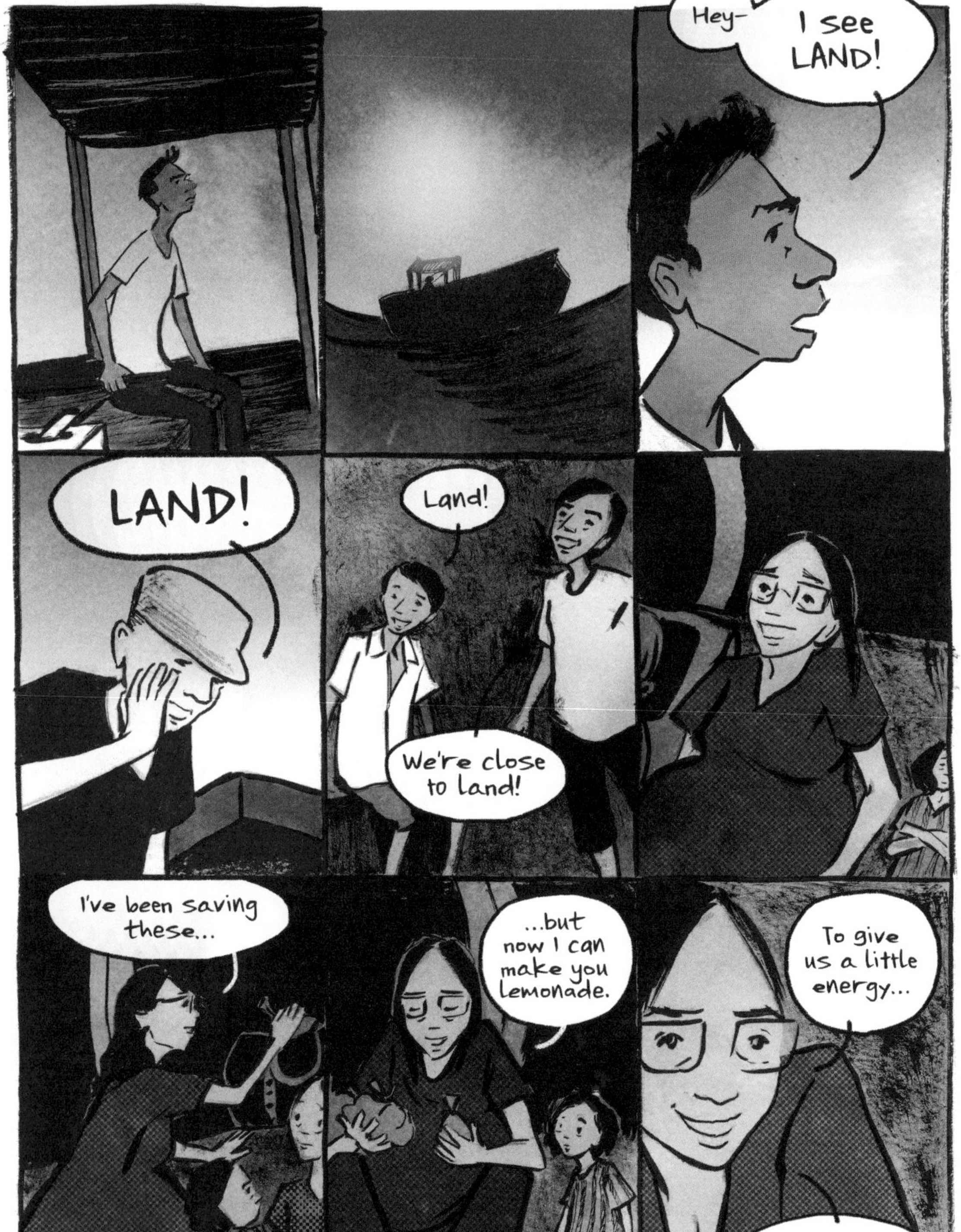
Hey-
I see LAND!
LAND!
Land!
We're close to land!
I've been saving these...
...but now I can make you lemonade.
To give us a little energy...
...and to celebrate!

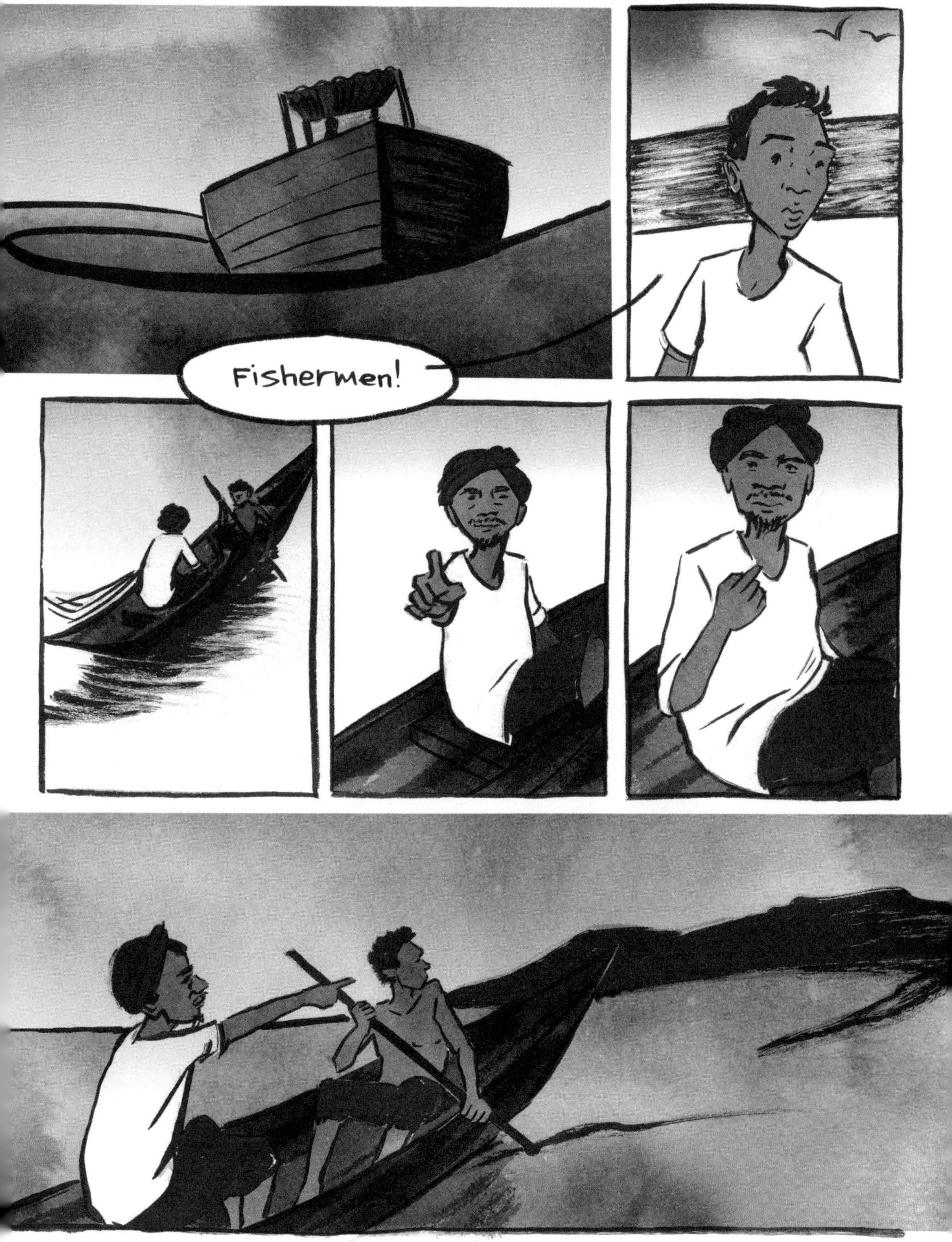
Fishermen!

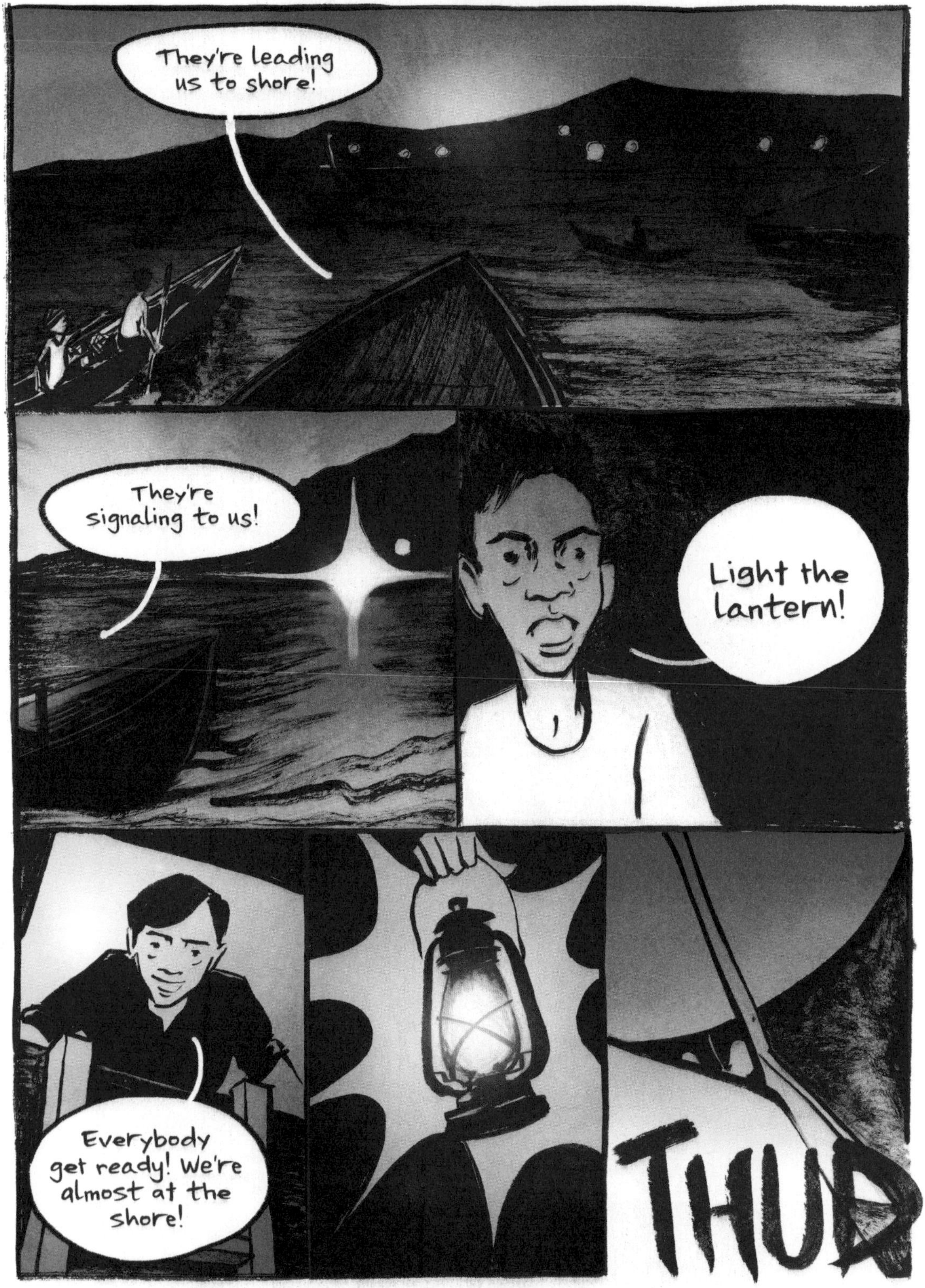
They're leading us to shore!
They're signaling to us!
Light the lantern!
Everybody get ready! We're almost at the shore!
THUD

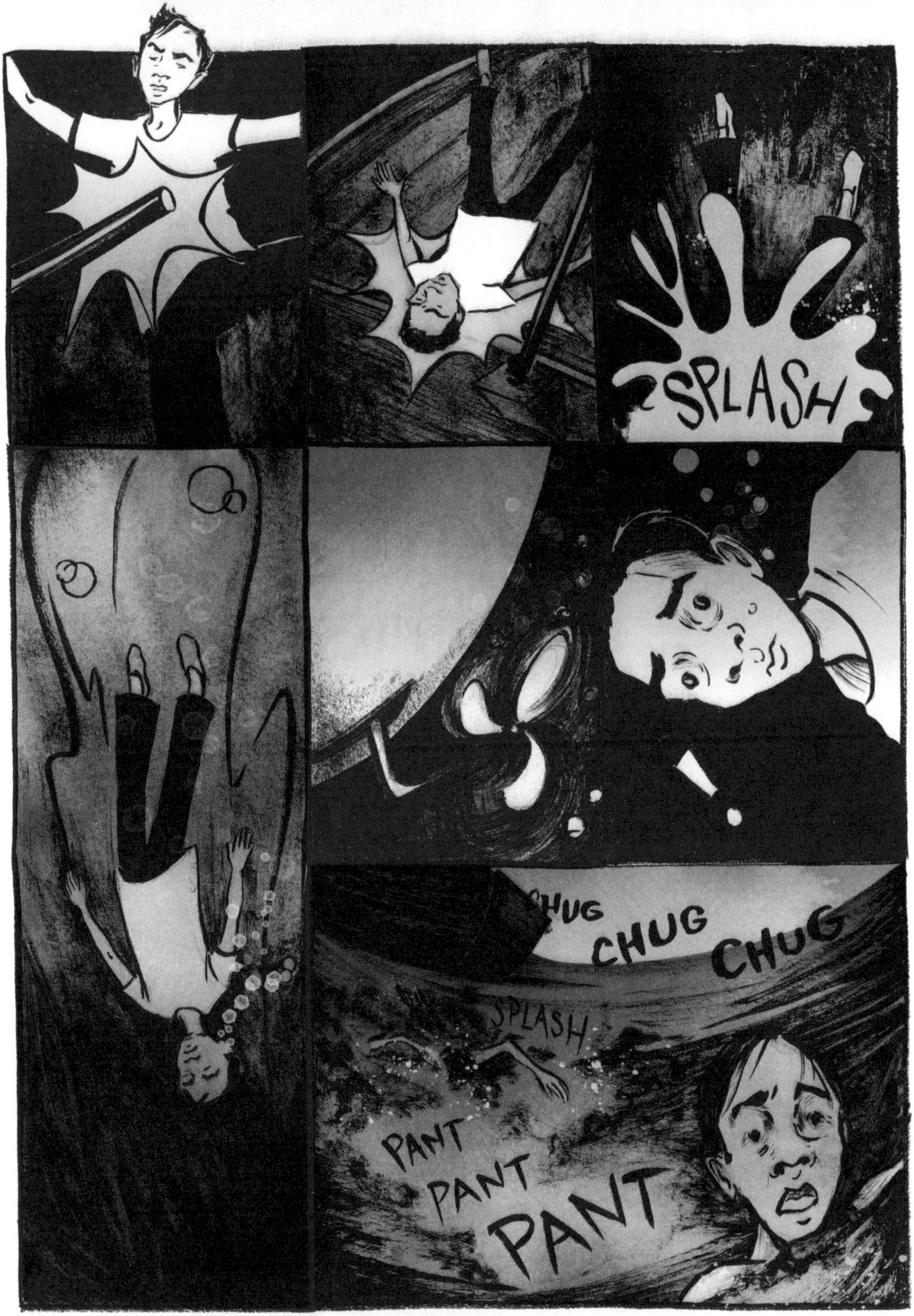
SPLASH
CHUG
CHUG
CHUG
SPLASH
PANT
PANT
PANT

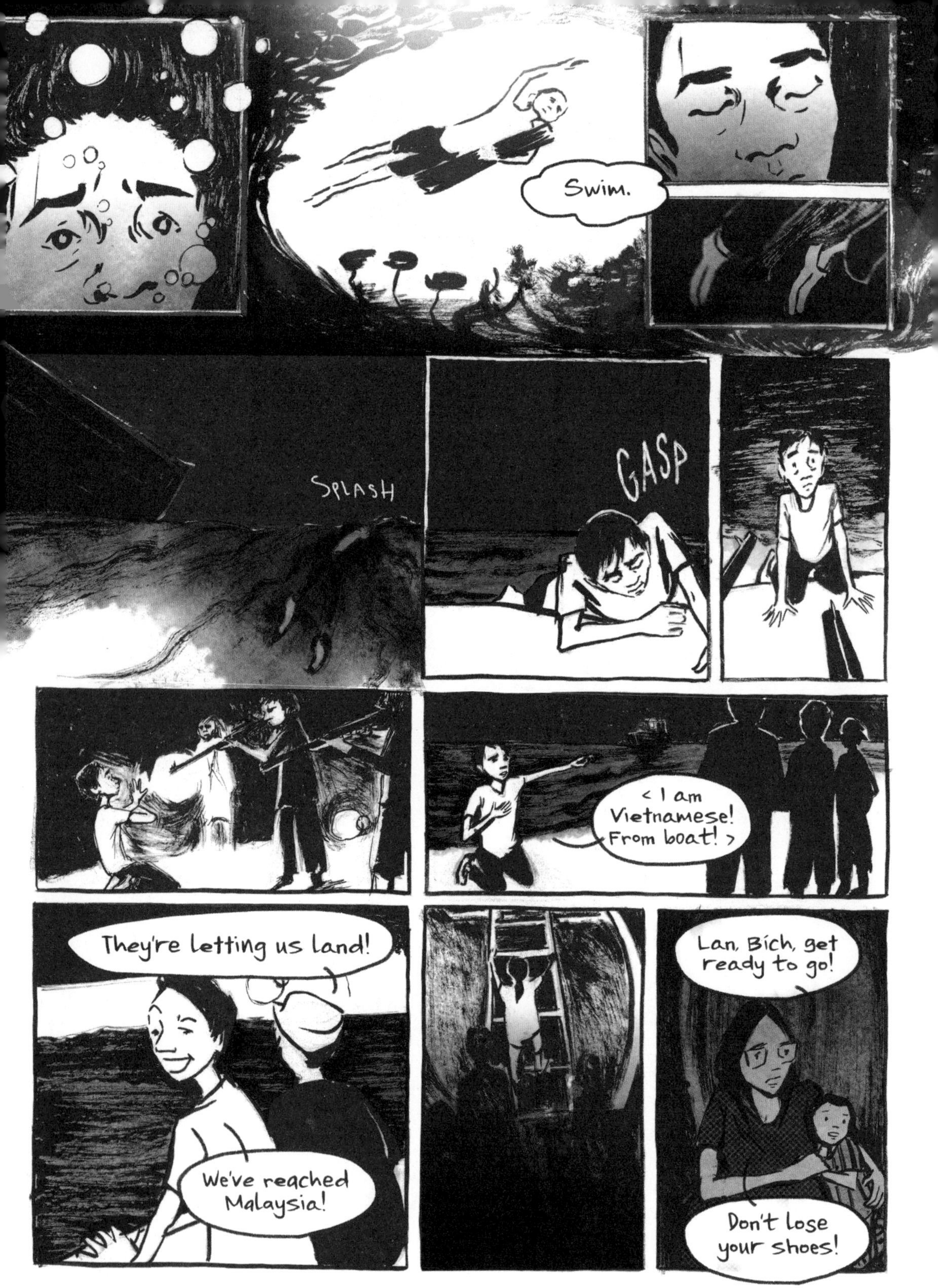
Swim.
SPLASH
GASP
< I am Vietnamese! From boat! >
They're letting us land!
We've reached Malaysia!
Lan, Bich, get ready to go!
Don't lose your shoes!

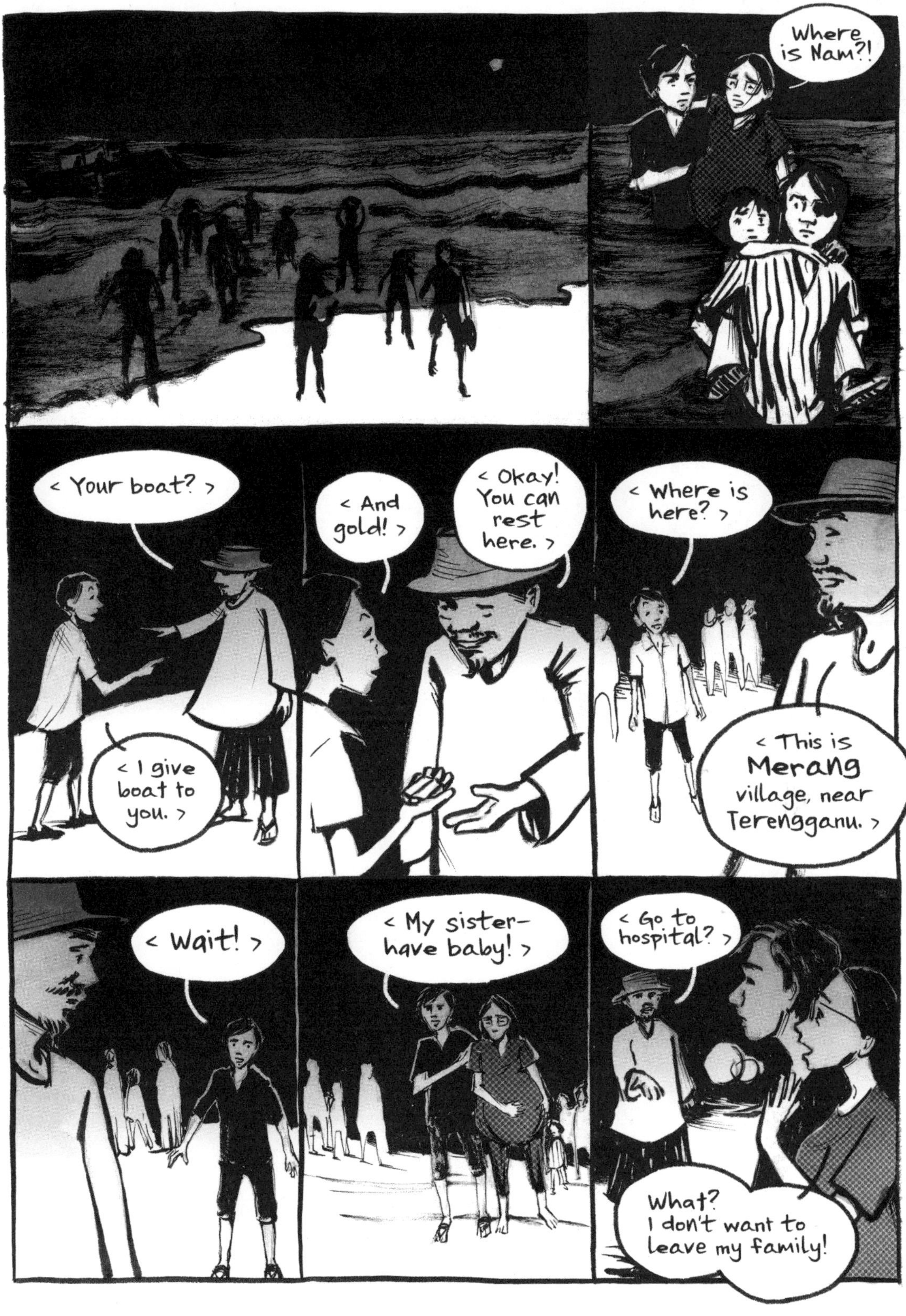
Where is Nam?!
< Your boat? >
< I give boat to you. >
< And gold! >
< Okay! You can rest here. >
< Where is here? >
< This is Merang village, near Terengganu. >
< Wait! >
< My sister- have baby! >
< Go to hospital? >
What? I don't want to leave my family!

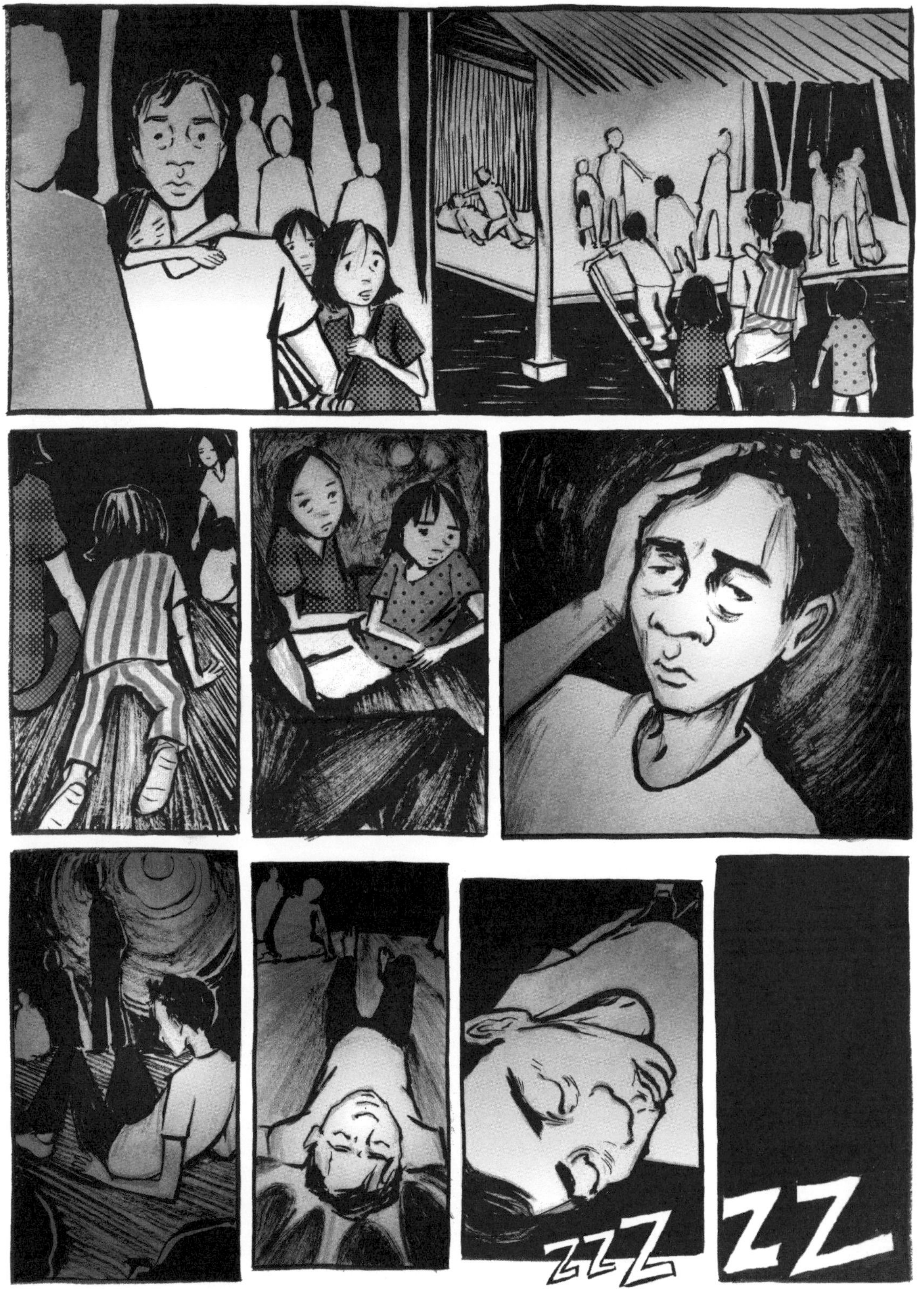
ZZZ ZZ

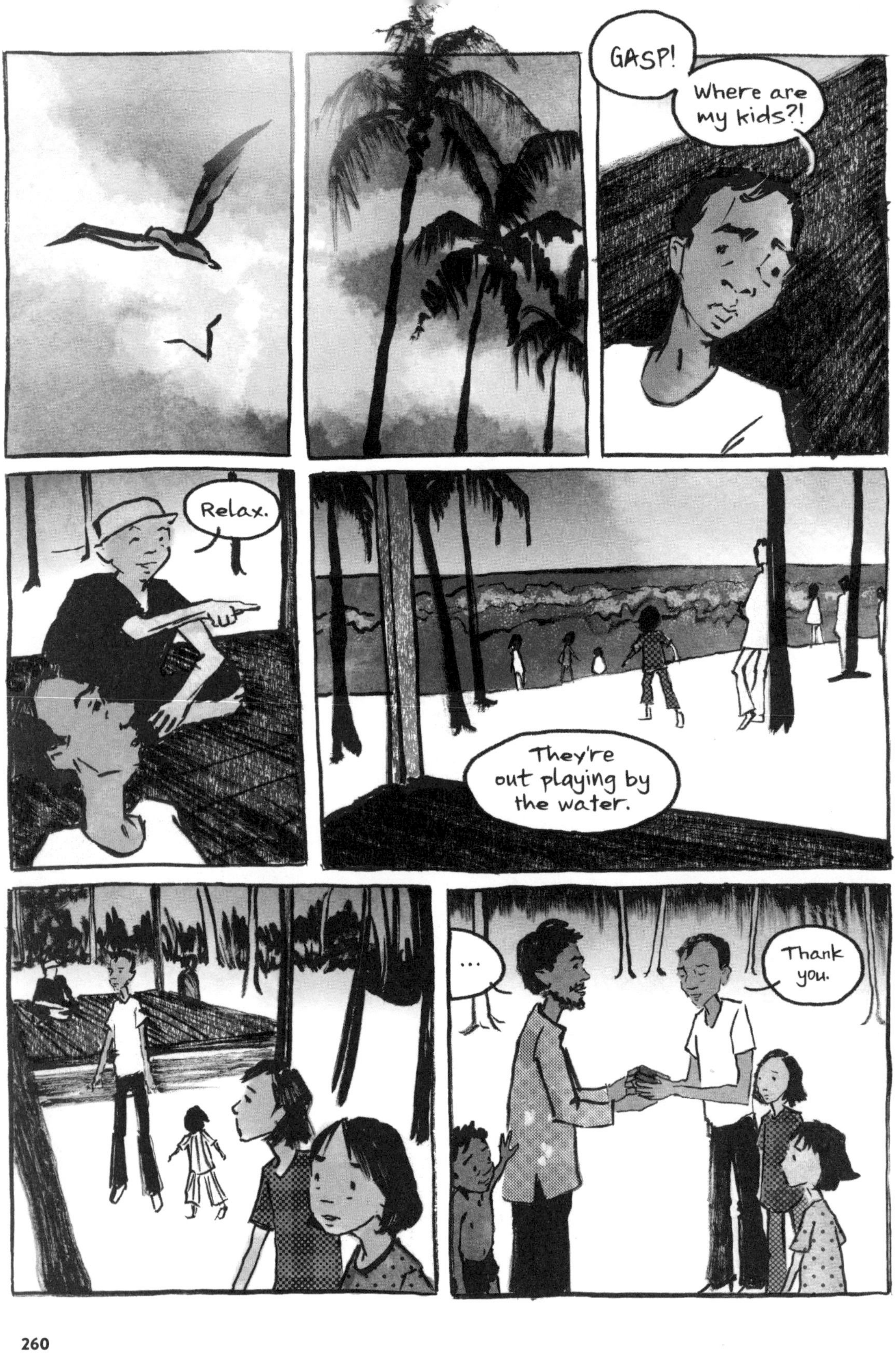
GASP!
Where are my kids?!
Relax.
They're out playing by the water.
...
Thank you.

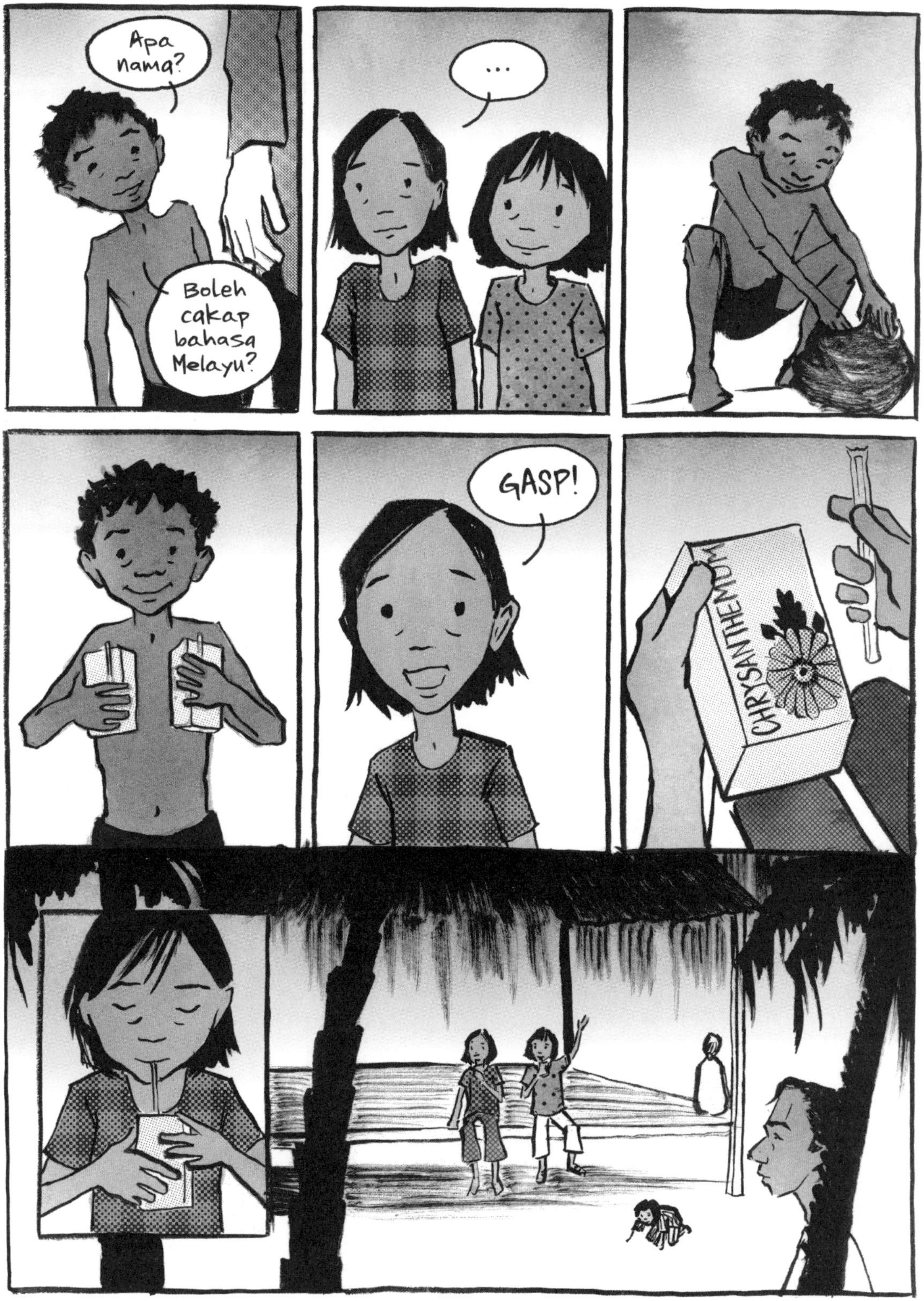
Apa nama?
Boleh cakap bahasa Melayu?
...
GASP!
CHRYSANTHEMUM

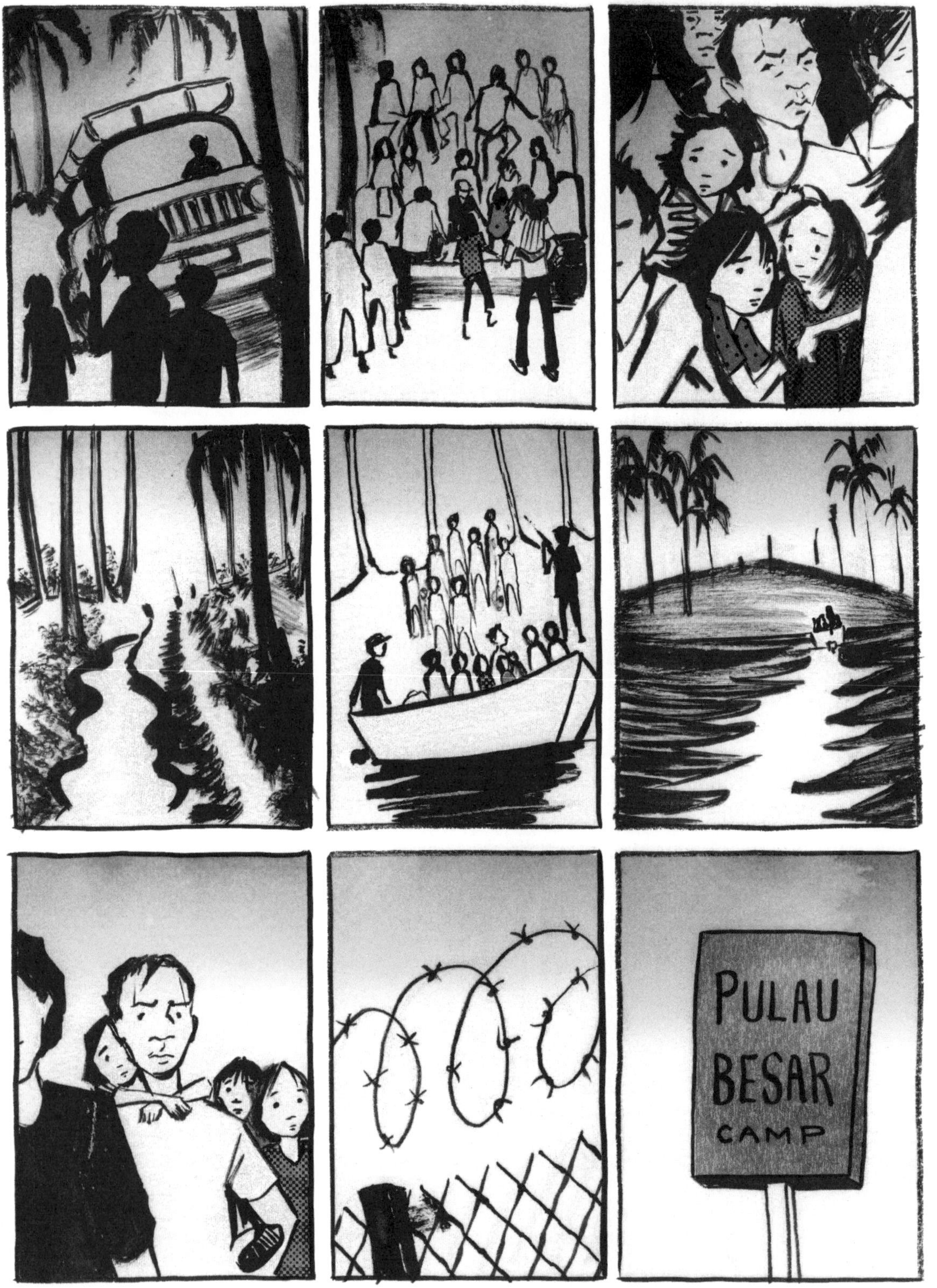
PULAU BESAR
CAMP

CHAPTER 8
THE SHORE

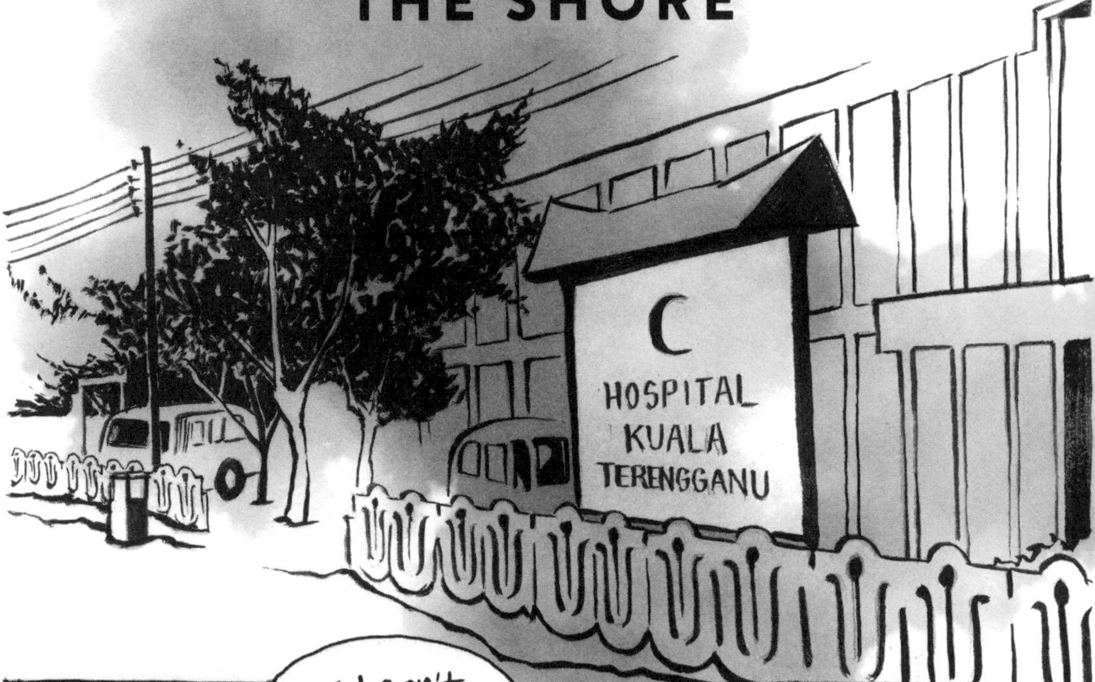
HOSPITAL
KUALA
TERENGGANU

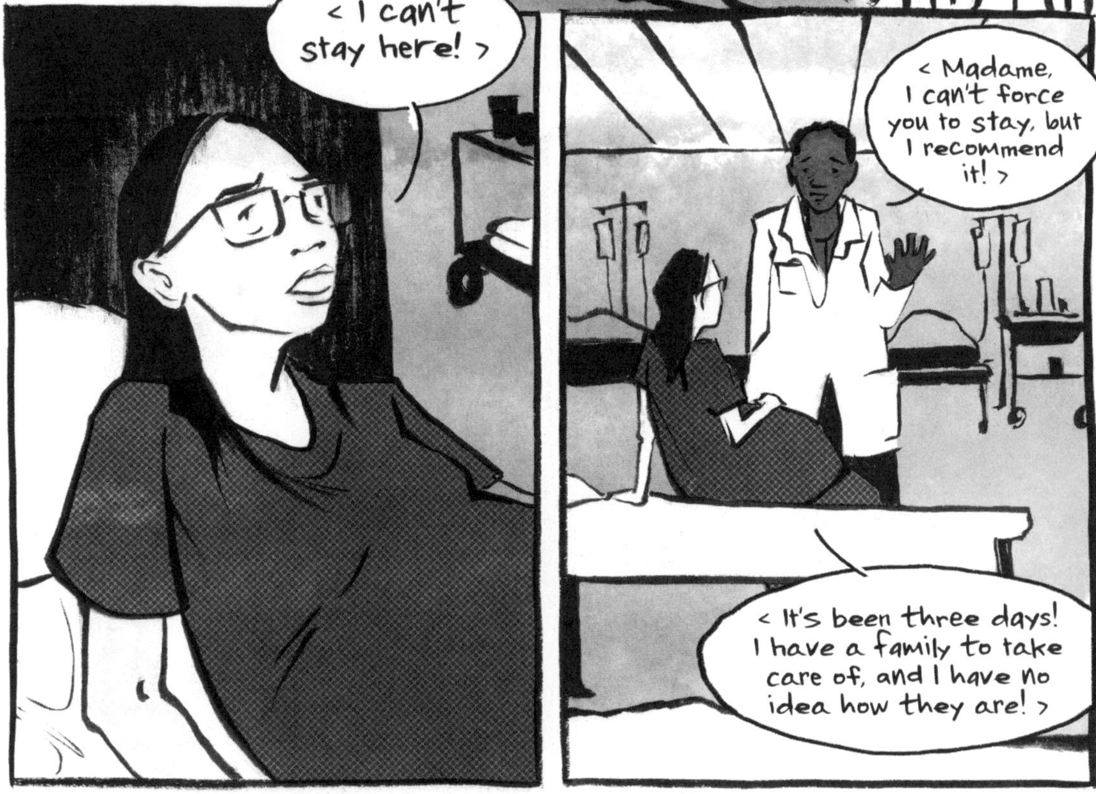
< I can't stay here! >
< Madame, I can't force you to stay, but I recommend it! >
< It's been three days! I have a family to take care of, and I have no idea how they are! >

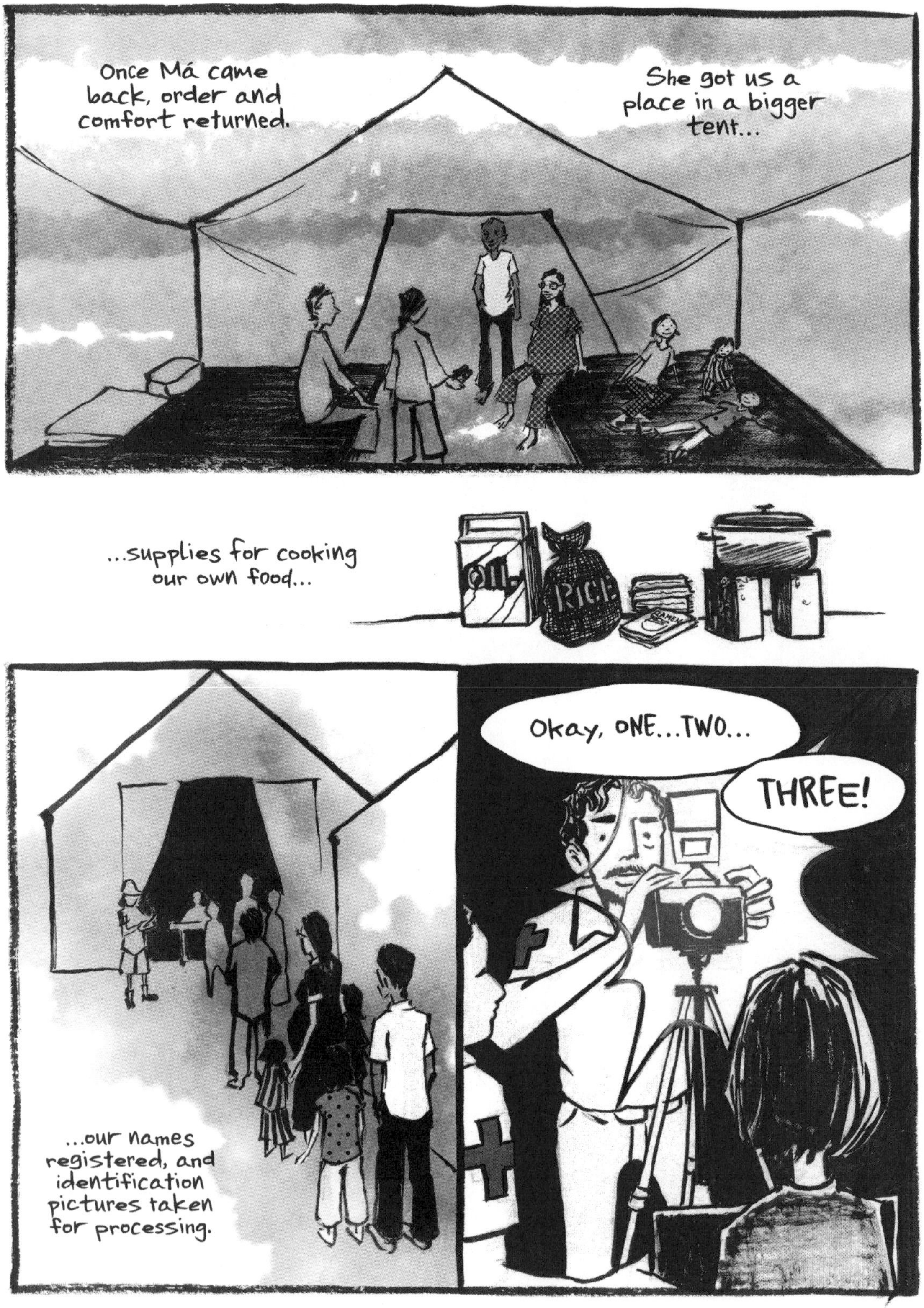
Once Má came back, order and comfort returned.
She got us a place in a bigger tent...
...supplies for cooking our own food...
OIL
RICE
...our names registered, and identification pictures taken for processing.
Okay, ONE...TWO...
THREE!

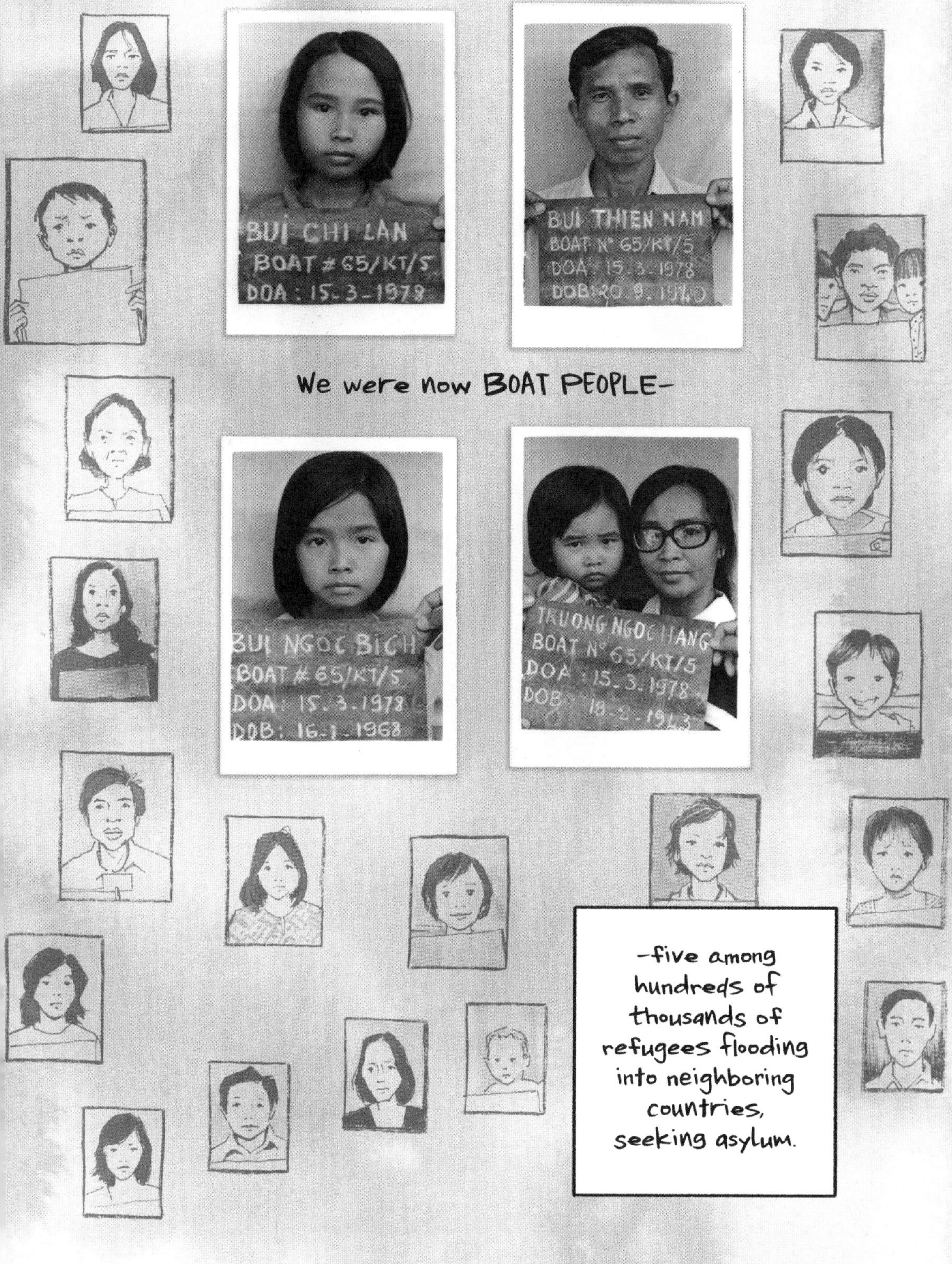
BUI CHI LAN
BOAT # 65/KT/5
DOA: 15-3-1978
BUI THIEN NAM
BOAT Nº 65/KT/5
DOA: 15-3-1978
DOB: 20-9-1940
We were now BOAT PEOPLE-
BUI NGOC BICH
BOAT # 65/KT/5
DOA: 15-3-1978
DOB: 16-1-1968
TRUONG NGOC HANG
BOAT Nº 65/KT/5
DOA: 15-3-1978
DOB: 18-2-1943
-five among hundreds of thousands of refugees flooding into neighboring countries, seeking asylum.

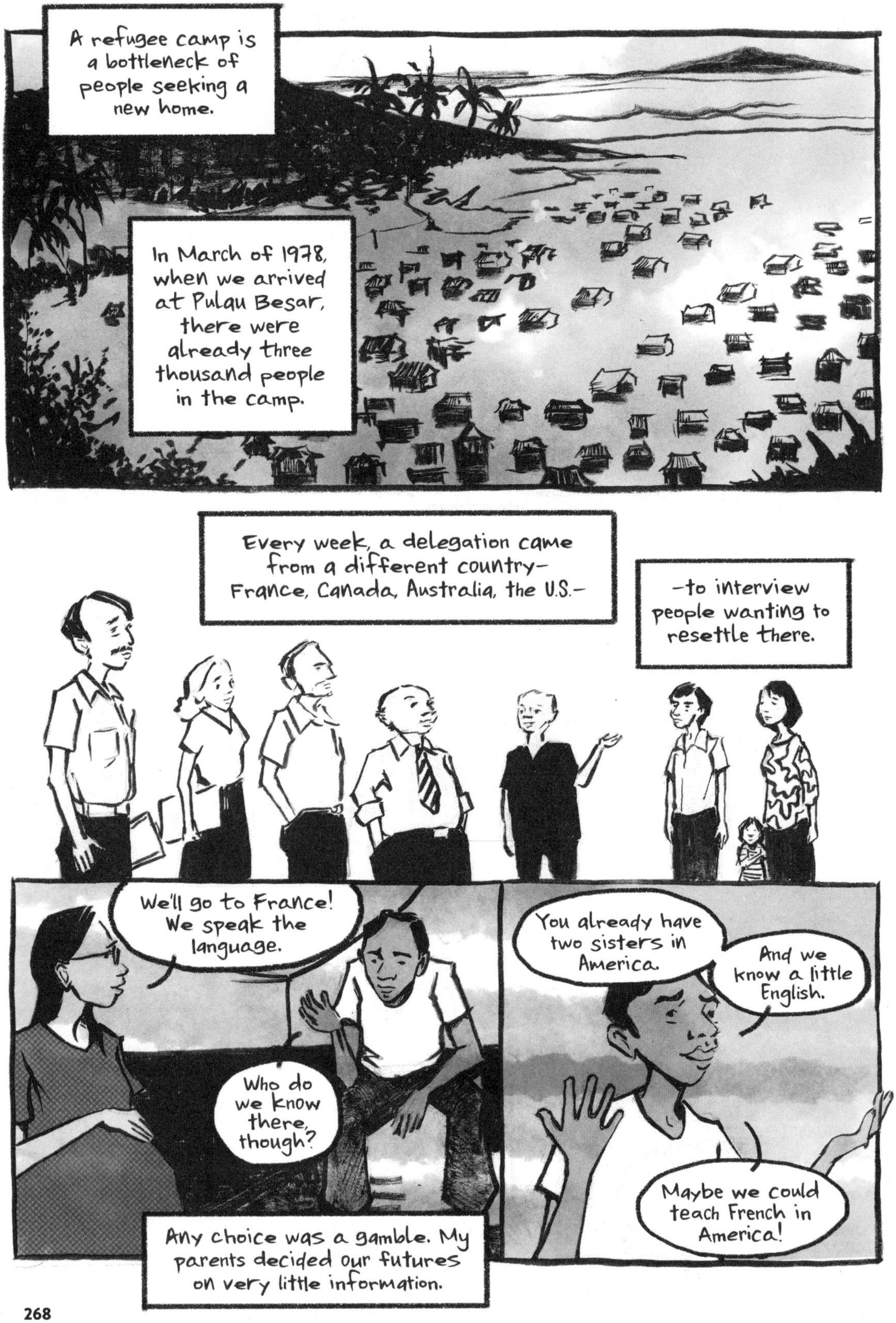

A refugee camp is a bottleneck of people seeking a new home.
In March of 1978, when we arrived at Pulau Besar, there were already three thousand people in the camp.
Every week, a delegation came from a different country- France, Canada, Australia, the U.S.-
-to interview people wanting to resettle there.
We'll go to France! We speak the language.
Who do we know there, though?
Any choice was a gamble. My parents decided our futures on very little information.
You already have two sisters in America.
And we know a little English.
Maybe we could teach French in America!

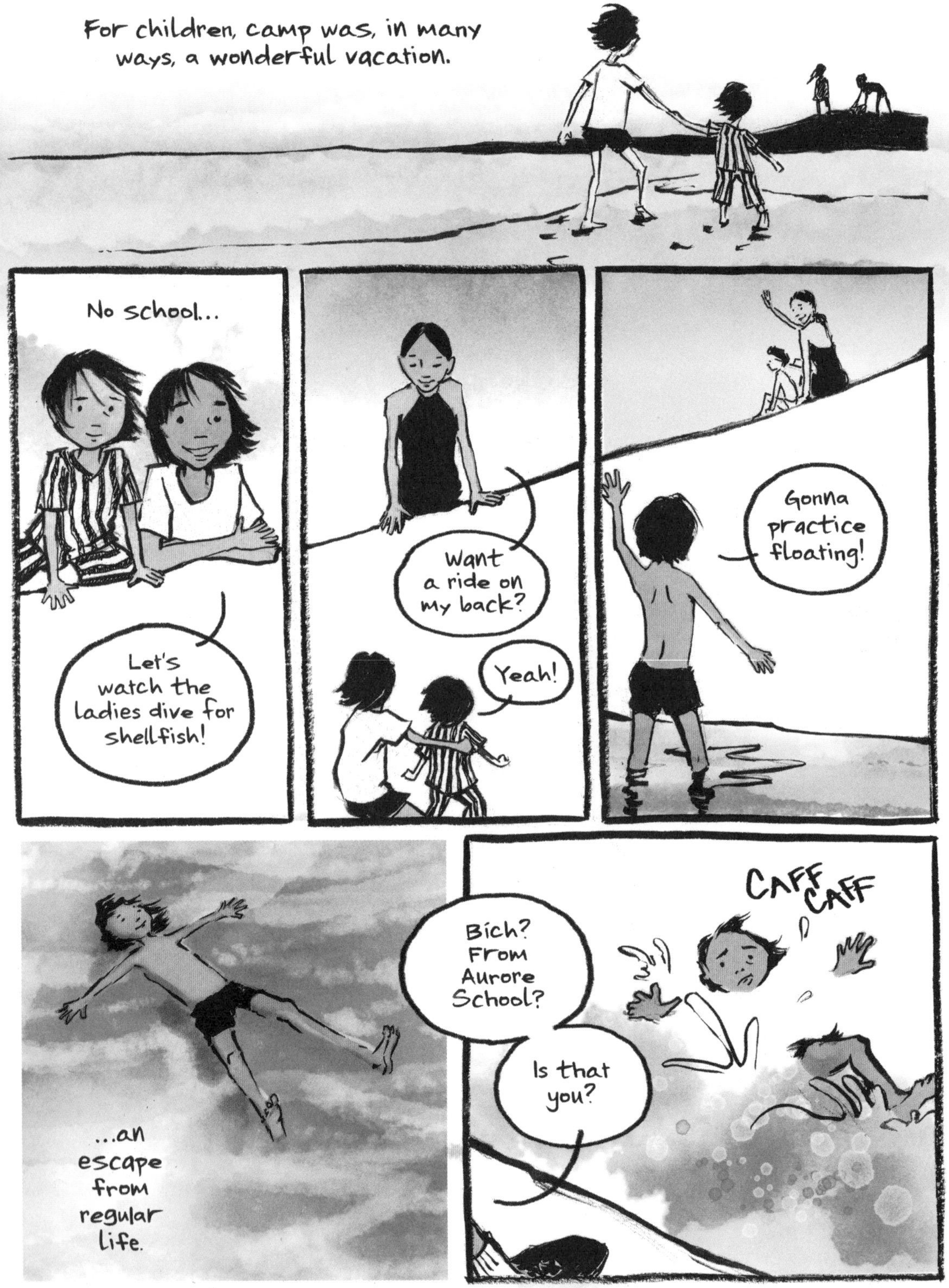
For children, camp was, in many ways, a wonderful vacation.
No school...
Let's watch the ladies dive for shellfish!
Want a ride on my back?
Yeah!
Gonna practice floating!
...an escape from regular life.
CAFF CAFF
Bich? From Aurore School?
Is that you?

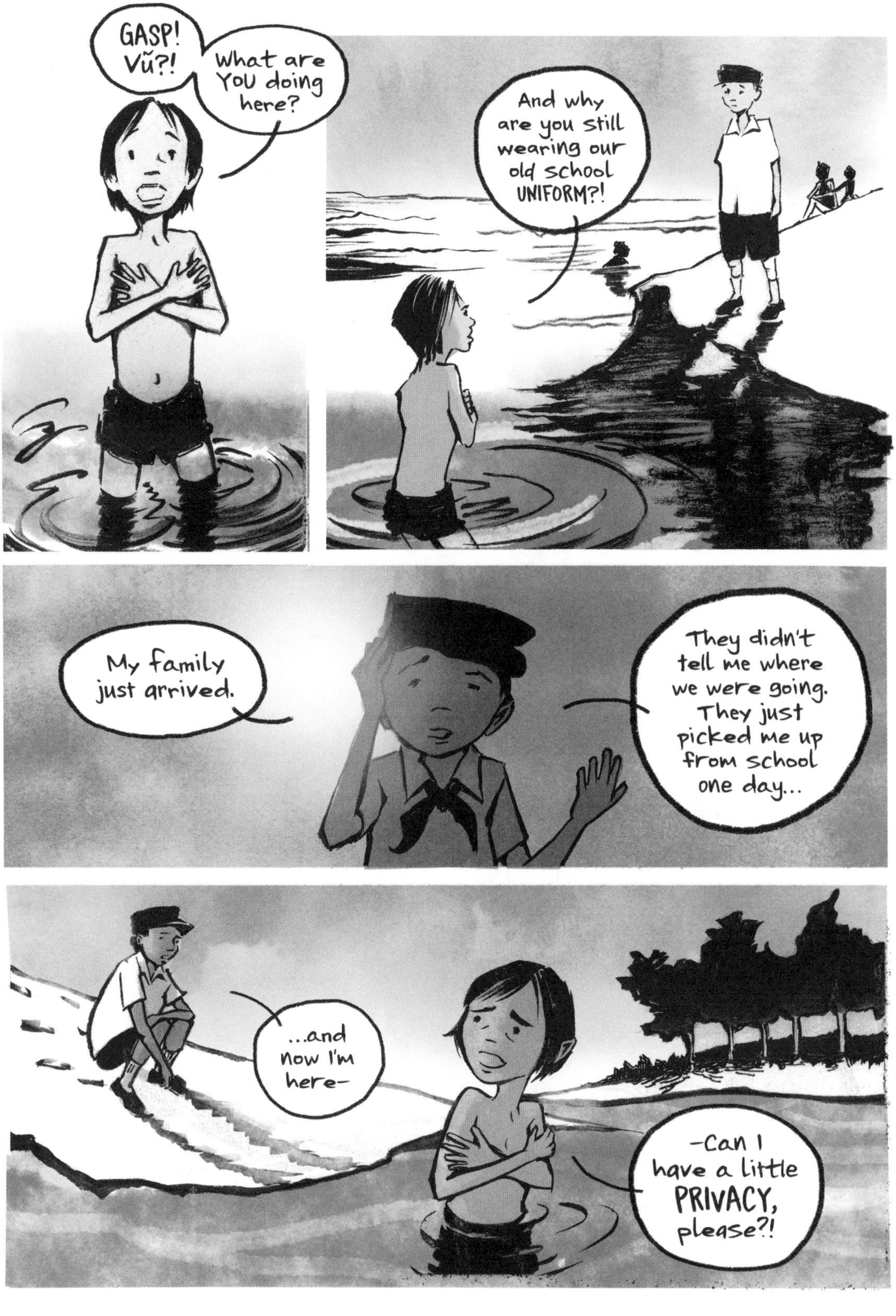
GASP! Vũ?!
What are YOU doing here?
And why are you still wearing our old school UNIFORM?!
My family just arrived.
They didn't tell me where we were going. They just picked me up from school one day...
...and now I'm here-
-Can I have a little PRIVACY, please?!

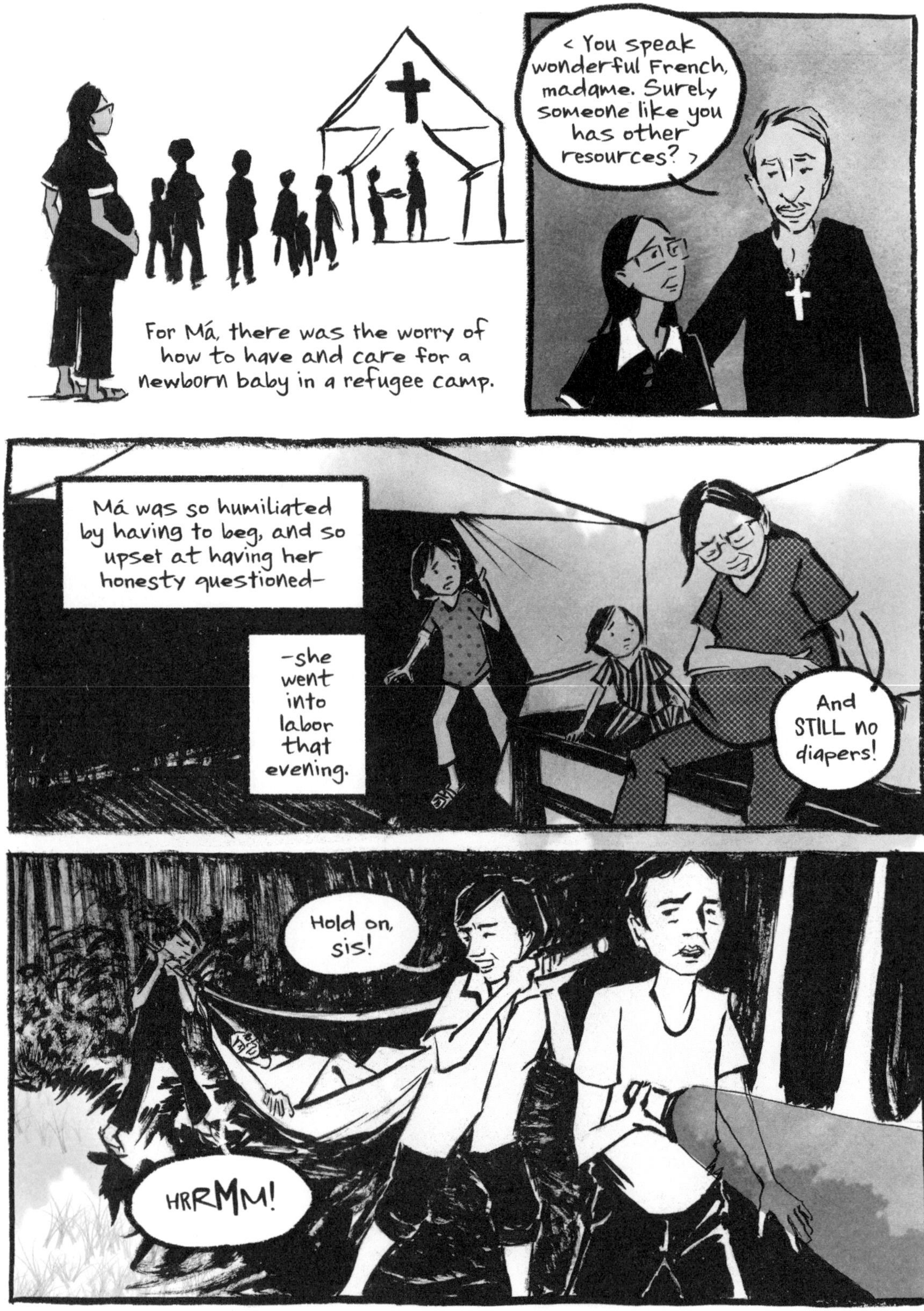
For Má, there was the worry of how to have and care for a newborn baby in a refugee camp.
< You speak wonderful French, madame. Surely someone like you has other resources? >
Má was so humiliated by having to beg, and so upset at having her honesty questioned-
-she went into labor that evening.
And STILL no diapers!
Hold on, sis!
HRRMM!

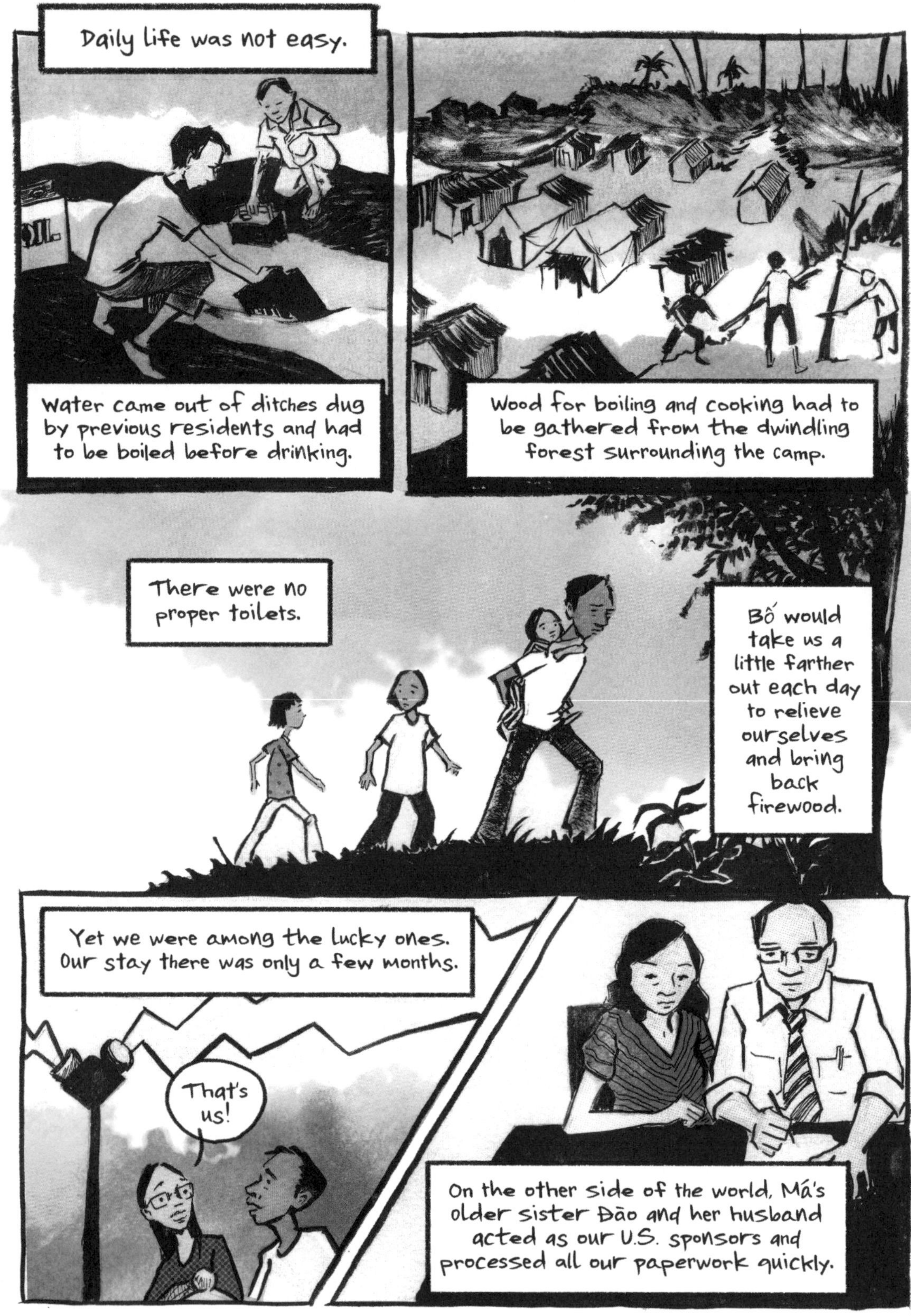
Daily life was not easy.
Water came out of ditches dug by previous residents and had to be boiled before drinking.
Wood for boiling and cooking had to be gathered from the dwindling forest surrounding the camp.
There were no proper toilets.
Bố would take us a little farther out each day to relieve ourselves and bring back firewood.
Yet we were among the lucky ones. Our stay there was only a few months.
That's us!
On the other side of the world, Má's older sister Đào and her husband acted as our U.S. sponsors and processed all our paperwork quickly.

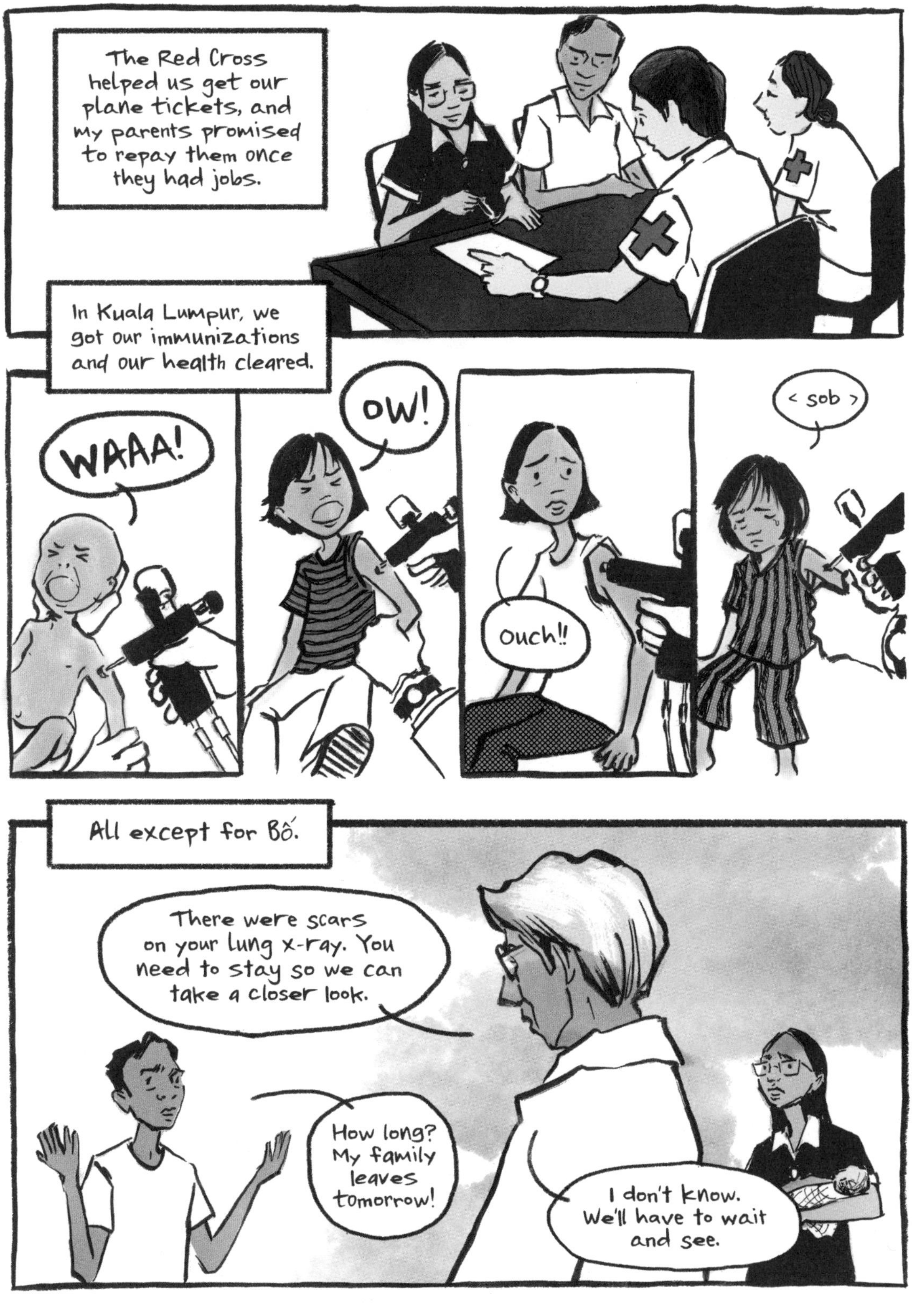

The Red Cross helped us get our plane tickets, and my parents promised to repay them once they had jobs.
In Kuala Lumpur, we got our immunizations and our health cleared.
WAAA!
OW!
Ouch!!
< sob >
All except for Bố.
There were scars on your lung x-ray. You need to stay so we can take a closer look.
How long? My family leaves tomorrow!
I don't know. We'll have to wait and see.

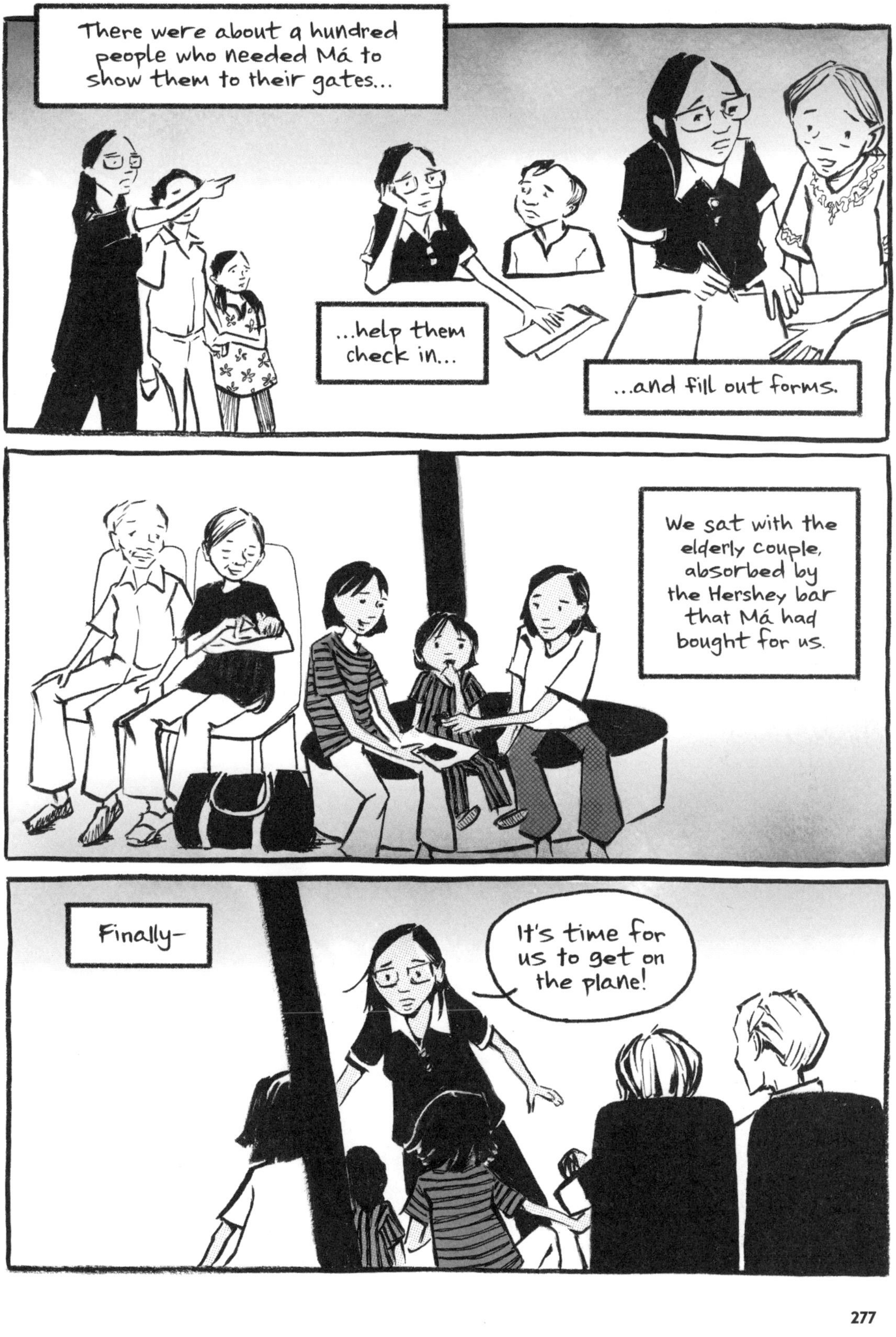
There were about a hundred people who needed Má to show them to their gates...
...help them check in...
...and fill out forms.
We sat with the elderly couple, absorbed by the Hershey bar that Má had bought for us.
Finally-
It's time for us to get on the plane!

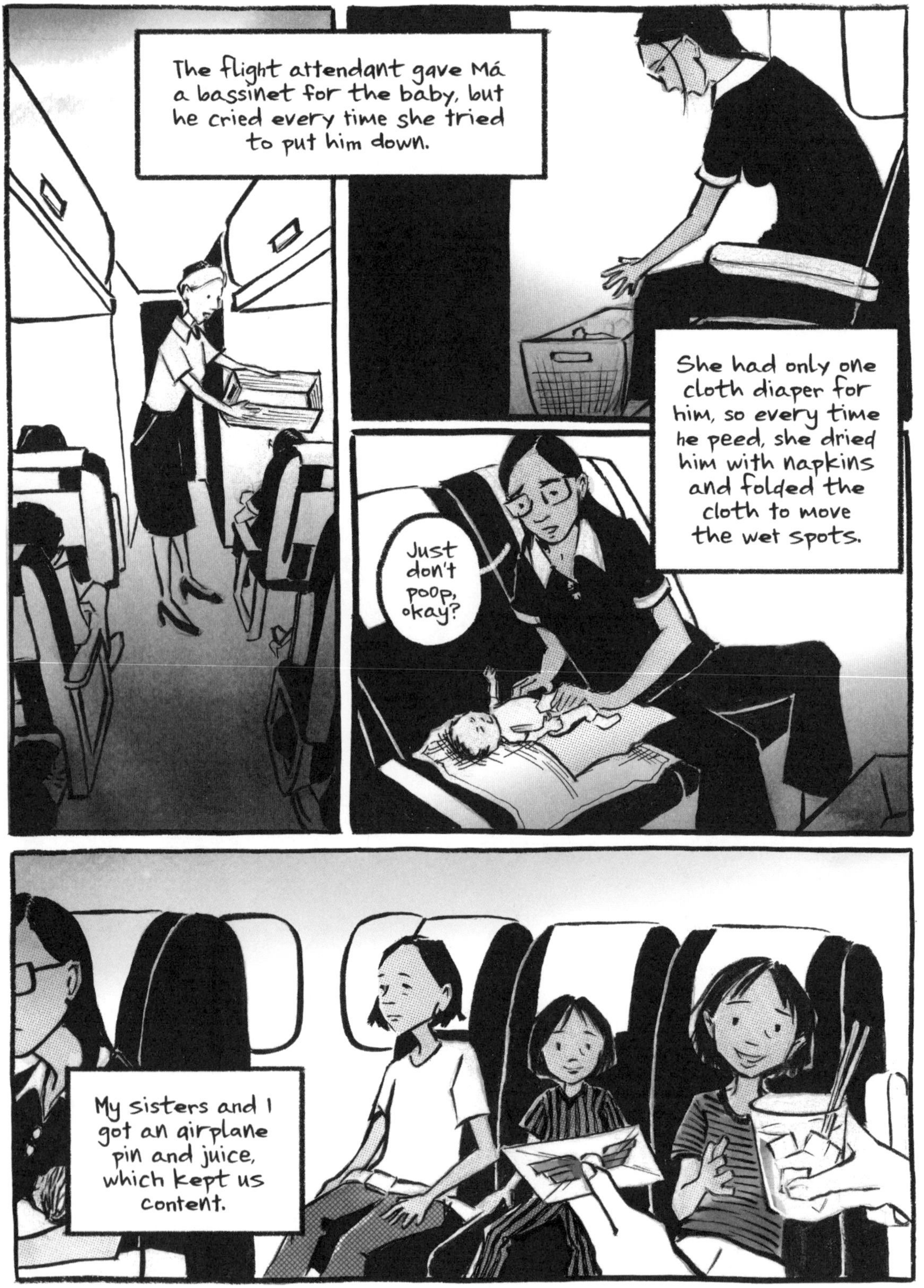
The flight attendant gave Má a bassinet for the baby, but he cried every time she tried to put him down.
She had only one cloth diaper for him, so every time he peed, she dried him with napkins and folded the cloth to move the wet spots.
Just don't poop, okay?
My sisters and I got an airplane pin and juice, which kept us content.

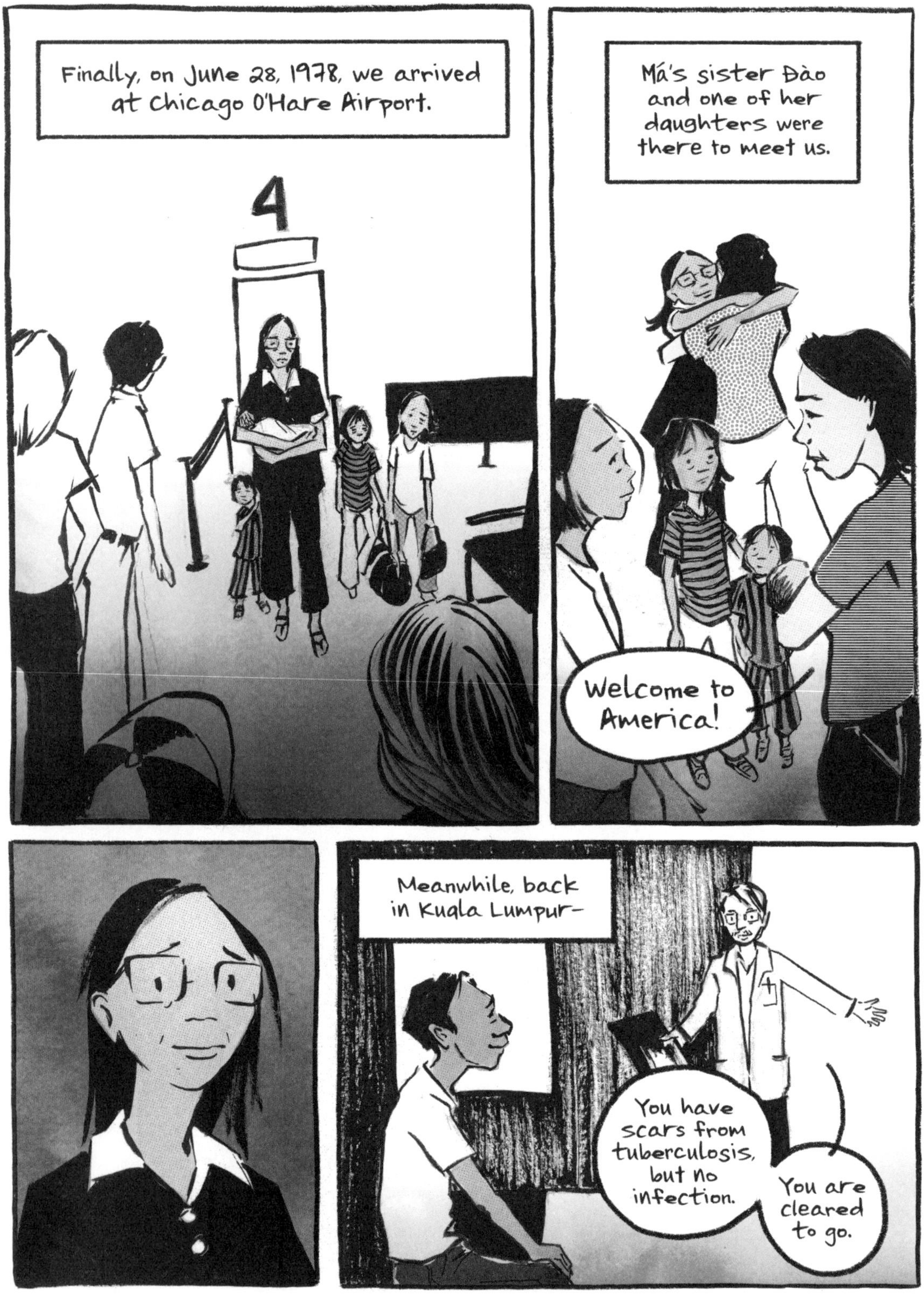
Finally, on June 28, 1978, we arrived at Chicago O'Hare Airport.
4
Má's sister Đào and one of her daughters were there to meet us.
Welcome to America!
Meanwhile, back in Kuala Lumpur-
You have scars from tuberculosis, but no infection.
You are cleared to go.

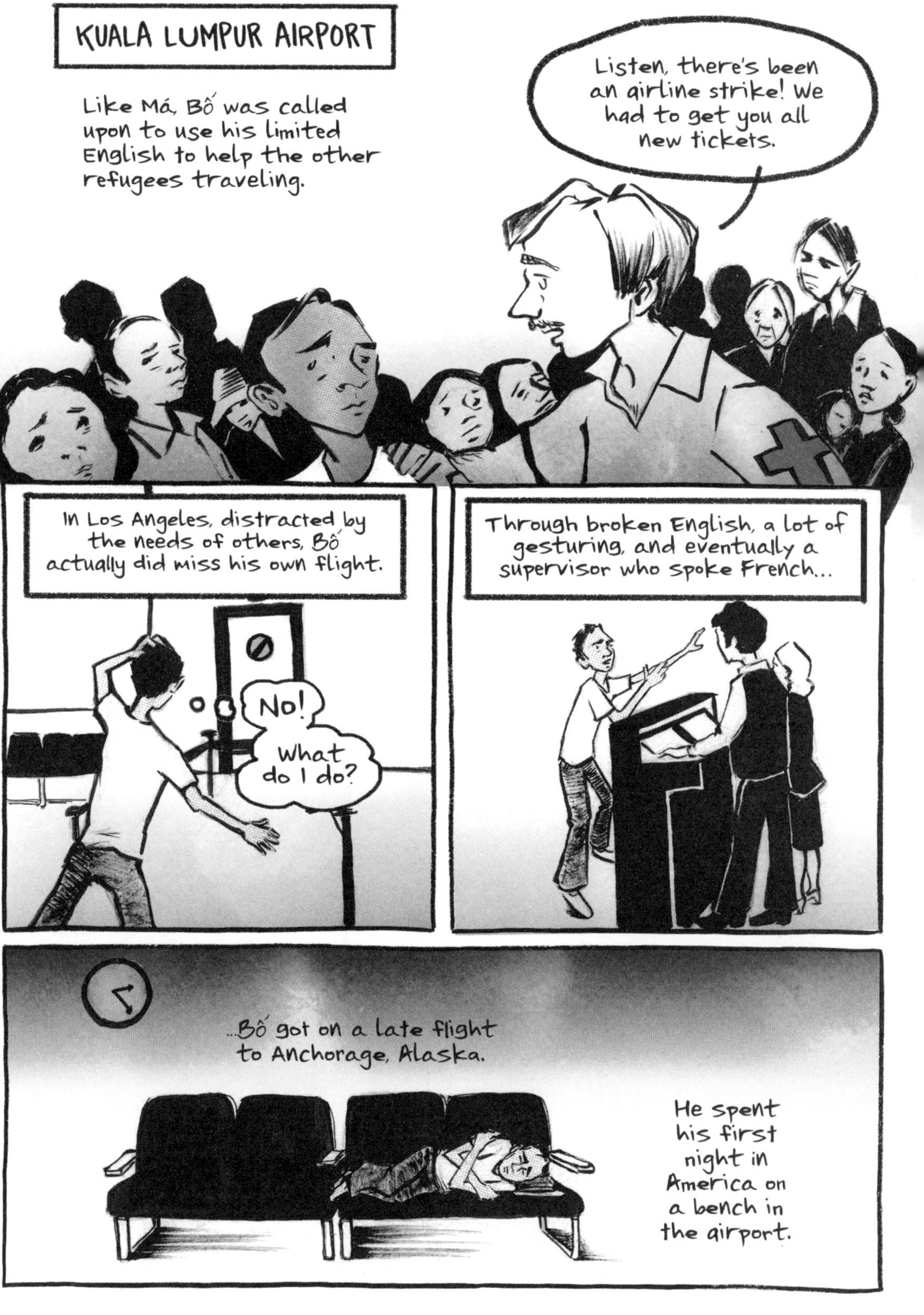
KUALA LUMPUR AIRPORT
Like Má, Bố was called upon to use his limited English to help the other refugees traveling.
Listen, there's been an airline strike! We had to get you all new tickets.
In Los Angeles, distracted by the needs of others, Bố actually did miss his own flight.
No!
What do I do?
Through broken English, a lot of gesturing, and eventually a supervisor who spoke French...
...Bố got on a late flight to Anchorage, Alaska.
He spent his first night in America on a bench in the airport.

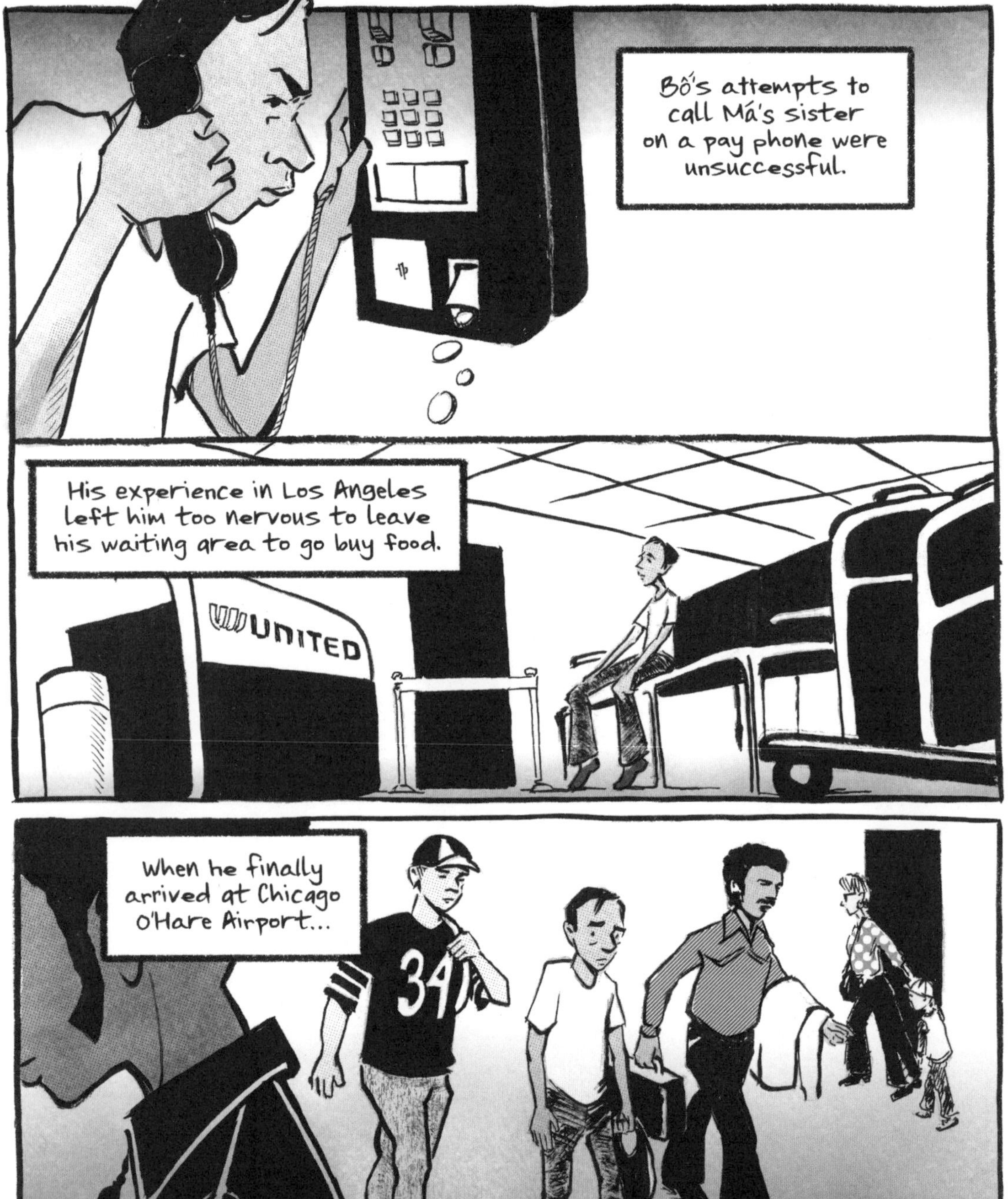
Bố's attempts to call Má's sister on a pay phone were unsuccessful.
His experience in Los Angeles left him too nervous to leave his waiting area to go buy food.
UNITED
When he finally arrived at Chicago O'Hare Airport...
34
...his belly was as empty as his morale was low.

283

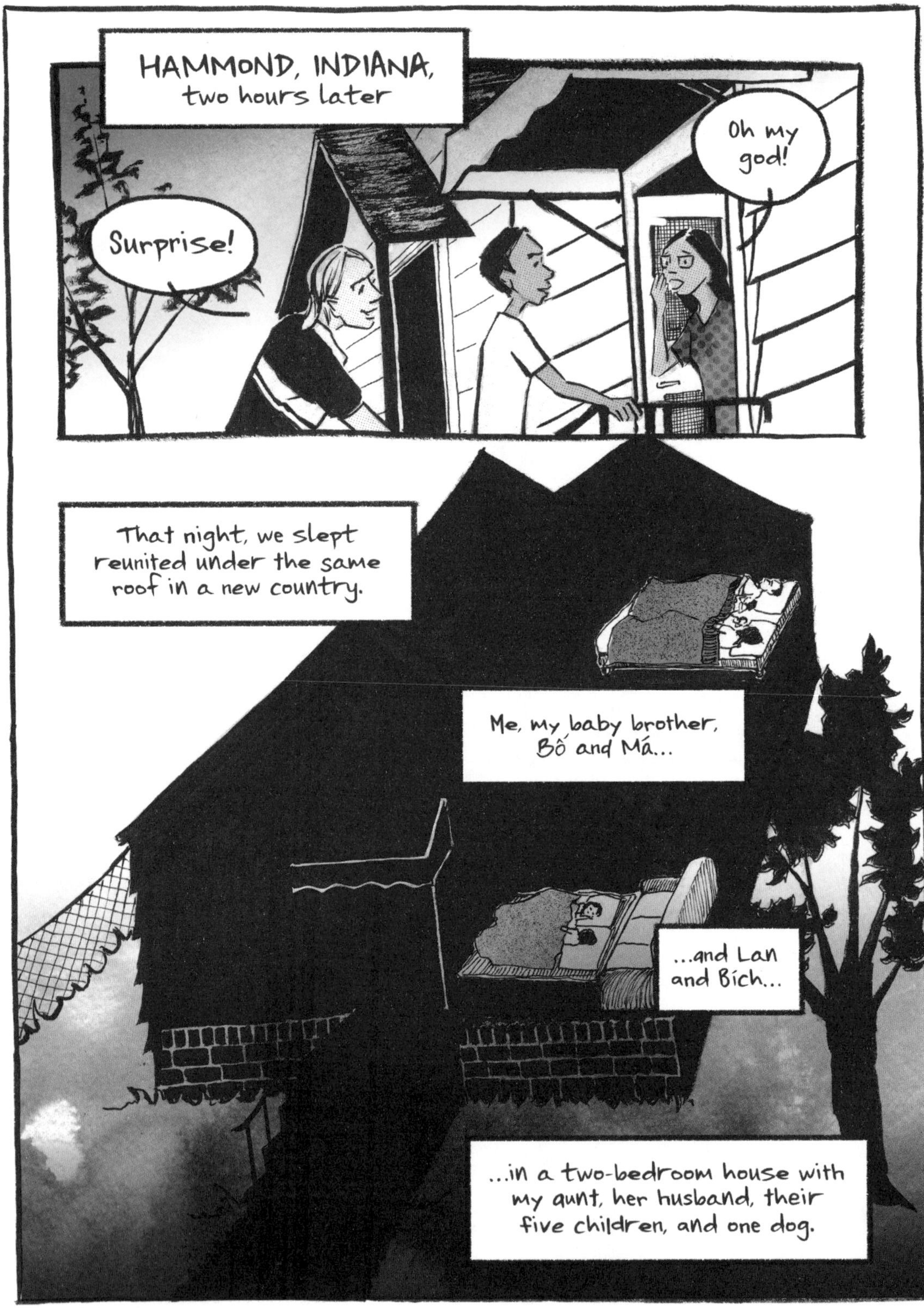
HAMMOND, INDIANA,
two hours later
Surprise!
Oh my god!
That night, we slept reunited under the same roof in a new country.
Me, my baby brother, Bố and Má...
...and Lan and Bích...
...in a two-bedroom house with my aunt, her husband, their five children, and one dog.

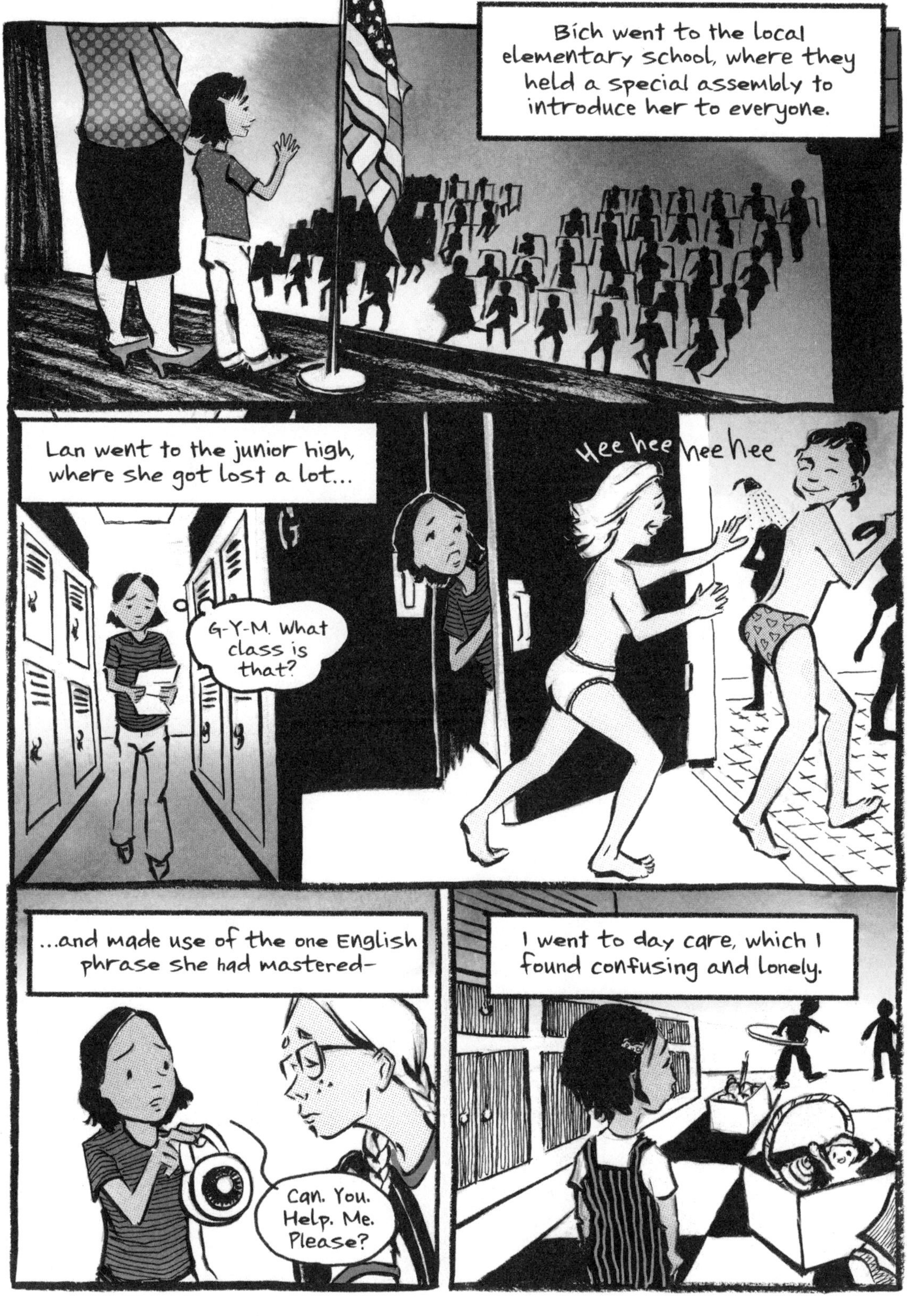
Bich went to the local elementary school, where they held a special assembly to introduce her to everyone.
Lan went to the junior high, where she got lost a lot...
G-Y-M. What class is that?
Hee hee hee hee
...and made use of the one English phrase she had mastered-
Can. You. Help. Me. Please?
I went to day care, which I found confusing and lonely.

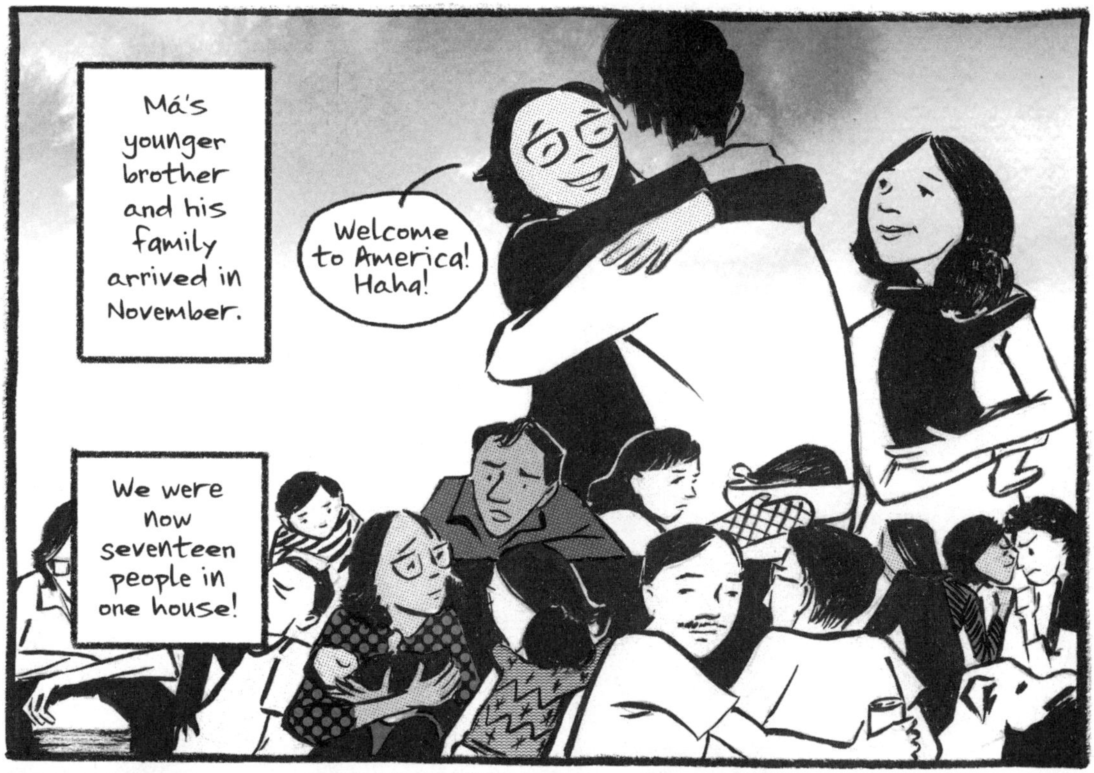
Má's younger brother and his family arrived in November.
Welcome to America! Haha!
We were now seventeen people in one house!

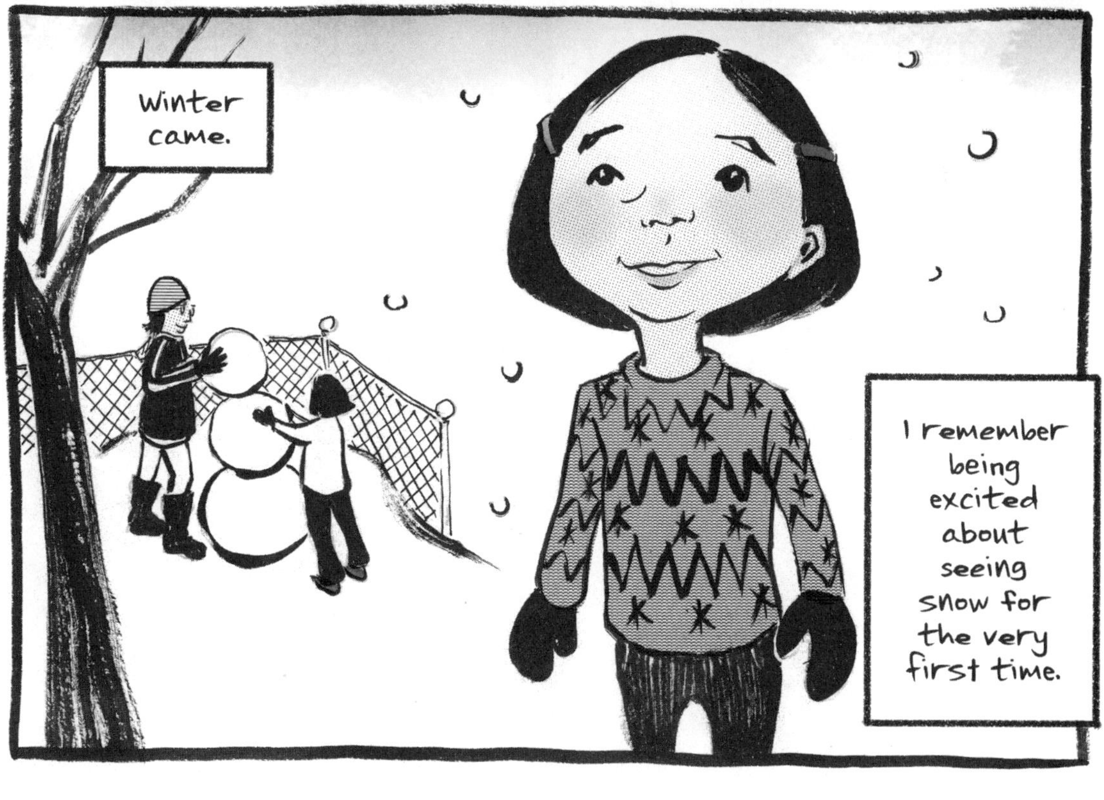
Winter came.
I remember being excited about seeing snow for the very first time.

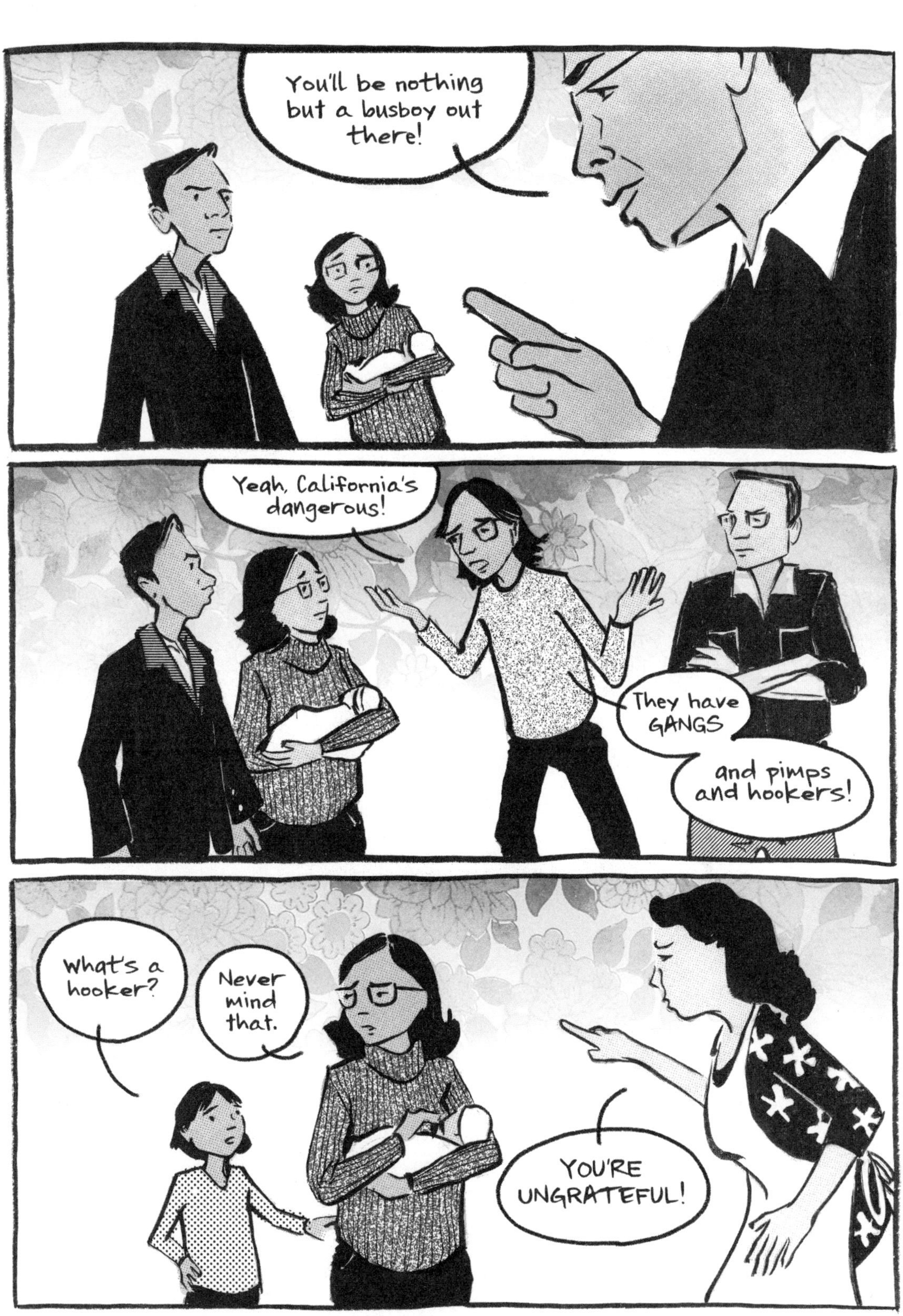
You'll be nothing but a busboy out there!
Yeah, California's dangerous!
They have GANGS
and pimps and hookers!
What's a hooker?
Never mind that.
YOU'RE UNGRATEFUL!

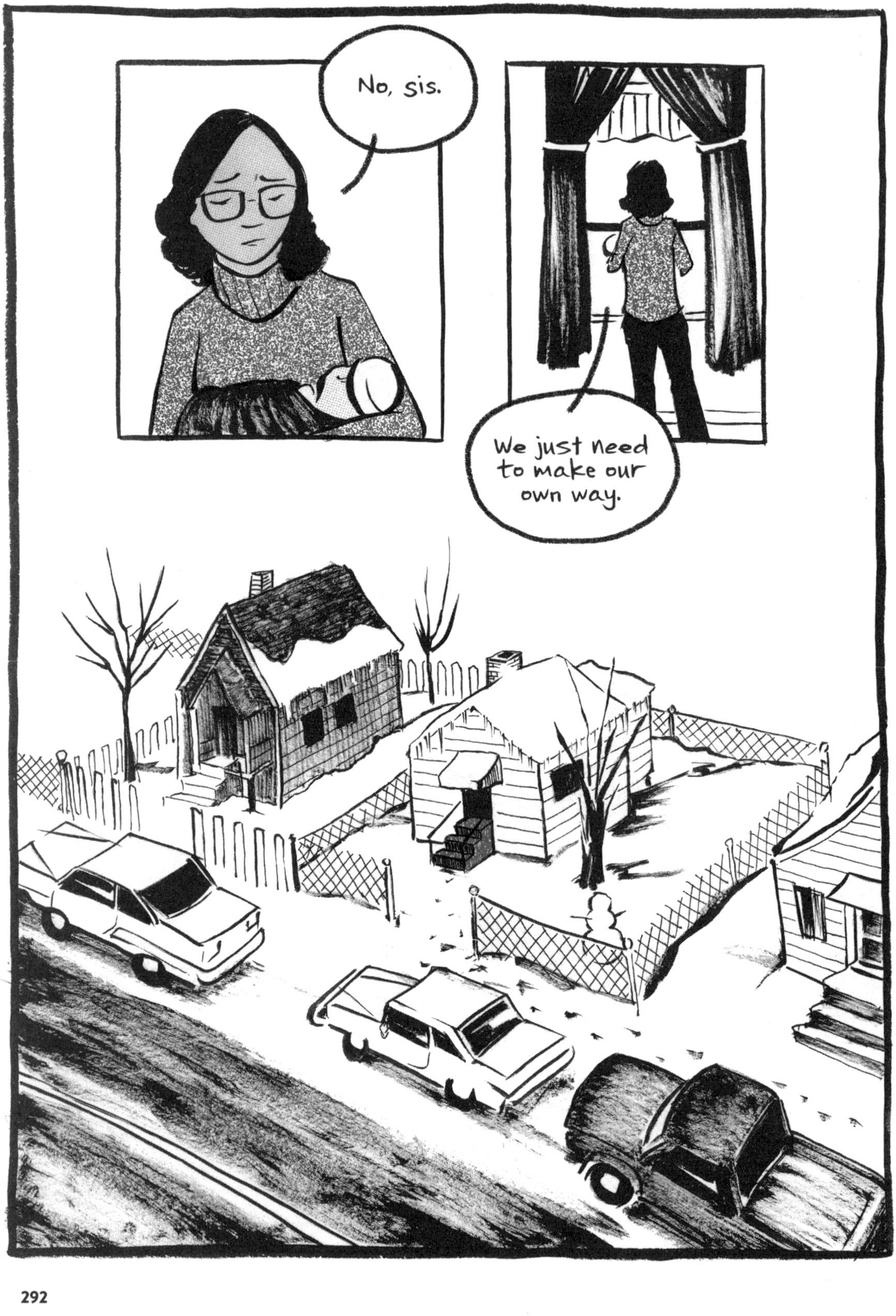
No, sis.
We just need to make our own way.

CHAPTER 9
FIRE AND ASH

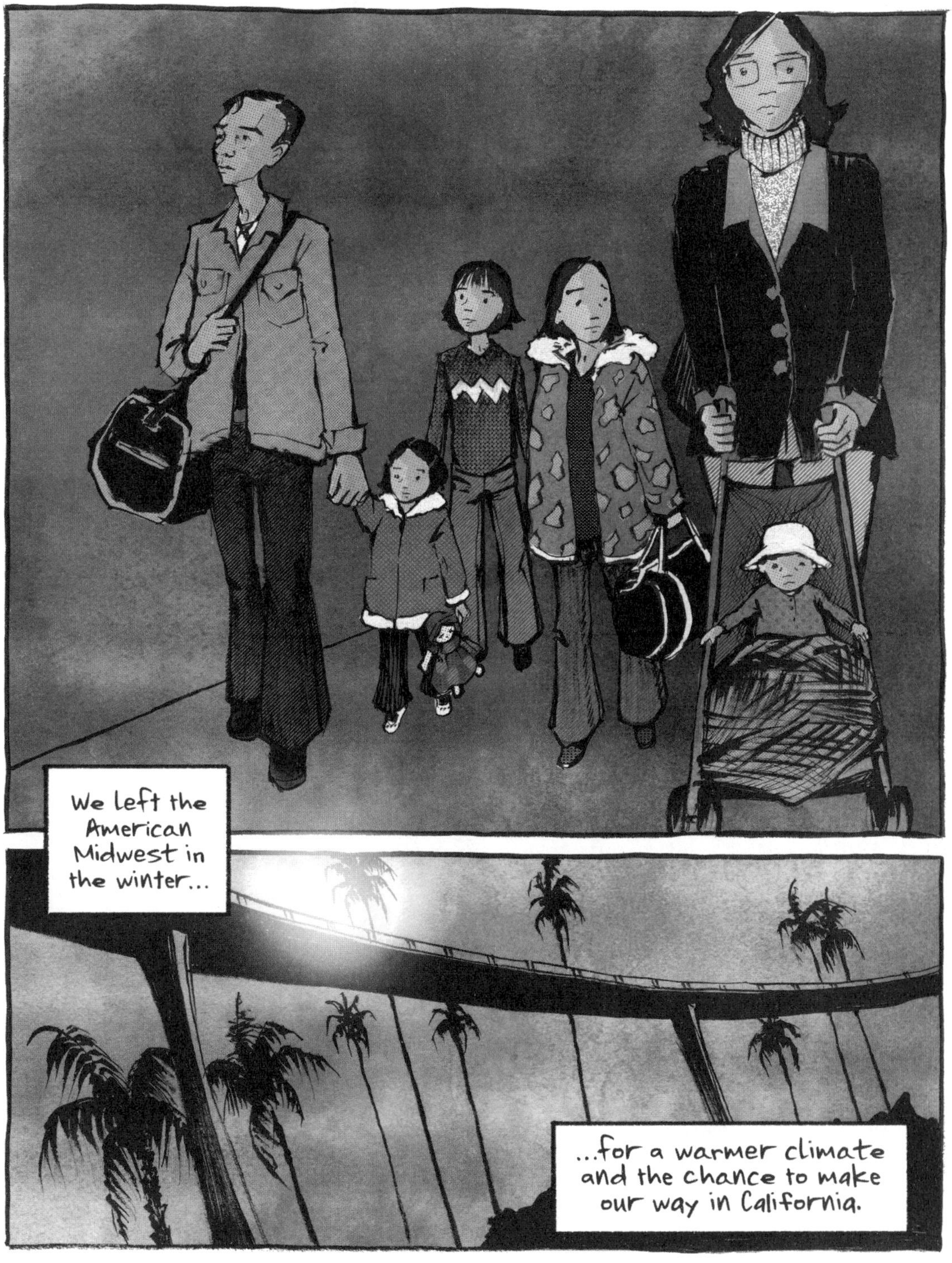
We left the American Midwest in the winter...
...for a warmer climate and the chance to make our way in California.

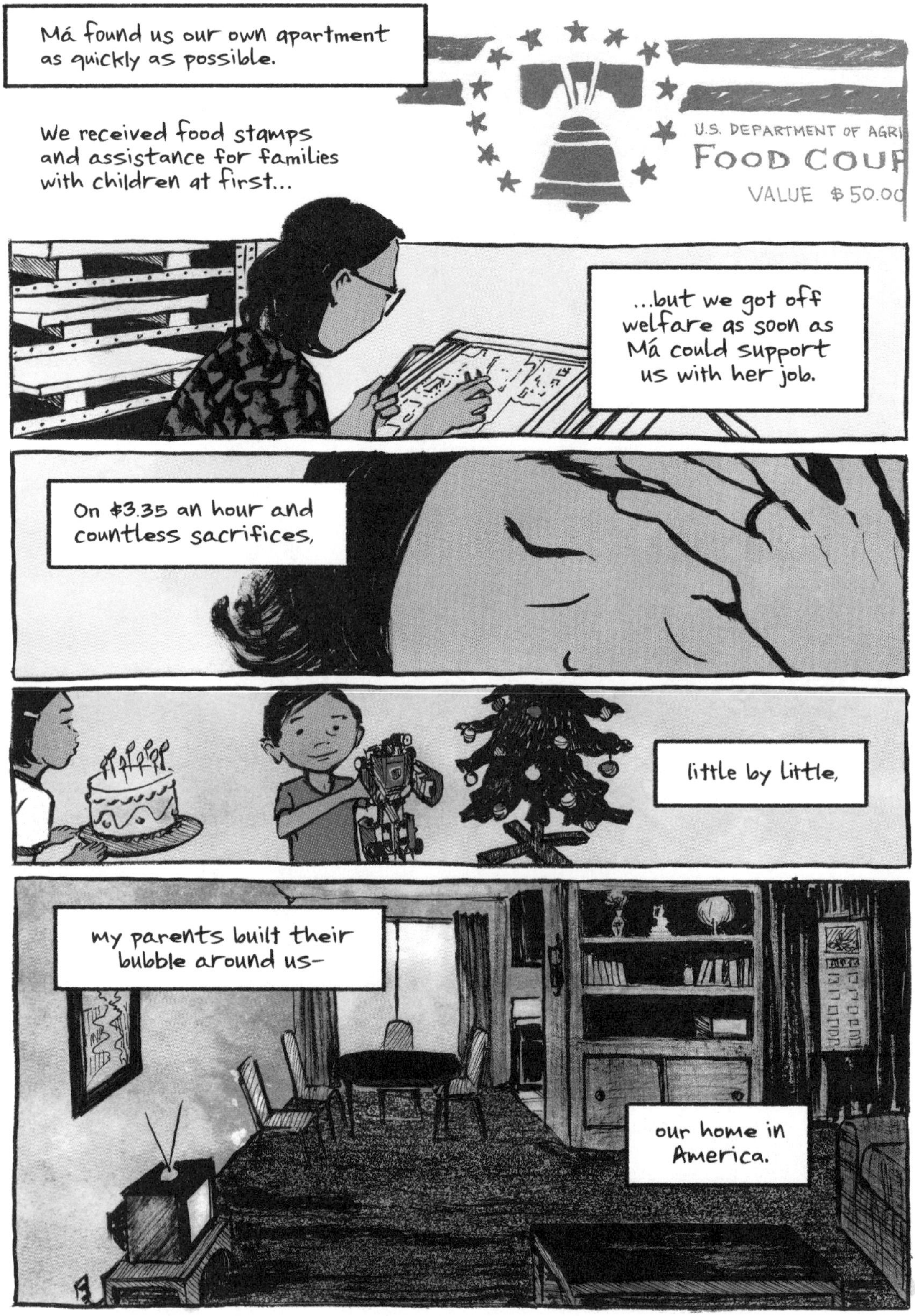
Má found us our own apartment as quickly as possible.
We received food stamps and assistance for families with children at first...
U.S. DEPARTMENT OF AGRI
FOOD COUP
VALUE $50.0
...but we got off welfare as soon as Má could support us with her job.
On $3.35 an hour and countless sacrifices,
little by little,
my parents built their bubble around us–
our home in America.

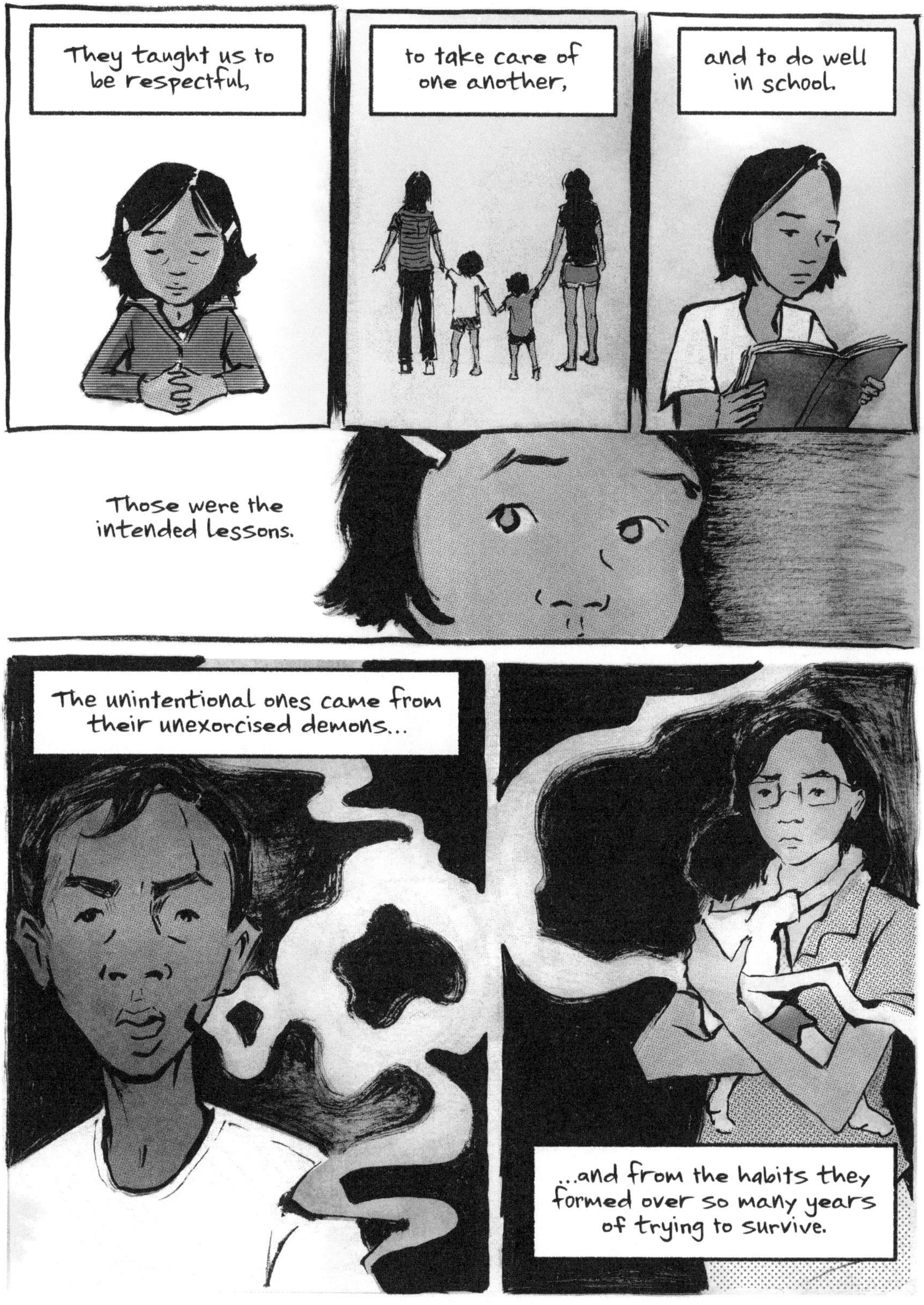
They taught us to be respectful,
to take care of one another,
and to do well in school.
Those were the intended lessons.
The unintentional ones came from their unexorcised demons...
...and from the habits they formed over so many years of trying to survive.

IMPORTANT DOCUMENTS

Our most important possession was this unassuming brown file folder—

—in which my parents placed the most essential pieces of our identity.

Our birth certificates, translated and notarized,

our green cards,

and our Social Security cards.

When we began school, we were each given a brown folder of our own.

Bui Phuong Thi

Into this folder went our report cards,

Bui, Thi

Bui, Tam

certificates and awards,

CITIZEN OF THE MONTH

January 1981

Thi

Bui

and the annual class picture.

No individual school pictures. Those were too expensive.

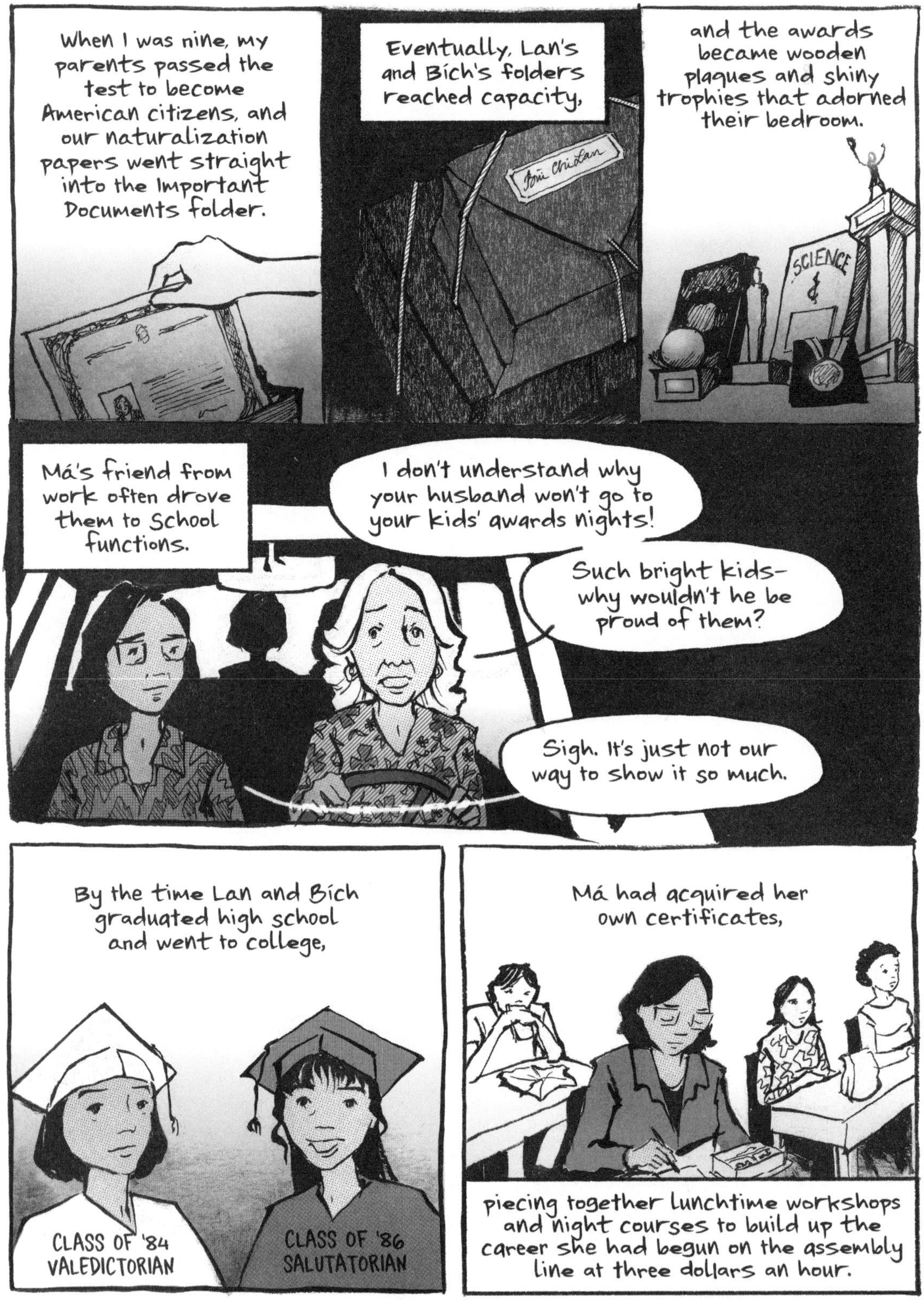

When I was nine, my parents passed the test to become American citizens, and our naturalization papers went straight into the Important Documents folder.
Eventually, Lan's and Bích's folders reached capacity,
and the awards became wooden plaques and shiny trophies that adorned their bedroom.
SCIENCE
Má's friend from work often drove them to School functions.
I don't understand why your husband won't go to your kids' awards nights!
Such bright kids- why wouldn't he be proud of them?
Sigh. It's just not our way to show it so much.
By the time Lan and Bích graduated high school and went to college,
CLASS OF '84 VALEDICTORIAN
CLASS OF '86 SALUTATORIAN
Má had acquired her own certificates,
piecing together lunchtime workshops and night courses to build up the career she had begun on the assembly line at three dollars an hour.

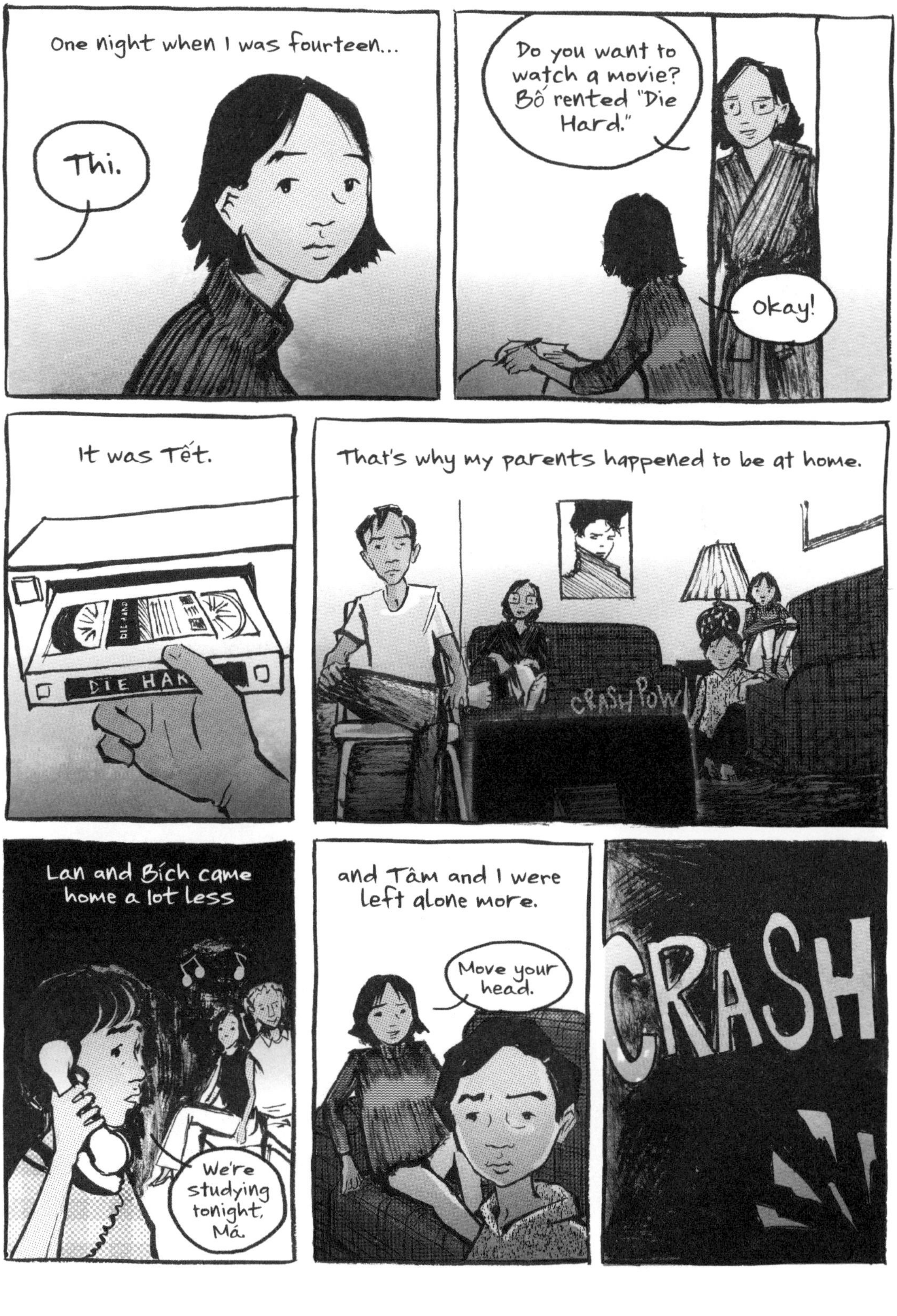
One night when I was fourteen...
Thi.
Do you want to watch a movie? Bố rented "Die Hard."
Okay!
It was Tết.
DIE HARD
DIE HAR
That's why my parents happened to be at home.
CRASH POW
Lan and Bích came home a lot less
We're studying tonight, Má.
and Tâm and I were left alone more.
Move your head.
CRASH

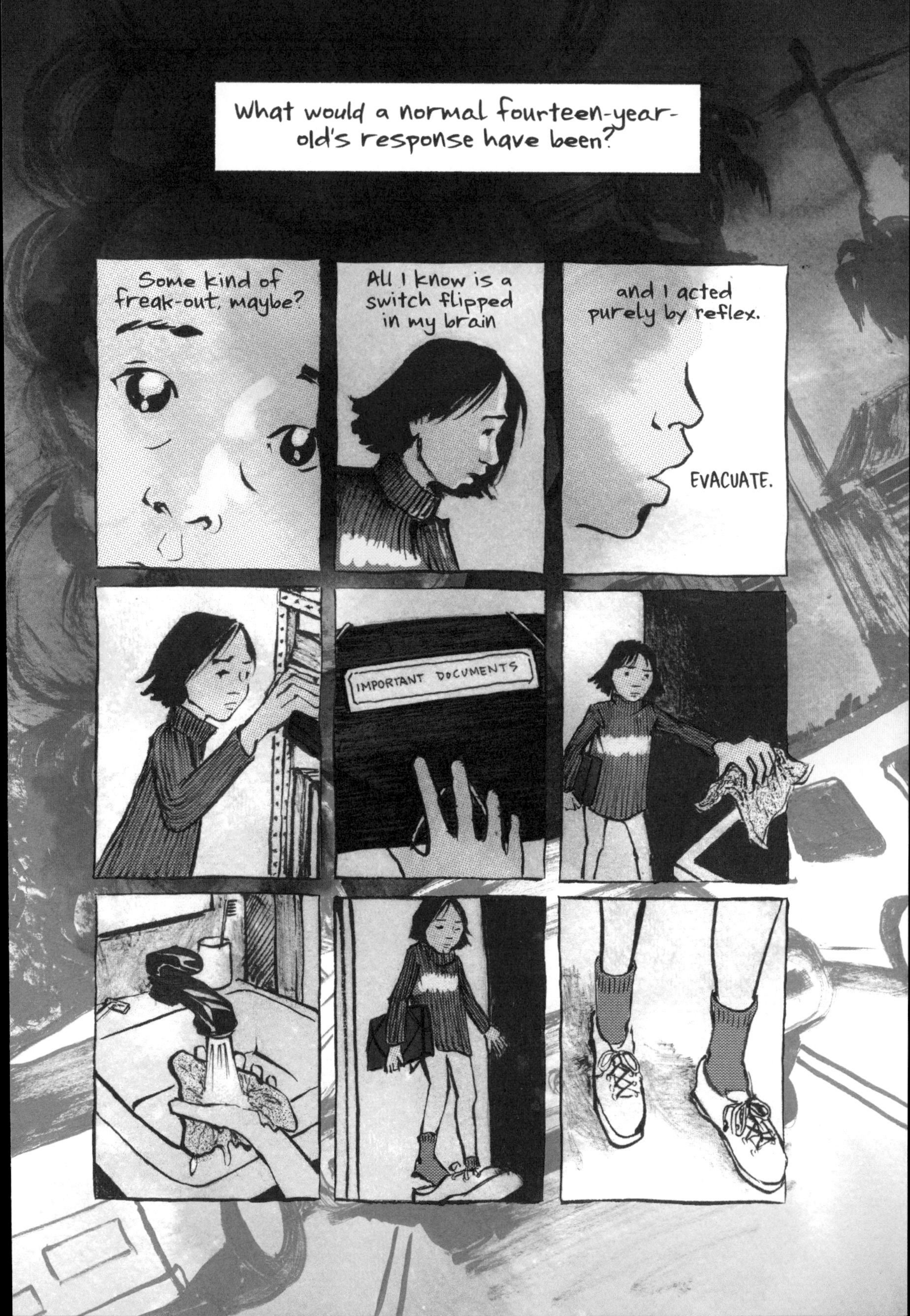
What would a normal fourteen-year-old's response have been?
Some kind of freak-out, maybe?
All I know is a switch flipped in my brain
and I acted purely by reflex.
EVACUATE.
IMPORTANT DOCUMENTS

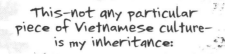

This—not any particular piece of Vietnamese culture—is my inheritance:

the inexplicable need and extraordinary ability to RUN when the shit hits the fan.

My Refugee Reflex.

CHAPTER 10

EBB AND FLOW

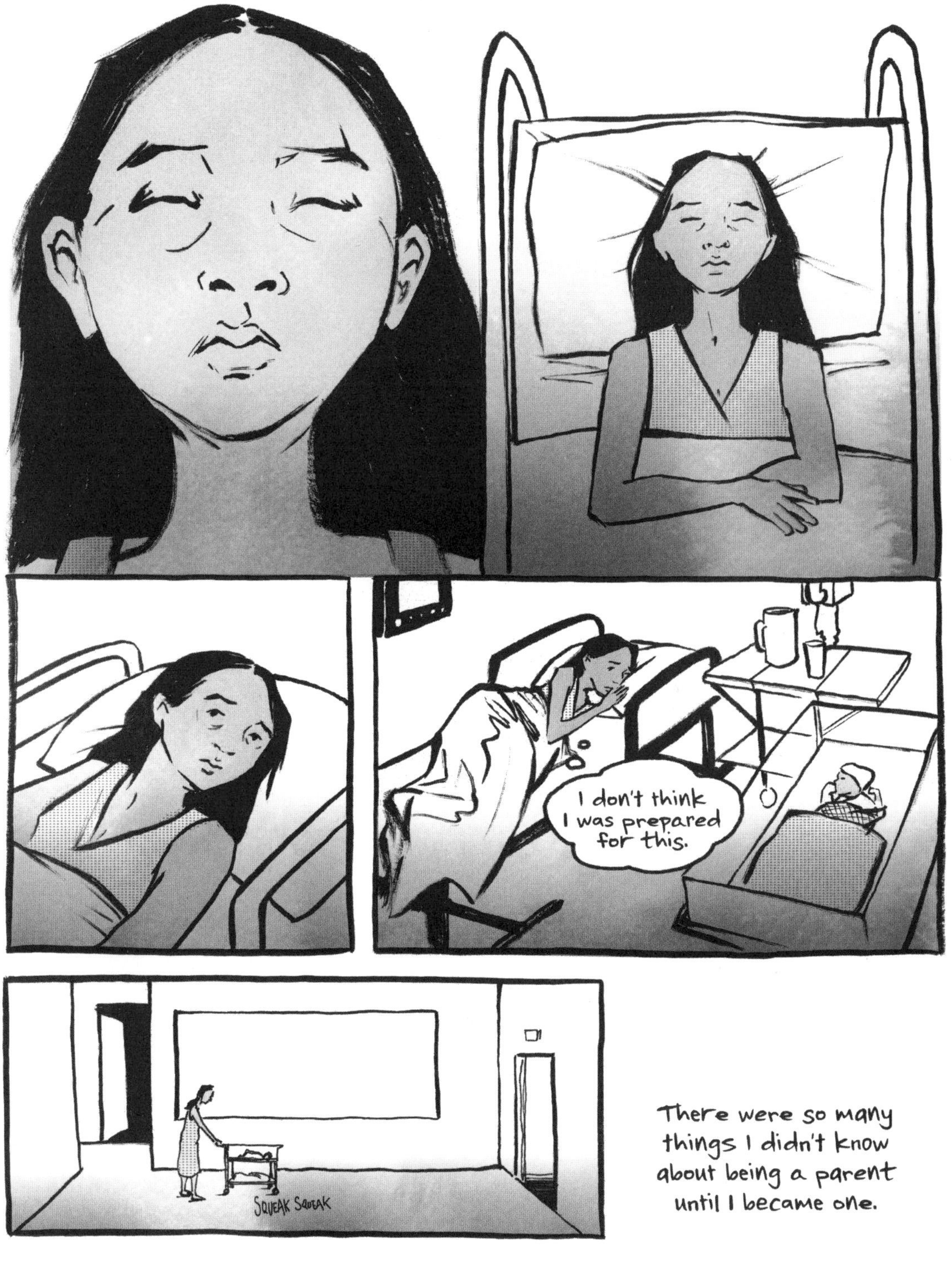
I don't think I was prepared for this.
SQUEAK SQUEAK

There were so many things I didn't know about being a parent until I became one.

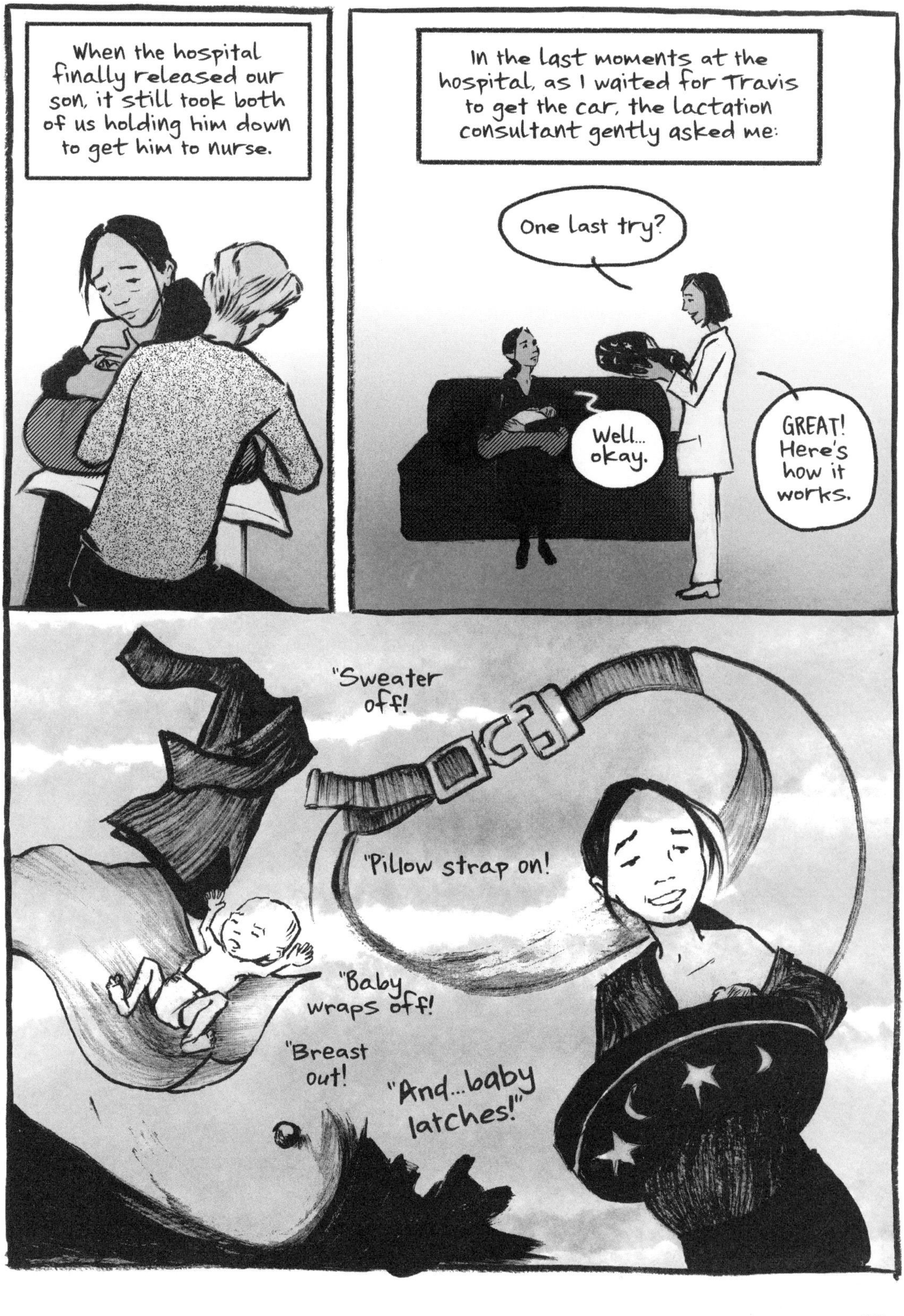
When the hospital finally released our son, it still took both of us holding him down to get him to nurse.
In the last moments at the hospital, as I waited for Travis to get the car, the lactation consultant gently asked me:
One last try?
Well... okay.
GREAT! Here's how it works.
"Sweater off!
"Pillow strap on!
"Baby wraps off!
"Breast out!
"And...baby latches!"

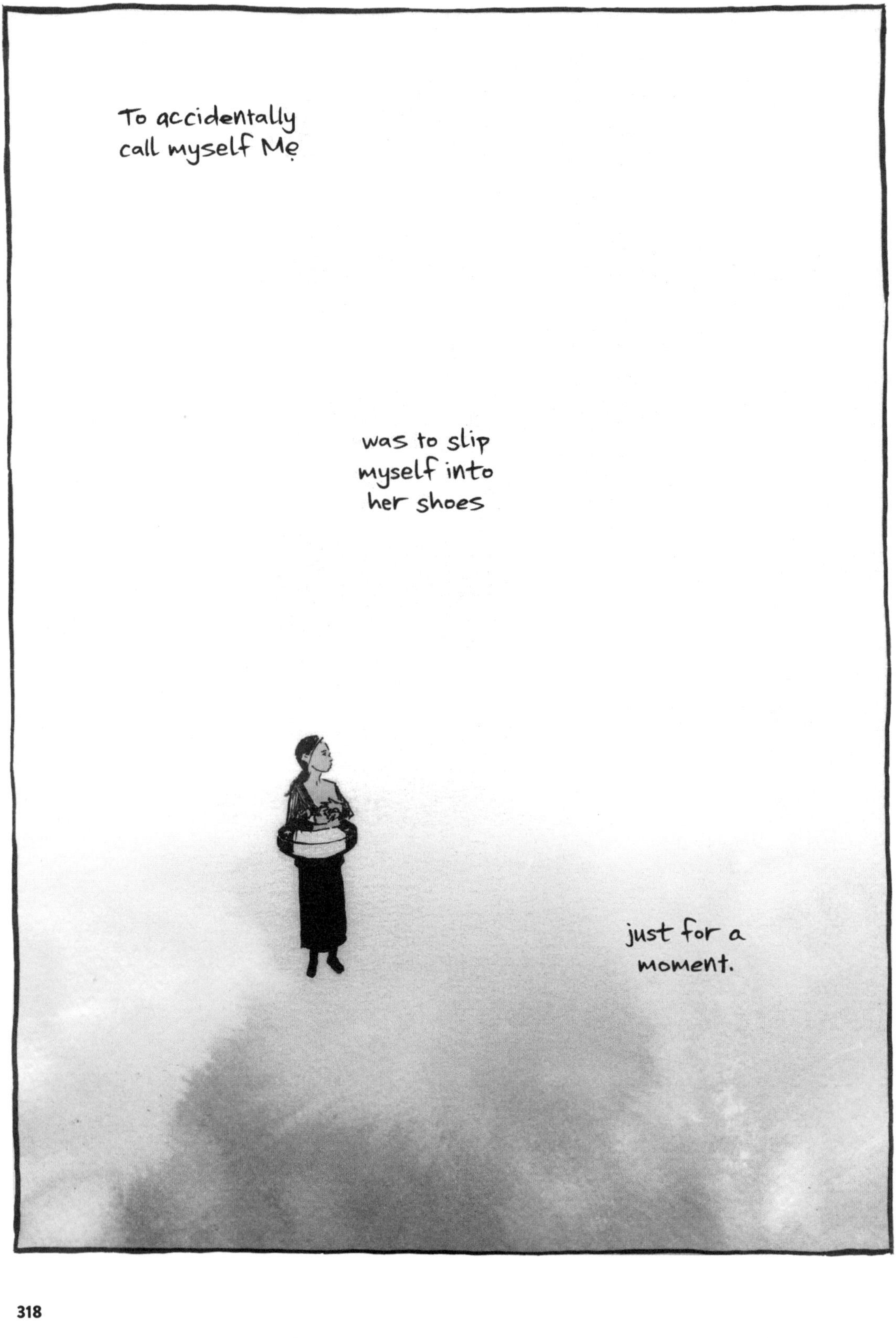
To accidentally call myself Mẹ
was to slip myself into her shoes
just for a moment.

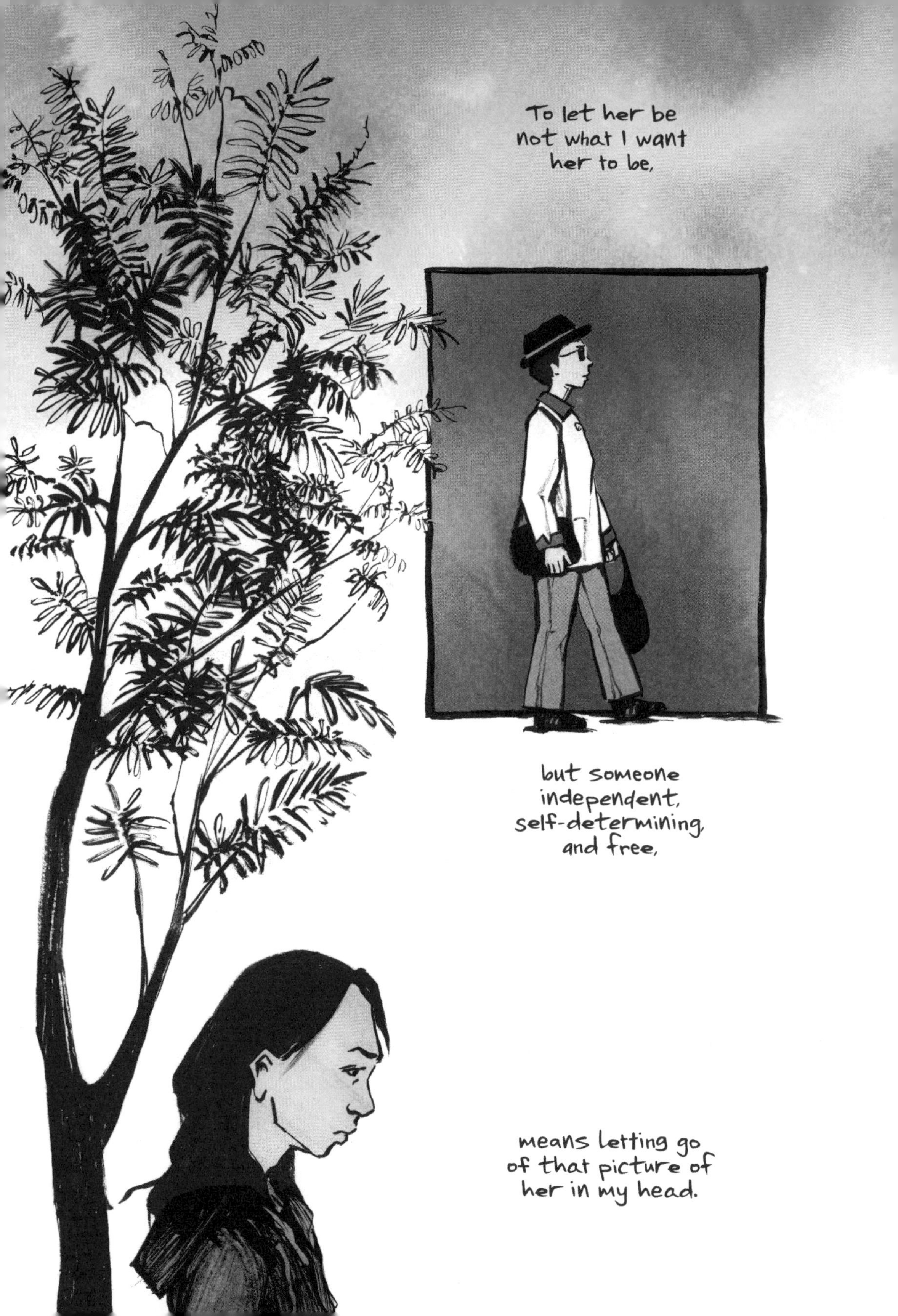

To let her be not what I want her to be,
but someone independent, self-determining, and free,
means letting go of that picture of her in my head.

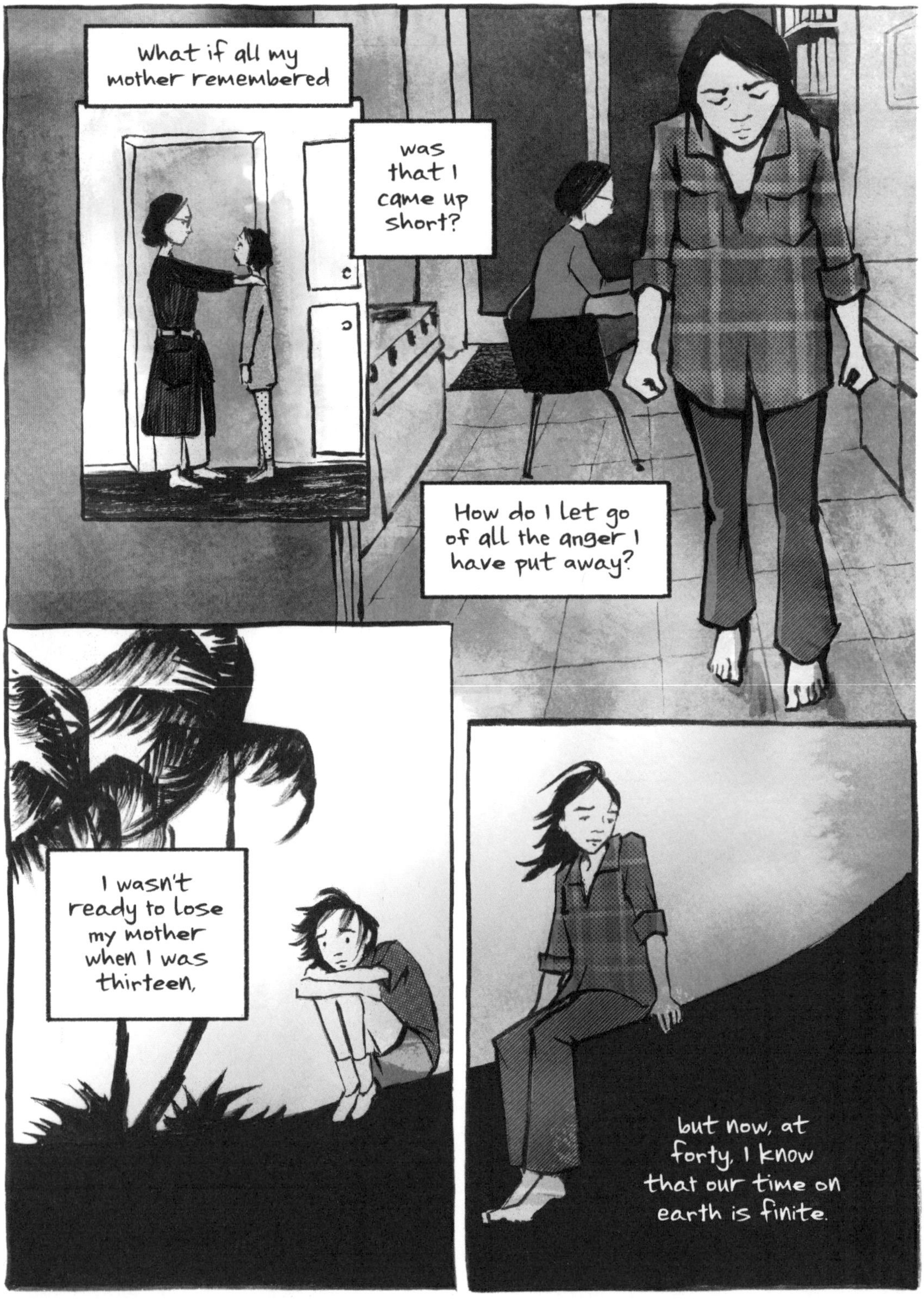
What if all my mother remembered
was that I came up short?
How do I let go of all the anger I have put away?
I wasn't ready to lose my mother when I was thirteen,
but now, at forty, I know that our time on earth is finite.

What becomes of us after we die?
Do we live on in what we leave to our children?

Nguyễn Văn Minh
2008

Trương Thị Nhân
2002

Bùi Hữu Khởi
2011

Vũ Thị Huu
1996

Bùi Thị Miện
1979

Bùi Hữu Tường
1974

How much of ME is
my own, and how
much is stamped
into my blood and
bone, predestined?

I used to imagine
that history had
infused my parents'
lives with the dust
of a cataclysmic
explosion.

That it had
seeped through
their skin and
become part of
their blood.

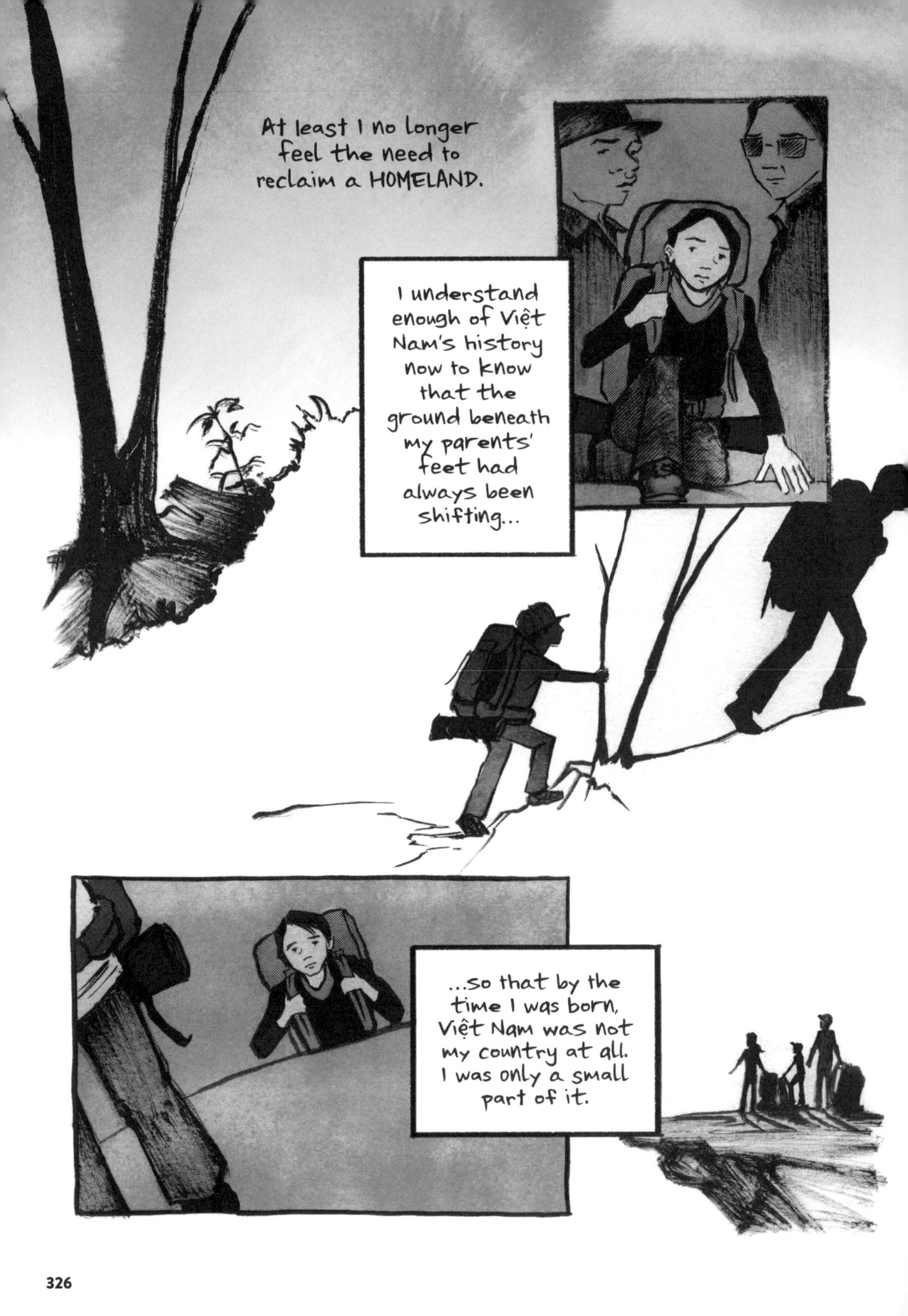
At least I no longer feel the need to reclaim a HOMELAND.
I understand enough of Việt Nam's history now to know that the ground beneath my parents' feet had always been shifting...
...so that by the time I was born, Việt Nam was not my country at all. I was only a small part of it.

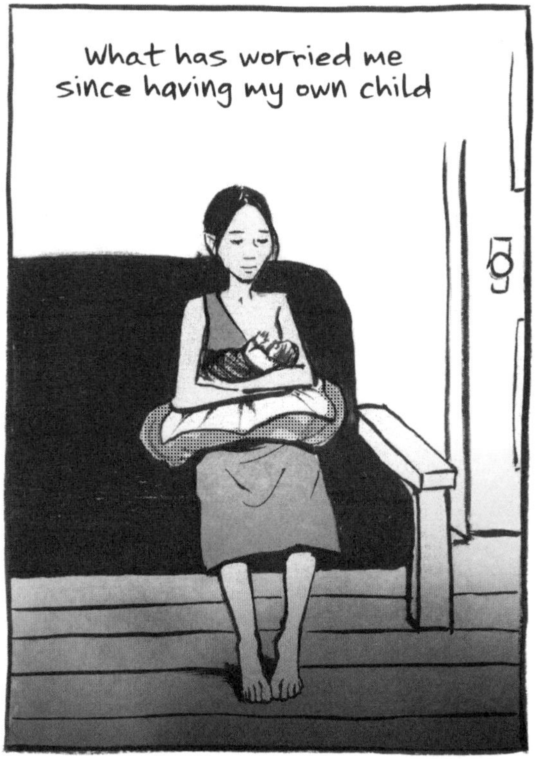
What has worried me
since having my own child

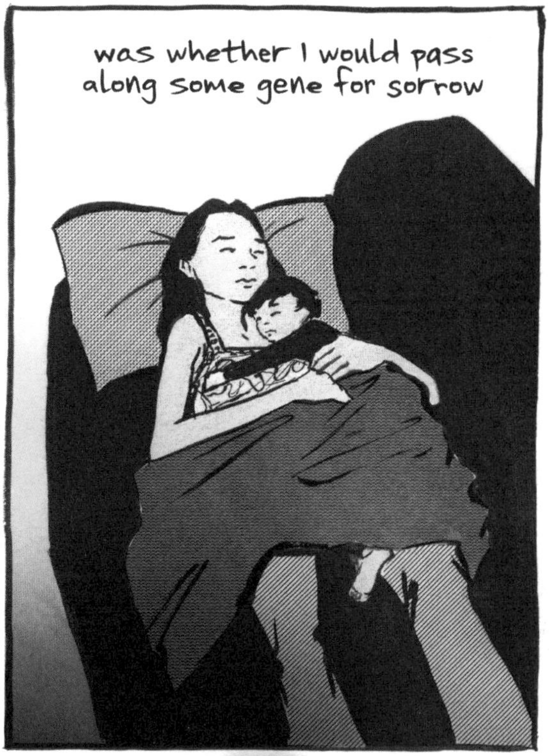
was whether I would pass
along some gene for sorrow

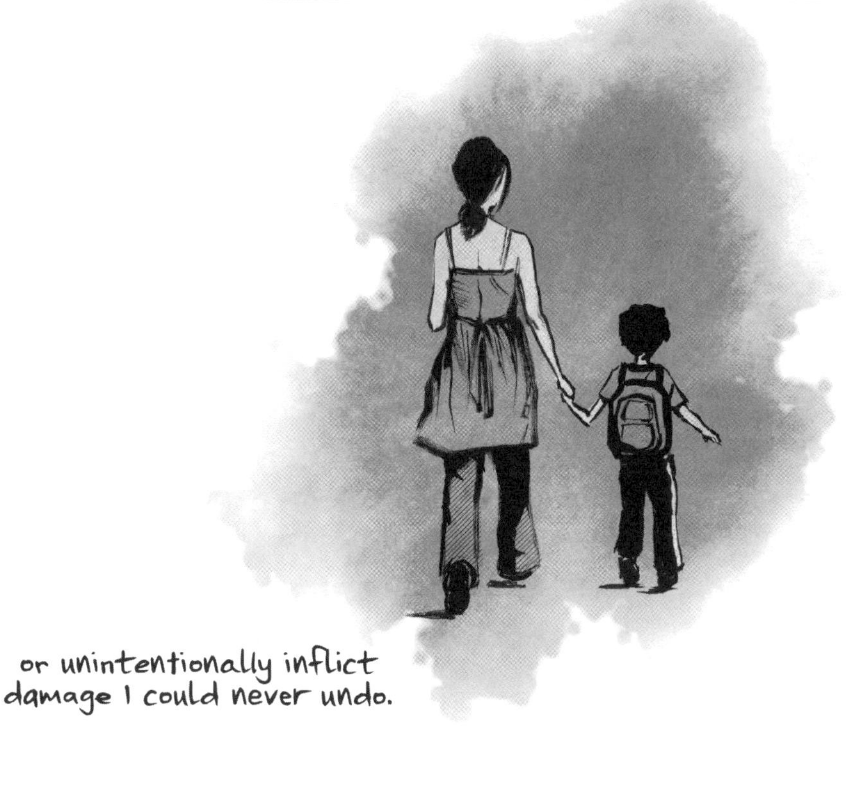
or unintentionally inflict
damage I could never undo.

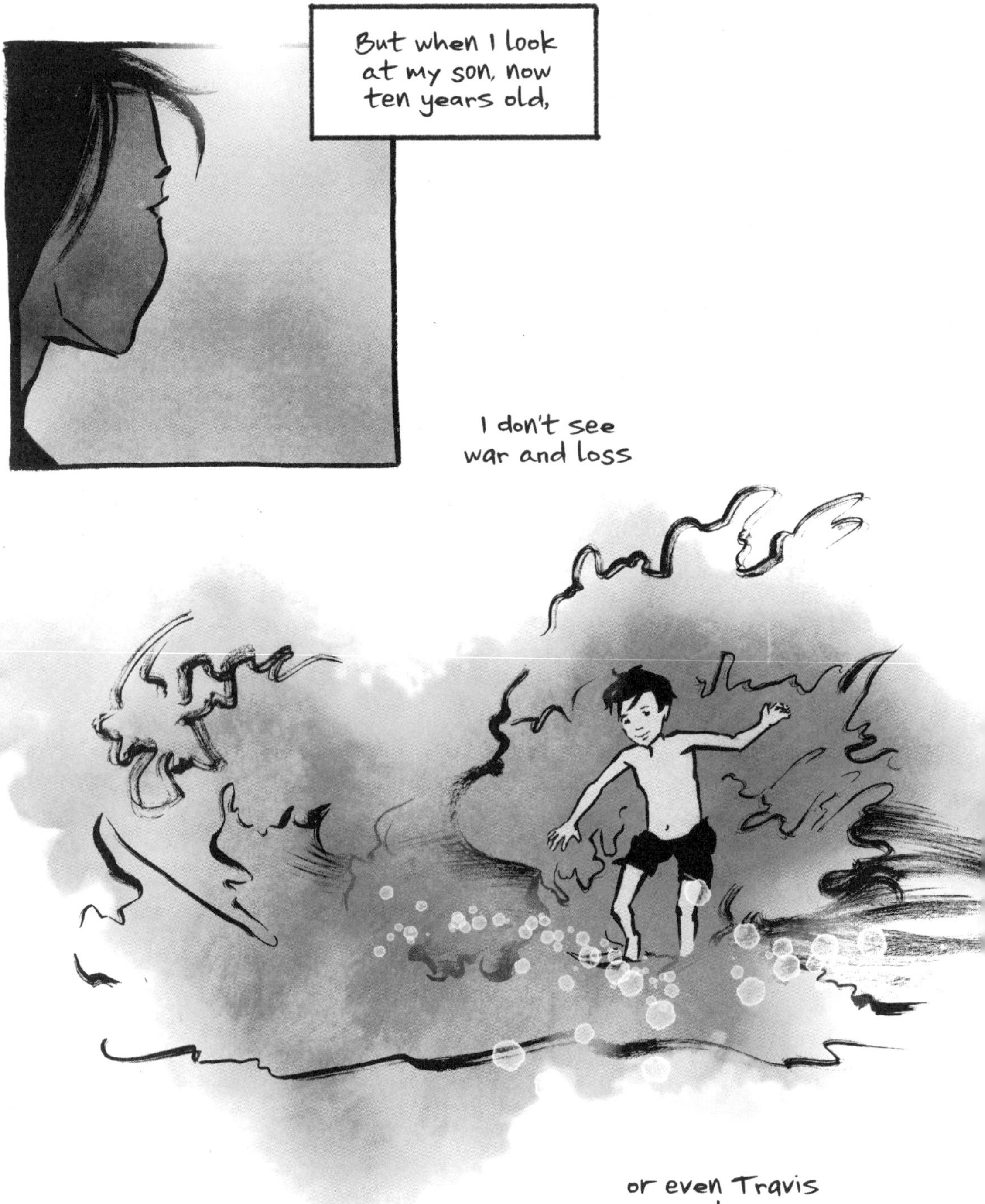
But when I look at my son, now ten years old,
I don't see war and loss
or even Travis and me.